LIAONING MUSEUM

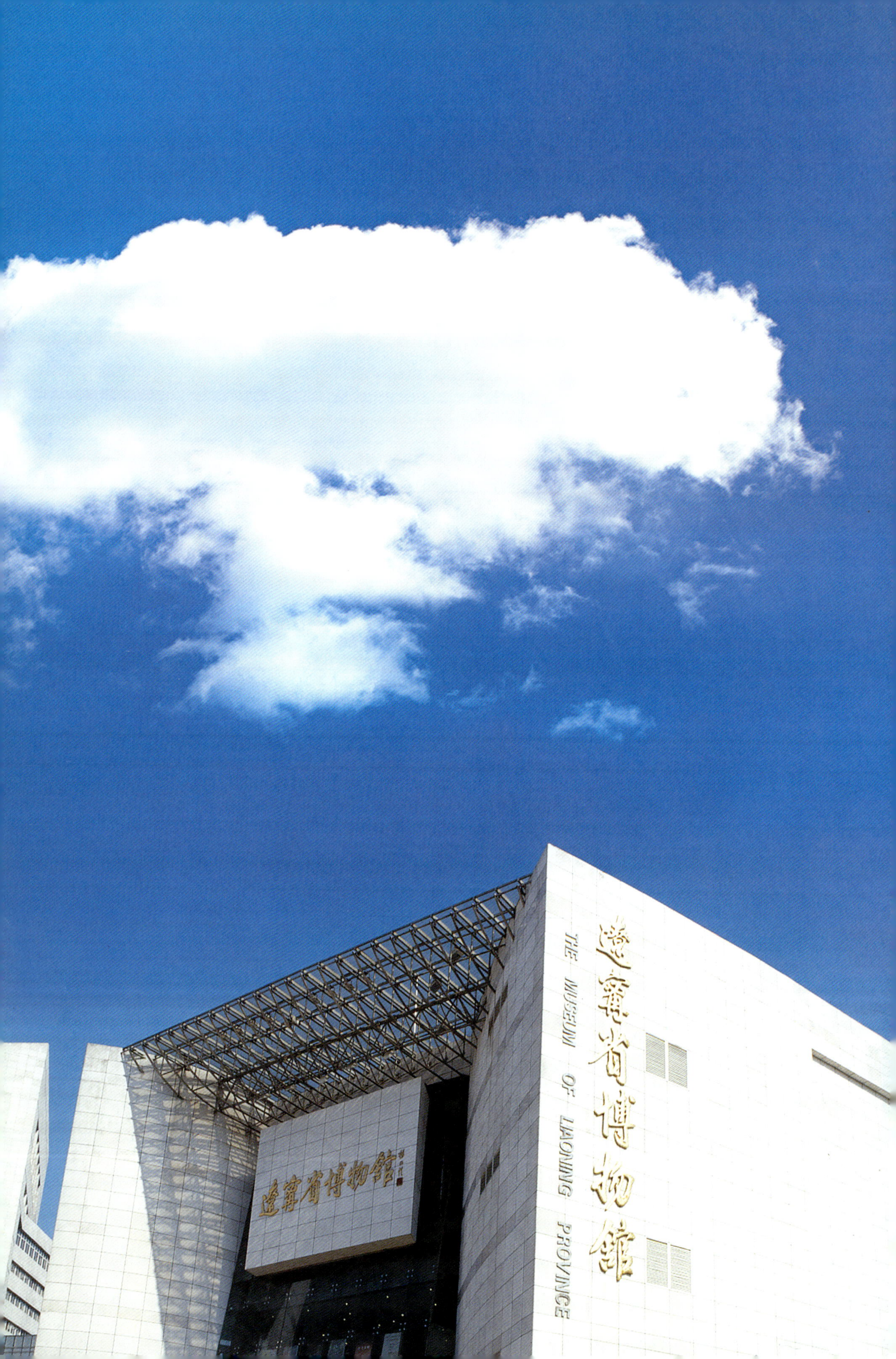
遼寧省博物館
THE MUSEUM OF LIAONING PROVINCE
遼寧省博物館

LIAONING MUSEUM

Liaoning Museum

In collaboration with London Editions, Hong Kong

Editor in Chief: Ma Baojie

Deputy Editors in Chief: Zhang Li, Liu Yun and Lin Li

Responsible Editor: Liu Yun

Co-ordinating Editors: Antony White and Cui Jing

Chinese Editor: Yang Ting

English Translator: Alastair Morrison

English Editor: Julie Pickard

Design: Yuan Yinchang and Li Jing

ISBN: 978-7-80204-487-6

First published in 2008 by

Chang Zheng Publishers

Liaoning Provincial Museum

In collaboration with London Editions, Hong Kong

Distributed worldwide outside China by

Scala Publishers Limited

Northburgh House,

10 Northburgh Street,

London EC1V 0AT

United Kingdom

Tel: 44 (0) 207 490 9900

Plans

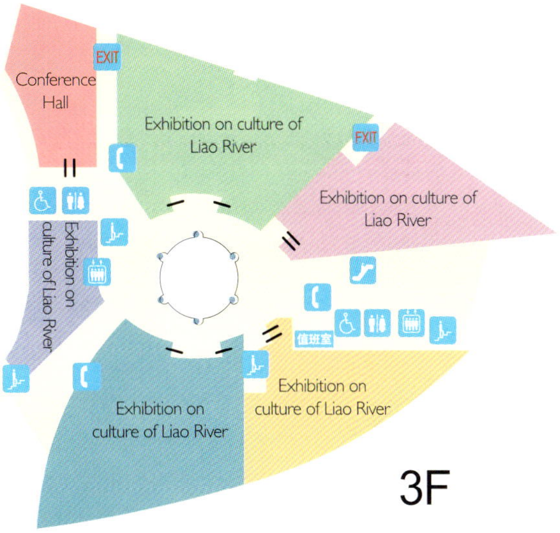

3F

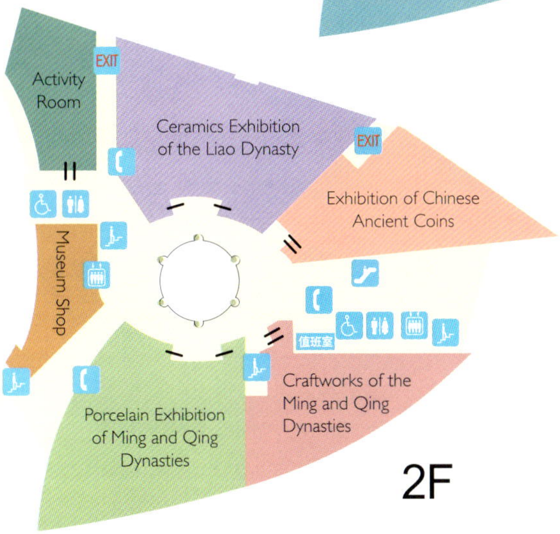

2F

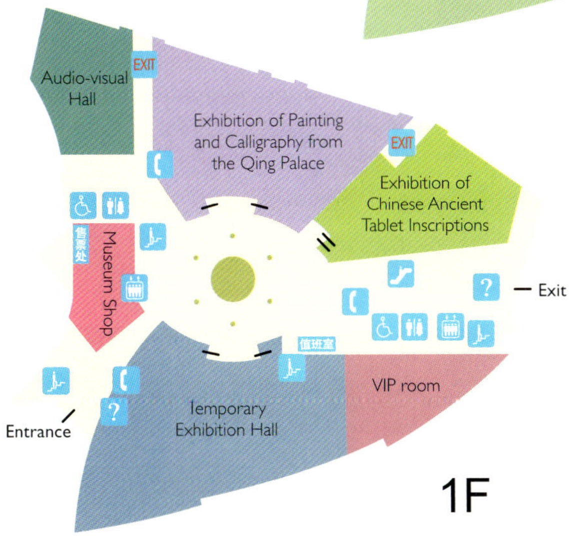

1F

contents

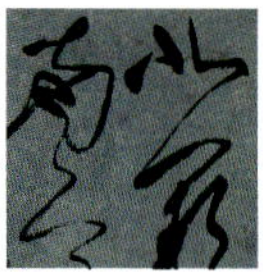

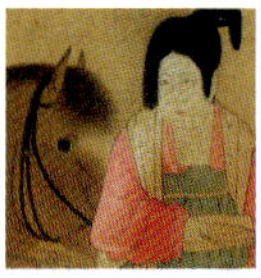

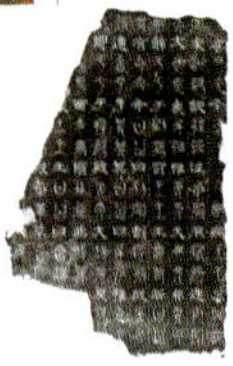

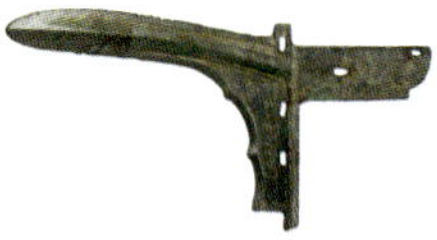

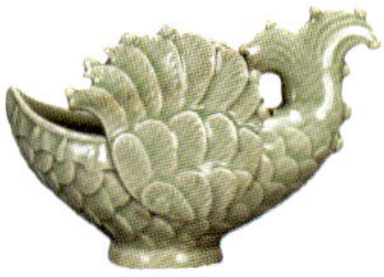

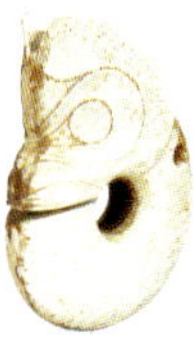

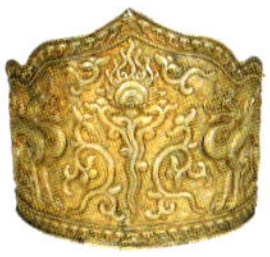

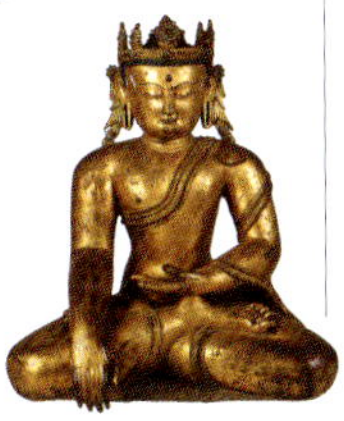

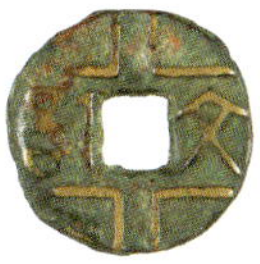

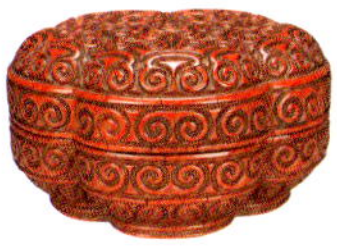

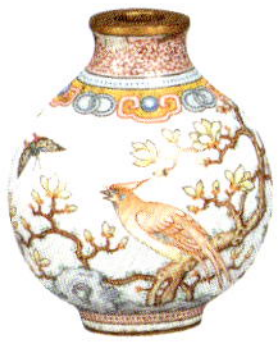

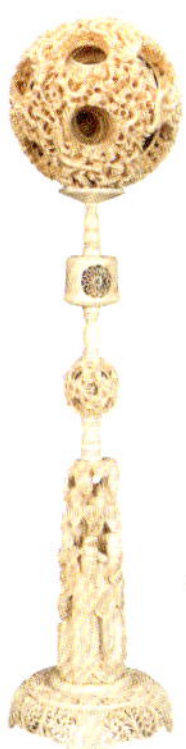

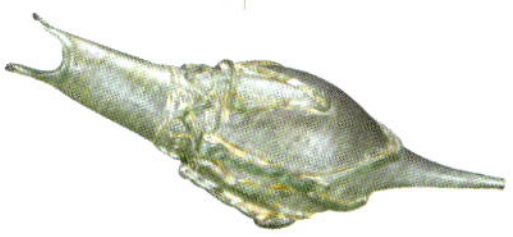

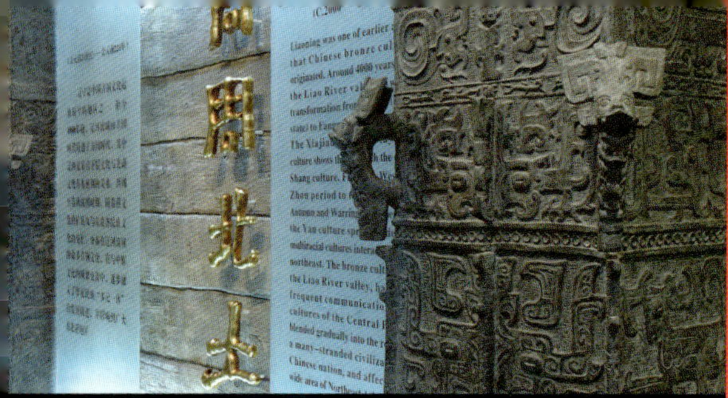

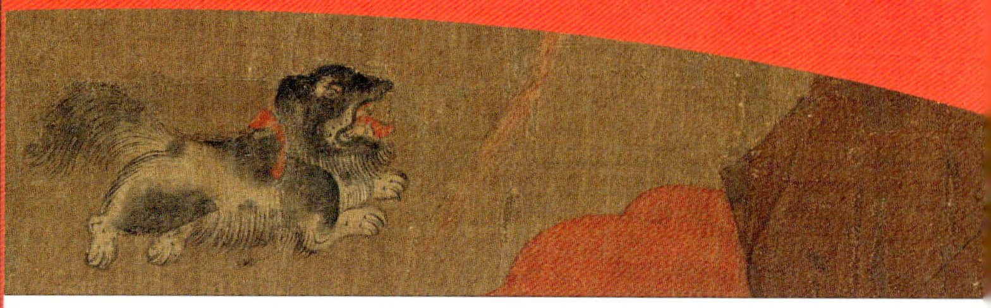

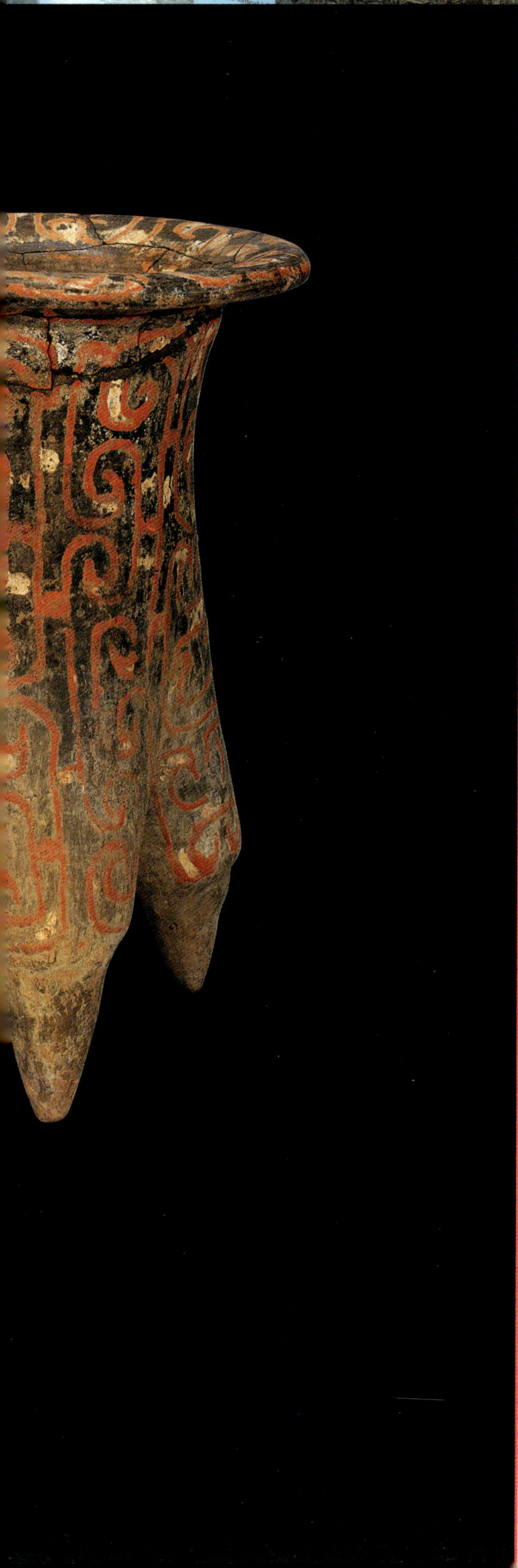

Introduction

The Liaoning Provincial Museum holds an important collection of great artistic and historical value. It is one of China's major cultural institutions for conservation, research and exhibitions. The museum was formally known as the Northeast Museum and was founded in 1949, the largest museum of its kind to be established in the People's Republic of China. Situated on the southeast side of City Government Square in the heart of Shenyang, the Liaoning Provincial Museum opened fully to the public on 12 November 2004. 30,000 square metres in size, the building symbolises the jade 'pig dragon' of the Neolithic Hongshan Culture. The museum has over 115,000 precious items in its collection, including paintings, calligraphy, tapestries, textiles, jade, bronzes, ceramics, grave tablets, prints, historical maps and coins.

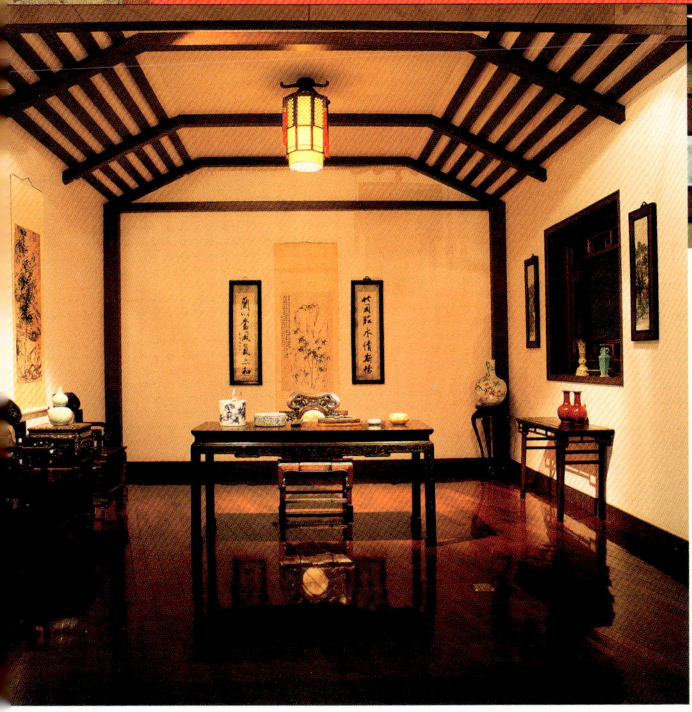

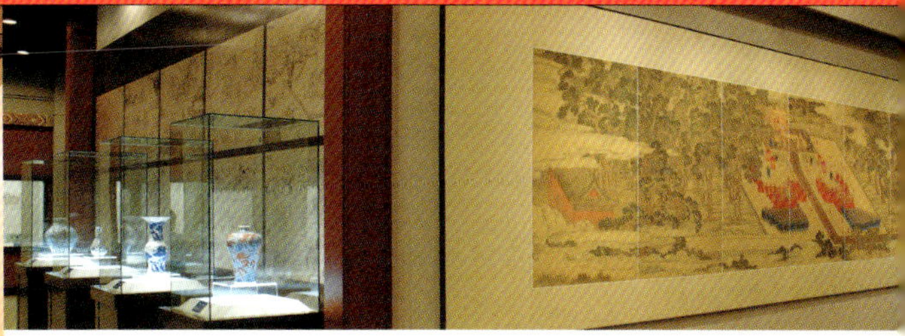

The museum has specialists in research, authentication, museum management, education, cultural exchange, exhibitions and conservation. The museum publishes more than ten academic books and exhibition catalogues every year, and has worked on national conservation projects. The multi-media auditorium is equipped with simultaneous interpreting and film projection facilities, and the library contains over 100,000 volumes on art and history. Items exhibited come from the museum collections and recent archaeological finds in the region, supported by research findings in history and material culture. A number of specialist galleries document the history of the region from early civilisation through the Shang, Zhou and Khitan, to the rise of the Manchus. Finally there is a gallery of 8,500 square metres for temporary exhibitions.

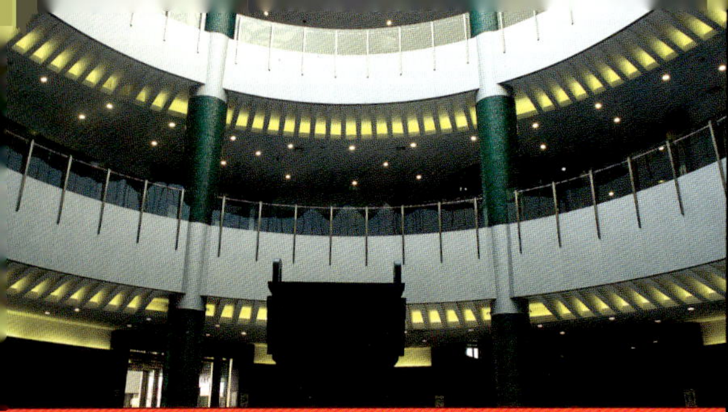

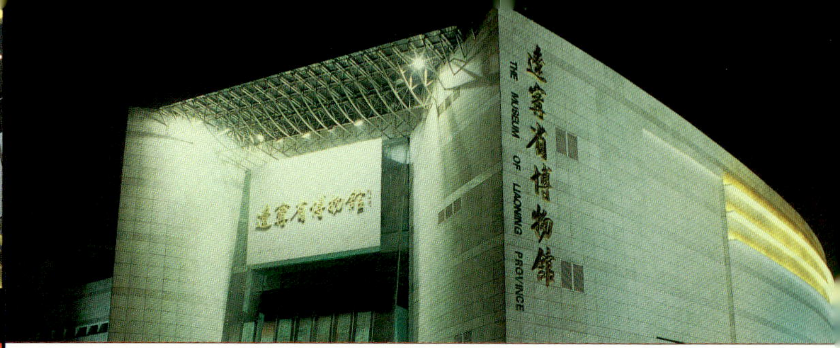

Preface

Liaoning Provincial Museum was the first museum to be established in the People's Republic of China in 1949. It has since become a well-designed modern museum, making it one of China's top-ranking museums, excelling in collection management, conservation, research and exhibitions. The museum collections contain around 120,000 objects, ten thousand of which are precious masterpieces mostly excavated from the Liaoning region. The most significant of these pieces include calligraphy and painting from the Jin, Tang, Song and Yuan periods, tapestry and embroidery from the Song, Yuan, Ming and Qing periods, Hongshan Culture jade, Shang and Zhou bronzes, Liao ceramics, grave tablets from all periods, and Ming and Qing prints, historical maps and money from the *Collection of Ancient Coins* by Li Zuoxiang of the late Qing.

The calligraphy and painting collection in the Liaoning Provincial Museum is celebrated in China and internationally for its quality and beauty. The Jin, Tang, Song and Yuan calligraphy and paintings removed from the Forbidden City in Beijing by the last Qing emperor, Puyi, which were dispersed in the northeast of China, and finally arrived at the Northeast Museum (present-day Liaoning Provincial Museum) are now the most important part of the collection, making the museum the leading holding institution of collections dispersed from the Forbidden City. These include

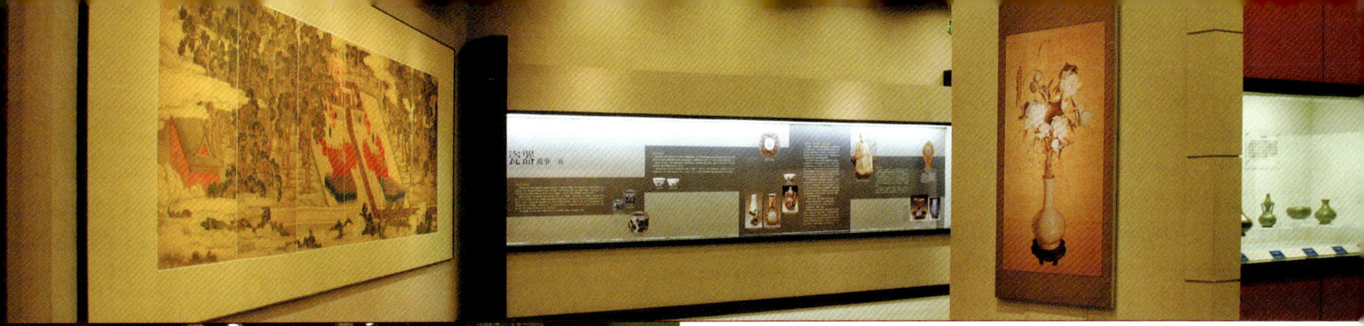

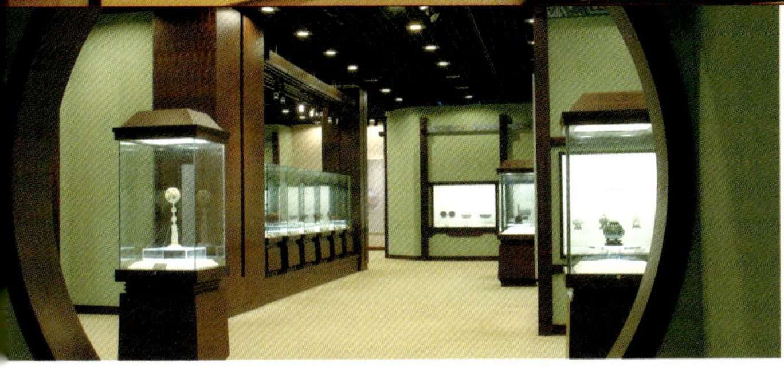

the earliest extant copy of the *Eulogy to Cao E*, the most reliable copy of the *Copy of a Calligraphy by Wang Xizhi*, Zhang Xu's only extant work, the *Gu Shi Si Tie in Cursive Script*, the figure painting that shows the realism of Tang art, *Court Ladies Adorning Their Hair with Flowers*, the representative work *Waiting for Ferry by the Mountain in Summer* by Dong Yuan of the southern landscape school, the *The Thousand Character Classic in Cursive Script* and *Auspicious Cranes* by the Song Huizong Emperor. All are extremely rare works.

Another special part of the collection are the famous and rare silk tapestries and embroidery from the Song, Yuan, Ming and Qing dynasties, most of which were collected through the life-long passion and resources of the early Republican collector and politician Zhu Qiqian, recorded in the *Record of Cunsu Studio Silk and Embroidery*. Works such as the Northern Song silk tapestry *Purple Luan and Magpie*, Southern Song *Painting of Camellia with Butterfly* by Zhu Kerou, *Round Fan with Peony Pattern* and *Astriding a Crane over Yaotai*, and the Ming, *Qixiang Building figures Scroll, Hair Embroidery* show the most notable achievements in silk tapestry and embroidery of their respective periods.

The bronze collection at the Liaoning Provincial Museum is outstanding in quality and scope. Part of the collection is composed of pieces handed down the generations such as the *Three 'pulling' daggers* in Luo Zhenyu's former collection, and the set of musical bells of the Northern Song. The other part of the collection comes from archaeological excavations since 1949 in the Ling river area of western Liaoning where items such as Shang and Zhou bronzes and short swords were found, showing the development of bronze technology and art in north China. Collections of ancient ceramics include coloured Neolithic pottery, Liao and Jin dynasty pieces as well as Jingdezhen ceramics from the Yuan, Ming and Qing dynasties. The collection also contains artefacts from a particular branch of Chinese ceramic history, Liao ceramics, the scope and quality of which are unrivalled anywhere in China or internationally. Excavations of Hongshan Culture jade pieces show the achievements of Chinese civilisation over five thousand years. Other categories of items include grave tablets, Ming and Qing prints and historical maps, as well as items typical of the nomadic culture of the steppe such as horse tack, gold and silver objects and coins dating from all periods in Li Zuoxian's *Collection of Ancient Coins*.

The Liaoning Provincial Museum collection reflects the achievements of Chinese culture and art throughout history and provides a rich resource for studying this legacy. We are confident that readers from China and abroad will appreciate the value of these collections through this catalogue and will discover the beauty and special qualities of each object.

Ma Baojie
Director of Liaoning Provincial Museum

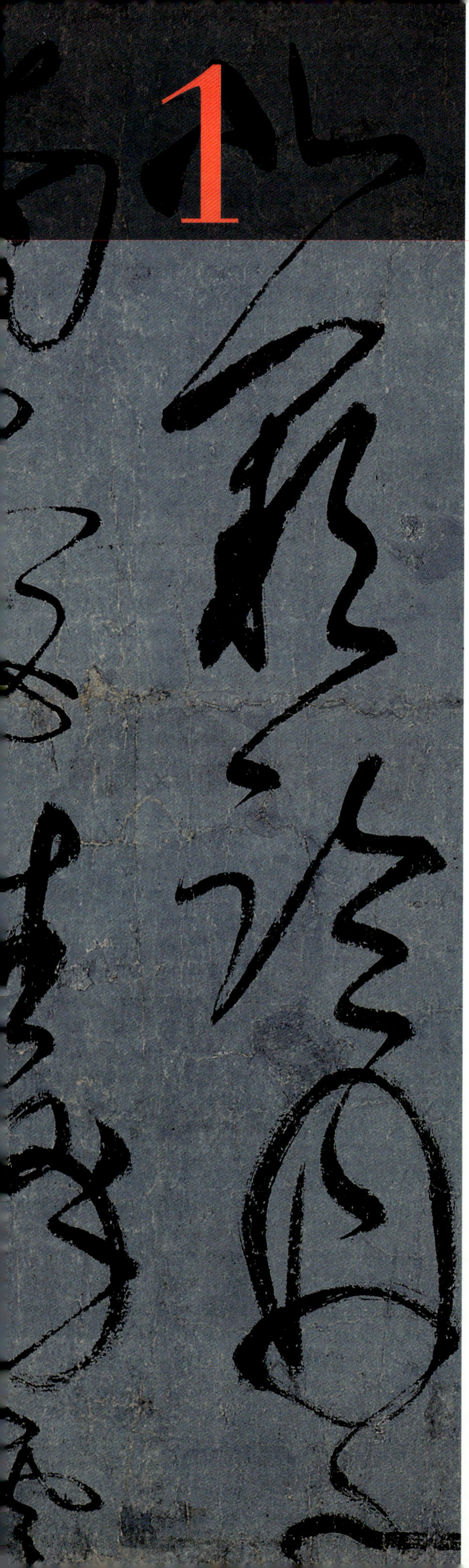

1

Calligraphy

The art of calligraphy in China has been constantly refined and developed as an essential component of the history of writing. From the Shang dynasty onwards, Chinese calligraphy has gradually become a special art form, developed over countless dynasties.

Historical calligraphy in the Liaoning Provincial Museum collection ranges from the Eastern Jin dynasty to the Ming and Qing dynasties. It is a complete collection of high quality, enjoying its special reputation from the dispersed collections of works from the Jin dynasty, through the Tang, Song and Yuan dynasties from the Qing palace in Shenyang. These rare examples show graphically the main trends of the development of Chinese calligraphy.

By the Wei, Jin and North and South dynasties, the regular style, running script and modern cursive style had more or less been formed. This led to the appearance of profoundly influential calligraphy masters such as Zhong Yao, Wang Xizhi and Wang Xianzhi. The *Eulogy to Cao E* of the Eastern Jin is the earliest extant work of regular script calligraphy and is a classic example of the change from official style to regular style, showing that the regular style was already mature by the Eastern Jin. Examples of original calligraphy from the family of Wang Xizhi, collected by his descendent Wang Fangqing and presented to Empress Wu Zetian as a book, provide an accurate representation of the period, and a reliable source for research into Eastern Jin calligraphy, particularly that of Wang Xizhi and Wang Xianzhi. The Tang dynasty was a high point in the development of Chinese calligraphy. Masters of regular script such as Ouyang Xun, Yu Shinan, Yan Zhenqing and Liu Gongquan inherited from the Wei and Jin the twin tradition of black ink calligraphy and stone inscription, and gradually broke away from the free-moving style of the Wang clan towards a more serious style. The *Meng Dian Tie* is one of Ouyang Xun's late works, and is the only original work surviving in Ouyang Xun's own hand. It shows the rigorous artistic style of the calligrapher. The work of two masters at the end of the High Tang, Zhang Xu and Huai Su, broke with tradition by turning cursive stroke into wild cursive stroke, laying the way for the form of wild cursive script. *Gu Shi Si Tie* is an extant example of Zhang Xu's wild cursive style, and serves as an illustration of the change from cursive to wild cursive script. *Lun Shu Tie* shows another side of Huai Su's cursive style and is useful for research.

Tang calligraphy emphasised style. It is followed by the mature calligraphy of the Song dynasty that emphasised meaning. The most notable exponents of this style were the four masters Su Shi, Huang Tingjian, Mi Fu and Cai Xiang. Song dynasty emperors were keen patrons of calligraphy, the father and son Huizong Zhao Ji and Gaozong Zhao Gou being the most exceptional. Huizong was skilled at slender gold style and cursive style. The *Thousand Character Classic in Cursive Script Text* is a fine example of his cursive script. From this work the development of cursive script can be traced back to Huai Su, and the clear artistic talent of the painter can be seen. Gaozong was the most skilled of the emperors who practised calligraphy. His honed skill can be seen in the *Inscription in Cursive Script about the Nymph of the Luo River*. Many literati were also fine calligraphers and the Liaoning Museum contains works of the following big names such as Ouyang Xiu, one of the eight masters of the Tang and Song, Lu You the patriotic poet, Zhu Xi the neo-Confucian and the anti-Yuan Wen Tianxiang. The continued tradition of the Southern Song is represented by Yuan artists such as Zhao Mengfu and Xian Yushu. They continued styles from the Wei and Jin, and were heavily influenced by the Wang family style. Zhao Mengfu's poem and painting of *River Mist and Craggy Peaks*, *Ode to the Sound of Autumn*, *Returning Home* and *Heart Sutra* and Xian Yushu's *Collection of Verse by Wang Anshi*, his *Copy and Supplement to Gao Xian's Thousand Character Classic*, and works by others such as Zhang Yu and Yang Weizhen have their own special characteristics.

The Ming and Qing dynasties marked an important stage in the development of Chinese calligraphy, showing diverse strands of development, with a number of famous individuals emerging including the four Wu Zhong masters Zhu Yunming, Wen Zhengming, Wang Chong and Chen Daofu. There are Dong Qichang, Zhang Ruitu, Huang Daozhou, Ni Yuanlu of the late Ming period, and calligraphers from the end of the Ming such as Wang Duo, Fu Shan, Weng Fanggang, Liu Yong, Liang Tongshu, Wang Wenzhi, Jin Nong, Zheng Xie, Deng Shiru, Yi Bingshou, He Shaoji, and Zhao Zhiqian. The quantity and excellence of work by the above names determine the outstanding quality of the Liaoning calligraphy collection. GUO DAN

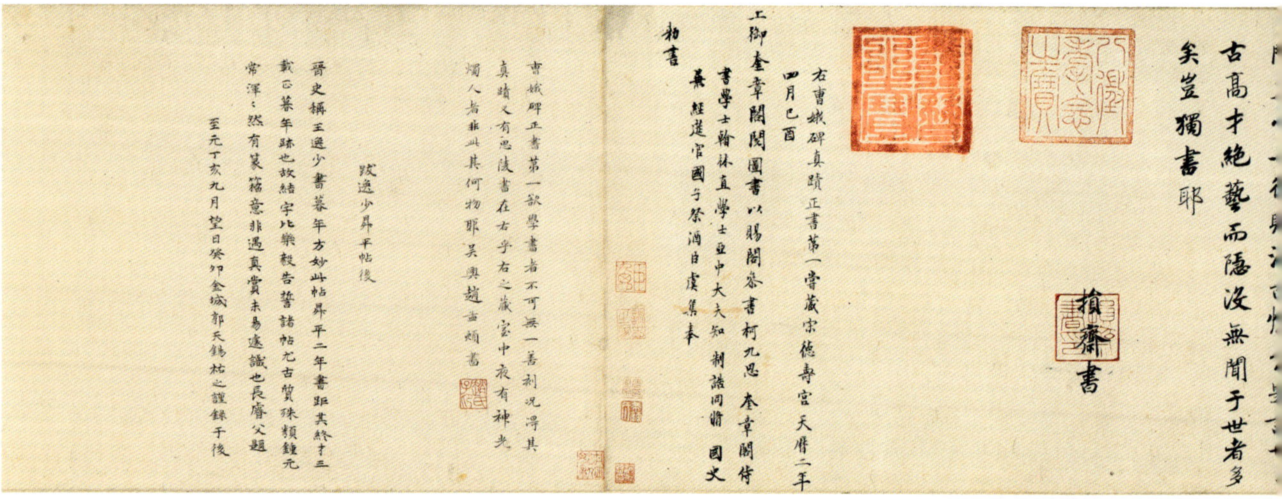
古高才絕藝而隱沒無聞于世者多
矣豈獨書耶
損齋書
右曹娥碑真蹟正書第一嘗藏宋德壽宮天曆二年
四月己酉
上御奎章閣閱圖書以賜閣參書柯九思奎章閣侍
書學士翰林直學士亞中大夫知制誥同脩國史
兼經筵官國子祭酒臣虞集奉
勅書
曹娥碑正書第一欲學書者不可無一善刻況得其
真蹟又有思陵書在右乎右之藏室中夜有神光
燭人者非此其何物耶吳興趙孟頫書
跋逸少昇平帖後
晉史稱王逸少書暮年方妙此帖昇平二年書距其終才三
載正暮年跡也故結字比樂毅告誓諸帖尤古質殊類鍾元
常渾渾然有篆籀意非遇真賞未易遽識也長睿父題
至元丁亥九月望日癸卯金城郭天錫祐之謹錄于後

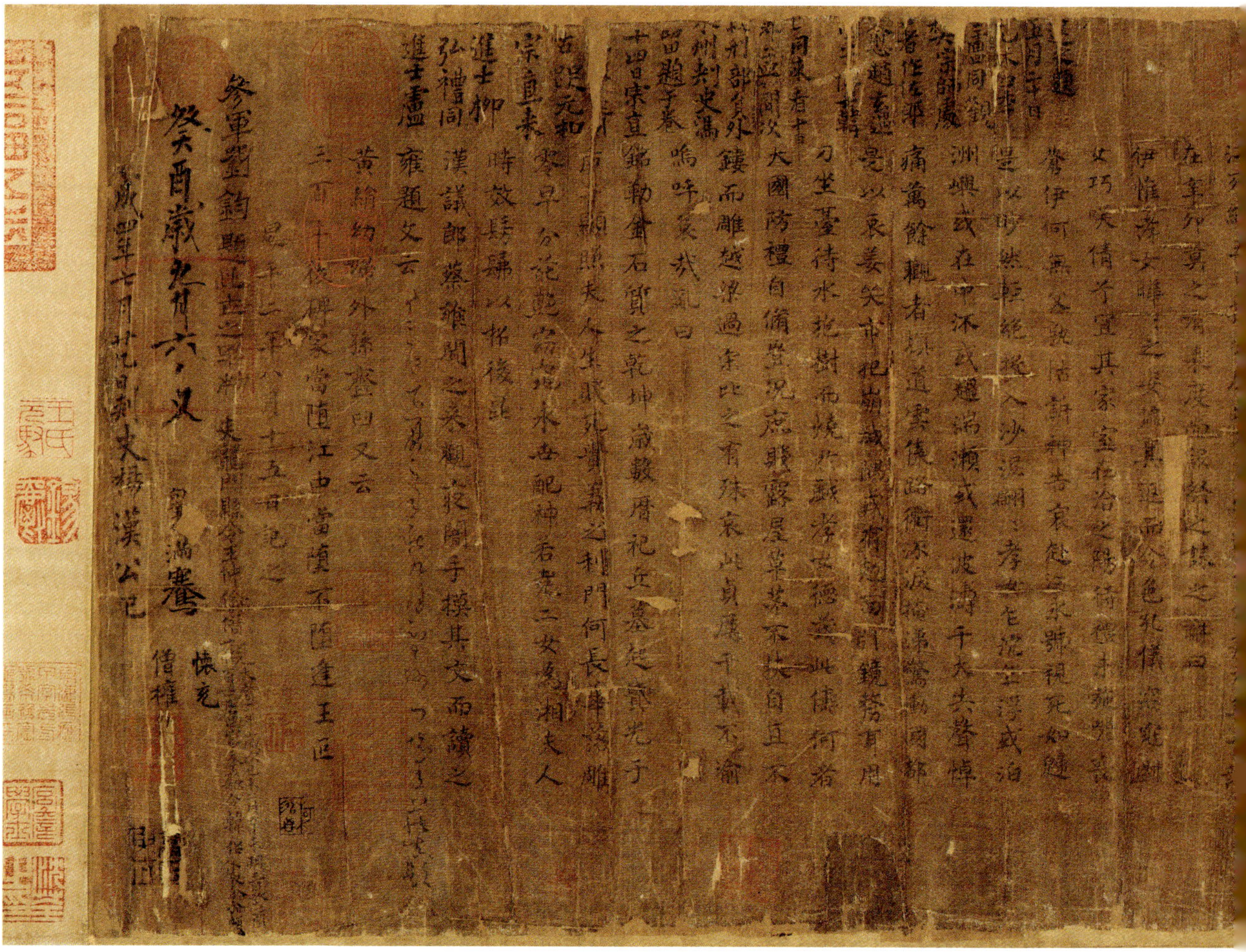

1 *Eulogy to Cao E*, regular script

Unknown
Eastern Jin dynasty (317–420)
Hand scroll, ink on silk
Height 32.3 cm, Width 54.3 cm

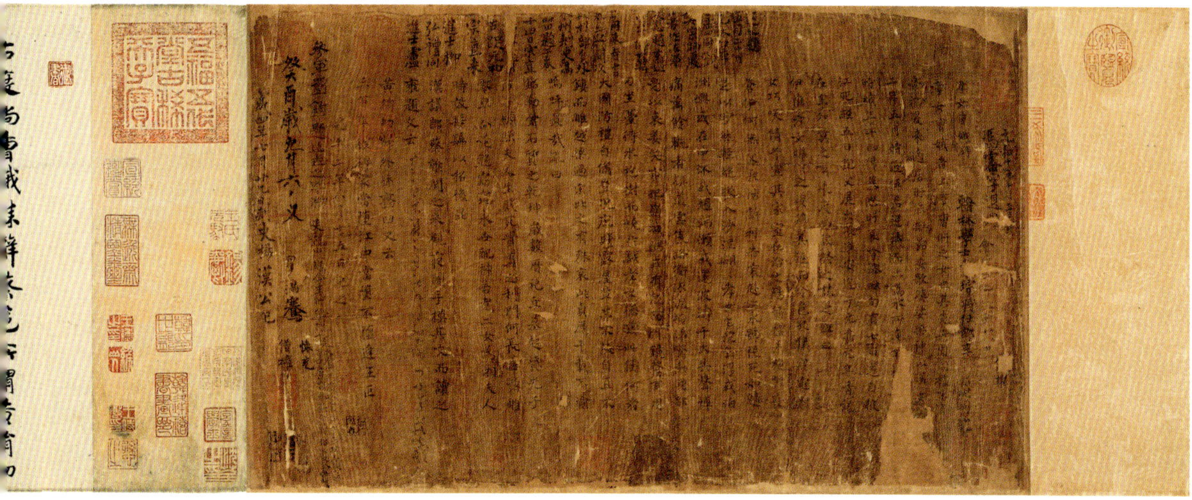

1

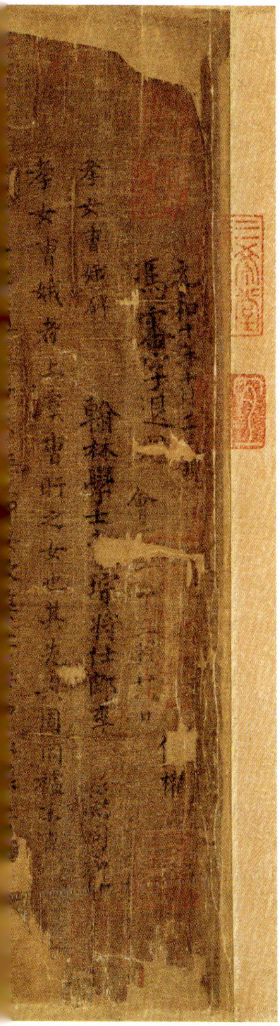

The *Eulogy to Cao E* is an example of calligraphy in black ink in regular script from the Eastern Jin. Since there is an inscription 'Shengping 2nd year' at the end of the scroll, it is also called the *Shengping Tie*. Cao E, of the Eastern Han, threw herself into a river to search for her drowned father. In AD 151 the head of Shangyu County wrote some lines to record her filial behaviour, and had a stele carved for her. More information about her can be found in the *Later Book of Han, Biographies of Notable Women*. The text in the *Eulogy to Cao E* is a copy of the stele inscription. Since this scroll followed the stele inscription, it was called the *Cao E Stele*. The calligraphy of the stele is in small cursive script, with pressure exerted on the brush and flat joined-up characters. It still has elements of the official script. From this the characteristics of the early stage of cursive script and joined-up characters can be seen. This scroll was originally attributed to Wang Xizhi, but by the Song dynasty Gaozong Zhao Gou had shown it to be the unknown work of a calligrapher from the Jin dynasty.

There are inscriptions by the Southern Liang dynasty collectors Huai Chong, Seng Quan, the Tang literary scholar Han Yu, and the calligrapher Huai Su. At the end of the scroll are colophons by the Song Gaozong Emperor, Yuan Yuji, Zhao Mengfu, Qiao Kuicheng, Huang Shiweng, Song Ben, Ming Jianghui, the Qing Kangxi Emperor, Shen Quan and Gao Shiqi. This scroll also has over ten collectors' seals at the bottom. Guo Dan

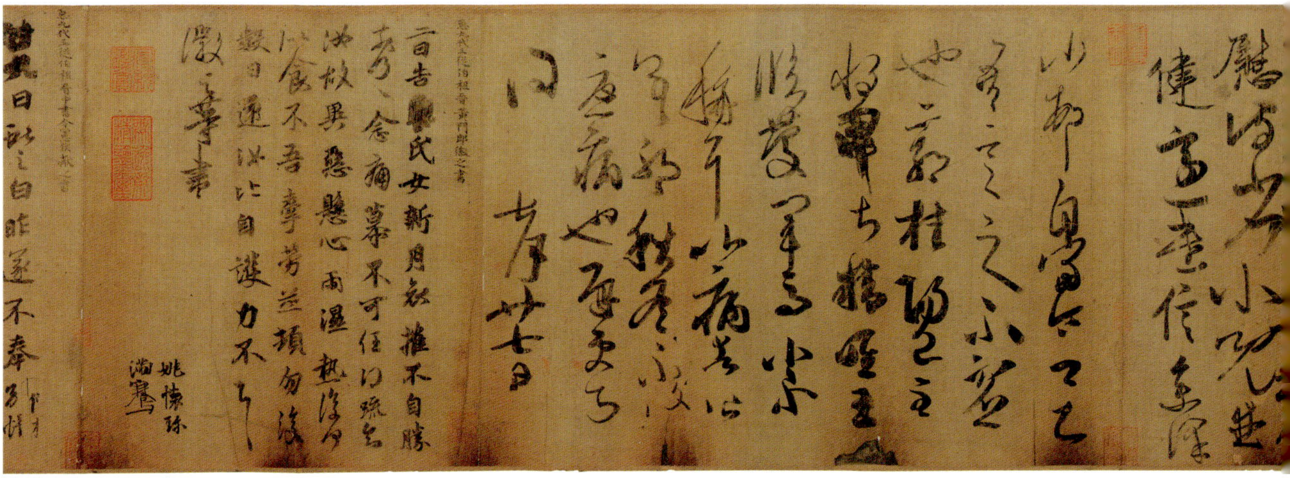

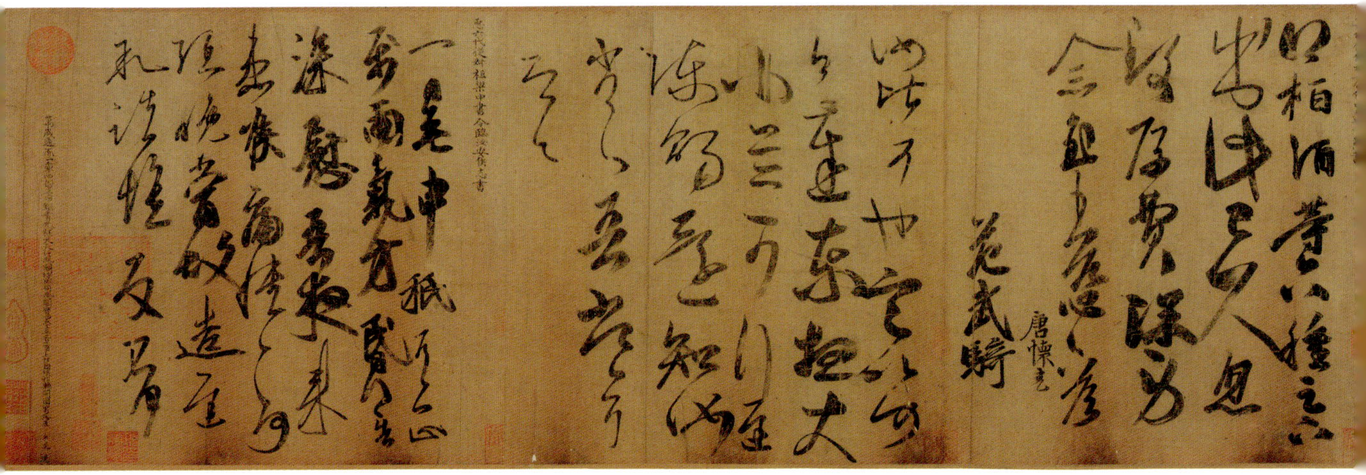

2 *Copy of a Calligraphy by Wang Xizhi*, regular script

Unknown
Tang dynasty (618–907)
Hand scroll, ink on paper
Height 26.3 cm, Length 253.8 cm

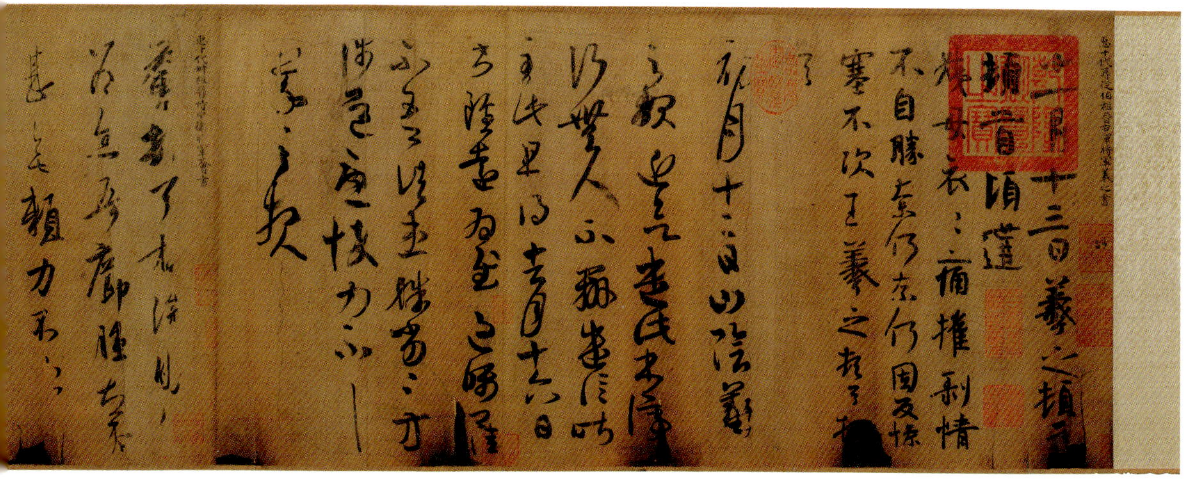

2

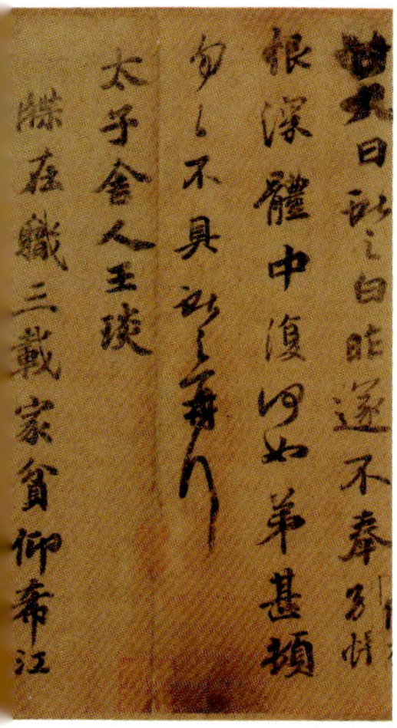

In the second year of the reign of the Tang Empress Wu Zetian (697), she was presented with a collection of original calligraphy works by a descendent of Wang Xizhi named Wang Fangqing. The collection contained works by both father and son, Wang Xizhi and Wang Xian, and twenty-eight other works by Wang family members. Wu Zetian ordered these to be copied and kept in her palace, and ordered Cui Rong to record this in the *Collections of Treasures of the Wang Family*. The originals that Wang Fangqing presented have not survived; there are only ten copies of calligraphy by Wang Xizhi, Wang Hui, Wang Huizhi, Wang Xianzhi, Wang Sengqian, Wang Ci and Wang Zhi. As the date *wansui tong* year (697) has been signed on the scroll, it is also known as the *Wansui Tongtian Tie*. The scroll has colophons by Tang Huaichong, Yao Huaizhen and Xu Sengquan of the Southern Liang dynasty. At the beginning and end of the scroll are the ancestors and rank of Wang Fangqing and details of the presentation of the work at court. Among these lines, the characters for *chen*, *tian*, *nian*, *yue*, *ri* and *guo* are all new Wu Zhou characters. Calligraphy by Wang Xizhi in the original ink was already rare by the Northern Song period, and the number of Tang copies of his work continues to diminish. This scroll has been beautifully copied, and has been praised as an outstanding likeness to the original. It shows the relationship between calligraphy styles that were practised during the Wei, Jin and Northern and Southern dynasties, and is a valuable resource for researching the development of Chinese calligraphy scripts. This scroll was damaged twice by fire and burn marks are still visible on the scroll today.

At the end of the scroll are colophons by Yue Ke of the Southern Song, Zhang Yu of the Yuan, Wen Weiming of the Ming, and Dong Qichang. Several collectors' seals are also visible on the scroll, including 'A newly carved seal of the history office', 'Literary office of the householder' and 'Zhong Xingxuan' of the Northern Song. Guo Dan

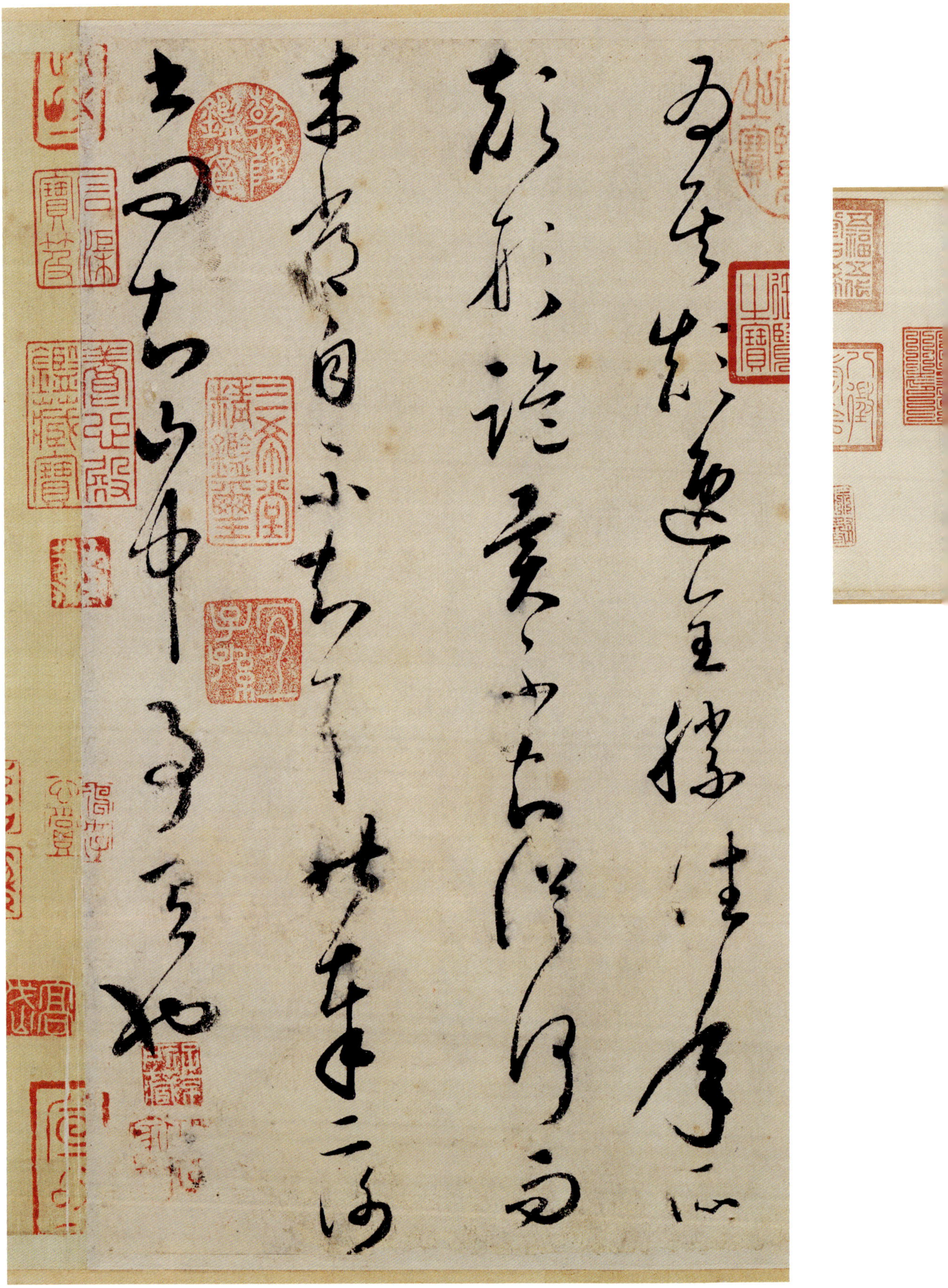

3 *Lun Shu Tie*, cursive script

Huai Su (725–785)
Tang dynasty (618–907)
Hand scroll, ink on paper
Height 38.5 cm, Width 40 cm

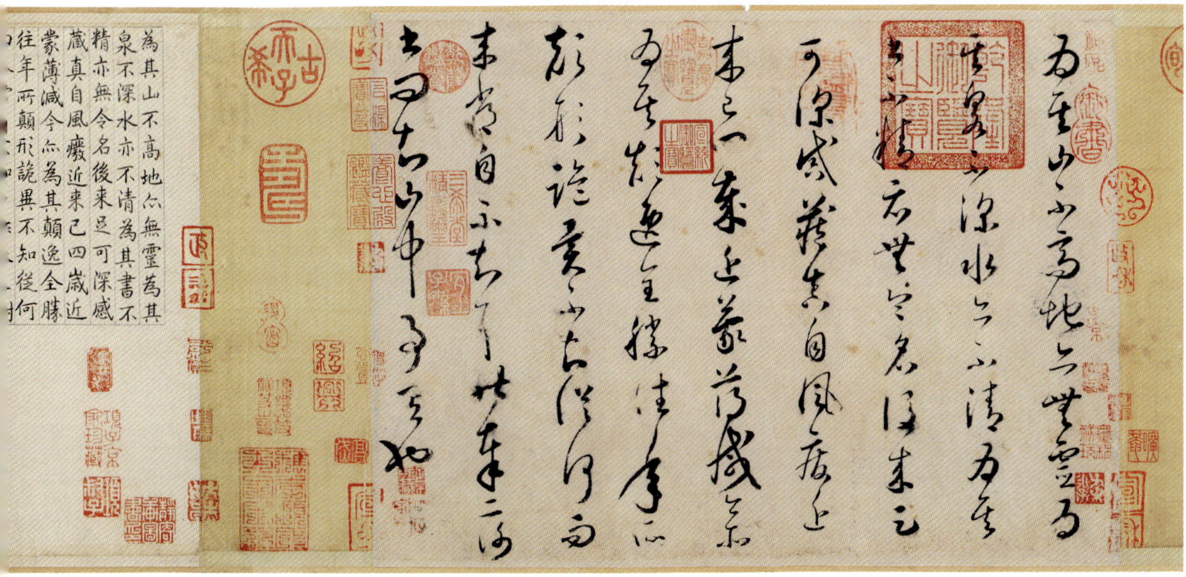

3

Huai Su, originally surnamed Qian and from Changsha (in present-day Hunan), was a Buddhist monk with the courtesy name *Zhan Zhen* (Treasury of Truth). In the history of Chinese calligraphy there are Crazy Zhang and Wild Su, where Zhang refers to Zhang Xu, the cursive script calligrapher of the Tang dynasty, and Su refers to Huai Su. Compared to other works in 'wild script' such as *Zi Xu Tie* and *Ku Sun Tie*, the *Lun Shu Tie* shows another side of Huai Su's cursive style. The brush strokes are very fine, in carefully executed cursive style. Looking at the whole object from top to bottom, Huai Su breaks with and adheres to convention, in a wild style. The origin of this style goes back no further than the Wei or Jin. In his *Observations on an Ordinary Life*, the early Qing collector Gu Fu surmised that this scroll is an early work of the calligrapher master Wang Xizhi, which is of great value to future research. GUO DAN

仲尼夢奠七十有二周王
九齡俱不滿百彭祖資
以導養樊重任性裁過
盈數終歸冥滅無有得
停住者未有生而不老

4 *Zhong Ni Meng Dian Tie*, running script

Ouyang Xun (557–641)
Tang dynasty (618–907)
Hand scroll, ink on paper
Height 26.5 cm, Width 34 cm

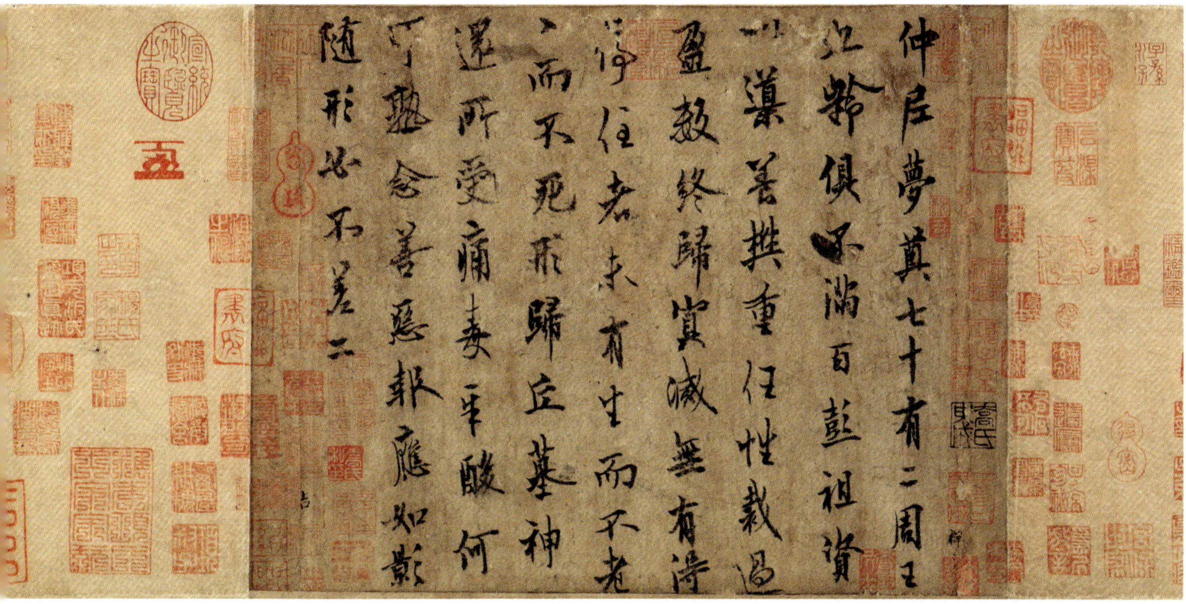

4

Ouyang Xun, who took the courtesy name Xinben, was from Linxiang, Tanzhou, the present-day Changsha in Hunan Province. He served as chief water clock watchman at court, was a scholar at the *Hongwenguan* (Academy of Culture), and received the title Governer of Bohai County. His calligraphy copied the style of the two Wangs, using the official script but unusually he painted self-portraits, invented the Ou style characters, and had a great influence on later generations. He was one of the four great calligraphy masters of the Tang dynasty.

This scroll has nine lines, with a total of seventy-eight characters. His characters flow with ease, with clear, joined-up script, with firm regular brush strokes. His writing is quick, with roundness hidden in square shapes and natural turns. Cursive script forms the main part of this scroll, which is an example of Ouyang Xun's original work.

Dai Jingying

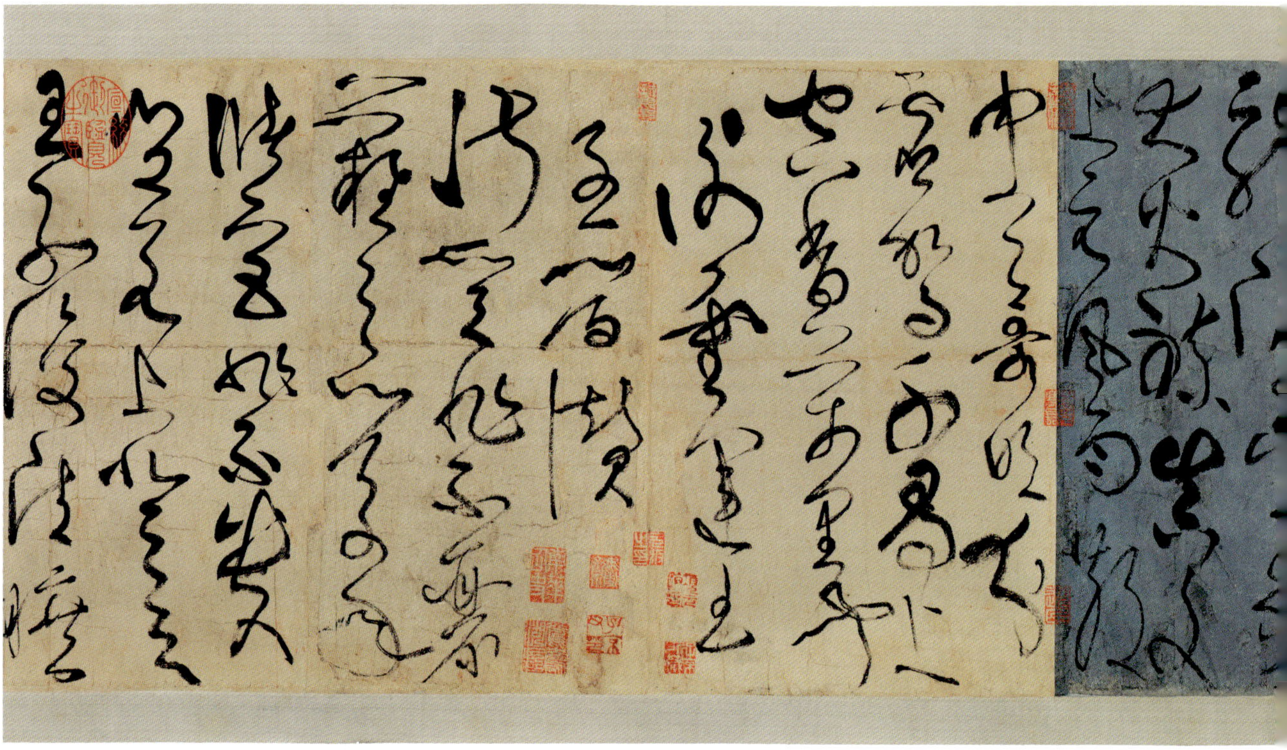

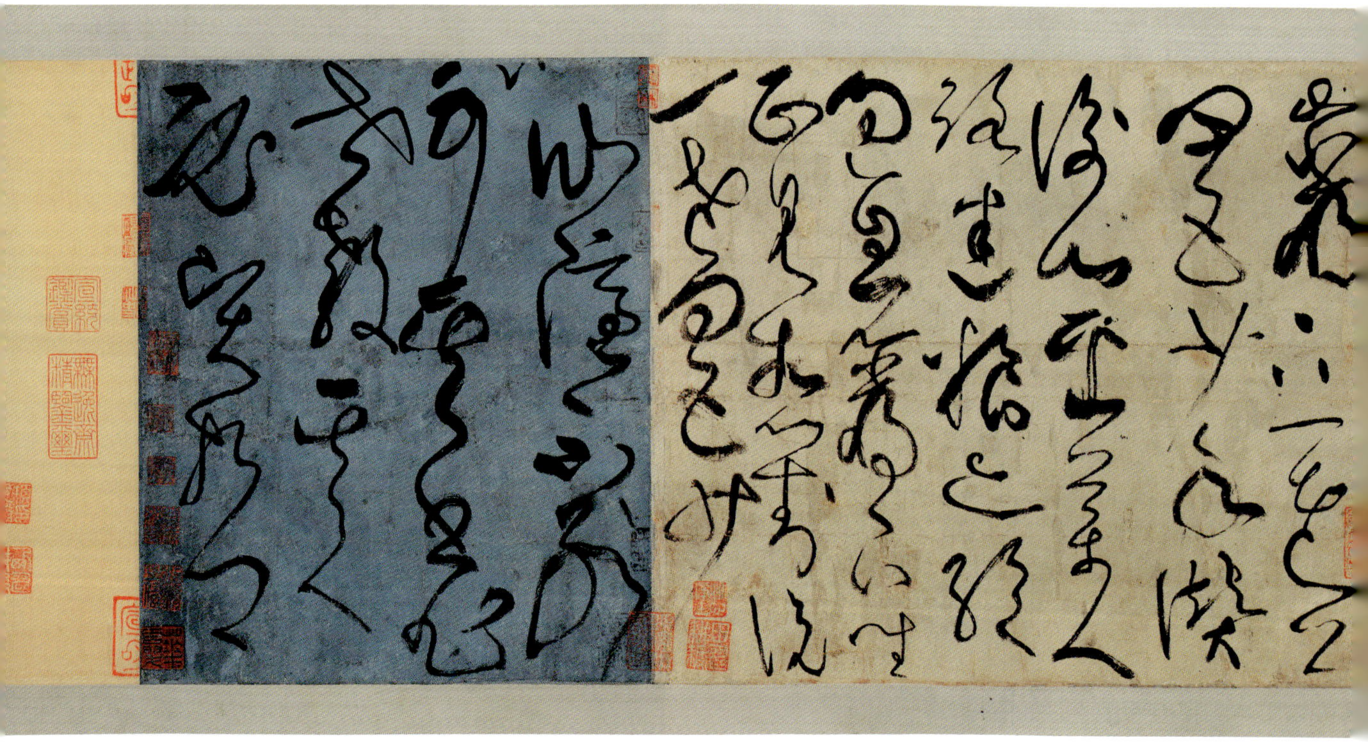

5 *Gu Shi Si Tie*, cursive script

Zhang Xu (dates unknown)
Tang dynasty (618–907)
Hand scroll, ink on paper
Height 29.5 cm, Length 195.2 cm

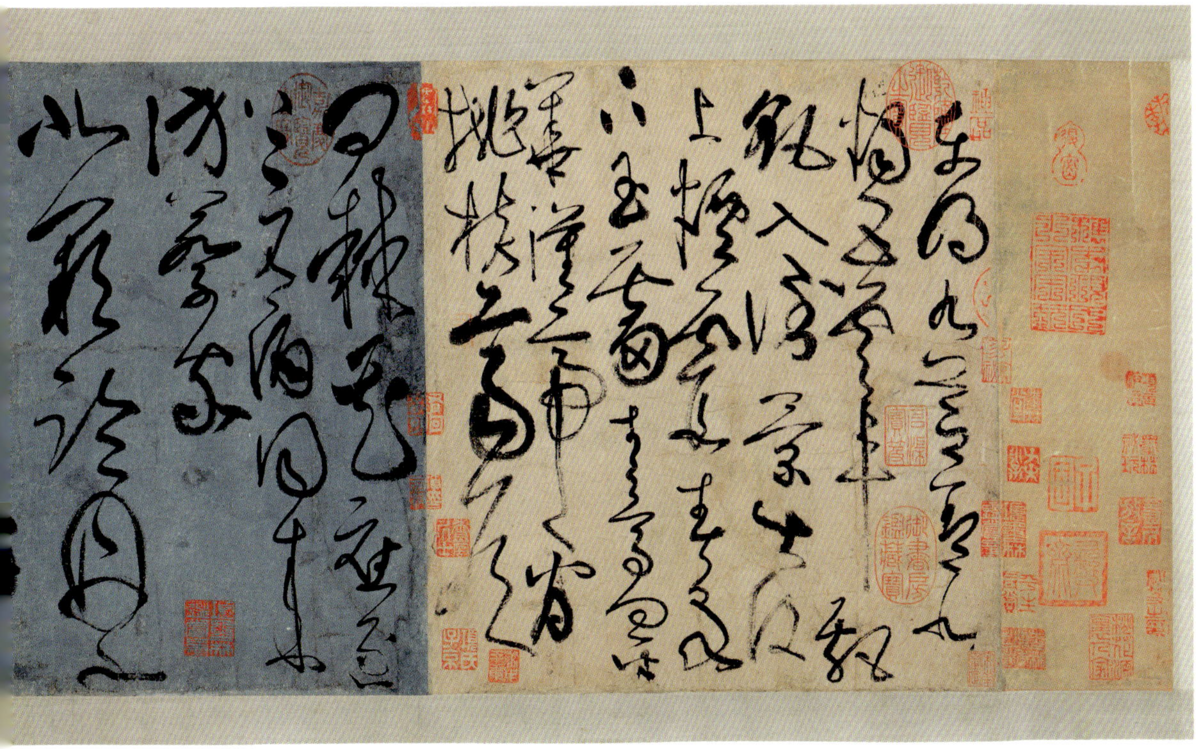

5

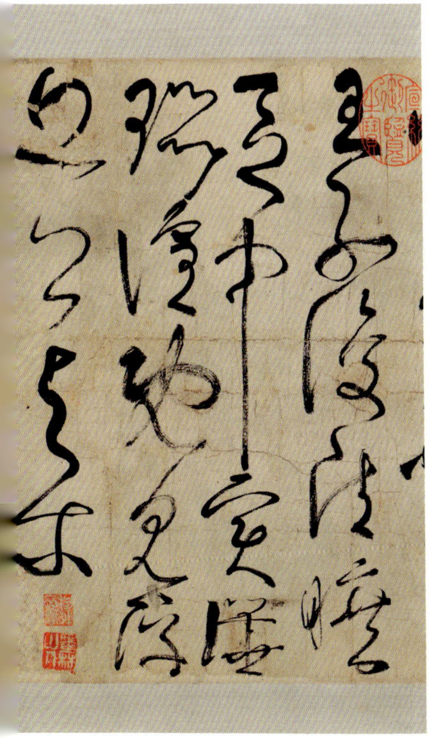

Zhang Xu's birth date is not clear, he was born during the time of the Tang Xuanzong Emperor, around the Kaiyuan and Tianbao years. His courtesy name was Bogao, and was from Wu (present day Suzhou in Jiangsu Province). He wrote poetry in *zhen* and cursive scripts, but was most famous for his cursive script, and was called the 'master of cursive script'.

The *Gu Shi Si Tie* records poems by Geng Xin and Xie Lingyun. There are forty lines of cursive script, in quick rushing strokes, as if jumping out in ambush, full of rhythm. The head of the brush is round, the brush strokes are firm in both horizontal and vertical strokes, and similar in style to seal characters. The cursive writing is closely executed, with lively movement, with rising and falling orderly waves. Although the style can be considered wild cursive script, the wildness is not strange and does not depart from the basic principles of cursive joined-up script. Dai Jingying

自唐末之亂士族亡其家譜今雖顯族名家多失
其世次譜學由是廢絶而唐之遺族往往有藏其舊譜者時得
見之而譜皆無圖豈其亡之抑前世簡而未備歟因采太史
公史記表鄭玄詩譜略依其上下旁行作為譜圖上自高祖下
止玄孫而別自為世使別為世者上承其祖為玄孫下系其
高祖凡世再別而九族之親備推而上之則知源流之所自旁

夫惟多久其勢必分此物之常理

昭陵以是年春晏駕十月復土時
厚陵再屬疾 兩宮情意未通故有攀髯路
斷憂國心危之句云
子頊出閤奏
入内内侍省取旨施行
右兩行元在歐陽公詩槀之陰殆中書所録旨揮盖
神宗以是年九月封淮陽郡王改賜今名十二月乙亥
出閤正當時事也
淳熙乙巳春 必大謹記

6 *Draft of a poem*, running script

Ouyang Xiu (1007–1072)
Northern Song dynasty (960–1127)
Hand scroll, ink on paper
Height 30.5 cm, Width 66.2 cm

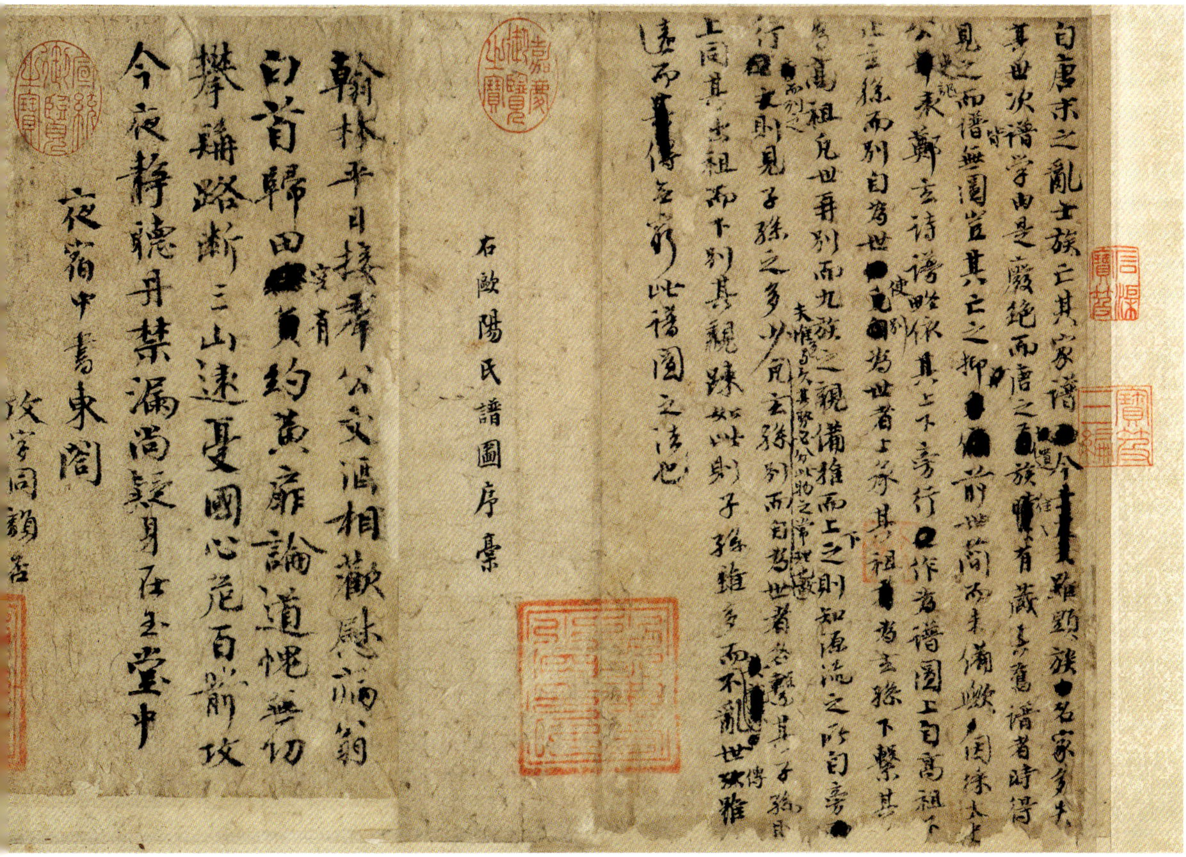

6

Ouyang Xiu, courtesy name Yongshu, first literary name Zuiweng, late literary name Jushi, was from Ji'an in Jiangxi. He had a vast knowledge of books, and wrote poetry comparable to that of Du Fu. He was the leader of the 'ancient writing' movement, and has been called one of the eight great masters of the Tang and Song dynasties.

This scroll is a draft of a poem by Ouyang Xiu. The composition is informal and light, the size of the characters is not constant or within the lines, the characters just flow downwards naturally, and are of great interest. The strokes are crisp and sharp, the rhythm of the rise and fall of the brush is clear, with complementary force and gentleness. The *Draft of a poem* epitomises the calligraphy style of this great master of the Northern Song. Dai Jingying

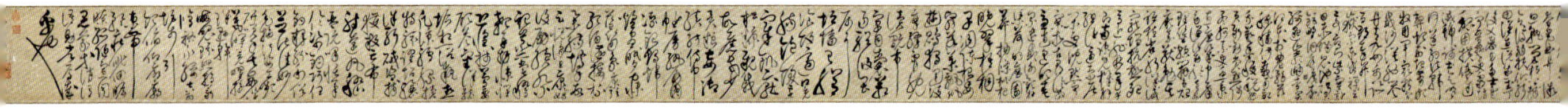

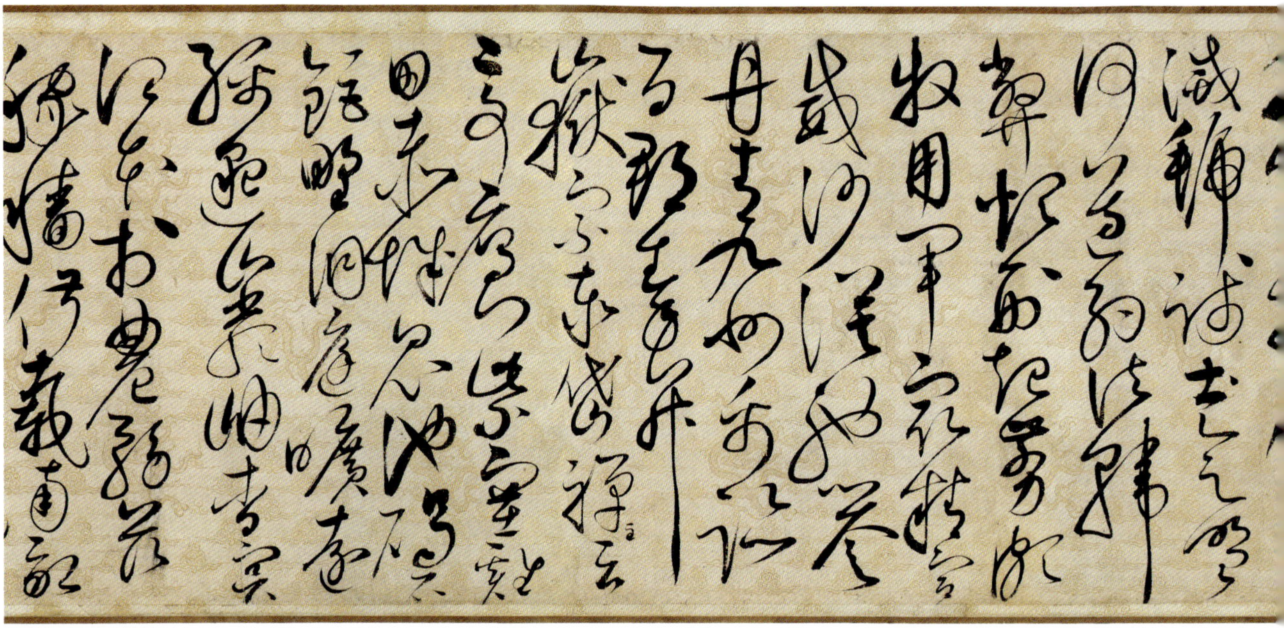

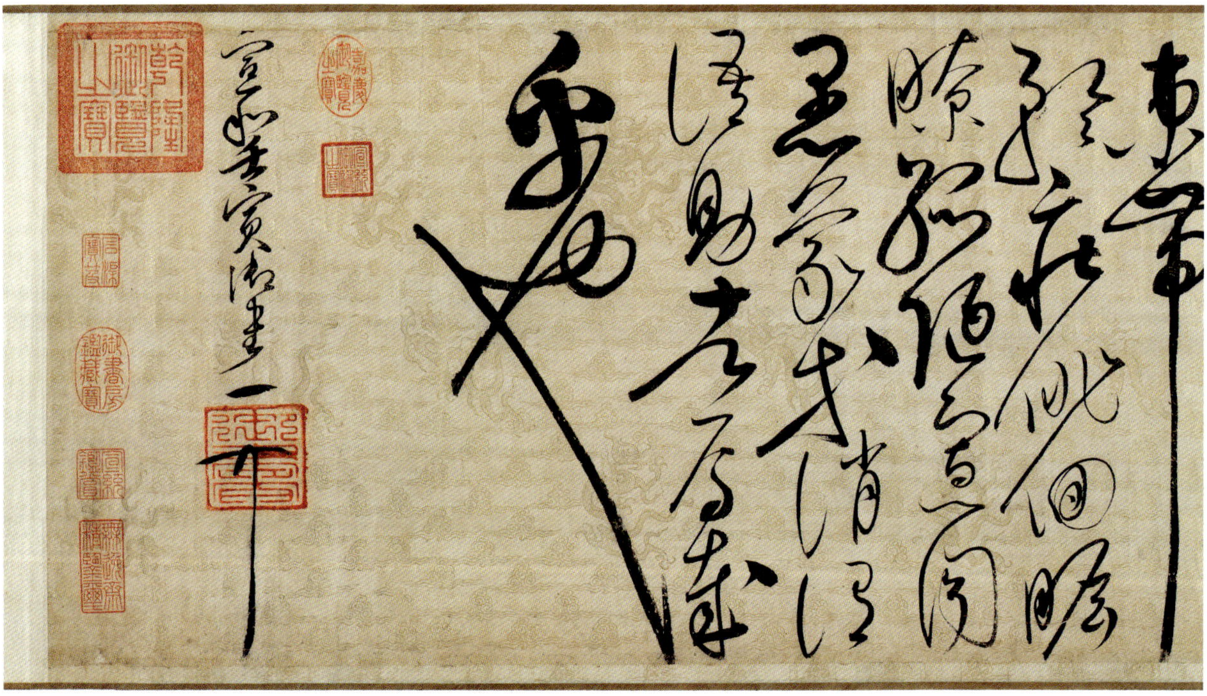

7 *The Thousand Character Classic*, cursive script

Zhao Ji (1082–1135)
Northern Song dynasty (960–1127)
Hand scroll, ink on paper
Height 31.5 cm, Width 1172.1 cm

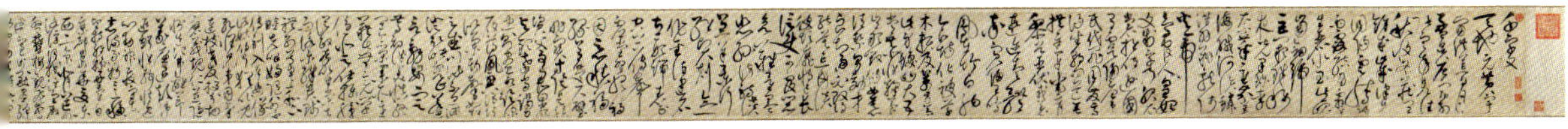

7

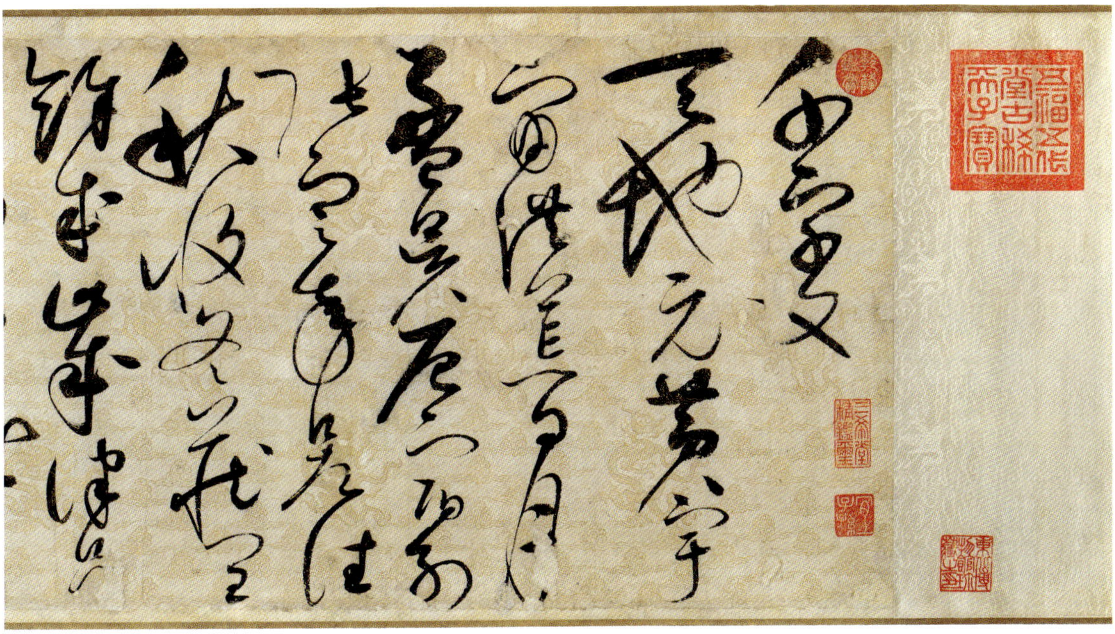

Zhao Ji was the last emperor of the Northern Song dynasty; his temple name was Huizong. Although Huizong was not a competent ruler, he was artistically accomplished, and was the most creative of the Song emperors in calligraphy and painting. He wrote in *zhen* script, running script and cursive script, and created a kind of regular script called 'the slender golden style'.

This *Thousand Character Classic* scroll is written on a twelve-metre-long golden scroll decorated with clouds and dragons. The cursive script is dynamic and unpredictable, executed in one breath of *qi*, and is a rare example of great work. The brushwork is calm yet rushing, firmly controlled, displaying heaviness and lightness of touch, fine and thick strokes, with smooth turns, blending change and harmony, like a lively piece of music evoked in calligraphy before the beholder's eye.

The *Thousand Character Classic* was written in the *xuanhe rengeng* year, 1122. It is a mature work of the forty-year old Zhao Ji, and is the only extant piece of his work, and is therefore extremely valuable. Dai Jingying

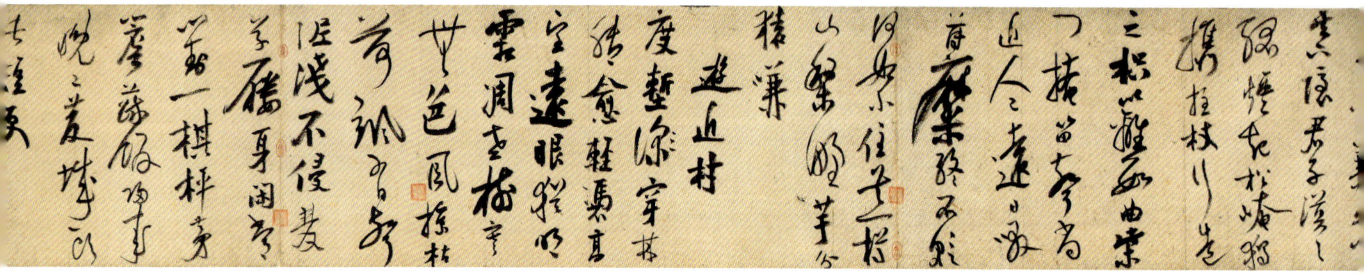

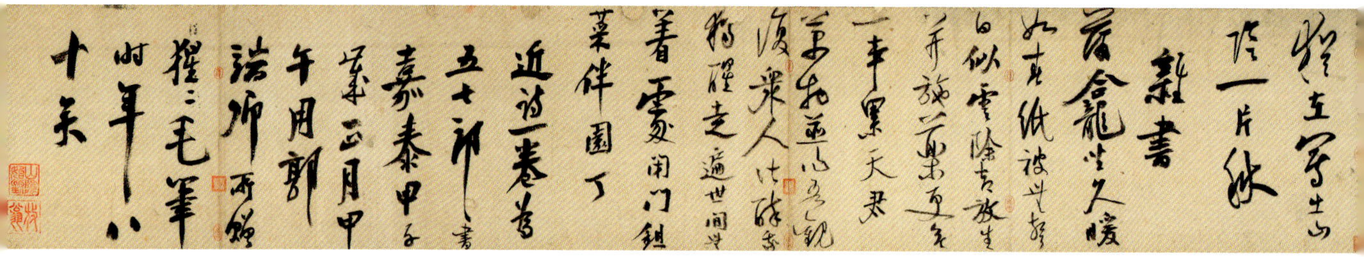

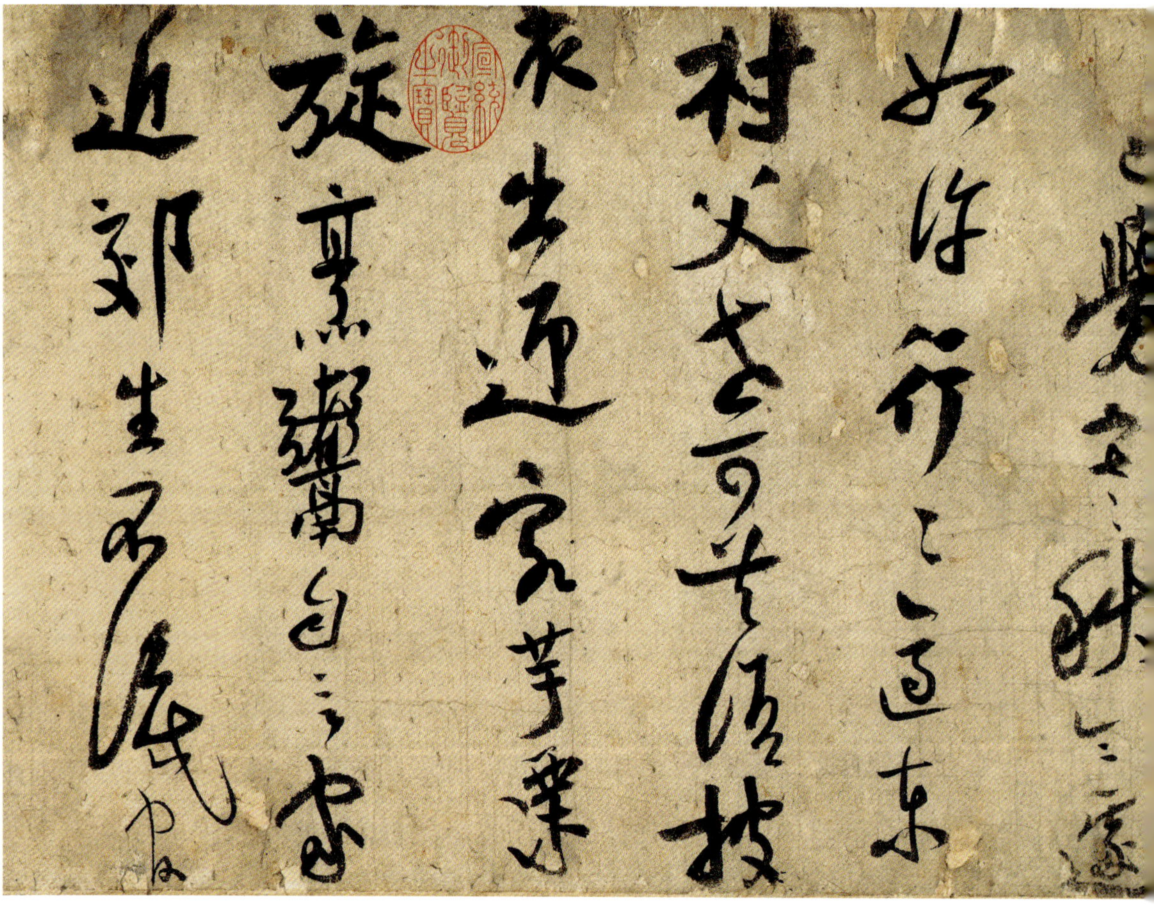

8 *Own poem*, running script

Lu You (1125–1210)
Southern Song dynasty (1127–1279)
Hand scroll, ink on paper
Height 31 cm, Width 701 cm

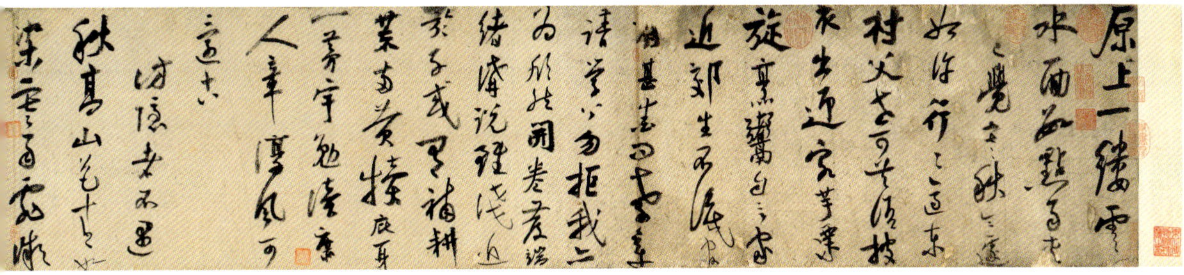

8

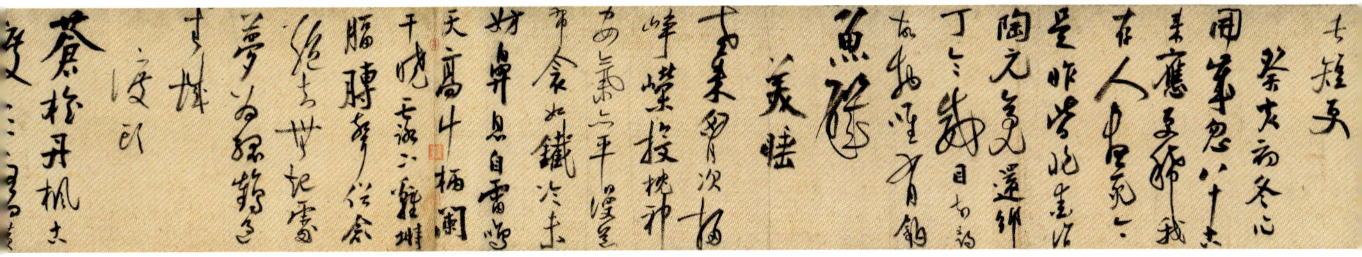

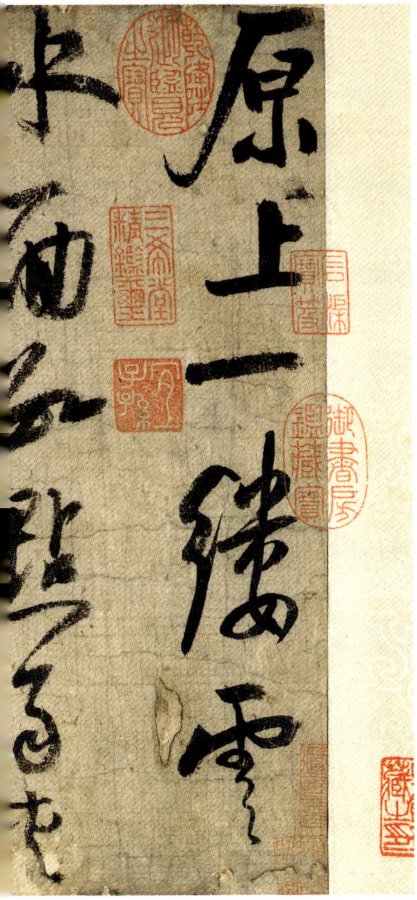

Lu You, famous poet of the Southern Song, courtesy name Wuguan, literary name Fangweng, was from Shanyang in Yuezhou (present-day Shaoxing in Zhejiang Province). This scroll was written in 1204 when Lu You returned home on his annual visit. He was eighty years old at the time. Liang Yan in the Qing dynasty wrote, 'Lu Fangweng's script, … is highly original', which sums up Lu You's work well. Looking at the whole scroll, the brushwork, the character joins, the *qi* in the lines and white spaces are all natural, giving a languid effect of beauty. GUO DAN

9 *The Fifth Book of the Thousand Character Classic*, cursive script

Sun Guoting (646–691)
Tang dynasty (618–907)
Hand scroll, ink on paper
Height 25.7 cm, Length 82.5 cm

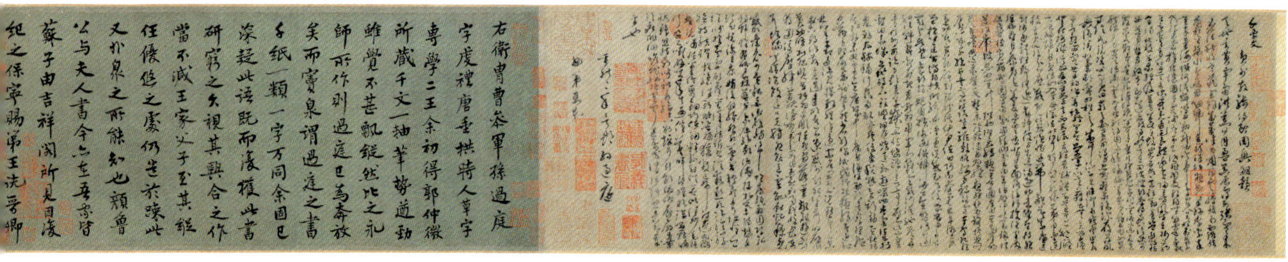

9

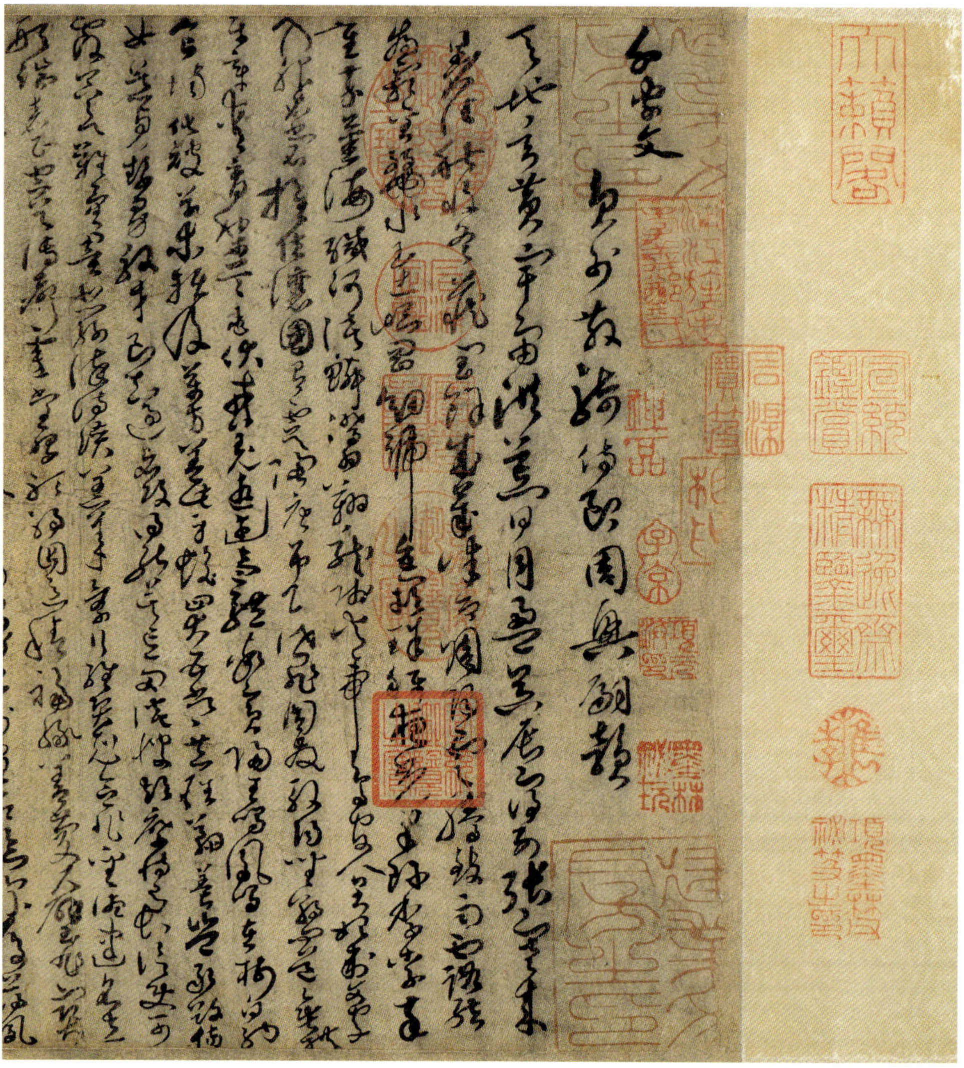

10 *Inscription about the Nymph of the Luo River*, cursive script

Zhao Gou (1107–1187)
Southern Song dynasty (1127–1279)
Hand scroll, ink on paper
Height 27.9 cm, Length 398 cm

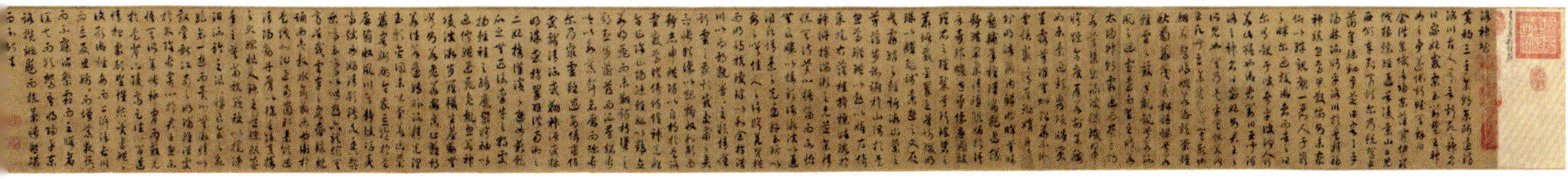

10

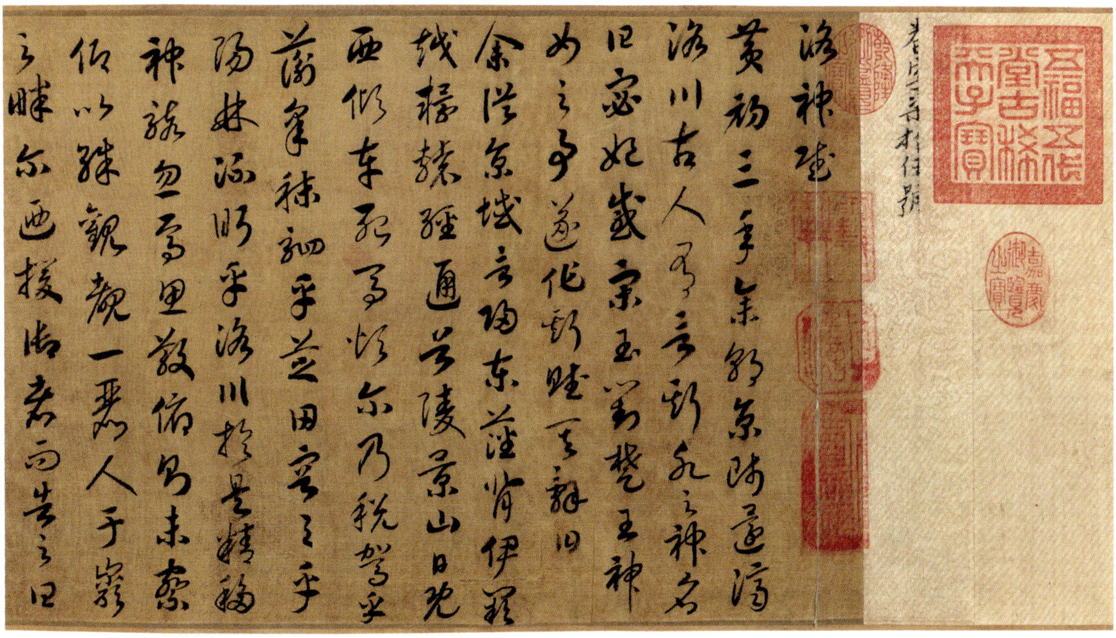

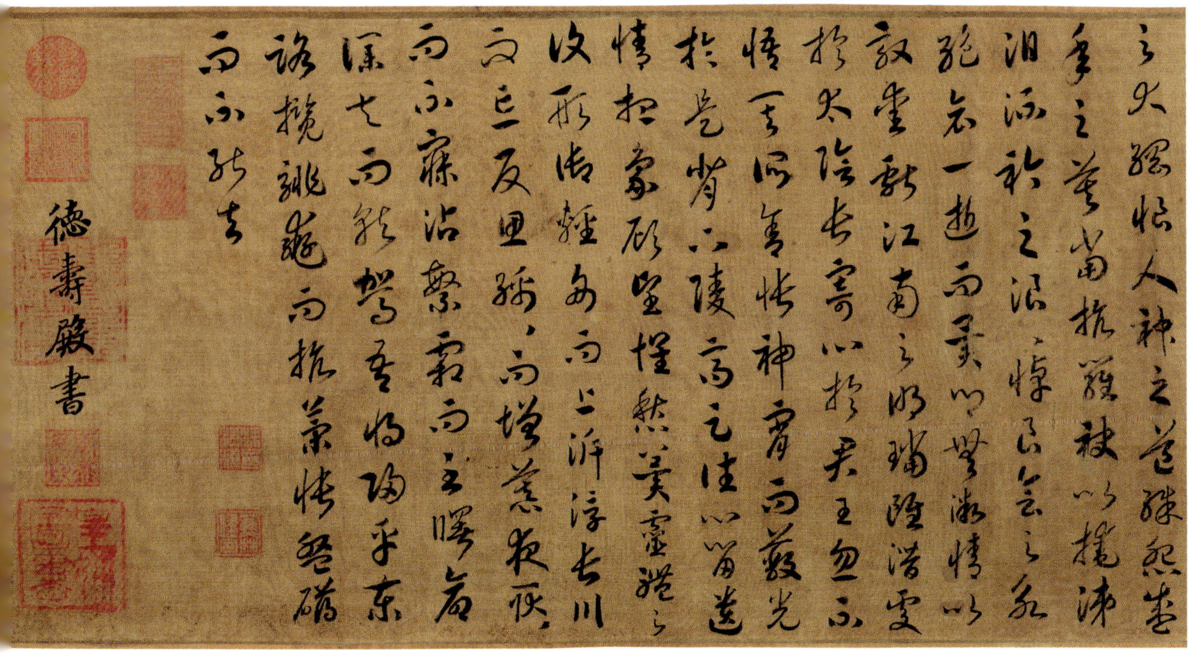

11 *Xing Shu Er Tie*, running script

Zhu Xi (1130–1200)
Southern Song dynasty (1127–1279)
Hand scroll, ink on paper
(First section) Height 33.5 cm, Length 45.3 cm
(Second section) Height 28.2 cm, Length 113.6 cm

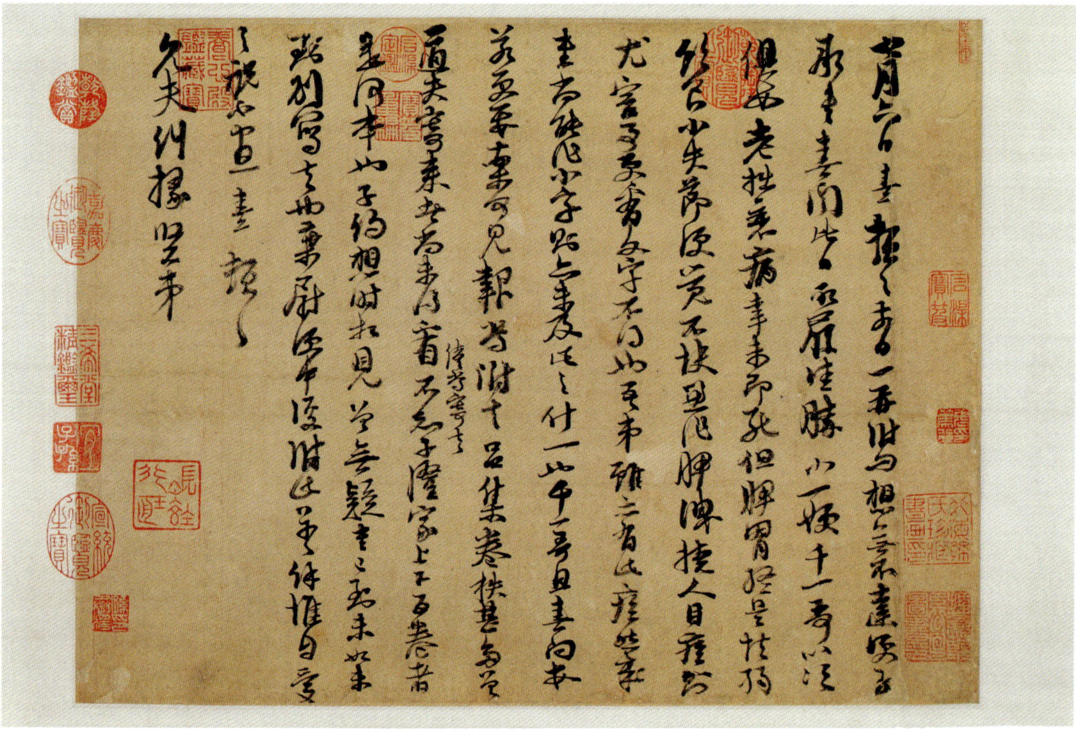

11

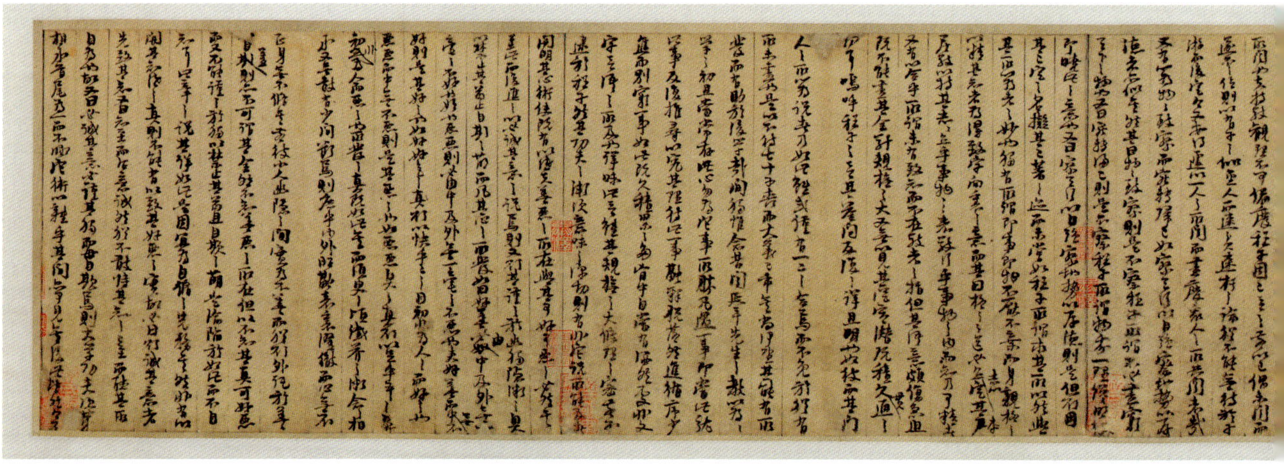

12 Poem by Du Fu, running script

Zhang Jizhi (1186–1266)
Southern Song dynasty (1127–1279)
Hand scroll, ink on paper
Height 34.6 cm, Length 1286.9 cm

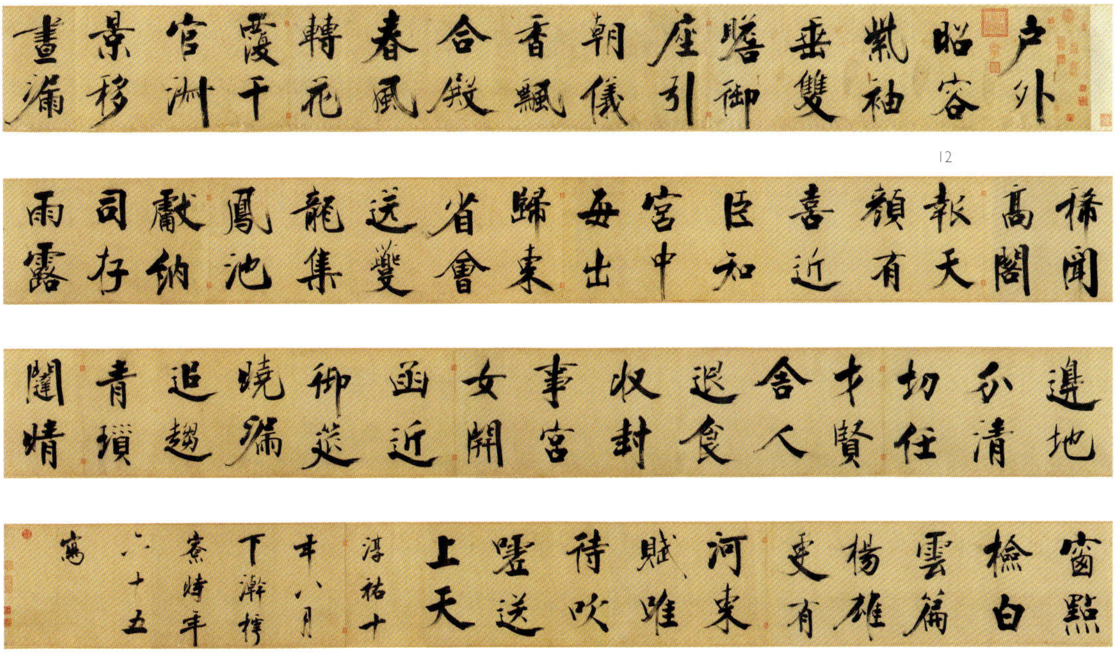

12

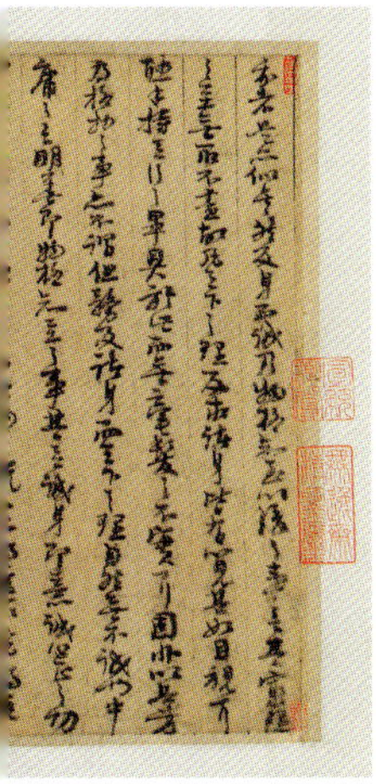

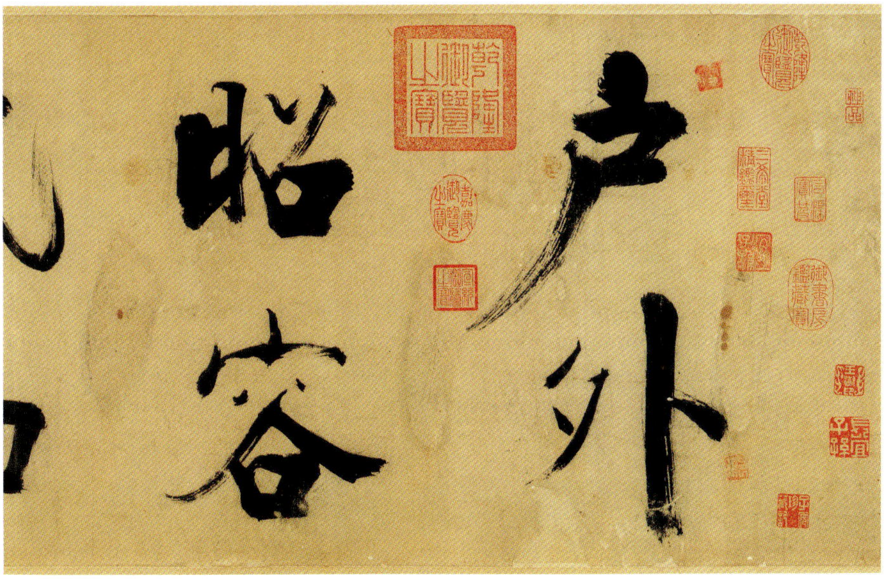

13 *Preface to Mu Ji Anthology*, cursive script

Wen Tianxiang (1236–1283)
Southern Song dynasty (1127–1279)
Hand scroll, ink on paper
Height 24.5 cm, Length 96.5 cm

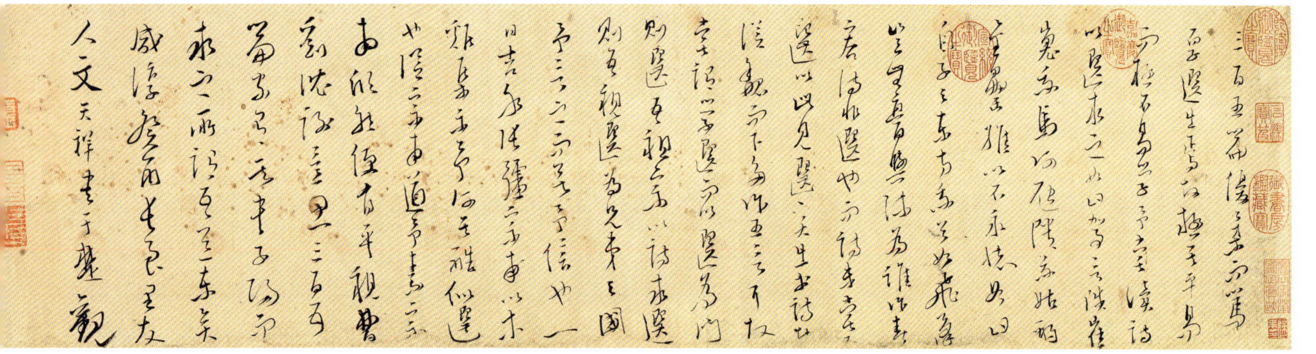

13

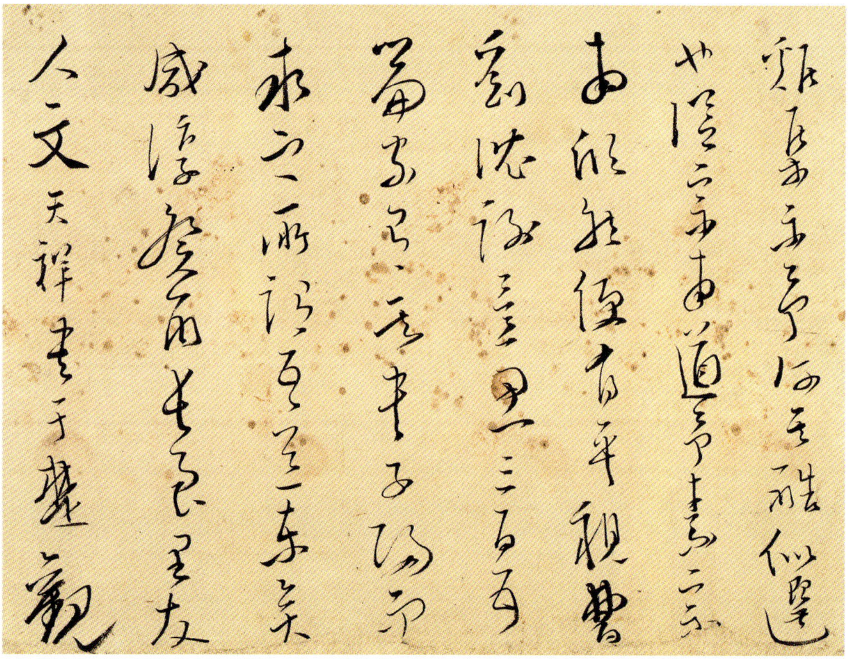

14 *Ode to the Sound of Autumn by Ouyang Xiu*, running script

Zhao Mengfu (1254–1322)
Yuan (1279–1368)
Hand scroll, ink on paper
Height 34.8 cm, Length 182.2 cm

15 *Collection of verse by Wang Anshi*, running script

Xian Yushu (1256–1307)
Yuan dynasty (1279–1368)
Hand scroll, ink on paper
Height 50 cm, Length 1,025 cm

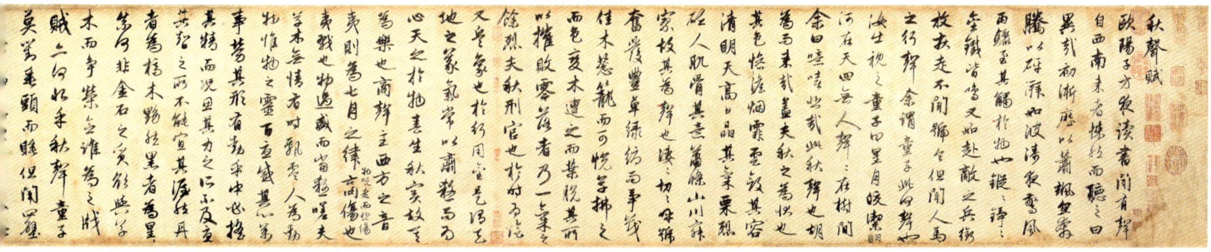

14

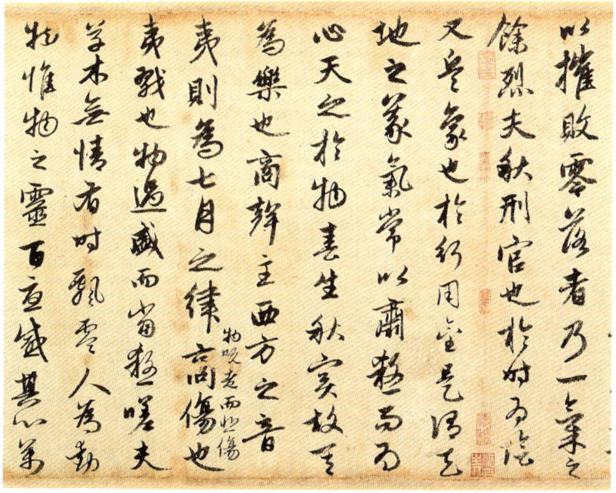

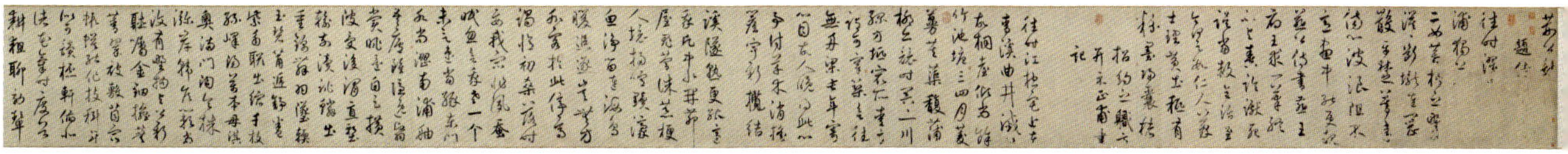

15

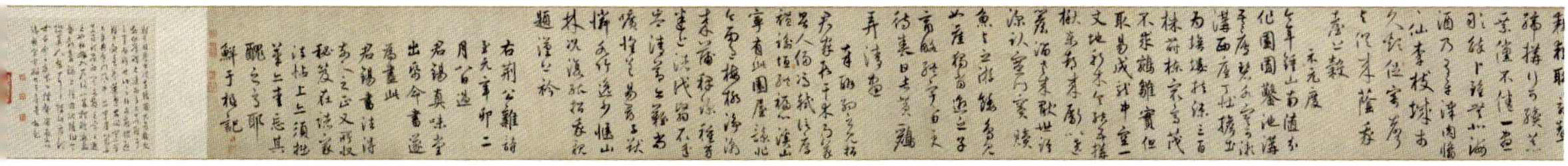

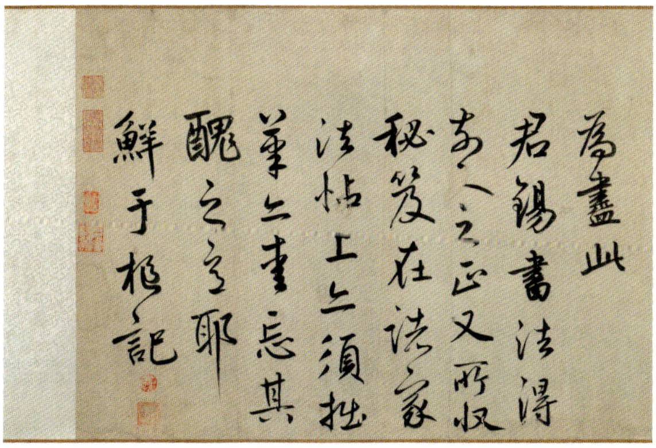

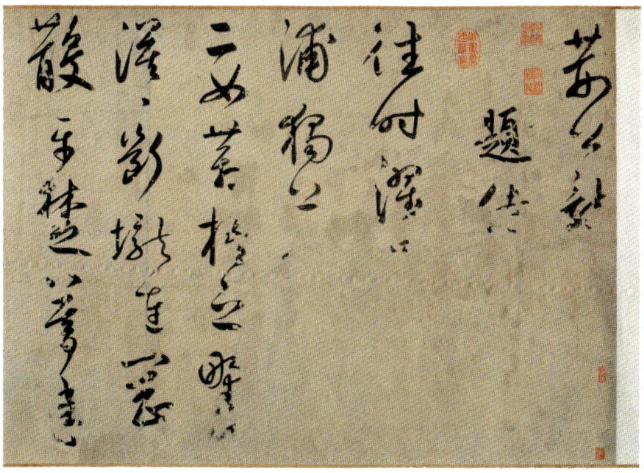

16 *Record of Travels of Su Dongpu*, regular script

Zhu Yunming (1460–1526)
Ming (1368–1644)
Hand scroll, ink on paper
Height 13.5 cm, Length 274 cm

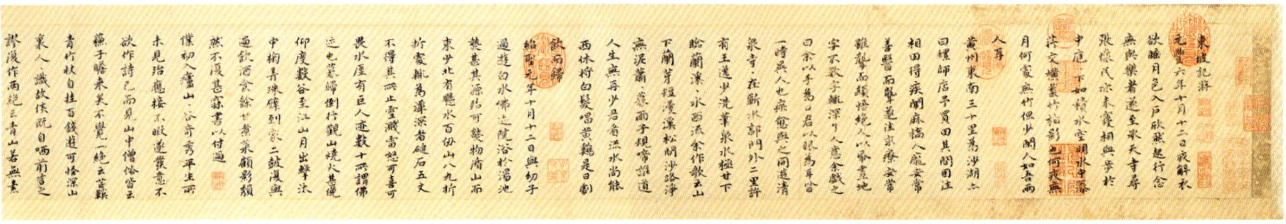

16

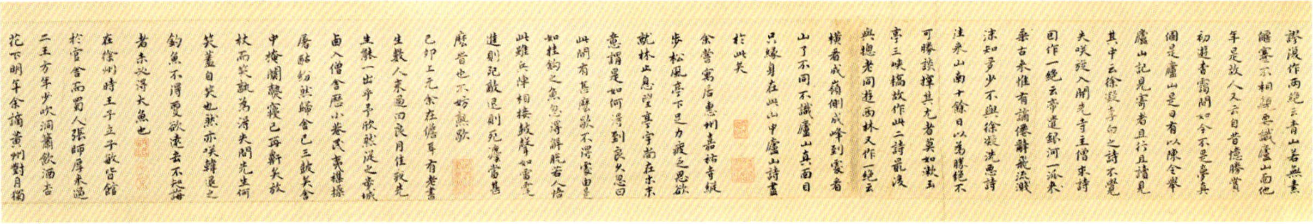

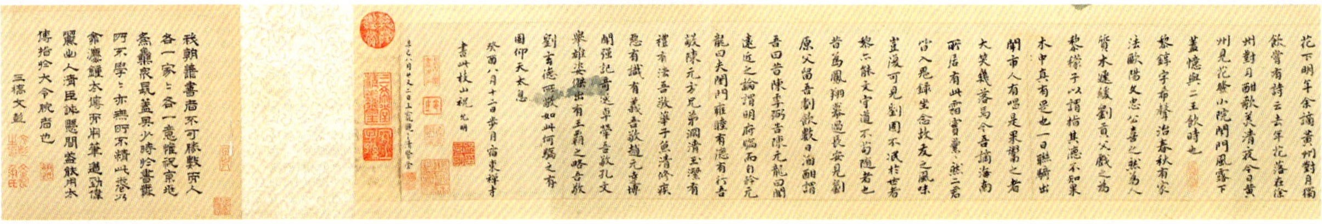

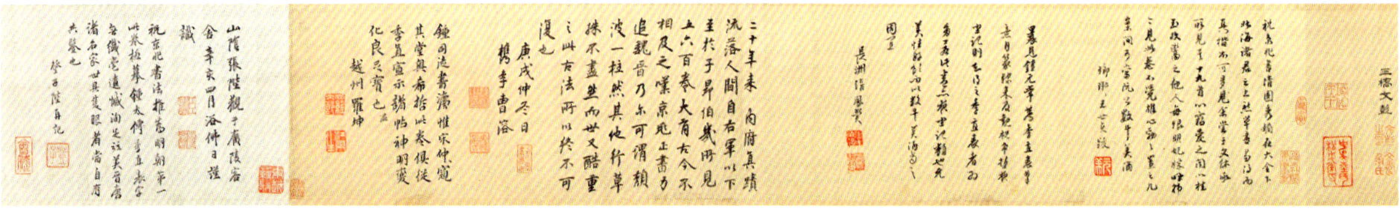

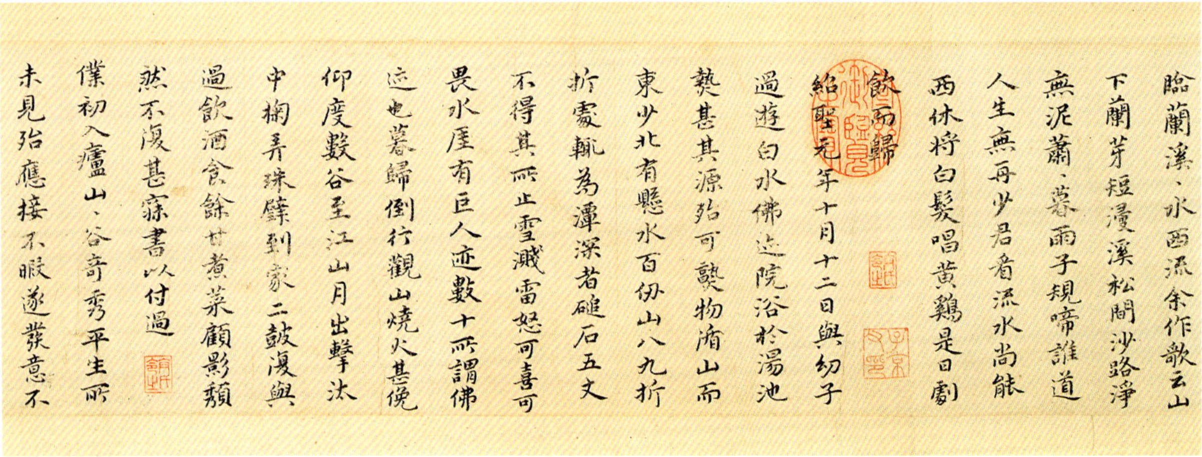

17 *Seven-Character Regulated Poem*, cursive script

Wen Zhengming (1470–1559)
Ming dynasty (1368–1644)
Hanging scroll, ink on paper
Height 315.5 cm, Length 98 cm

18 *Admonition of Diligent Administration and the Encouragement of Study*, regular script

Dong Qichang (1555–1636)
Ming dynasty (1368–1644)
Hanging scroll
Traced gold round lantern
Height 214.5 cm, Width 61.8 cm

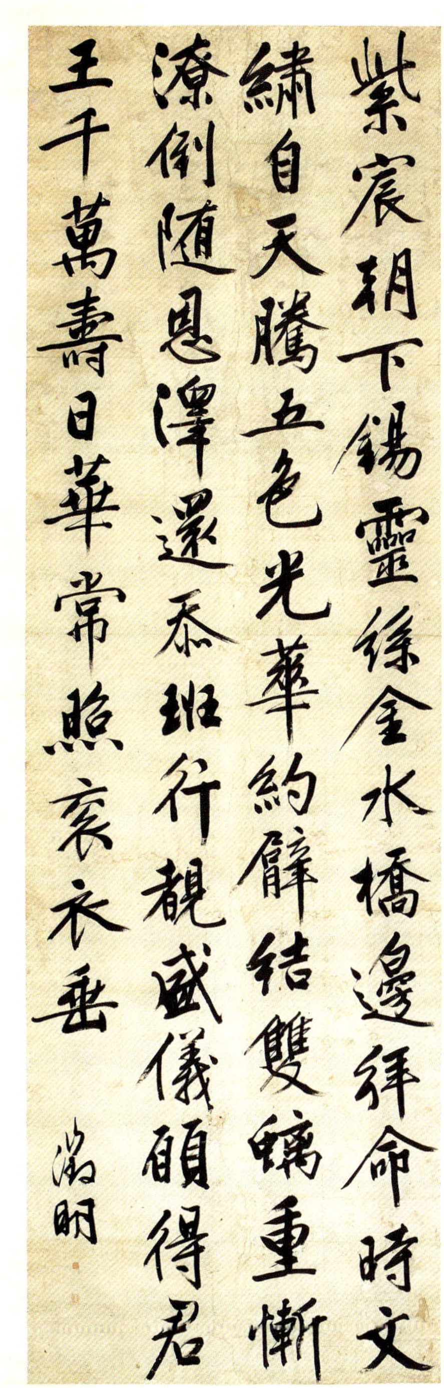

17

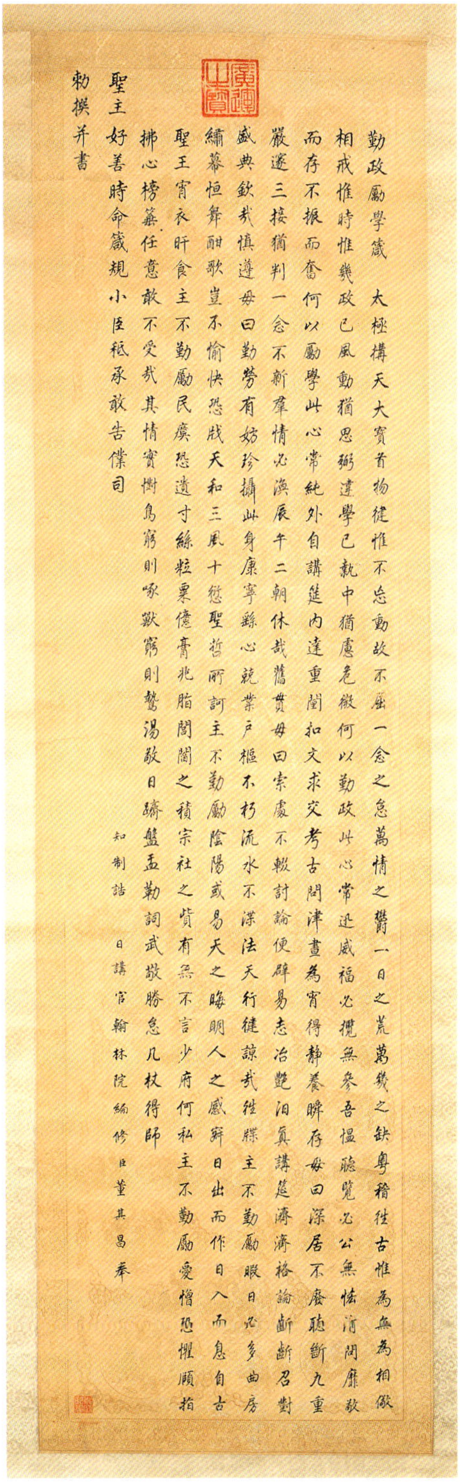

18

19 *At Wumen for Summer Retreat*, running script

Tang Yin (1470–1524)
Ming dynasty (1368–1644)
Hanging scroll, ink on paper
Height 138.2 cm, Width 31 cm

20 Copy of the Calligraphy of the Emperor Tang Taizong, cursive script

Wang Duo (1592–1652)
Qing (1644–1911)
Hanging scroll, ink on silk
Height 252 cm, Width 50 cm

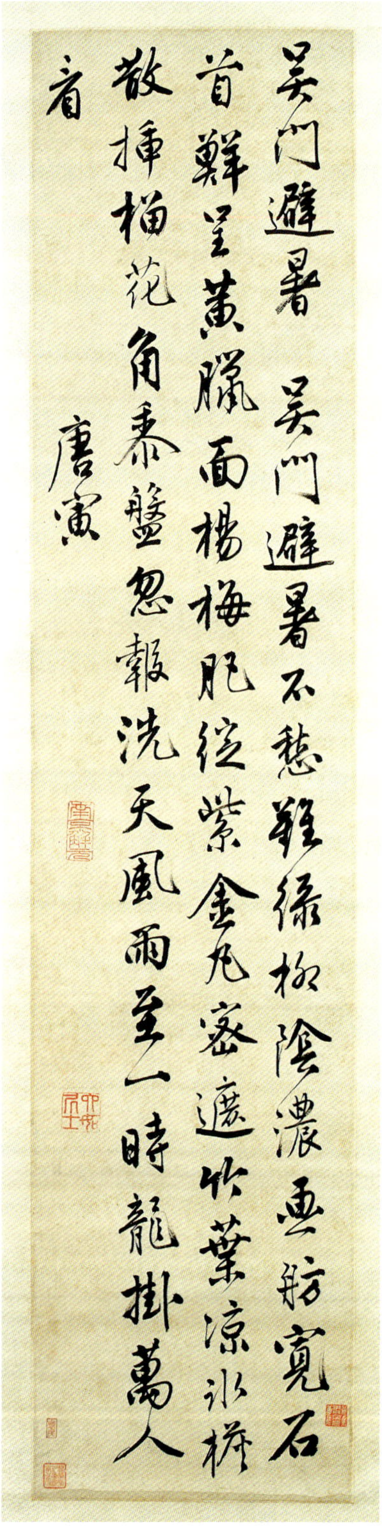

19

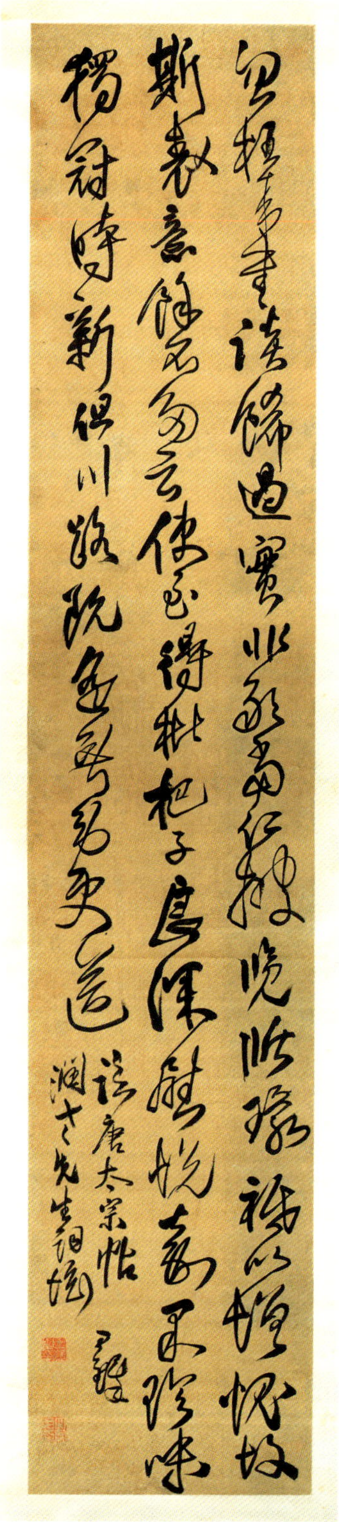

20

21 *Record of Yuan Jing Tower*, running script

Liu Yong (1719–1804)
Qing dynasty (1644–1911)
Hanging scroll, ink on silk
Height 165 cm, Length 56.1 cm

22 Letter of Su Shi to Mi Fu, running script

Zheng Xie (1693–1765)
Qing dynasty (1644–1911)
Hanging scroll, ink on paper
Height 171.8 cm, Length 56.1 cm

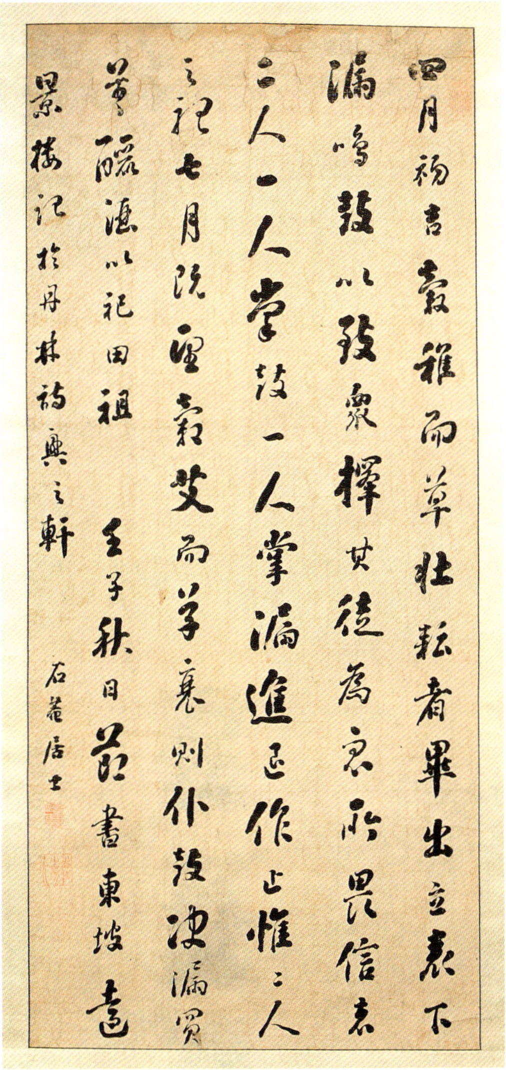

21

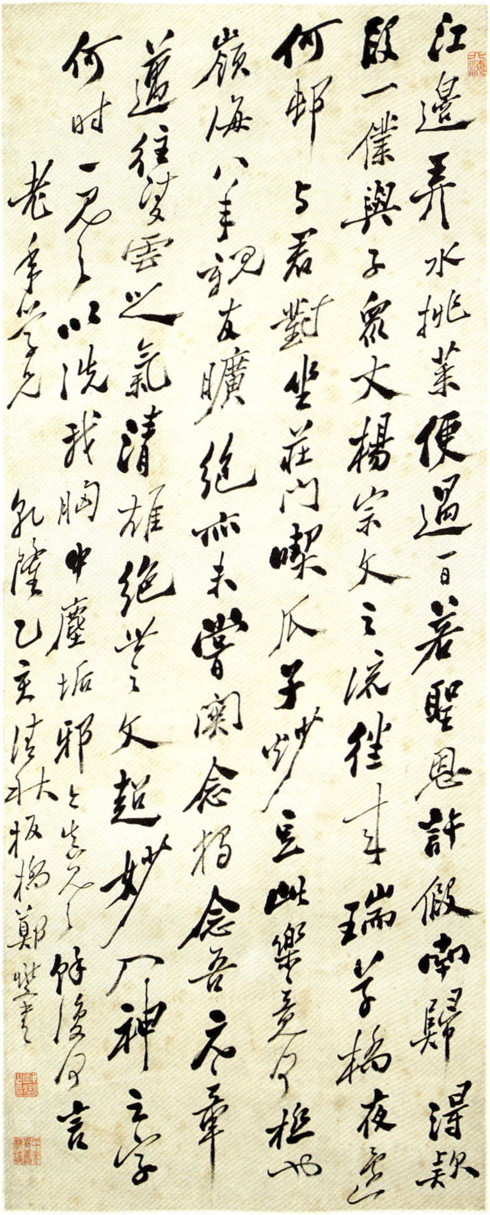

22

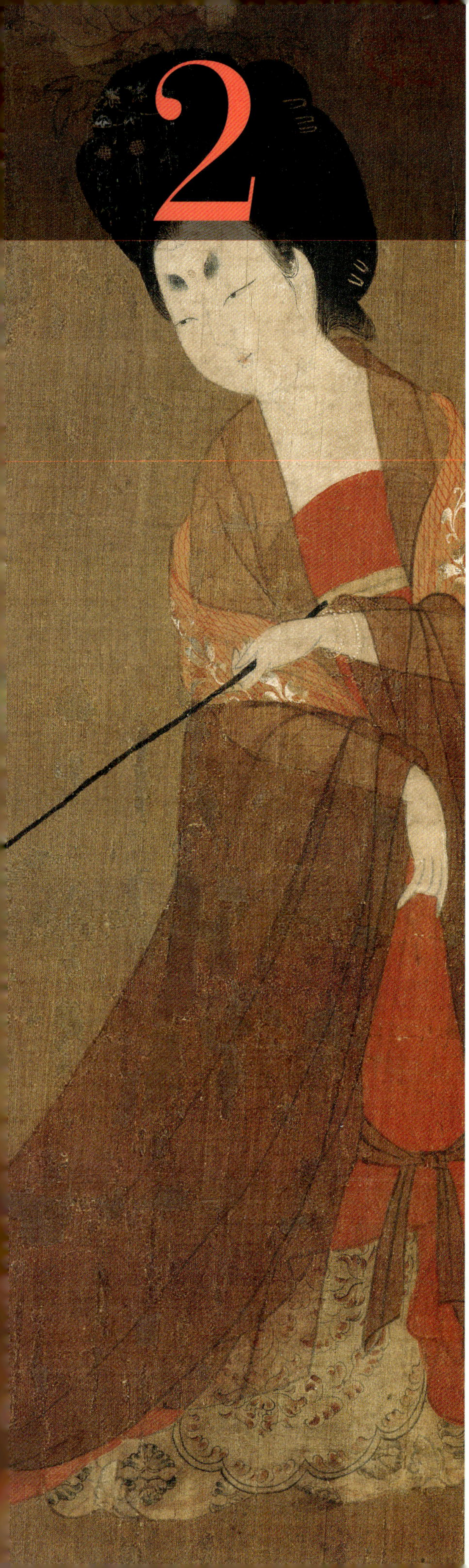

2

Painting

The Liaoning Provincial Museum has a rich collection of Chinese painting. After the Northeast Museum (the former name of the Liaoning Provincial Museum, which was changed to the present name in 1959) had been established in 1949, it received more than a hundred important pieces of the paintings that the last Qing emperor Puyi had brought with him on his escape from Beijing. The paintings came to the museum from the Northeast Bank. The museum continued to collect paintings that had been dispersed among the general public from the former collection of the Qing palace, making it one of the most important holding institutions of the paintings dispersed from the Qing palace. After this, it continued to enrich its painting collections through tomb excavations, collecting, purchases and donations from the public.

The Han–Wei tomb cluster on the outskirts of Liaoyang City has preserved a reasonably complete set of wall paintings. The subject matter of the paintings is diverse and the style mature. These paintings are excellent first-hand sources for researching the historical development of early Chinese painting. From the Eastern Jin onwards, silk hand scroll paintings gradually developed. One example that survives is a Song dynasty copy of Gu Kaizhi's *Nymph of the Luo River*, a rare example of a figure painting on silk.

Figure painting matured in the Tang dynasty with several masters emerging. Furthermore the paintings from the Tang dynasty are of an exceptional quality. *Court Ladies Adorning their Hair with Flowers* by Zhou Fang displays a high level of technique and beauty, and is a precious resource for understanding the history of Tang dynasty figure painting. *Lady of Guoguo on a Spring Outing* by Zhang Xuan, copied by a master of the Northern Song Xuan He art college, is also important for researching the history of Tang figure painting. Although the *Heavenly Horse* was painted by an unknown artist rather than by Han Gan, it is still a masterly and moving piece, and helps trace the development of Tang figure painting.

Landscape painting gradually matured during the Five Dynasties and Northern Song period, with the development of two styles, one in the north and one in the south. The assistant director of the Southern Tang art college, Dong Yuan, specialised in soft, naïve landscapes. A typical work of his, *Waiting for Ferry by the Mountain in Summer*, is a classic example of this style. Li Cheng is an important landscape painter in the northern school of the late Five Dynasties early Northern Song period, but almost none of his works survive. Thus since the provenance of *Dense Forest and Remote Mountains* is clearly documented, it is an important source for research into his painting style.

Very few extant works of Liao dynasty paintings survive. Two paintings, *Playing Chess in Remote Mountains* and *Magpie in Bamboo and Two Rabbits*, which were excavated in 1974 at number seven tomb of Liaoning Faku County Yemaotai, are rare first-hand sources for researching Liao dynasty painting. The *Two Steeds* by Yang Wei of the Jin dynasty art college is signed and is very rare.

Painting activity was very intense during the Song period with a surfeit of scholars and artists. Li Gonglin's white outline painting technique became fashionable for a time, Zhang Ji's *White Lotus Society* and *Shangshan Four Hermits and Huichang Nine Seniors* by an unknown artist are both products of following Li's style. Ma Hezhi of the Southern Song had a particular character, out of the many paintings of *The Classic of Poetry*, his most excellent is the *The Odes of Tang* in the Liaoning Museum collection. Yang Wujiu is renowned for painting ink plum blossom, after which the mantle passed to Xu Yugong whose *Plum and Bamboo in the Snow* is extremely rare as the only extant copy of his work, as well as containing ten poems of Yang's *Liu Shao Qing* at the end. The Southern Song religious painting *Dipankara Buddha's Bestowal of Prediction on Shakyamuni* is exquisitely executed, and contains influences from early periods.

Under the influence of Zhao Mengfu, painting styles changed in the Yuan dyansty as painters turned back to the techniques of the Jin and Tang dynasties, while scholars began to paint in great numbers. Zhao's *Arhat in Red Robe* of a monk from the Western regions is an important work of his figure painting. Zhao Mengfu's grandson, Wang Meng made significant achievements, *Taibai Mountain* is a fine example of his later work. The *Water Mill by Mountain Stream* by an unknown artist shows advanced technique in figure painting, and is an extremely rare masterpiece.

Continuing the tradition of the four Yuan masters, the Ming dynasty early period had Wang Fu's *Avalokitesvara*, Shen Zhen's *Zhulu Mountain Hut* in the same vein. The Xuande art college went back to the Southern Song style, with great masters, such as Ma Shi, Li Zai and Xia Zhi who together painted *Returning Home*, and Dai Jin's *The Six Patriarchs from Dharma to Huineng*, all of which are representative pieces of the period. In the middle of the Ming dynasty, the *Wumen* school was established, and four painters, Shen Zhou, Wen Zhengming, Tang Yin, Qiu Ying, became known, bringing about a change in style, the influence of which was felt until the end of the Ming. Qiu Ying's *Along The River During Qingming Festival* reflects many aspects of southern Chinese city life in Ming, and its significance is not restricted to art history. And the *Rustic Villa in the Forest* by Matteo Ricci, a Jesuit missionary who came to China in the late Ming, inaugurated a period of artistic exchange between the West and China, and is thus a very significant work.

Of the paintings by the four Wangs of the Qing dynasty, Wang Yuanqi's *Ten Views of the West Lake* is the most important, whereas Xu Yang's *Suzhou Prosperity* provides a historical record of local customs, depicting prosperous scenes of eighteenth-century Suzhou. Dong Baohou

1 *Court Ladies Adorning their Hair with Flowers*

Zhou Fang (730–800)
Tang dynasty (618–907)
Hand scroll, ink and colour on silk
Length 46 cm, Width 180 cm

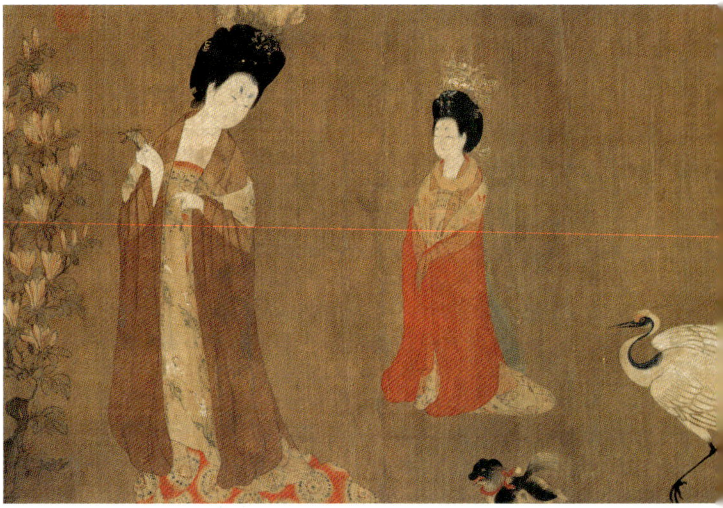

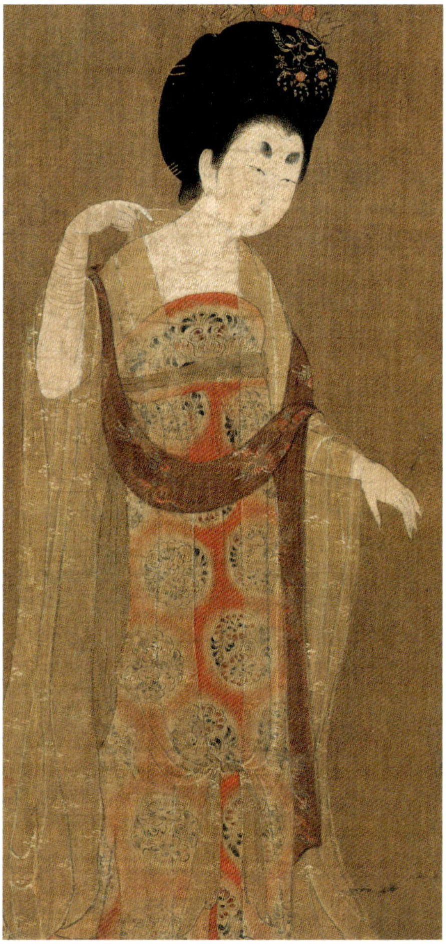

This painting on coarse silk is a hand scroll with added colours, with no background, depicting five court ladies adorning their hair with flowers. A maidservant is holding a fan in the courtyard. There are two small dogs and a white crane among the figures, and at the end of the painting there is a lake stone and magnolia buds. The court ladies are all plump, gentle and graceful, and are either playing with the dog, holding a flower, or catching a butterfly or in deep thought. All have aristocratic manners. The court ladies' puffy hair is tied up and adorned with peony, lotus flower and viburnum. They have full and round faces, and beautiful eyebrows. They have gold flowers between their eyebrows and red lips, and a serene expression. They are each wearing a transparent, loose outer garment with a wide neck, and a long dress that is fastened around the chest. They all have a shawl wrapped around their shoulders reaching their knees. The maidservant is holding a round fan in both hands, and is wearing a red dress and loose outer garment; her two hair buns are tied together with silk; she is smaller compared to the other figures.

Vivid realism is the predominant technique in this painting. The strokes are painted according to an advanced technique, and the

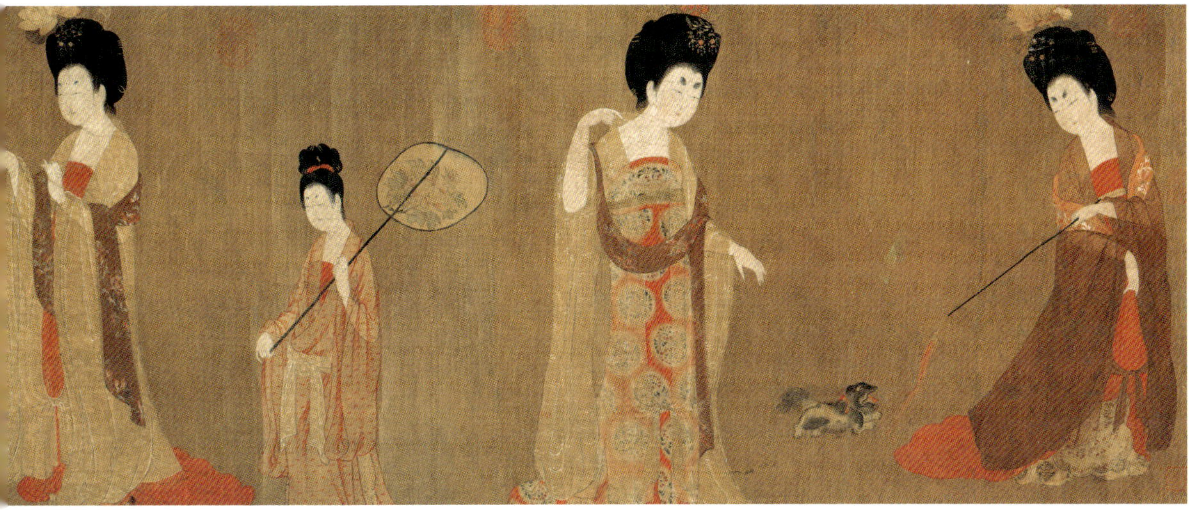

1

application of colour, the patterns and composition of the flowers and plants are all finely executed, although in comparison with works from the Five Dynasties and Song they are immature.

The *Court Ladies Adorning Their Hair with Flowers* was sent to the Palace Museum in 1972 for new backing. It was then discovered that it was not a complete piece, but had been joined together. The slightly smaller court lady on the left had clearly been added later, and, along with the small dog on the left and the crane, had been cut out from another painting and inserted. Some researchers believe this part originally belonged to a screen.

The lining on this painting does not have the seal of the painter, nor any dated inscription or colophon at either end. The earliest collector's seal is from the Southern Song with the year-characters *shao* and *xing* in red ink, and thus can be assumed to have been part of the palace collection of the Southern Song. At the end of the Southern Song it belonged to powerful minister Jia Sidao, and has the characters *yue sheng* from a gourd-shaped seal. The painting's preservation in the Yuan and Ming dynasties is unclear. During the early Qing it belonged to the collections of Liang Qingbiao and An Qi, after which it entered the Qing palace. At the fall of the Qing, it was lost from the palace, and after several detours ended up in the collections of the Liaoning Museum. The earliest record of this scroll in historical writing is in *Reflections on Ink* by An Qi of the Qing dynasty who believed it was by Zhou Fang of the Tang dynasty. After this *Records of Treasures at the Stone Canal* propagated An Qi's view, all recording the painting as *Court Ladies* by Zhou Fang, whereas *Court Ladies Adorning Their Hair with Flowers* is a recent name. Zhou Fang is an important painter of the mid to late Tang dynasty who painted aristocratic court ladies as well as *Avalokitesvara by Water Moonlight*. DONG BAOHOU

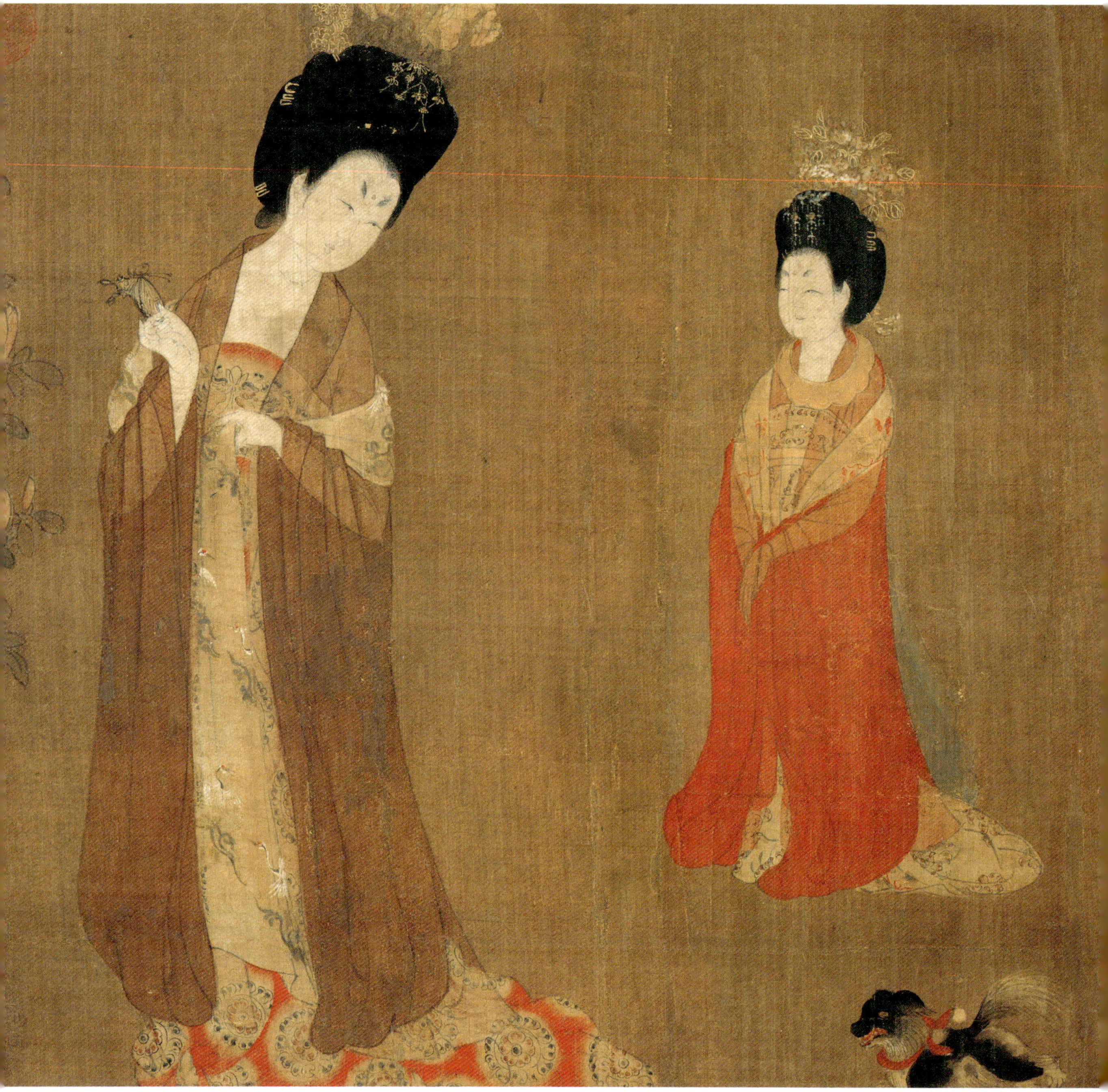

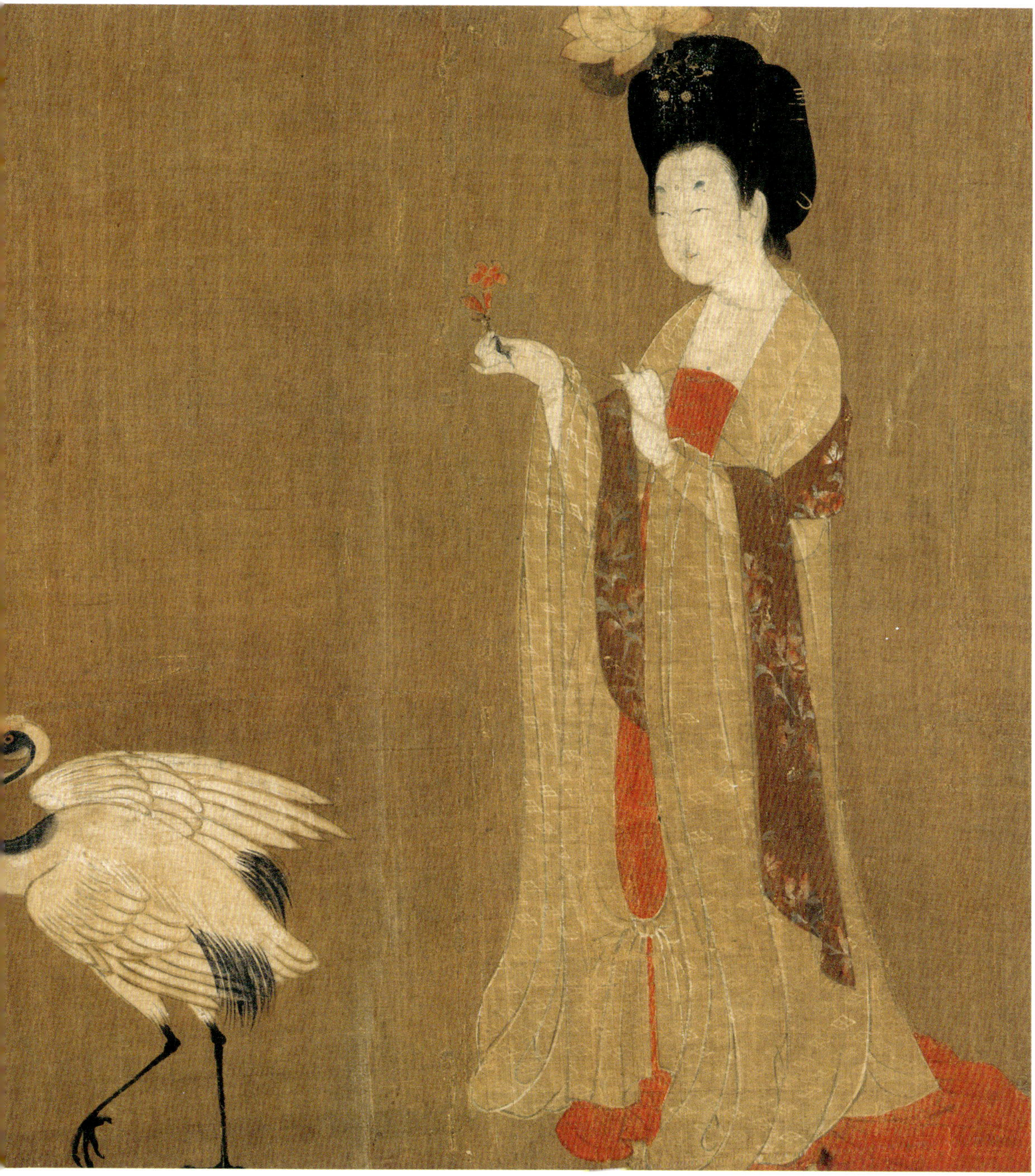

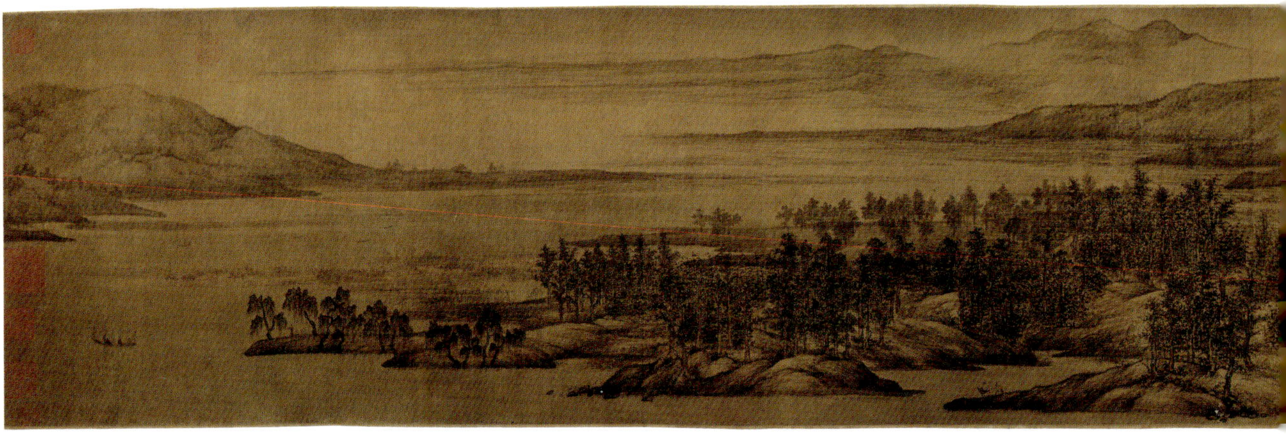

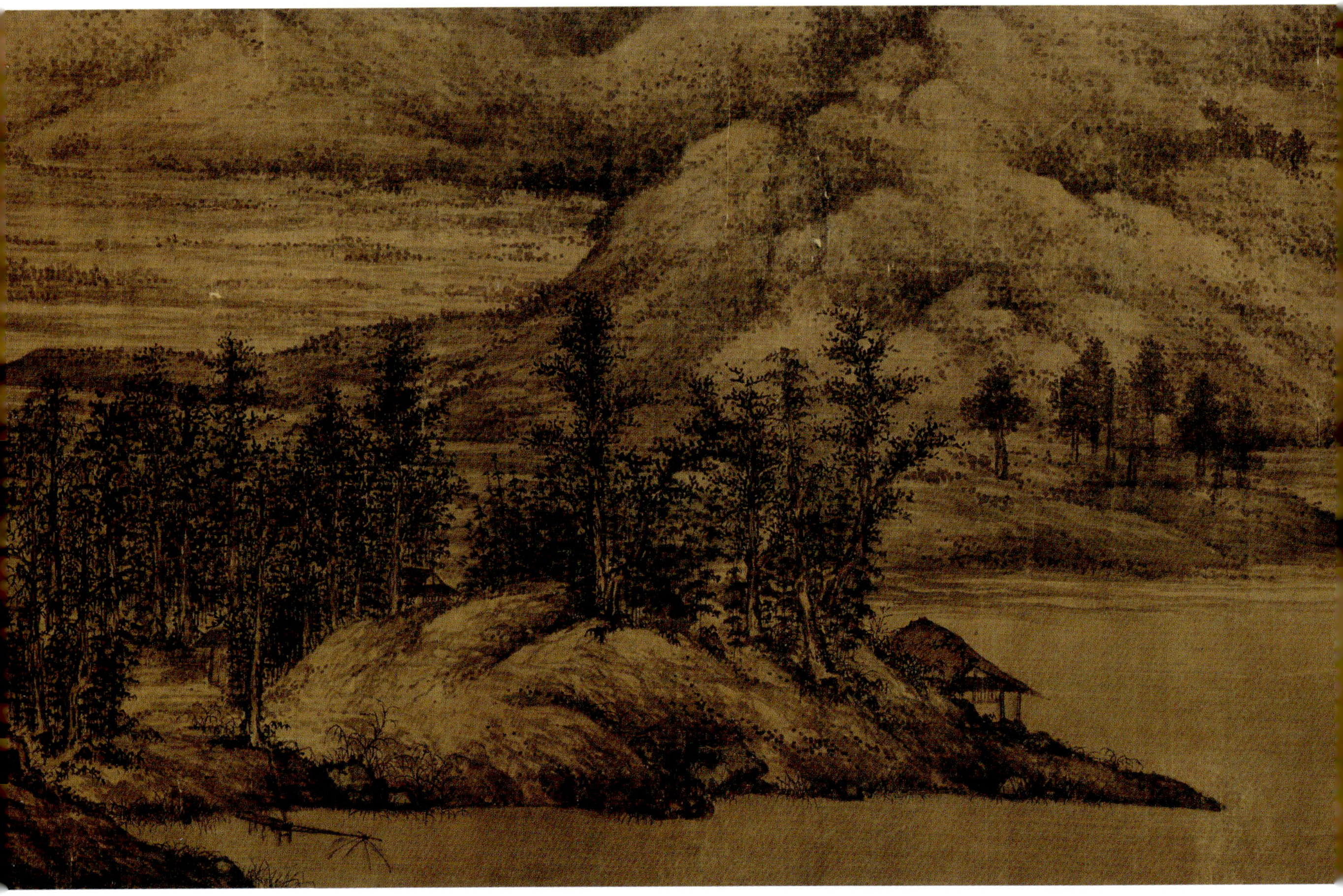

2 *Waiting for Ferry by the Mountain in Summer*

Dong Yuan (932–962)
Five Dynasties, (907–960)
Hand scroll, ink and colour on silk
Length 49.8 cm, Width 329.4 cm

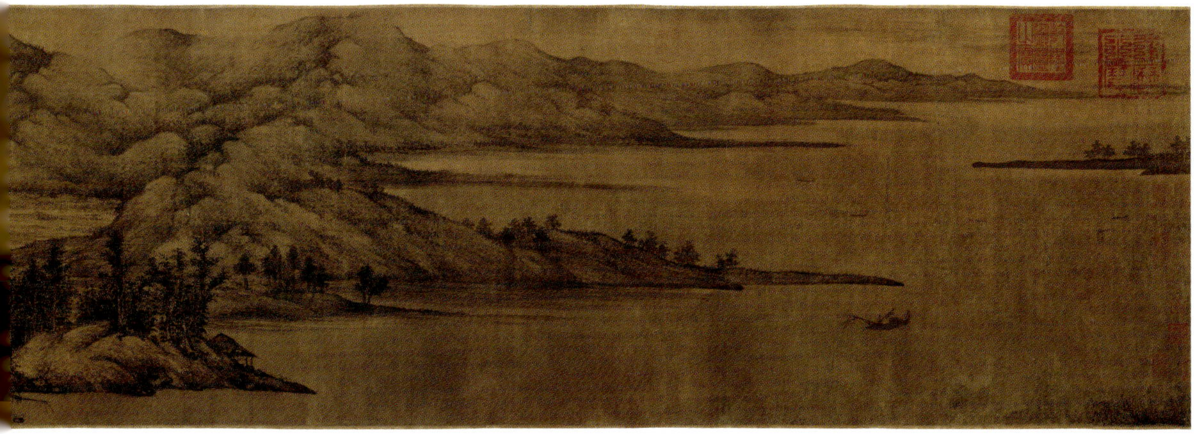

2

This painting depicts scenes from a summer day in south China, showing the rocky contours of the mountains. There are views into the distant mountains, water and mist, with clouds and mountains merging as one. On top of the crag are thinly scattered trees, with bamboo interspersed between them, as well as a few faint thatched cottages. There are several large rocks near the bank, and the traces of the colours applied are just visible. Water is depicted by leaving white spaces and adding a tiny amount of pale black ink, as if giving the impression of a dark reflection from the sky. There is sand at the end of the painting, and three officials dressed in red are hurrying towards the ferry crossing. The officials are waiting for the ferry to arrive. Nearby in the water a passenger ferry is slowing crossing, one man is rowing at the front, one man is turning the scull at the back, with four passengers sitting above among them are two officials dressed in red and there is a thatched pavilion on the right bank. In the water nearby there is a fishing-net with no one watching it. In the distance two fishermen are returning home, carrying fish and fishing equipment. There are six fishing boats on the river. The whole painting has been carefully conceived, the colour is simple and tasteful, the mountain slopes are clearly outlined, and the forest is delicately painted. The figures have only been outlined, but are clear and easily discerned, with no pretence at cleverness, just naïve, fully expressing the artistic spirit.

The poem at the beginning of this scroll has an inscription from Dong Qichang of the Ming dynasty, 'Dong Beiyuan summer scene at mountain pass waiting for the ferry.' At the end of the scroll are four inscriptions by Ke Jiusi, Yu Ji, Li Jiong and Ya Hu, all of the Yuan and who all think the painting is by Dong Yuan. Extant paintings by Dong Yuan are very few, and comparing this painting with his *Xiaoxiang River* at the Palace Museum and the *Summer Mountain Painting* at the Shanghai Museum, the mountains are round and solid, the water is extensive and still, the banks are shallow and straight, and the rocks almost disappear. Whether the trees are near or distant, they are all delicately depicted, the texturing methods are plain and the colours are predominantly simple and tasteful. The artistic style of the three paintings is basically the same, and seems to be the unique style of Dong Huan's latter years. DONG BAOHOU

3 *Heavenly Horse*

Unknown artist
Five Dynasties (907–960)
Hand scroll, ink and colour on silk
Length 27.5 cm, Width 122.5 cm

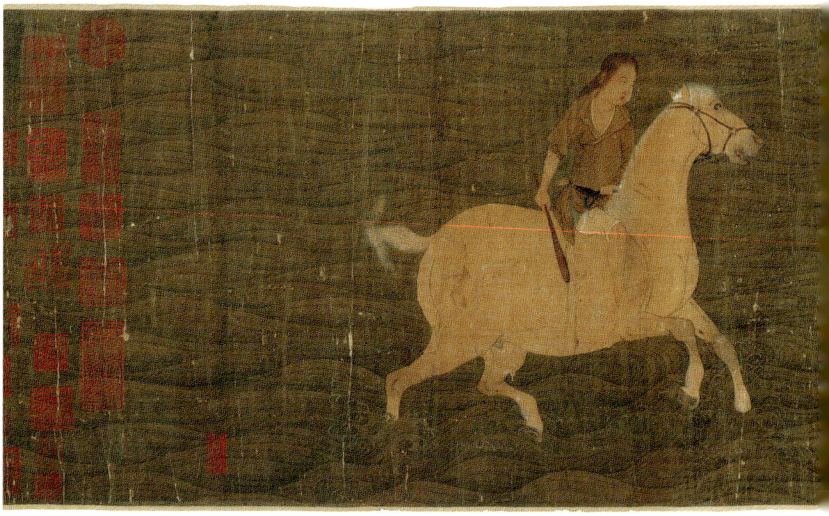

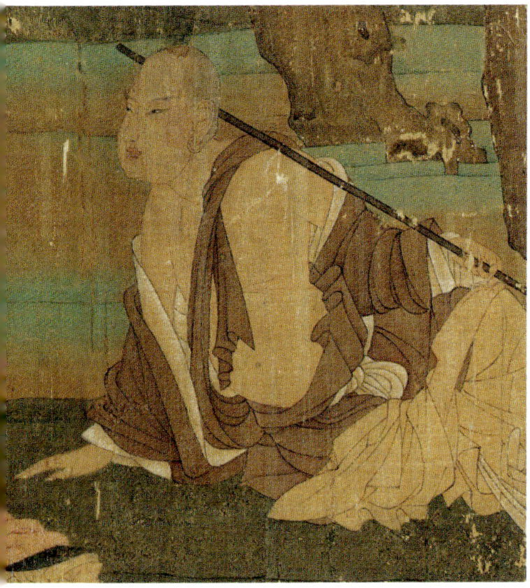

This painting vividly tells the story of Zhi Xun, the famous monk of the Jin dynasty, who loved horses. Zhi Xun was sitting on a rock by a riverbank; on another rock was a gentleman. The two men are sitting opposite each other with their bodies facing the water, staring with complete attention at a white horse leaping out of the water. The boy riding the horse has long hair, with one hand holding the reins, another hand holding the whip. A servant is standing behind Zhi Xun, with deep eyes and a high nose, and an eagle perched on his hand. The water has deep green waves, the rocky bank is rugged, painted with forceful lines and fresh colours. At the beginning of the scroll, between the water and on the yellow silk are five characters in golden script, 'Heavenly Horse painting by Han Gan'. This inscription seems to be by Guo Qujie, and its reasoning is unclear. Comparing extant works by Han Gan, this painting is likely to have been painted by someone from around the Five Dynasties and Northern Song period. DONG BAOHOU

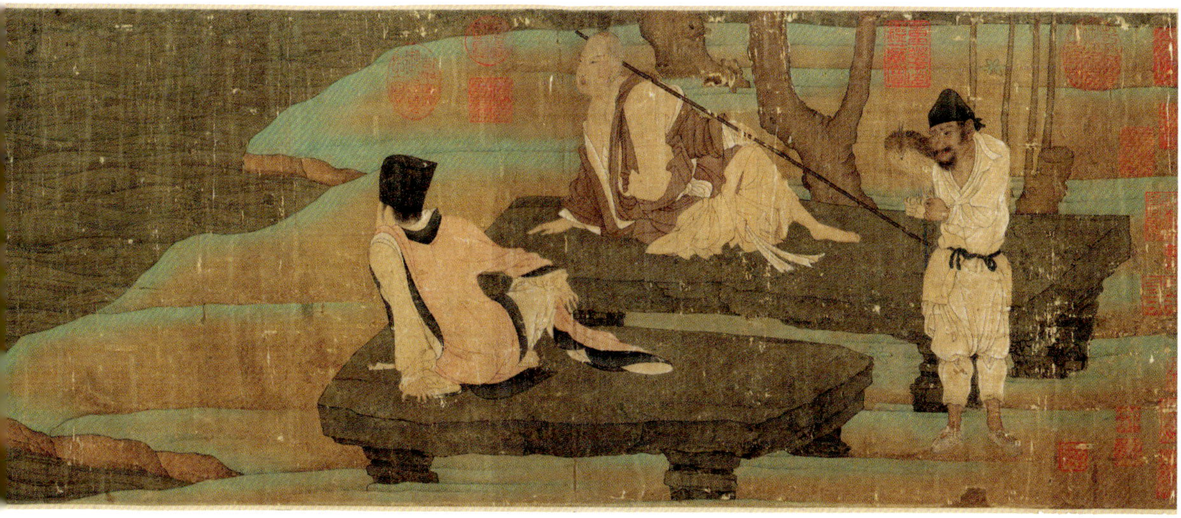

3

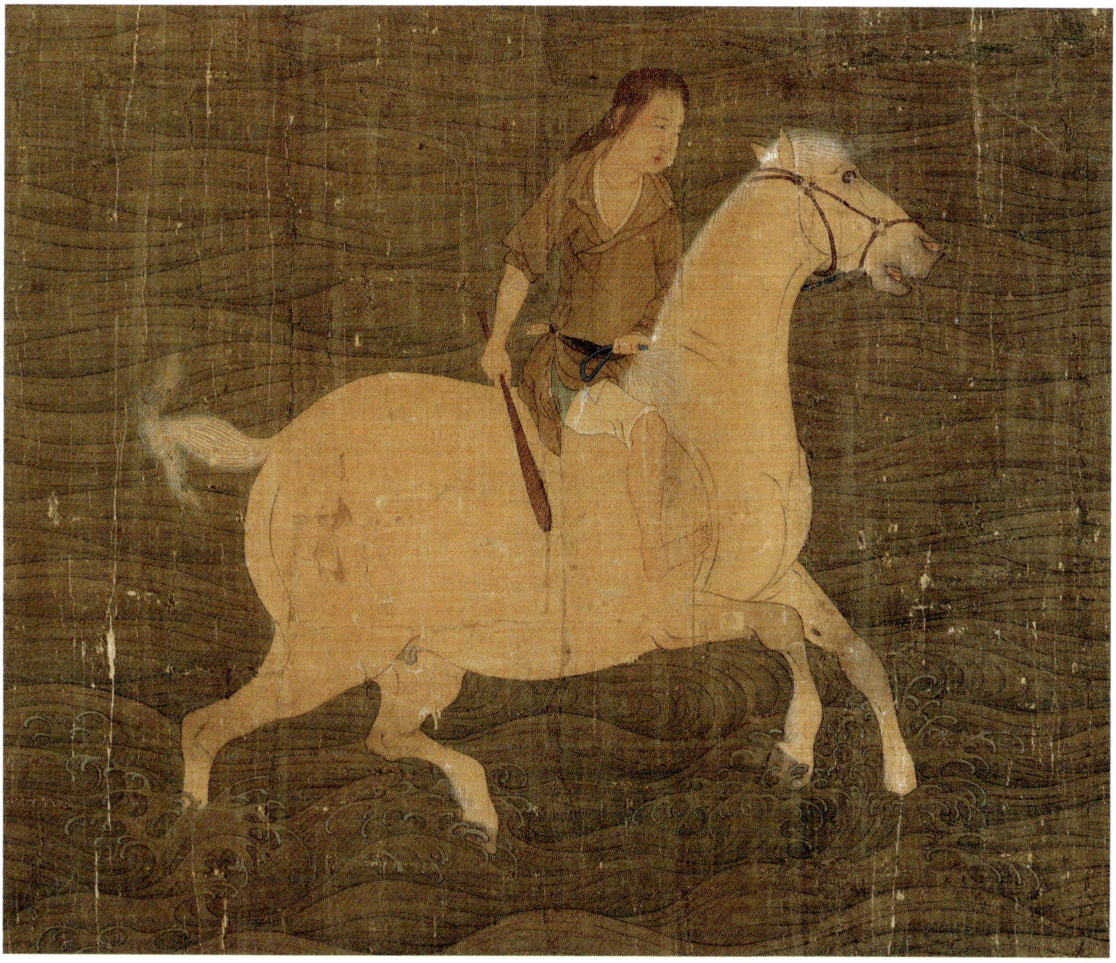

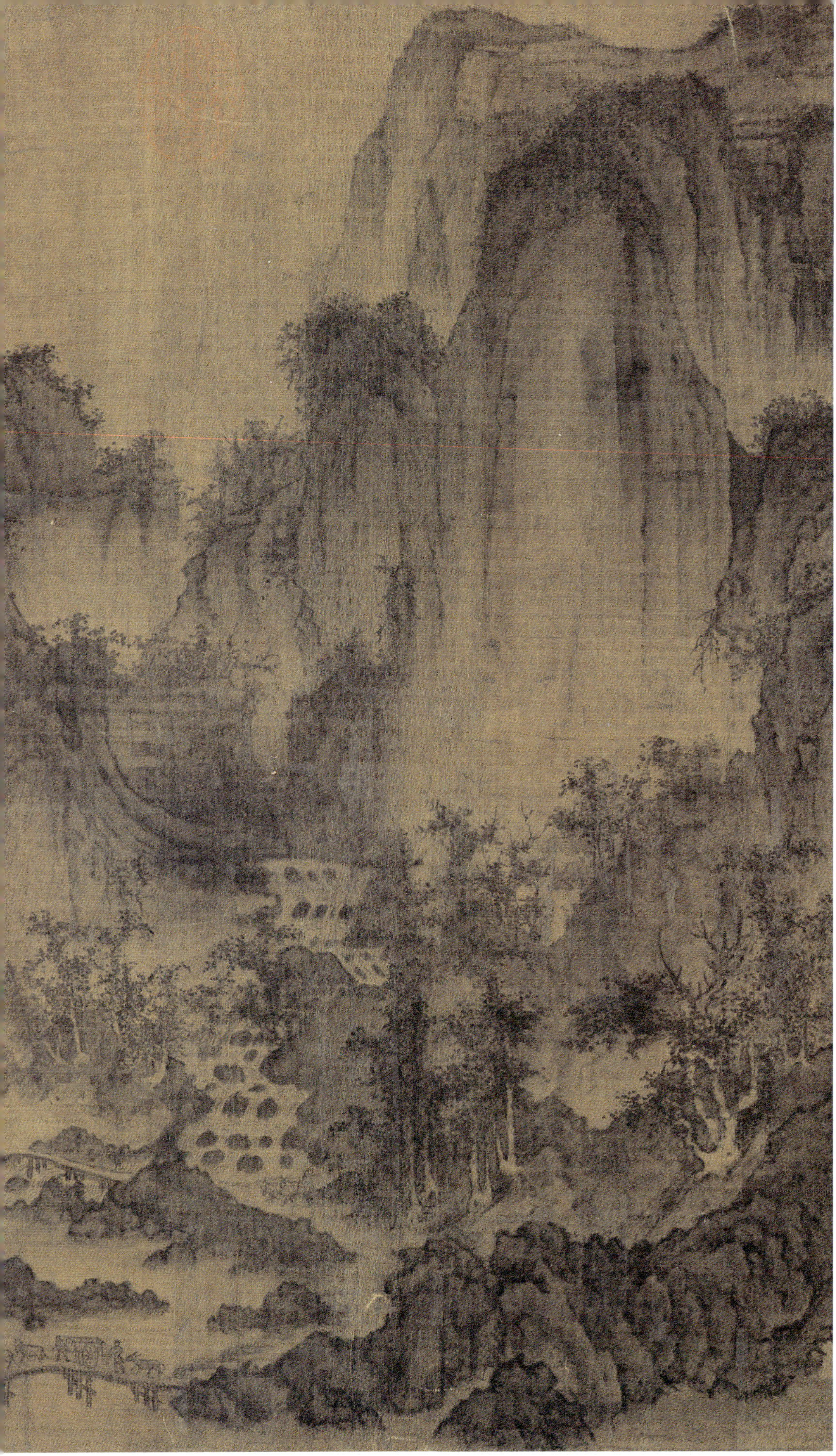
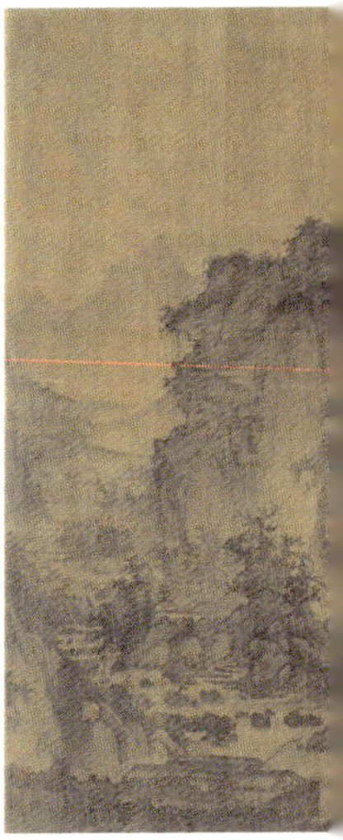

4 *Dense Forest and Remote Mountains*

Li Cheng (919–967)
Northern Song (960–1127)
Hand scroll, ink on silk
Length 45.2 cm, Width 143.2 cm

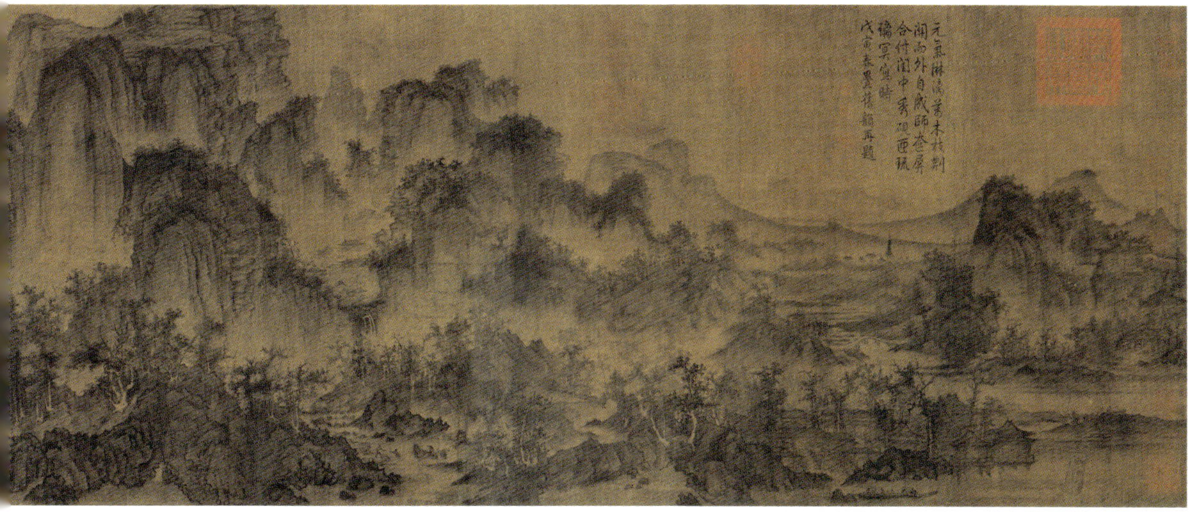

4

This painting uses black ink to depict a summer scene, with sharp mountain crags, lush forests, rising peaks and clear mountain woodland. In the foreground is a stream flowing under a bridge, and a light boat bobs on the waves, with the passengers barely visible. People walking with carts and horses are approaching, painted in neat formation. The people have only been sketched in outlines, with vivid postures. In the distance along the mountain ridge a waterfall drops majestically, the stream is in spate and halls and the shadows of pagodas are visible amidst the cloud vapour. The brush strokes are not visible, and are mainly heavy dots. The tops of the mountains and leaves are all represented with thick and delicate ink, with an animated rhythm.

There are poems written vertically by Qianlong on both sides of the painting, and also at the beginning of the scroll. At the beginning and end are poems by Xiang Ruobing of the Southern Song, Ni Zan of the Yuan and Zhang Tianjun of the Ming. From Xiang Ruobing's inscription of 1219 we know that this scroll once belonged to the collection of Lü Gongbi, secretary of Ying Zongshu of the Northern Song, and was handed down in their family. The date as well as the fact that Xiang Ruobing was a famous collector lend credibility to this line of transmission. Dong Baohou

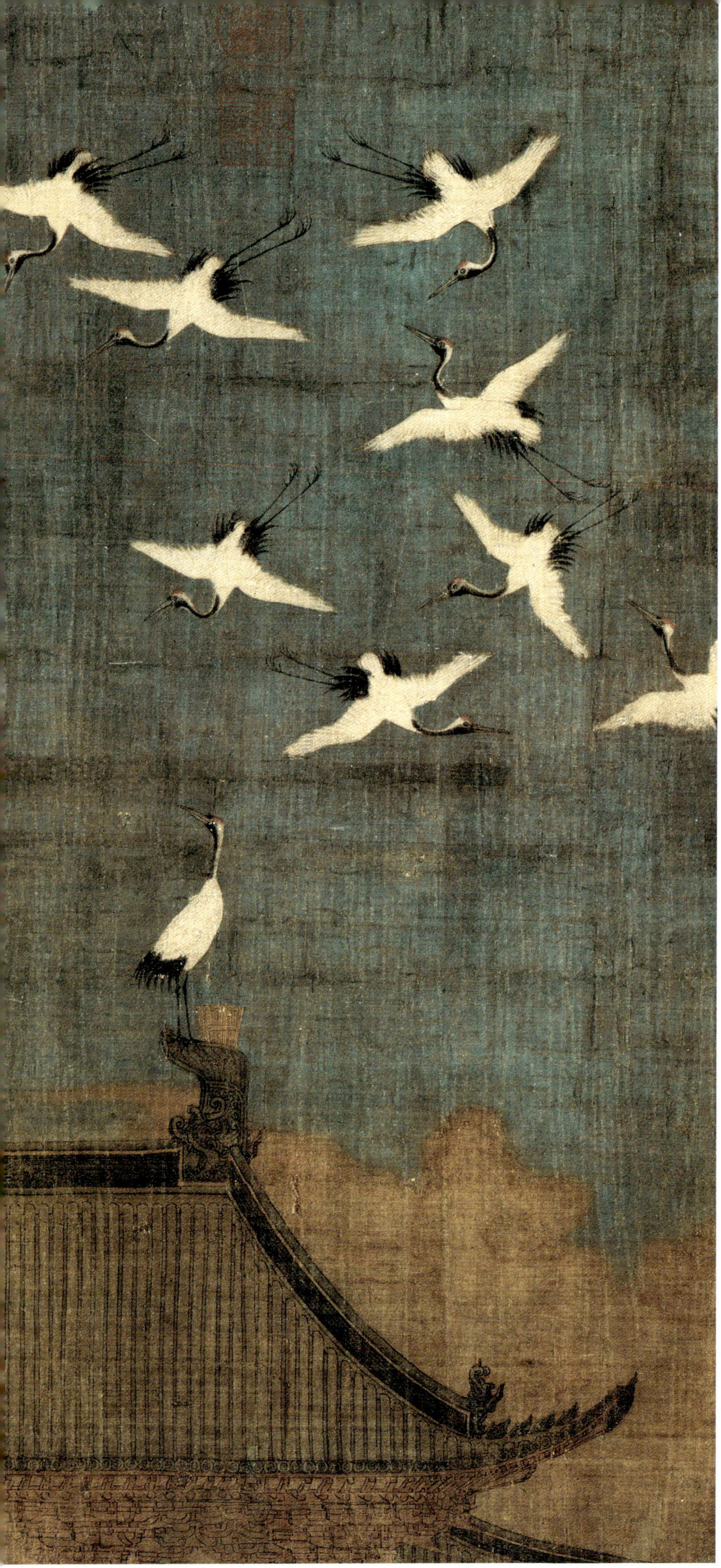

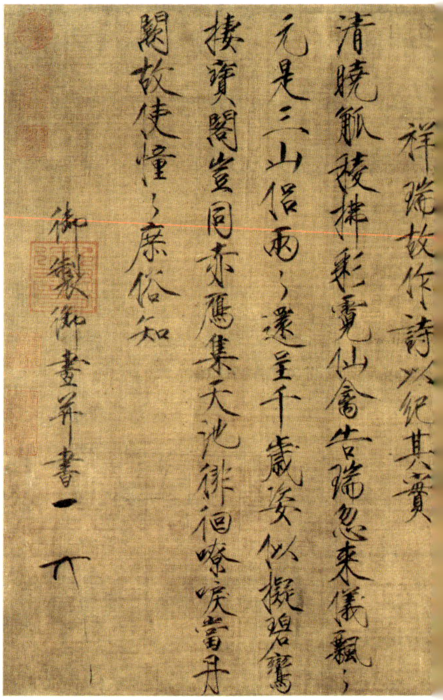
祥瑞故作詩以紀其實
清曉觚稜拂彩霓仙禽告瑞忽來儀飄ゝ
元是三山侶兩ゝ還呈千歲姿似擬碧鸞
棲寶閣豈同赤雁集天池徘徊嘹唳當丹
闕故使憧ゝ庶俗知
御製御畫并書

5 ***Auspicious Cranes***

Zhao Ji (1082–1135)
Northern Song dynasty (960–1127)
Hand scroll, ink and colour on silk
Length 51 cm, Width 138.2 cm

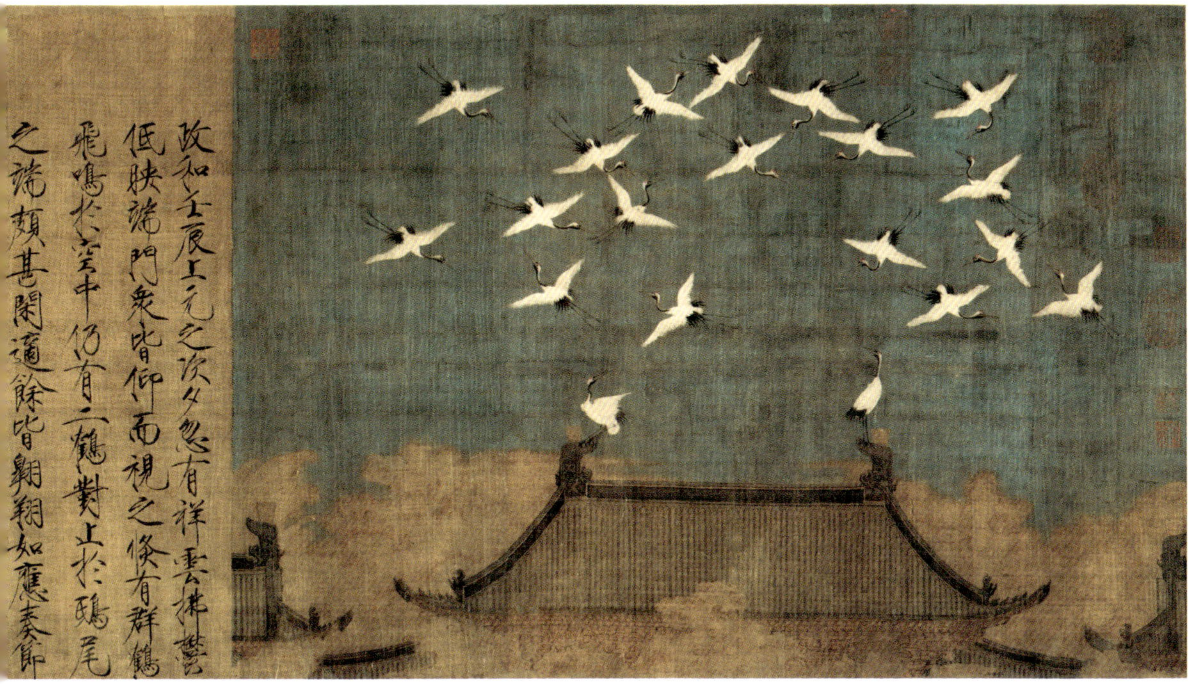

5

Zhao Ji was the Emperor Huizong of the Song dynasty, from Zhuozhou (in present-day Hebei Province), skilled at calligraphy and painting. He was particularly talented in painting landscapes and people, and excelled at birds and flowers.

This scroll shows the Xuande gate of Bianliang painted with coloured clouds, with eighteen flying cranes circling above the palace, each vividly holding its own position. On the roof of the hall there are two cranes standing on an 'eagle's tail', the one of the right is raising its neck in song, the one on the left is craning its neck looking around. They are painted very realistically, conveying emotion, ordered perspective and rhythm. The brushwork is exquisite across the whole painting, with careful thought going into every shape, giving an impression of clear spirit and delicate expression. At the end of the painting there is also a poem by the painter in slender gold script, as well as a postscript. The strokes are open and generous, slender and crisp, like the shape of bamboo and orchid, and the charm is apparent between the lines of the calligraphy. The end of the painting has been signed with the characters *tian xia yi ren* (one person under heaven). There are seals saying 'Viewed by the Emperor Qianlong', 'Stone Canal treasure' and 'Stone Canal collection'. WANG XIAOLIANG

6 Copy of Zhang Xuan's *Lady of Guoguo on a Spring Outing*

Unknown
Northern Song dynasty (960–1127)
Hand scroll, ink and colour on silk
Length 51.8 cm, Width 148 cm

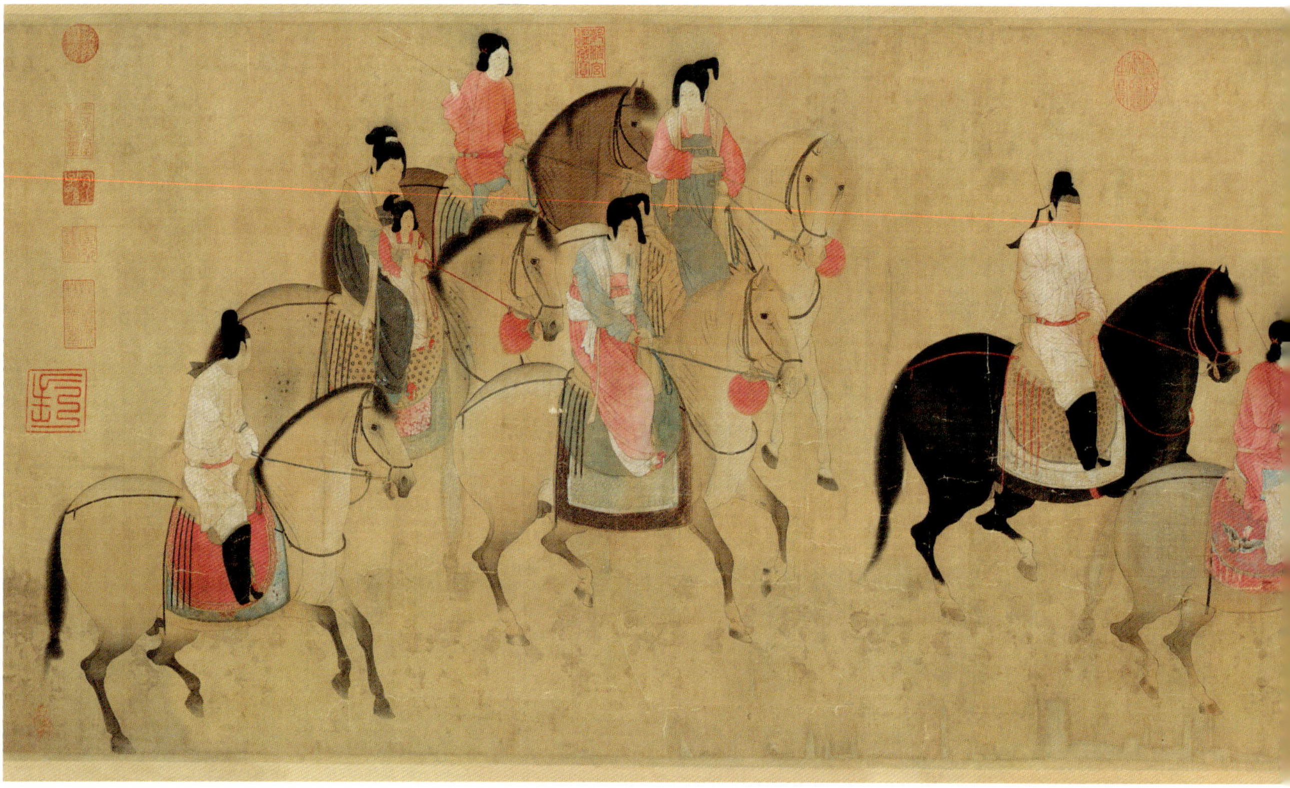

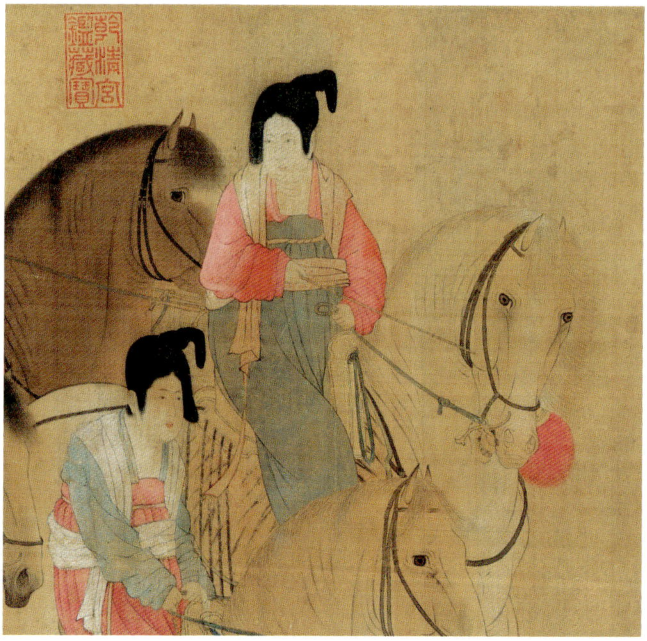

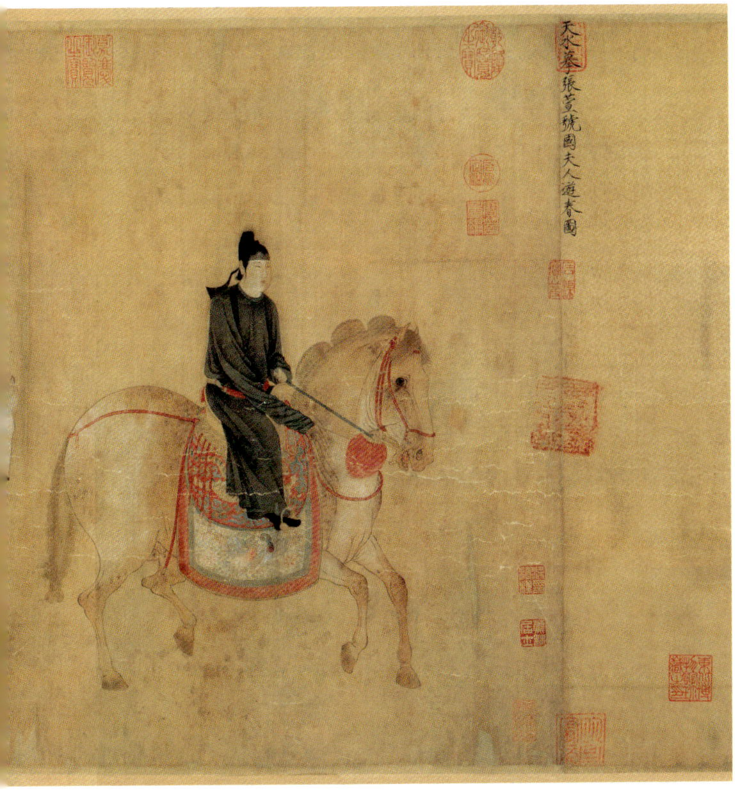

6

This is a copy of the scene from Zhang Xuan's *Lady of Guoguo on a Spring Outing*. There are nine figures on eight horses, all riding large tall horses, including court ladies, servants and nurses. The party is led by a middle-aged court lady in men's clothes riding a horse with its mane platted into three knots. She is followed closely by a court lady with hair tied in a double bun, with a eunuch dressed in white behind her. Next are two ladies riding beautiful horses with raised hoofs. The ladies both have round faces, with plump elegant figures and jet black hair hanging down tied in high buns. The three figures behind include an older nurse holding a little girl closely to her on the saddle, as if afraid of losing her. Flanking the nurse are a man and woman accompanying them. The main subject of the painting is striking, the scene is one of luxury and highly realistic. The painting is delicately executed on silk, the colours are deep, showing the ideals of Chinese feminine beauty.

At the front of the painting there is an inscription and seals of Wanyan Hao, Zhangzong Emperor of Jin, in slender gold style, 'Tian Shui copy of Zhang Xuan's *Lady of Guoguo on a Spring Outing*'. At the end is an inscription by Wang Duo of the Qing dynasty in 1649. It had belonged to the inner court of the Song, Jin, and Southern Song, to Shi Niyuan, Jia Sidao, Wang Changheng and Liang Qingbiao collections. It finally entered the Qing palace collection, and is recorded in the *Records of Treasures at the Stone Canal*. DONG BAOHOU

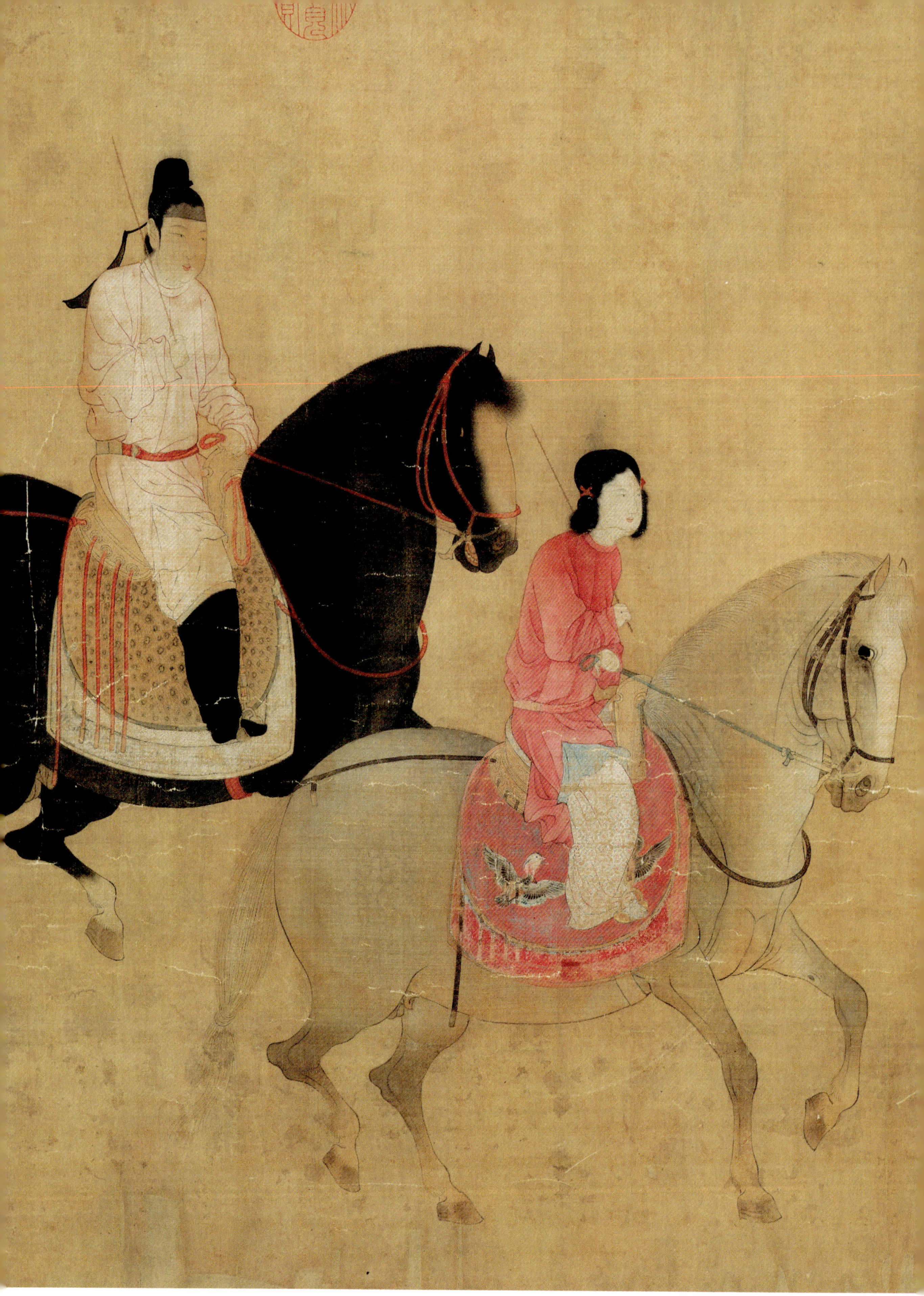

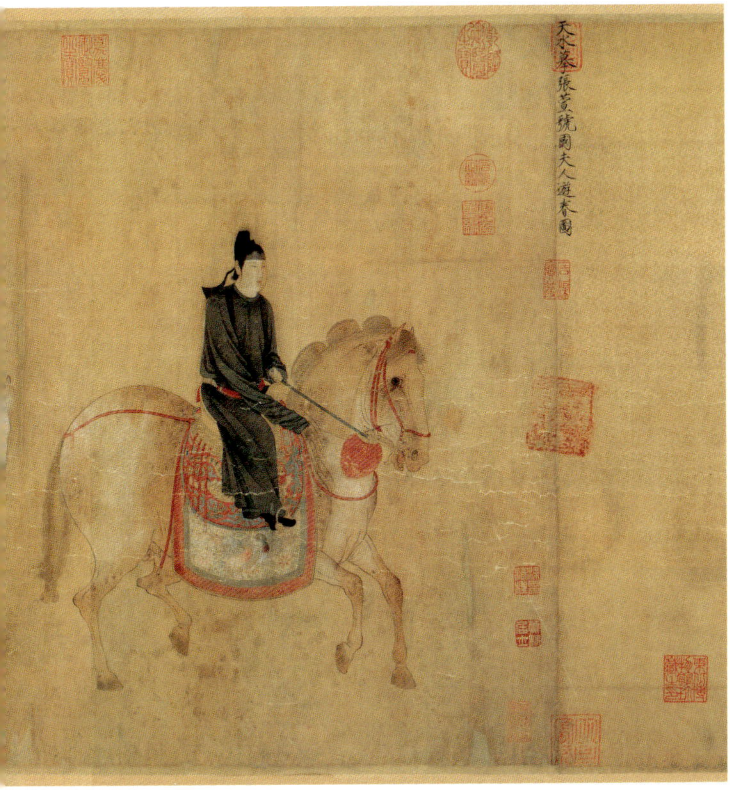

6

This is a copy of the scene from Zhang Xuan's *Lady of Guoguo on a Spring Outing*. There are nine figures on eight horses, all riding large tall horses, including court ladies, servants and nurses. The party is led by a middle-aged court lady in men's clothes riding a horse with its mane platted into three knots. She is followed closely by a court lady with hair tied in a double bun, with a eunuch dressed in white behind her. Next are two ladies riding beautiful horses with raised hoofs. The ladies both have round faces, with plump elegant figures and jet black hair hanging down tied in high buns. The three figures behind include an older nurse holding a little girl closely to her on the saddle, as if afraid of losing her. Flanking the nurse are a man and woman accompanying them. The main subject of the painting is striking, the scene is one of luxury and highly realistic. The painting is delicately executed on silk, the colours are deep, showing the ideals of Chinese feminine beauty.

At the front of the painting there is an inscription and seals of Wanyan Hao, Zhangzong Emperor of Jin, in slender gold style, 'Tian Shui copy of Zhang Xuan's *Lady of Guoguo on a Spring Outing*'. At the end is an inscription by Wang Duo of the Qing dynasty in 1649. It had belonged to the inner court of the Song, Jin, and Southern Song, to Shi Niyuan, Jia Sidao, Wang Changheng and Liang Qingbiao collections. It finally entered the Qing palace collection, and is recorded in the *Records of Treasures at the Stone Canal*. DONG BAOHOU

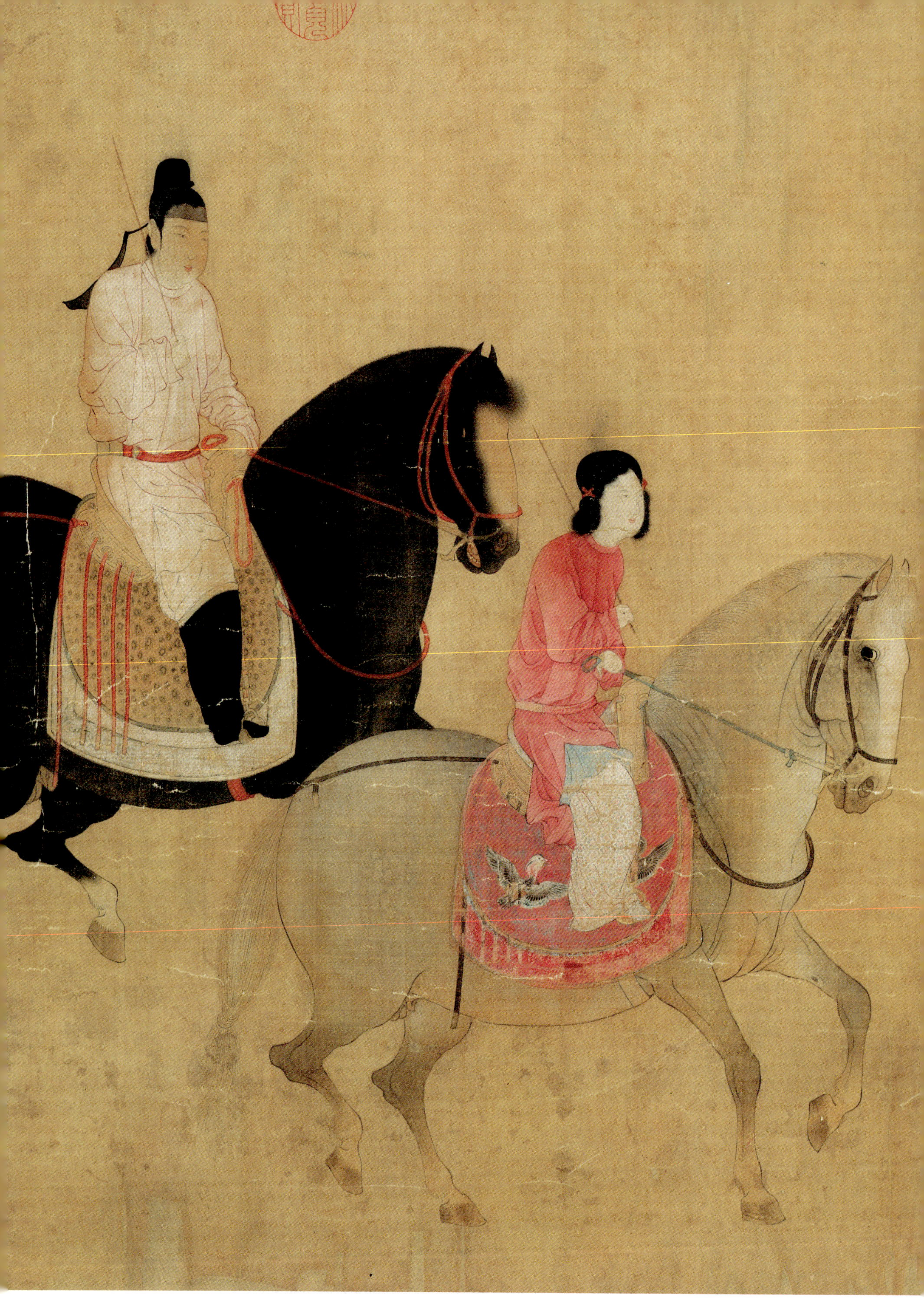

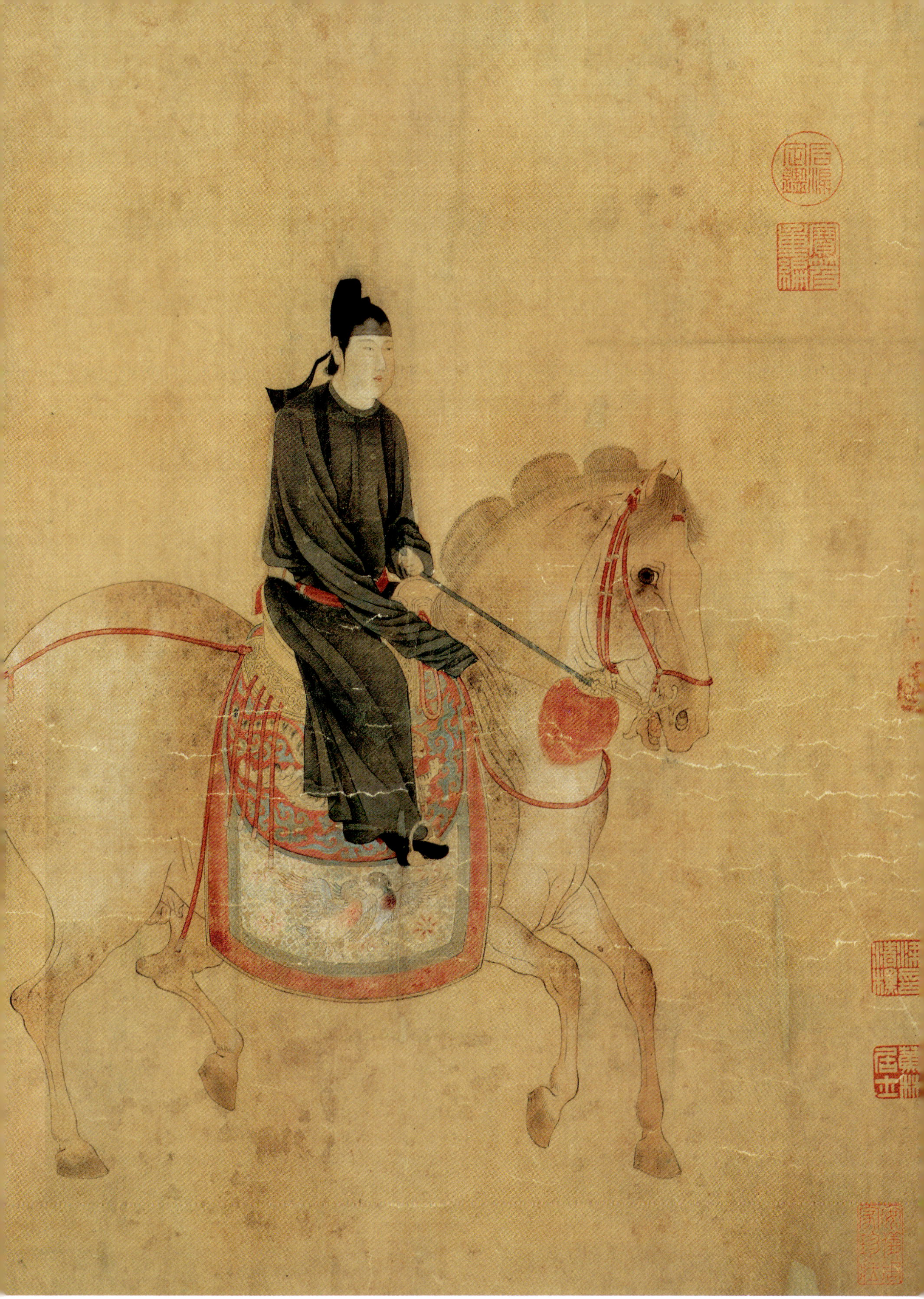

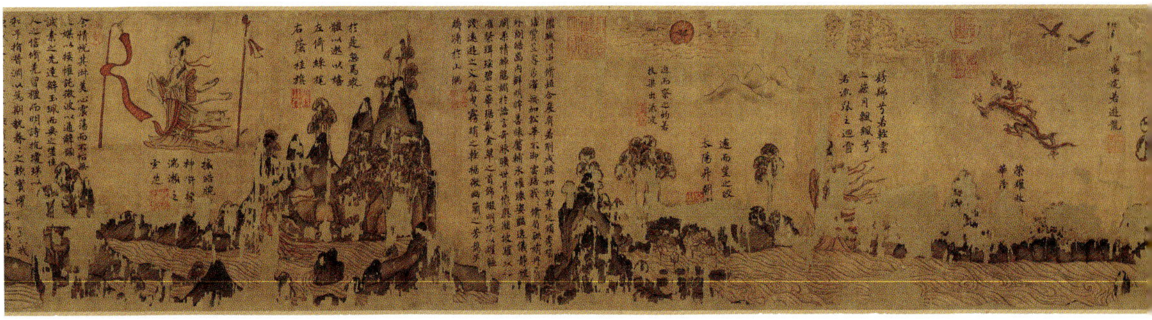

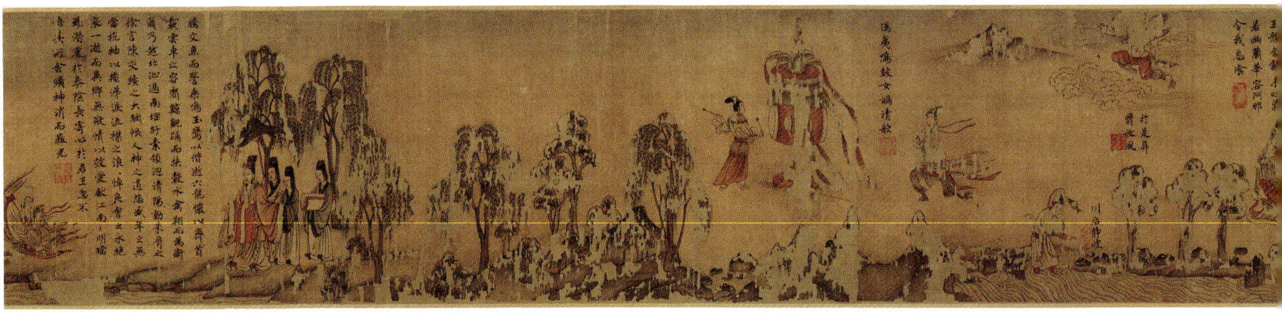

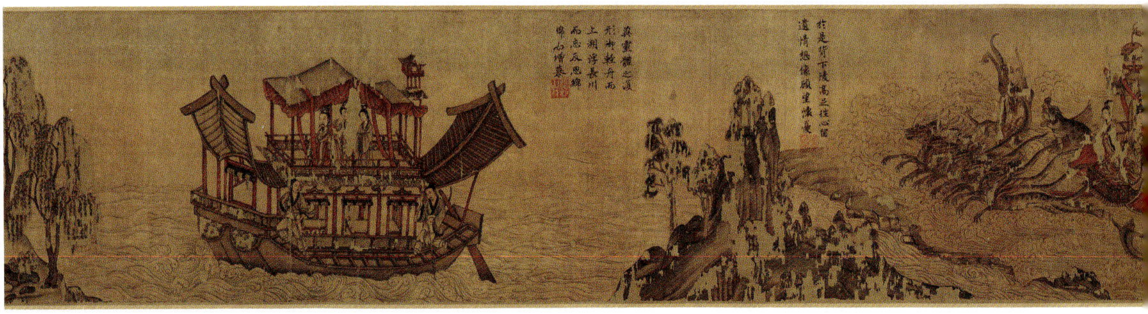

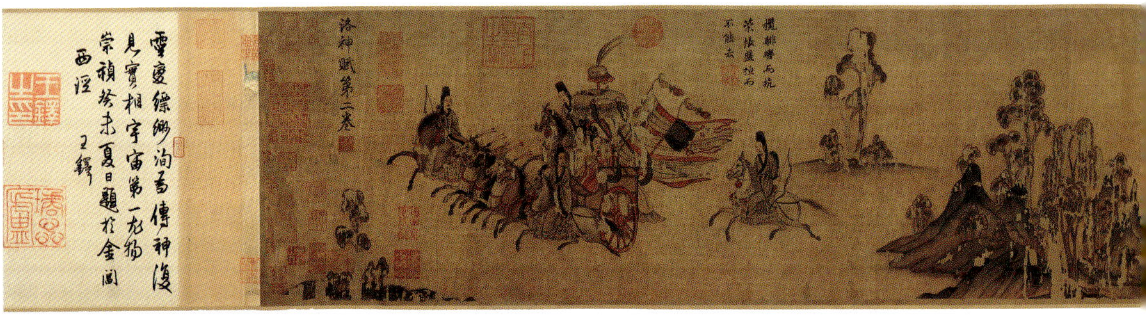
靈變縹緲洵爲傳神復
見寶相宇宙第一尤物
崇禎癸未夏日題於金閶
西涇　王鐸
洛神賦第一卷

7 Copy of *The Nymph of the Luo River*

Unknown
Northern Song dynasty (960–1127)
Hand scroll, ink and colour on silk
Length 26.3 cm, Width 641.6 cm

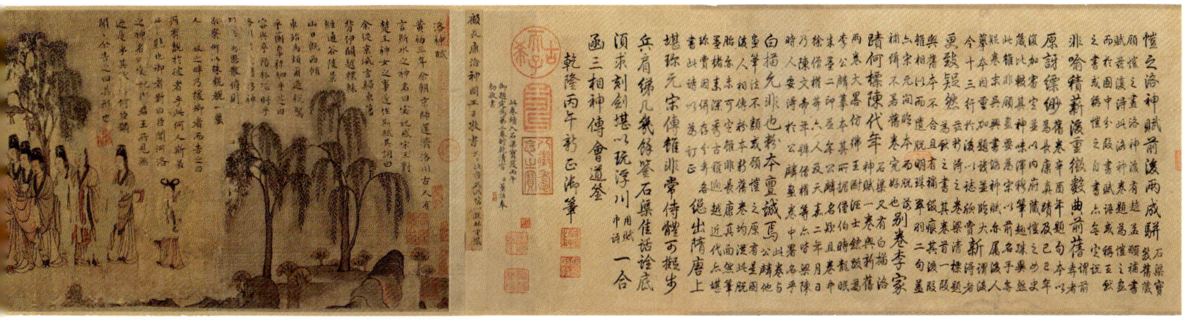

7

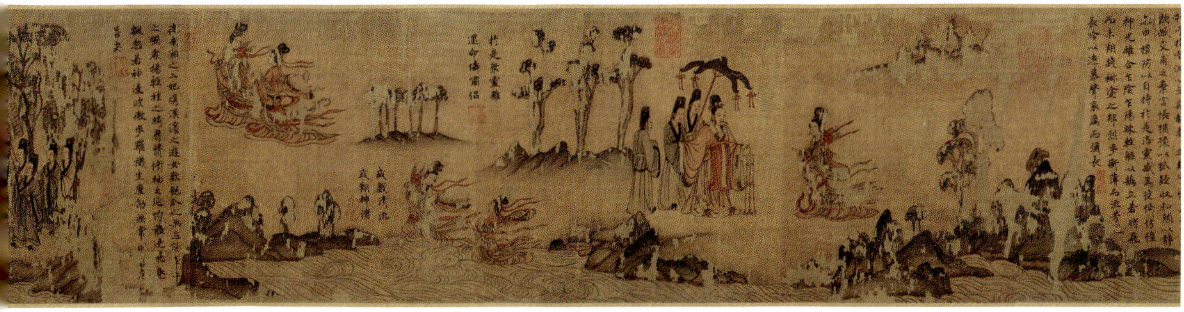

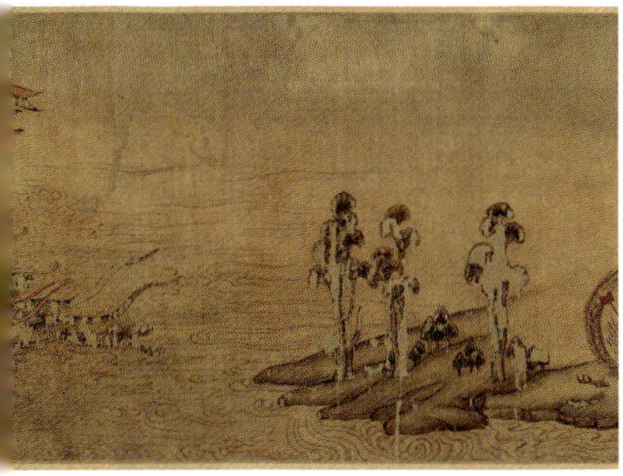

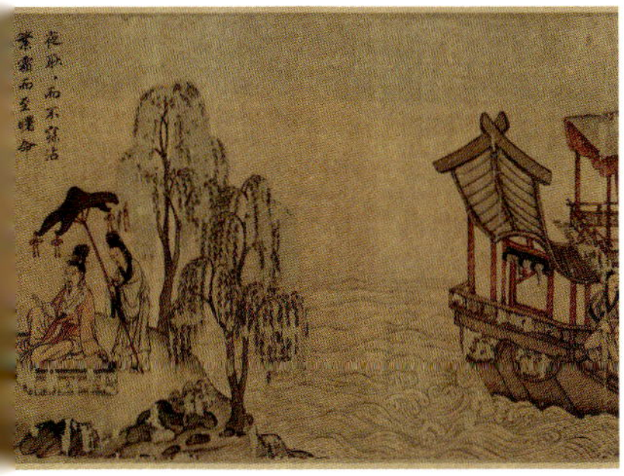

This scroll has the story of *The Nymph of the Luo River* by Cao Zhi of the Three Kingdoms, divided into twenty-two sections of coloured painted figures, landscapes, dragon and fish, horses and carts and mythical creatures. This has fully represented the intention of the original story. The shape of the figures is low and unassuming; folds in their clothing are depicted by simple, flowing brush strokes. The mountains and rocks are outlined, not dabbed, the trees often have leaves and are rarely detailed, and share the same style of the Wei and Jin described by Zhang Yanyuan in *A Record of Famous Painters of all the Dynasties*. Small regular script follows the painting, both high and low and with no fixed structure. It is likely that the painting was done first, followed by the calligraphy. Currently there are six known extant copies of *The Nymph of the Luo River*, all with basically the same execution, and all are Song copies. This copy is of a slightly higher standard than other examples. WANG YAJING

8 *White Lotus Society*

Zhang Ji
Northern Song dynasty (960–1127)
Hand scroll, ink on paper
Length 35 cm, Width 849 cm

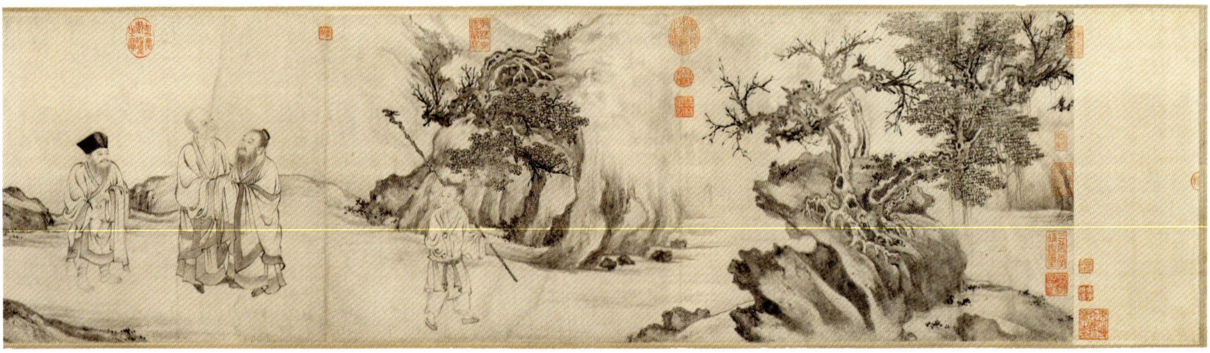

8

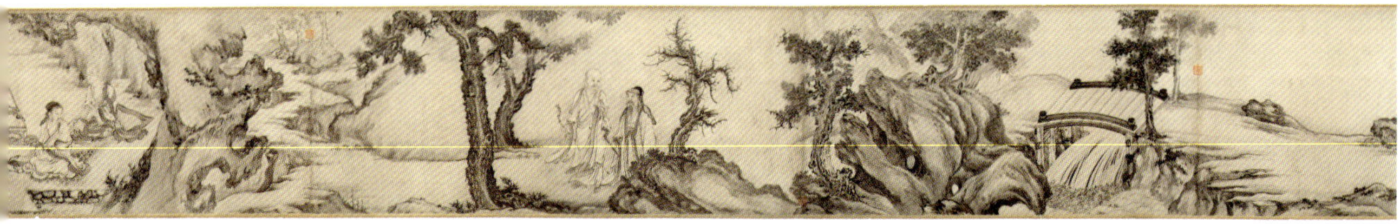

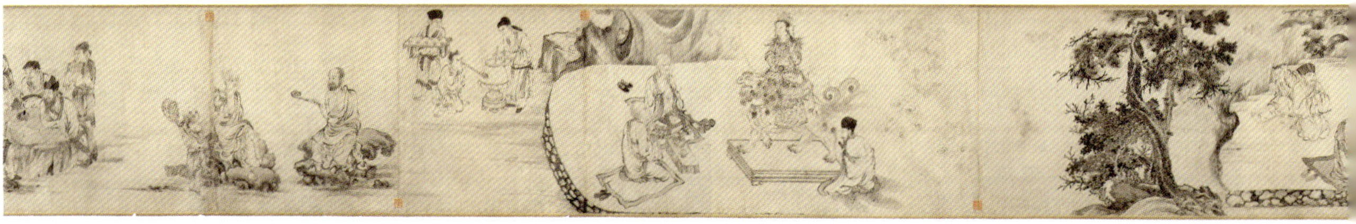

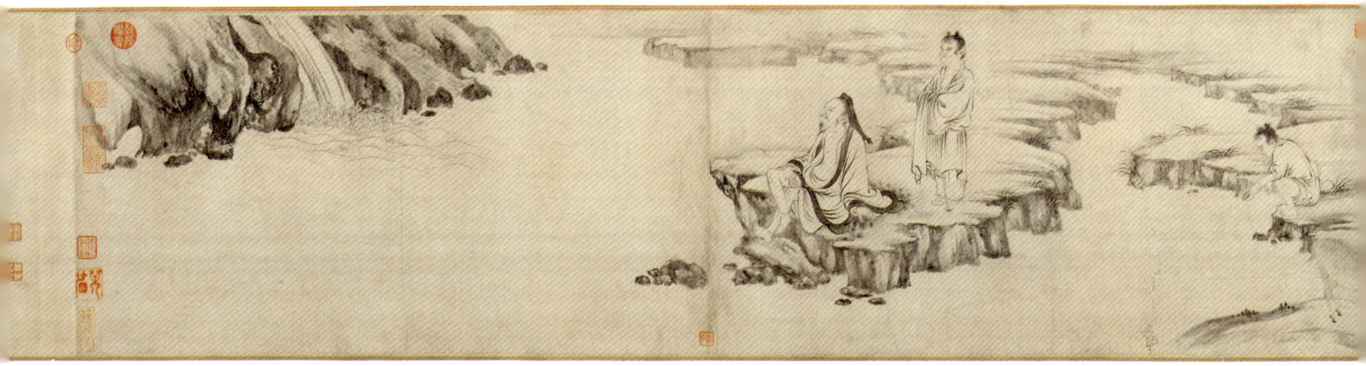

9 *Sandy Shore and Misty Trees*

Hui Chong (?c.1017?)
Southern Song dynasty (1127–1279)
Hand scroll, ink and colour on silk
Length 23.8 cm, Width 24.5 cm

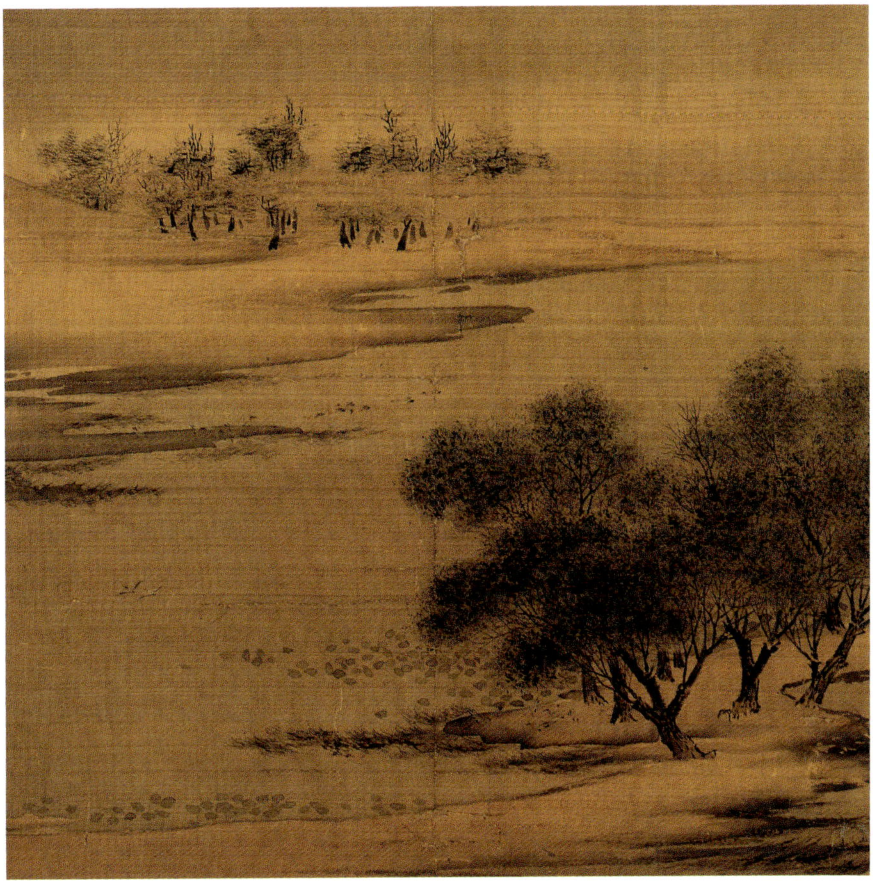

9

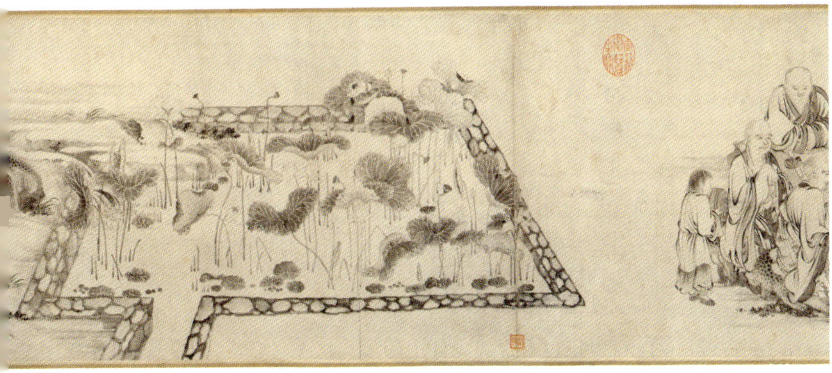

10 *Red Trees on Autumn Mountains*

Xiao Zhao (1130–1162)
Southern Song dynasty (1127–1279)
Hand scroll, ink and colour on silk
Length 28 cm, Width 28 cm

11 *Reading at the Window in Autumn*

Liu Songnian (1174–1224)
Southern Song dynasty (1127–1279)
Hand scroll, ink and colour on silk
Length 25.8 cm, Width 26 cm

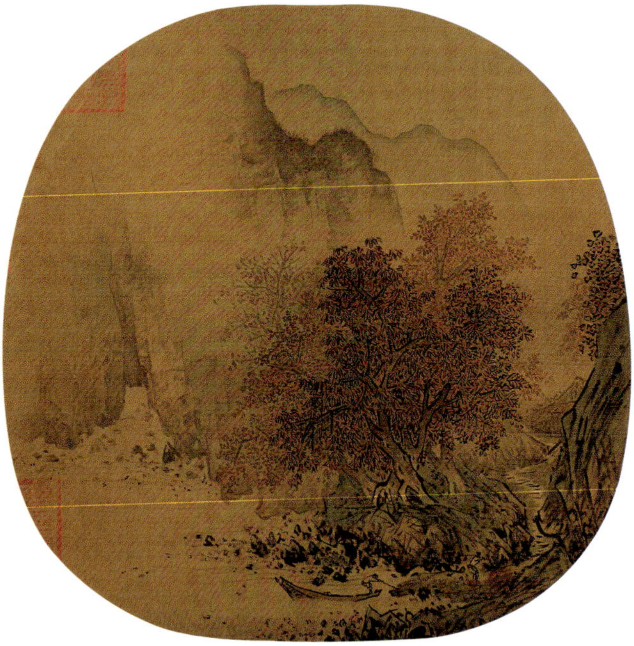

10

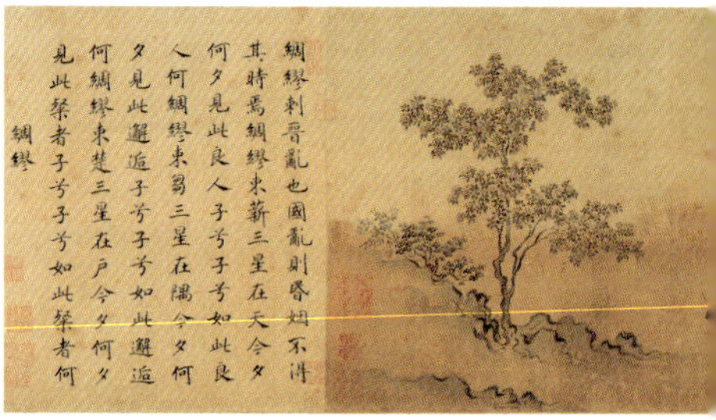

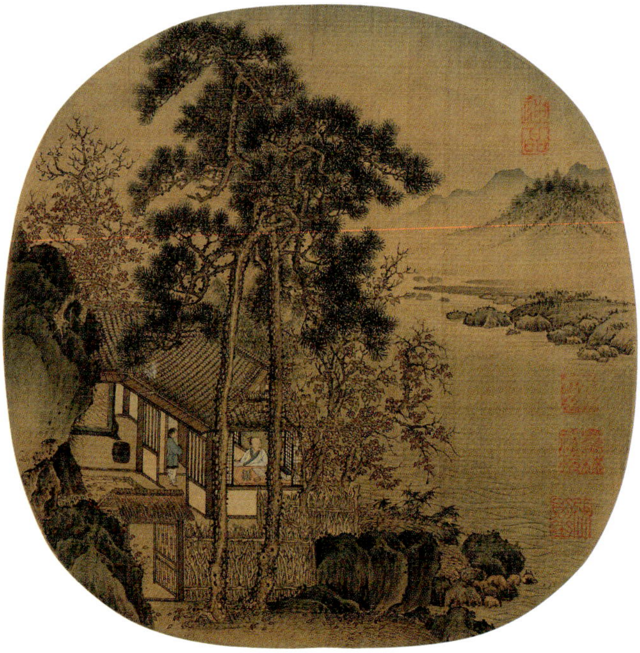

11

12 Illustrations to the Odes of Tang in Mao Poetry

Painter: Ma Hezhi (1131–1162)
Calligrapher: Zhao Gou
Southern Song dynasty (1127–1279)
Hand scroll, ink and colour on silk
Length 28.7 cm, Width 827.1 cm

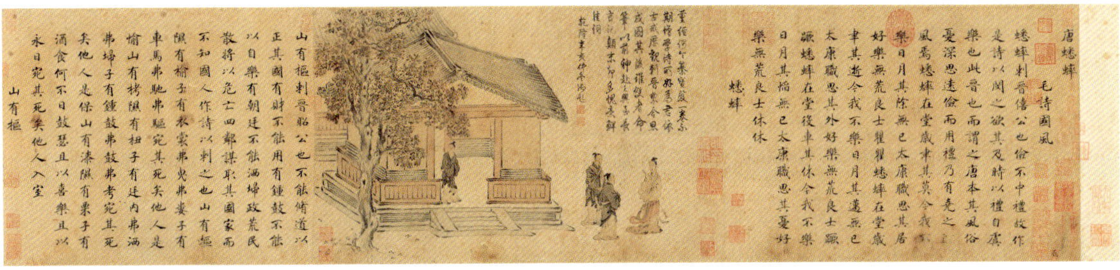

12

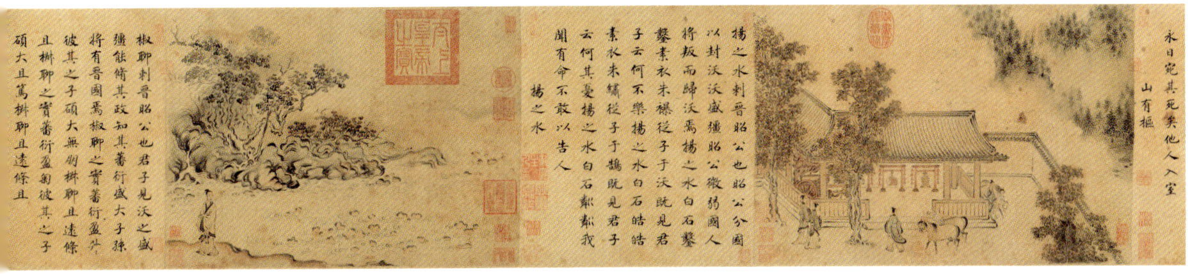

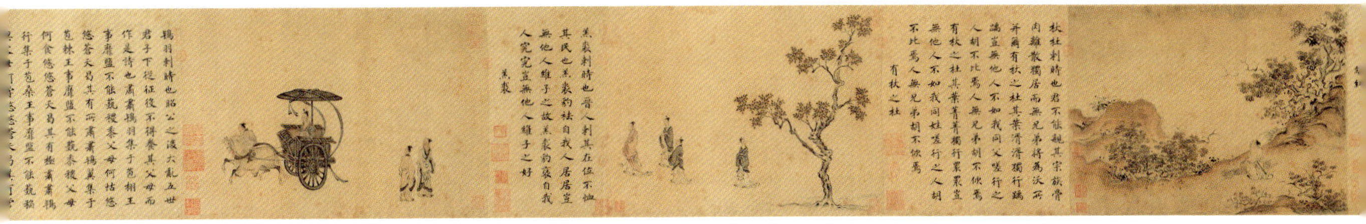

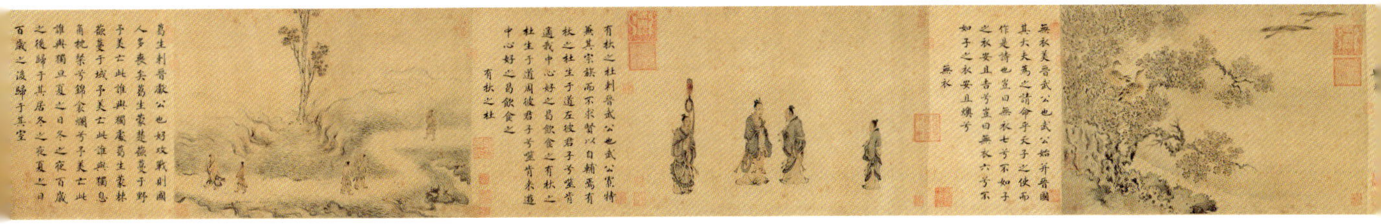

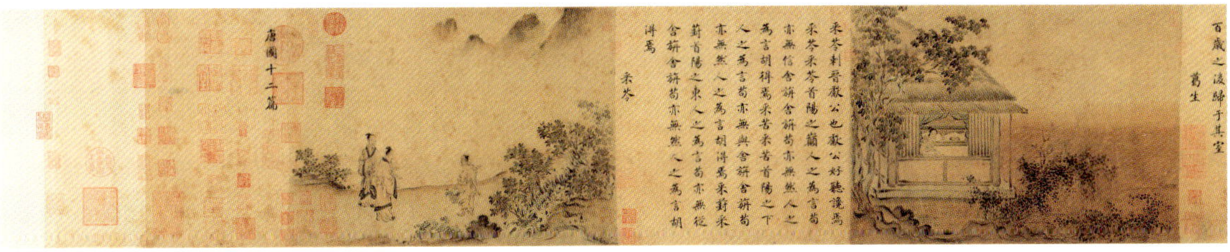

13 *Longevity Pine*

Ma Yuan (1190–after 1225)
Southern Song dynasty (1127–1279)
Hanging scroll, ink and colour on silk
Length 122 cm, Width 52.7 cm

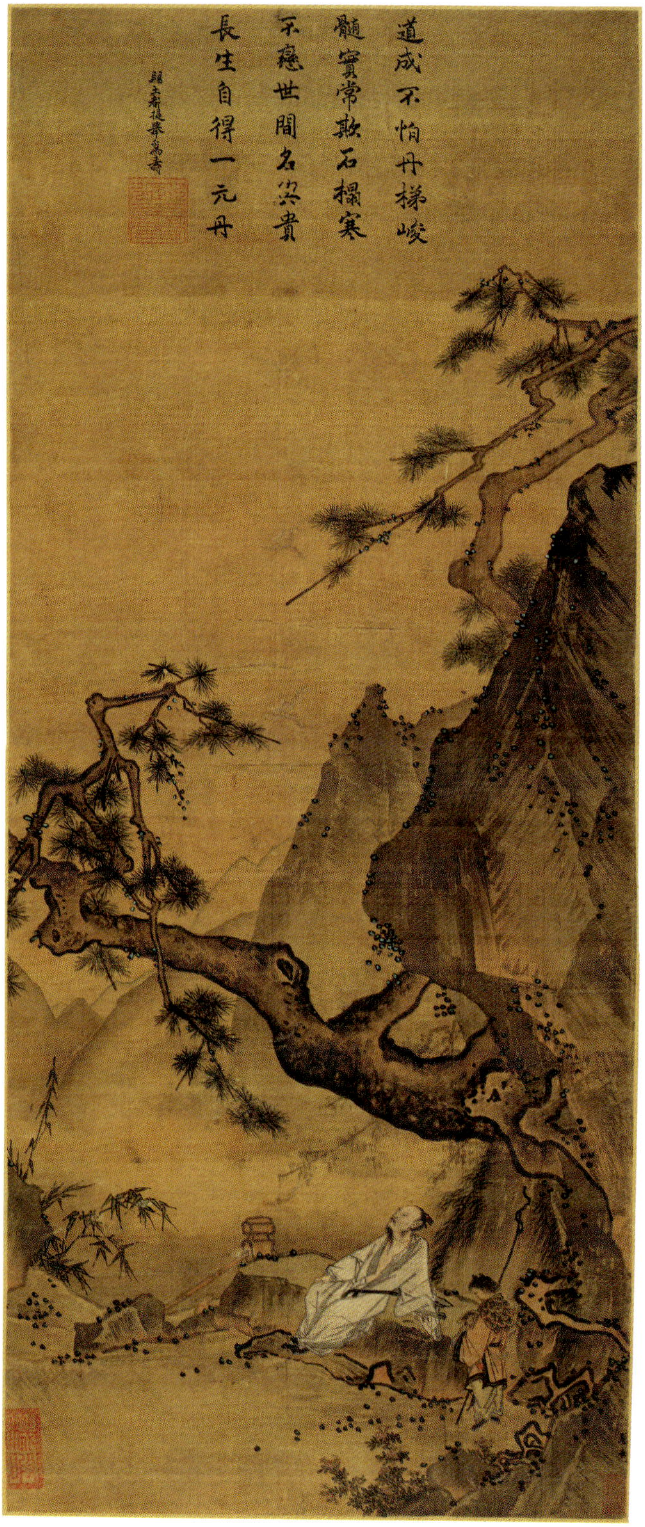

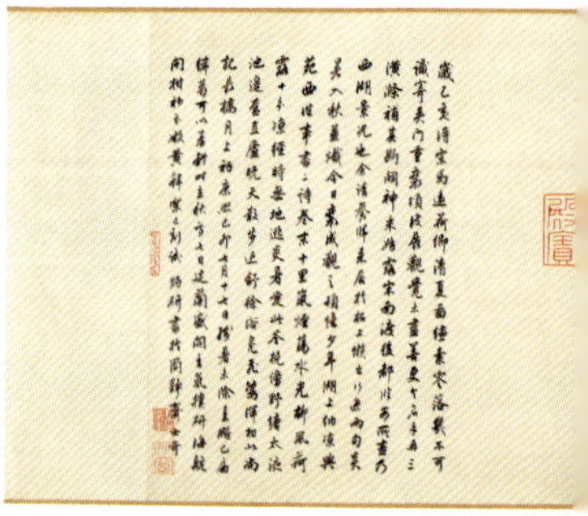

14 *Lotus Pond in Summer*

Ma Lin
Southern Song dynasty (1127–1279)
Hand scroll, ink and colour on silk
Length 41.7 cm, Width 323 cm

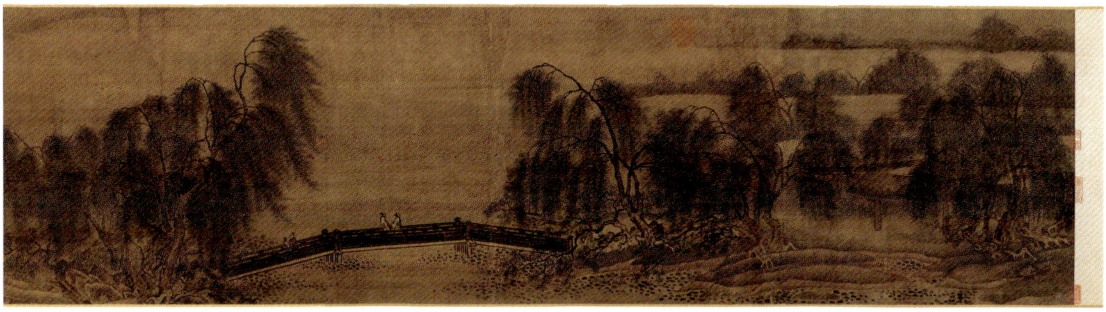

14

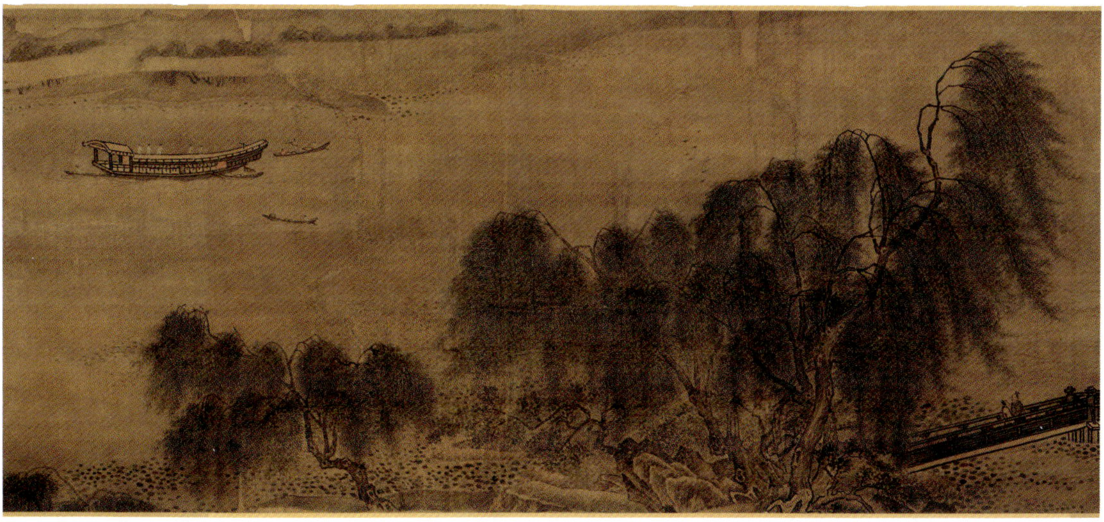

15 *Crows in Winter*

Unknown
Southern Song dynasty (1127–1279)
Hand scroll, ink and colour on silk
Length 28 cm, Width 116 cm

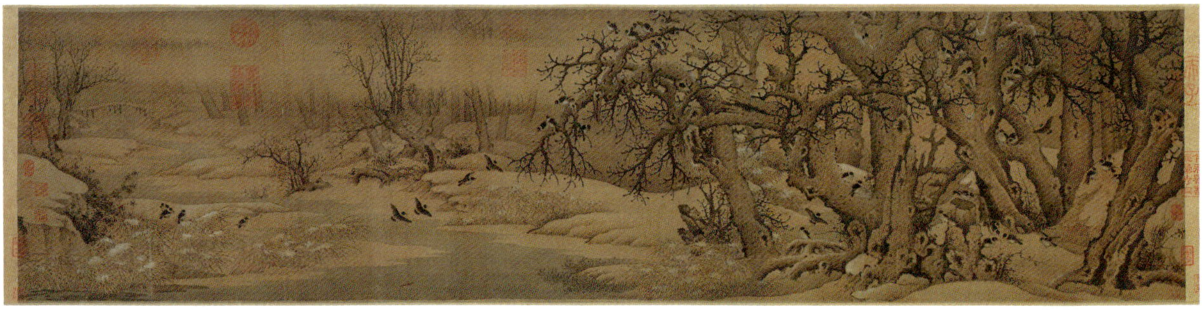

15

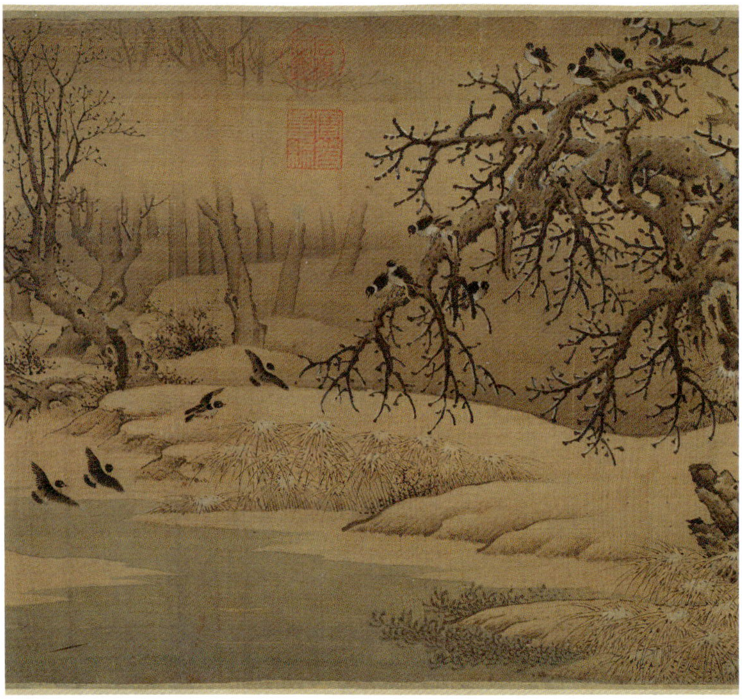

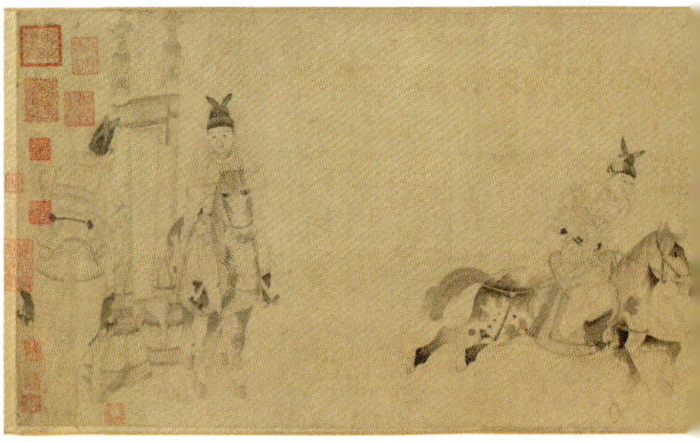

16 *Emperor Xuanzong Playing Polo*

Unknown
Southern Song dynasty (1127–1279)
Line drawing on paper
Length 32.1 cm, Width 230.5 cm

17 *Plum and Bamboo in the Snow*

Xu Yugong (b. 1141)
Southern Song dynasty (1127–1279)
Hand scroll, ink and colour on silk
Length 28 cm, Width 122 cm

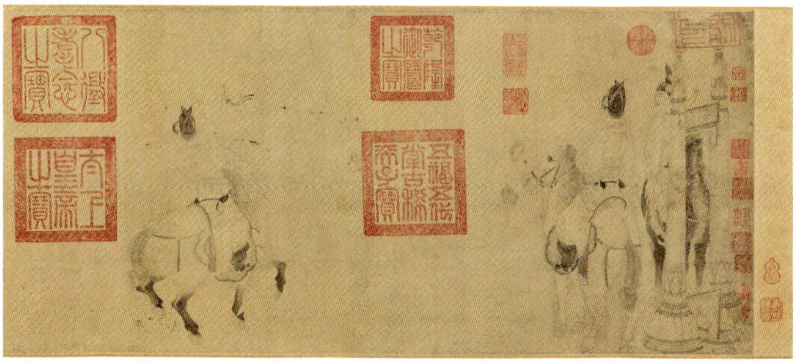

16

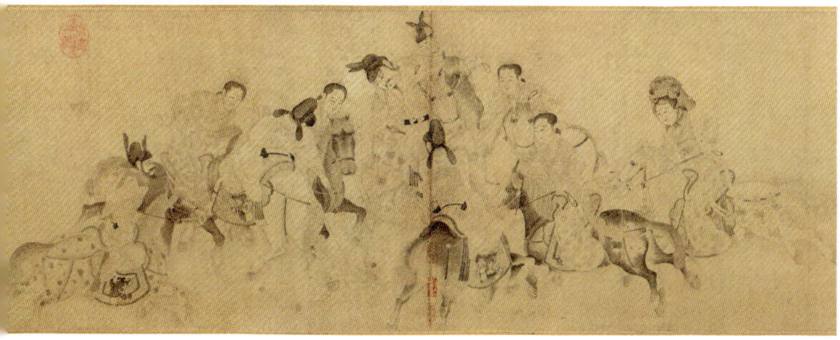

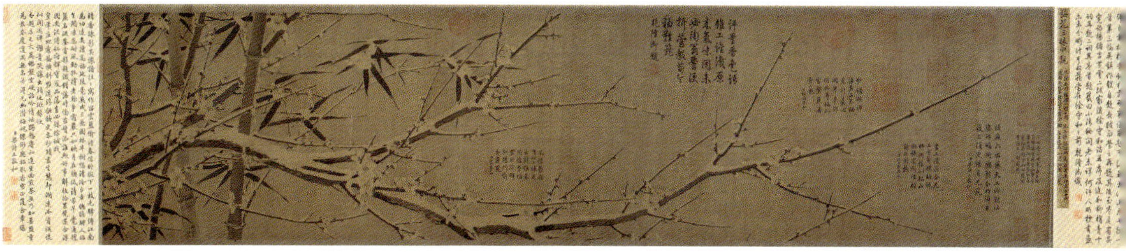

17

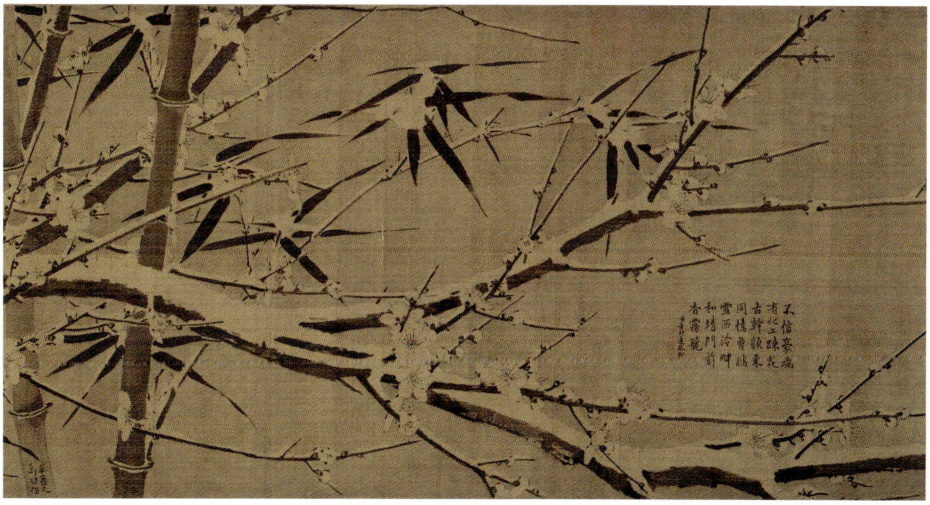

18 *Playing Chess in Remote Mountains*

Unknown
Liao dynasty (916–1125)
Hanging scroll, ink and colour on silk
Length 106.5 cm, Width 54 cm
Excavated in 1974 from the seventh Liao tomb at Yamaotai in Faku County in Liaoning Province

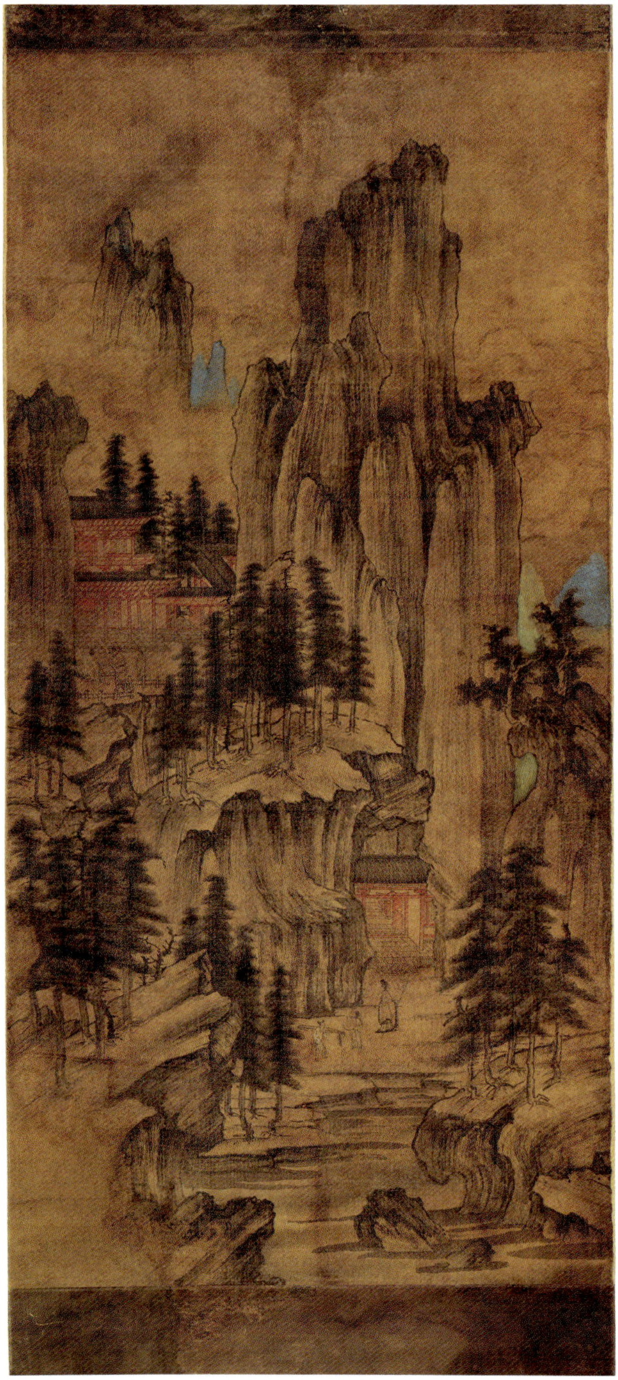

The whole painting has been executed in perspective. Clouds and mountains, trees and rocks, pavilions and water all merge as one. The pavilions in the painting are careful and neat, and courtyards are hidden among the mountains and rocks, in curvy lines. Two gentlemen are playing chess over a table in a courtyard and a child servant is waiting to one side. In the foreground, there is a gentleman carrying a stick, next to two children carrying a pot of alcohol and a *qin* (a stringed instrument) next to the stream, walking up the path. The two groups of people up and down the mountain are calling each other, the man waiting for his friend is playing chess, while the visitor has arrived with wine and a *qin*. Between the pavilions in the mountain, water flows down the stream, embellished with straight, luxurious pine trees. The scene in the painting is depicted accurately, the colour is fine, and the style is similar to that expounded by Ji Guan in his Landscape School in Central China in the Five Dynasties and Northern Song periods.

Although this painting has no signature or seal, the excavated tomb dates from the early Liao dynasty and the painting therefore should be no later than the Yingzong Yelü Xian Liao period (969–982), which is the Northern Song period of 976–983. This painting has provided an important example for researching the development and influence of landscape painting from Central China in the Five Dynasties and early Northern Song periods. WANG YAJING

19 *Magpie in Bamboo and Two Rabbits*

Unknown
Liao dynasty (916–1125)
Hanging scroll, ink and colour on silk
Painting lining, Height 106.5 cm, Width 54 cm
Excavated in 1974 from the seventh Liao tomb at Yamaotai in Faku County in Liaoning Province

20 *Two Steeds*

Yang Wei
Jin dynasty (1115–1234)
Hand scroll, ink and colour on silk
Painting lining, Length 24.8 cm, Width 80.8 cm

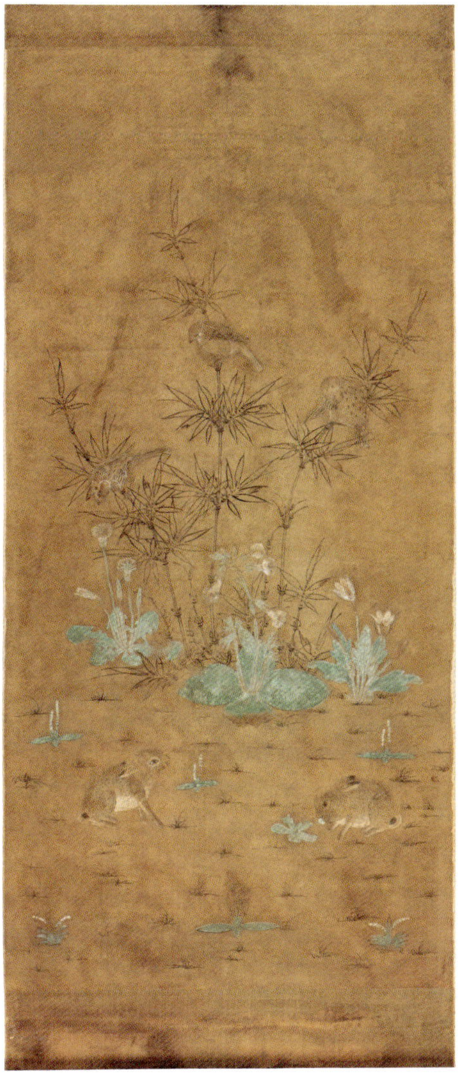

19

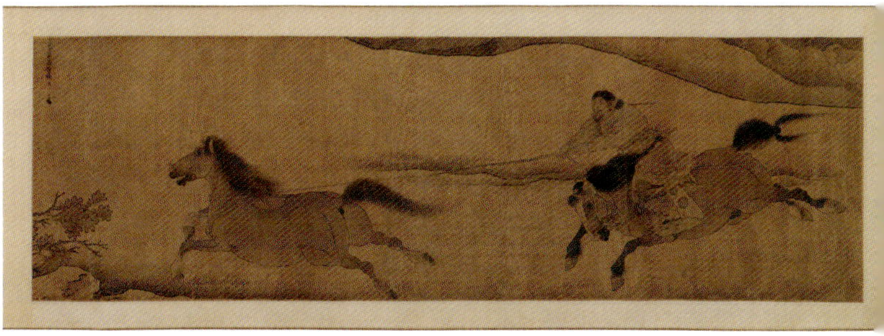

20

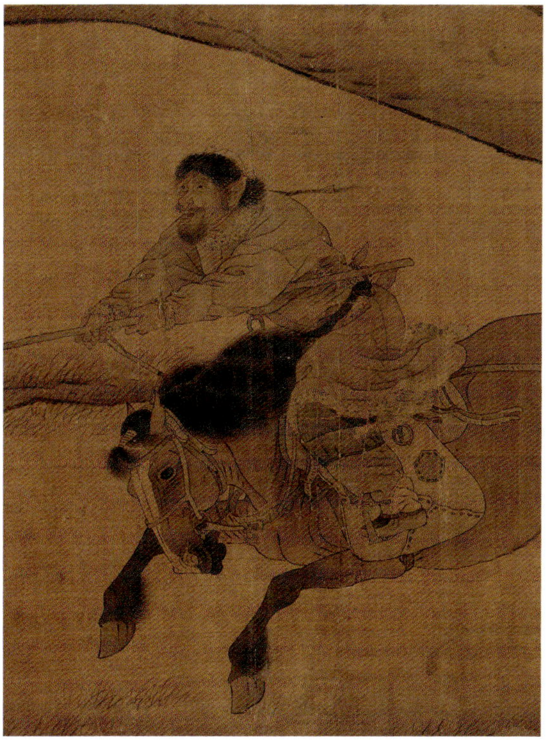

21 *Arhat in Red Robe*

Zhao Mengfu (1254–1322)
Yuan (1271–1368)
Hand scroll, ink and colour on paper
Length 26 cm, Width 52 cm

22 *Dipankara Buddha's Bestowal of Prediction on Shakyamuni*

Unknown
Yuan (1271–1368)
Hand scroll, ink and colour on silk
Length 26.2 cm, Width 382 cm

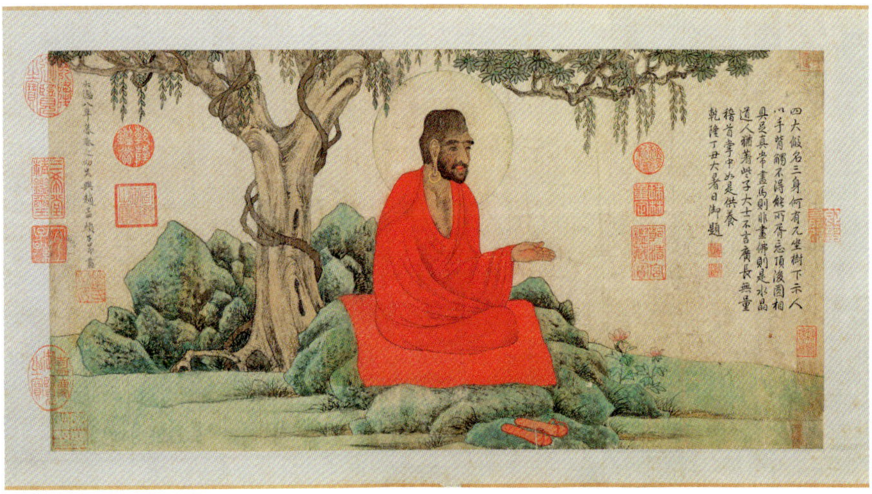

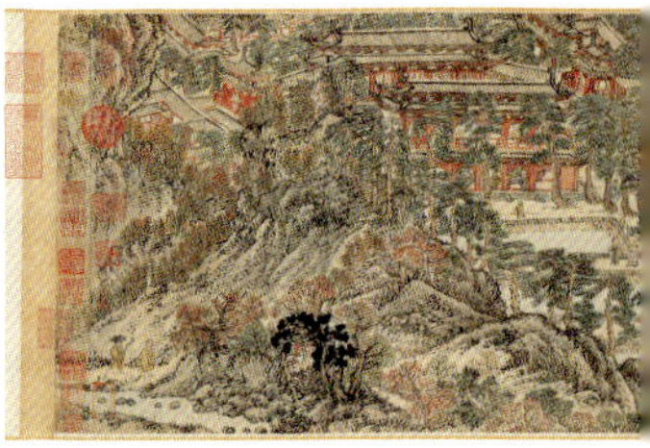

21

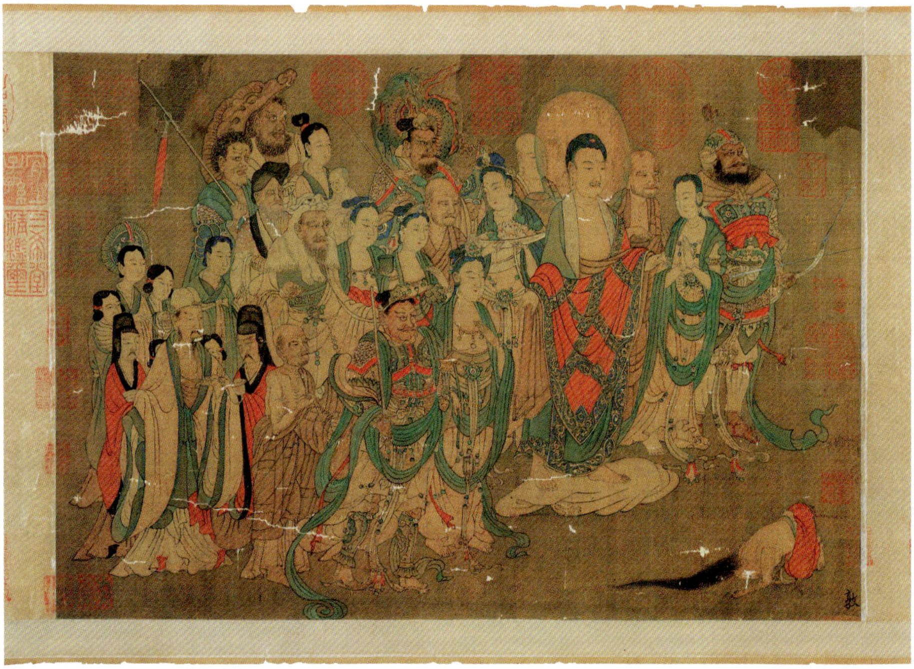

22

23 *Taibai Mountain*

Wang Meng (1308–85)
Yuan dynasty (1271–1368)
Hand scroll, ink and colour on paper
Length 28 cm, Width 238.2 cm

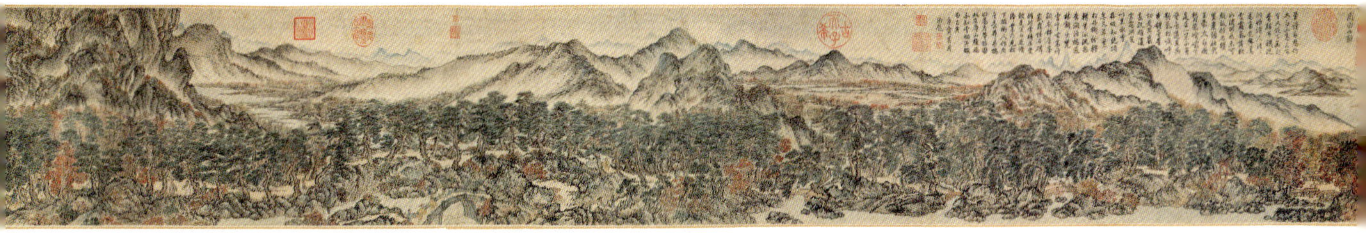

23

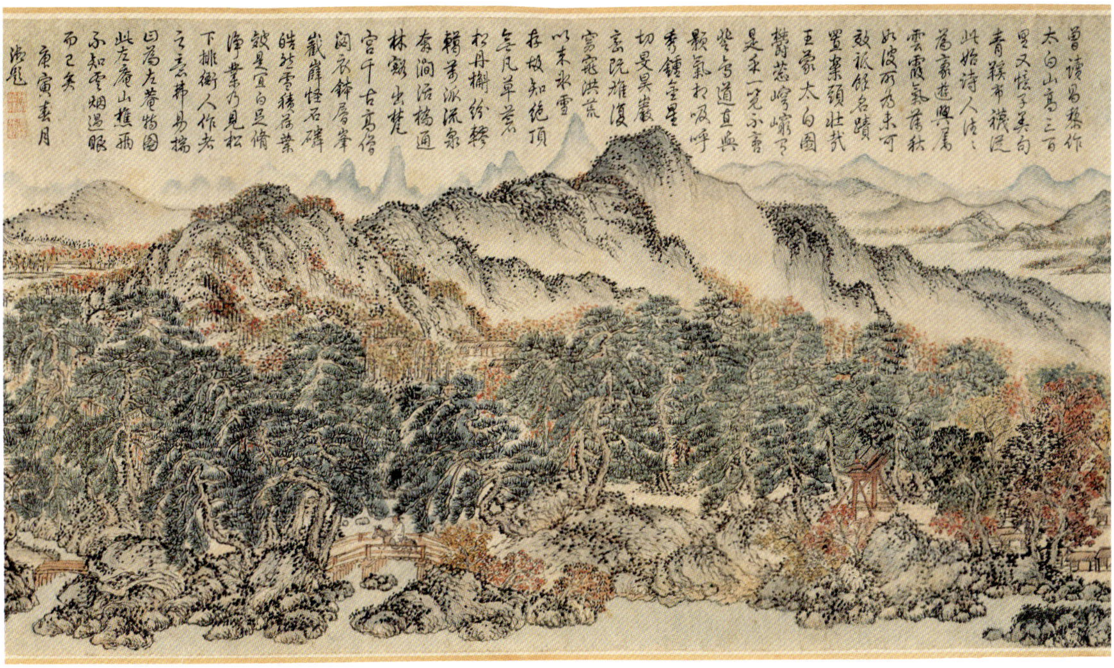

24 *The Six Patriarchs from Dharma to Huineng*

Dai Jin (1388–1462)
Ming (1368–1644)
Hand scroll, ink and faint colour on silk
Length 33.8 cm, Width 220 cm

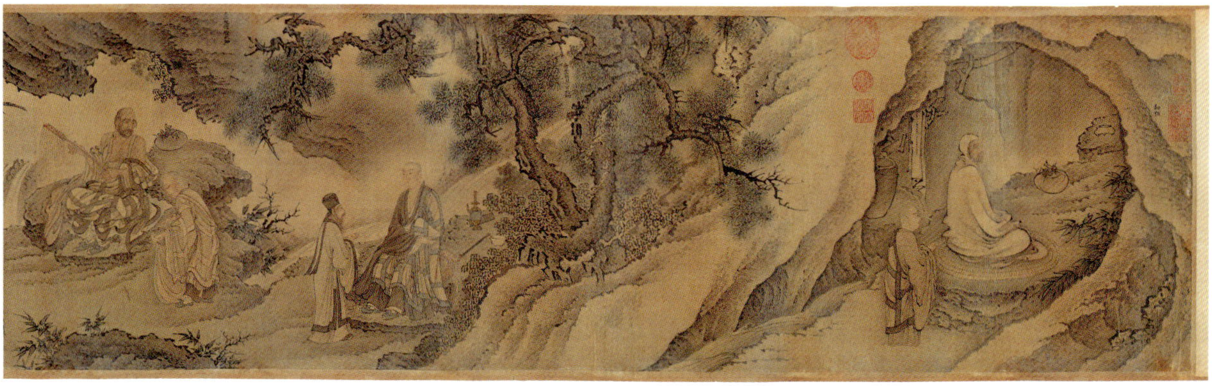

24

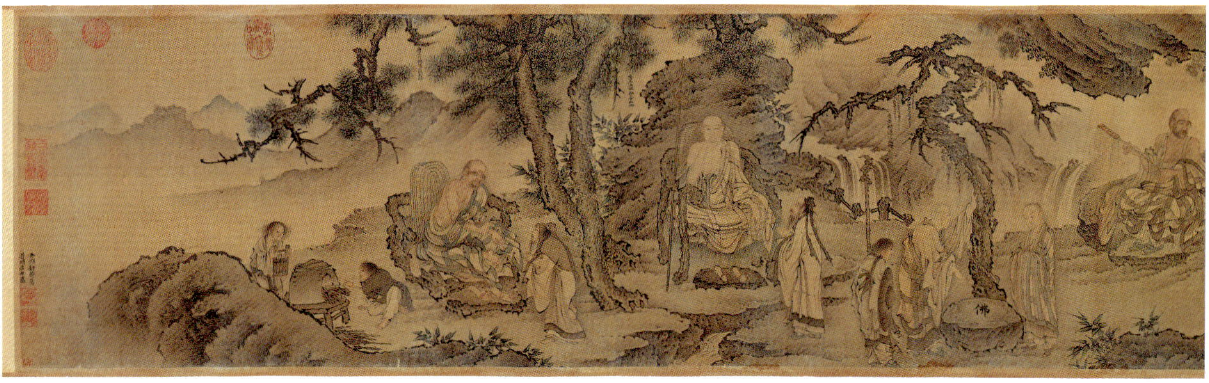

25 *Ten thousand year-old Pine Tree*

Ming Emperor Xuande Zhu Zhanji (1426–1435)
Hanging scroll, ink and colour on paper
Length 33 cm, Width 453 cm

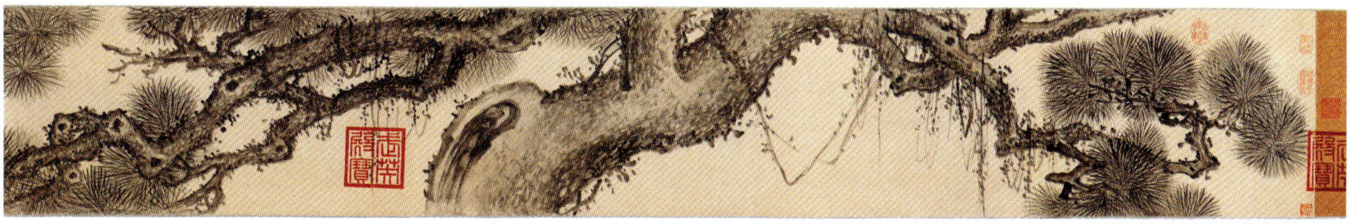

25

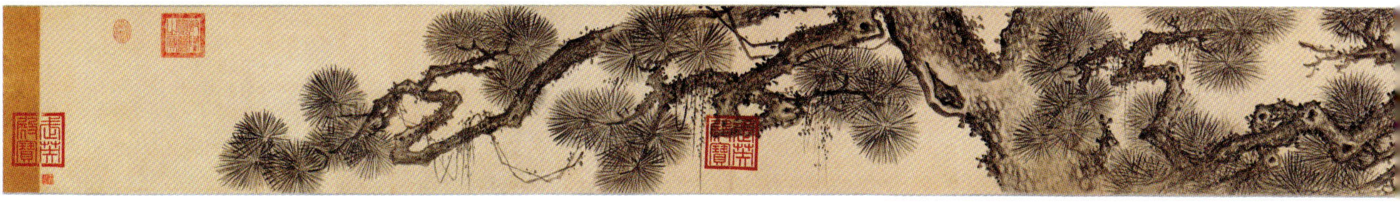

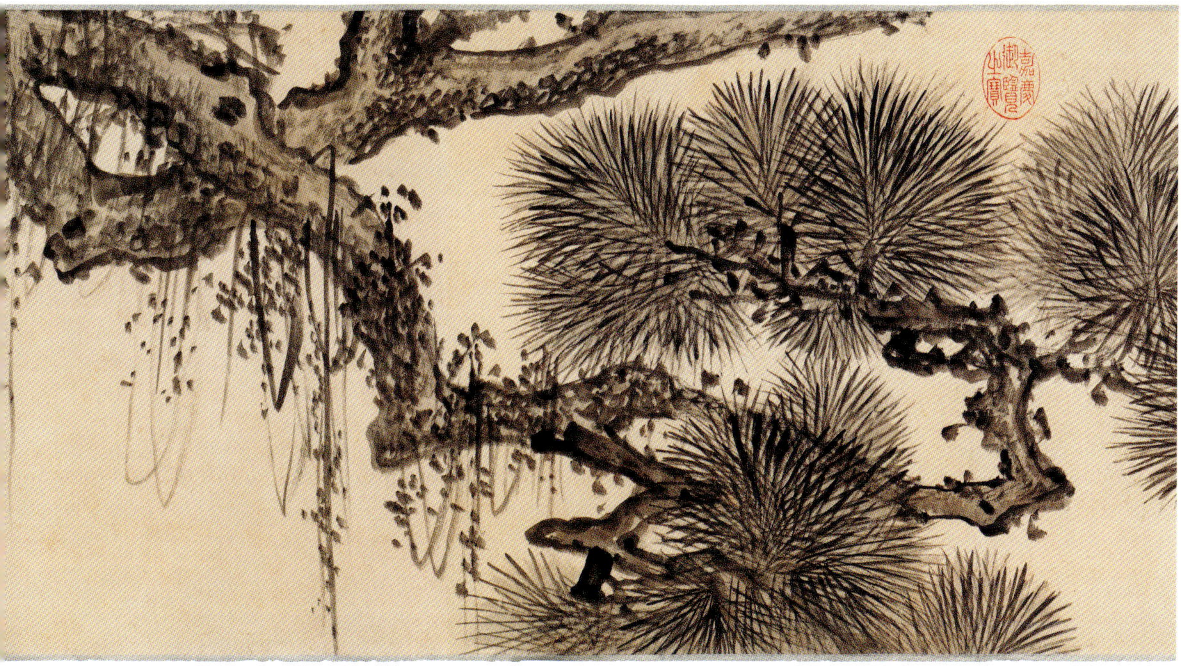

26 *Three paintings of the Poem Returning Home*

Ma Shi, Li Zai (b. 1431), Xia Zhi (1390–1450)
Ming dynasty (1368–1644)
Hand scroll, ink on paper
Length 27.7 cm, Width 643.9 cm

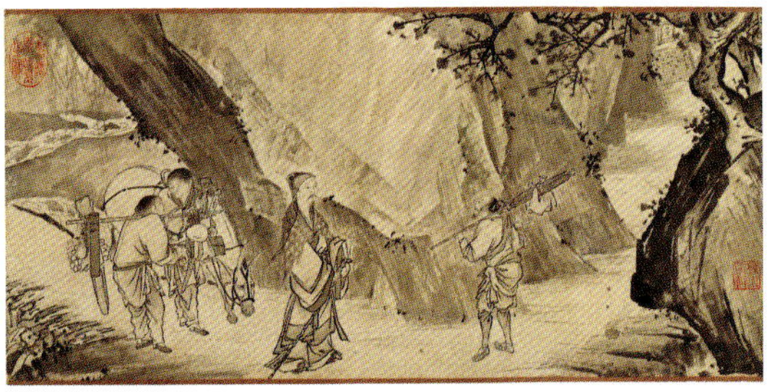

Ma Shi Asking the passengers about the way ahead

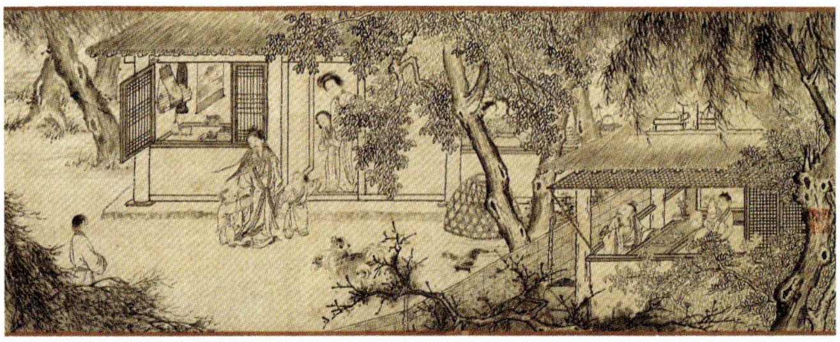

Ma Shi Children waiting at the gate

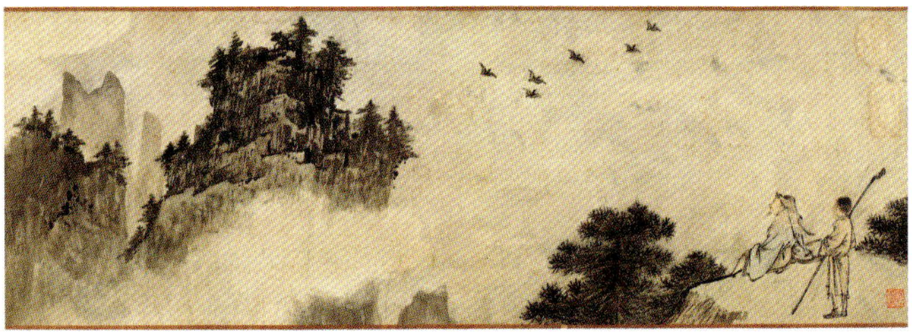

Li Zai Cloud floating out of the mountain side aimlessly

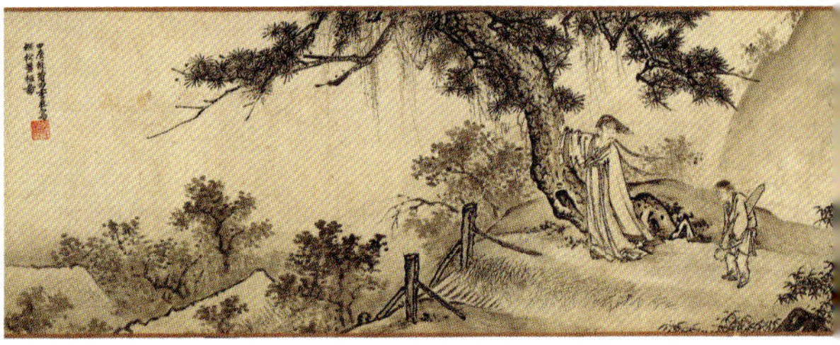

Li Zai I caressed a pine tree and lingered around

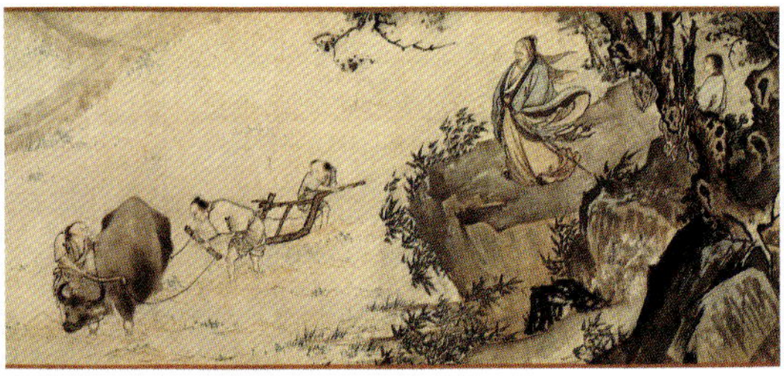

Ma Shi Peasants will tell me that spring is coming

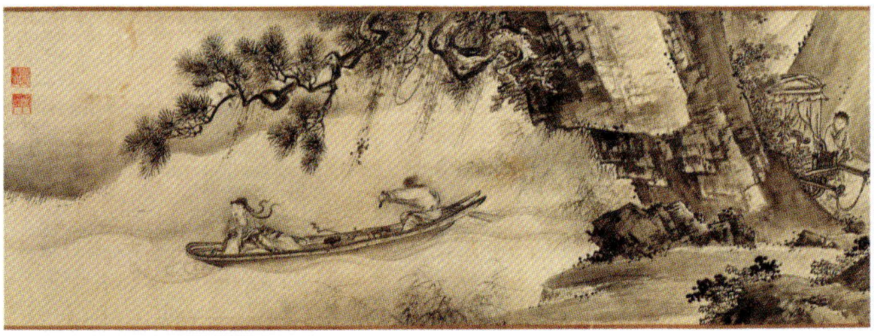

Xia Zhi I would ride a curtained cart

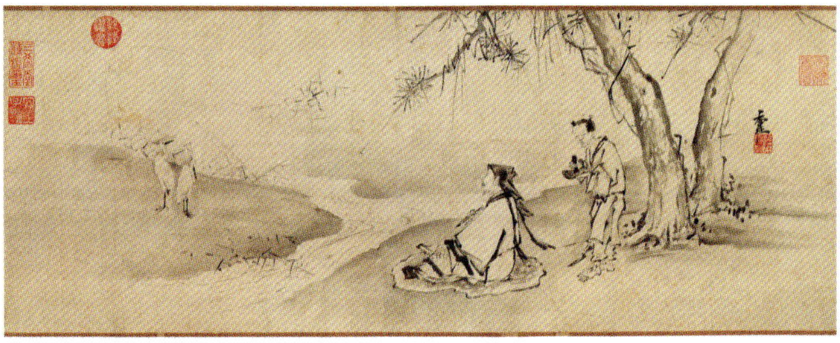

Li Zai Sitting by a clear riverside and composing poems

27 *Shitou Goose*

Lü Ji (b. 1477)
Ming dynasty (1368–1644)
Hanging scroll, ink and colour on silk
Length 192.5 cm, Width 106 cm

28 *Elegant Gathering in Wei Garden*

Shen Zhou (1427–1509)
Ming dynasty (1368–1644)
Hanging scroll, ink and colour on paper
Length 145.5 cm, Width 47.5 cm

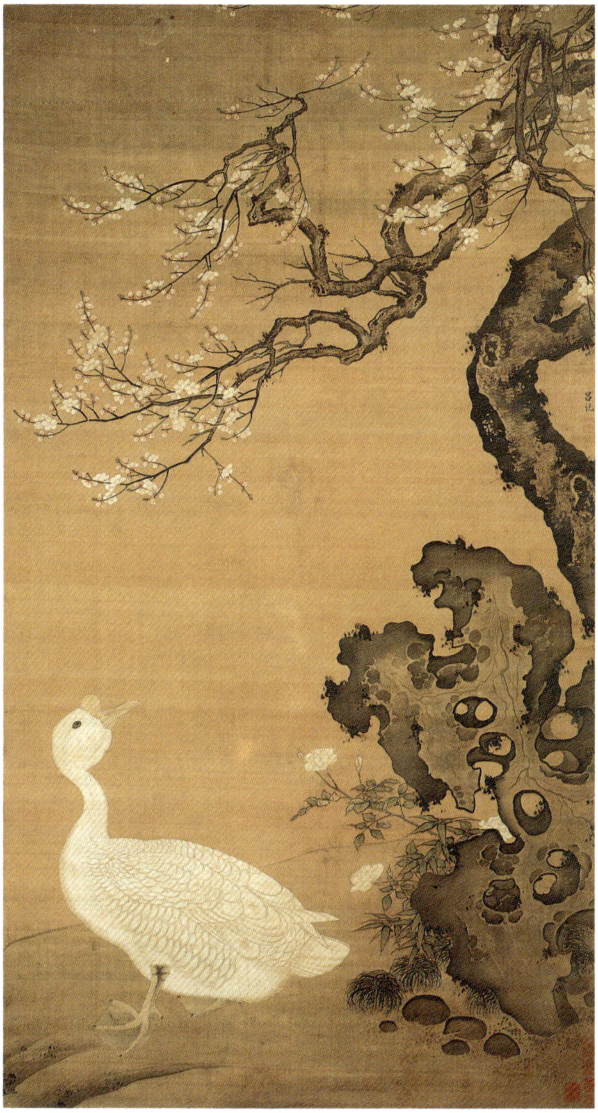

27

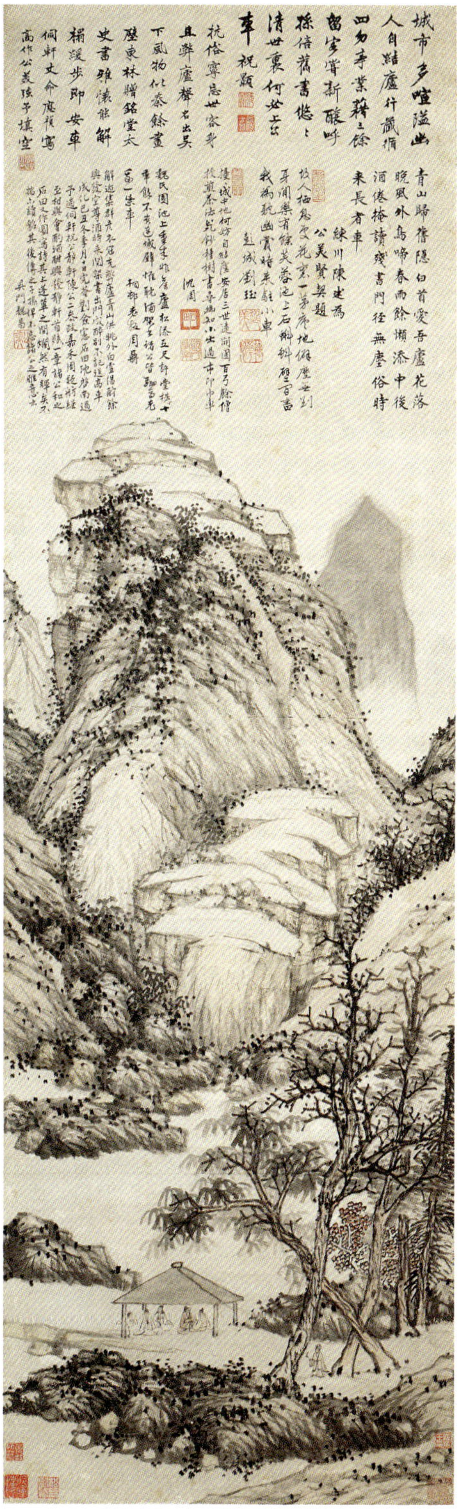

28

29 Wen Zhengming *Preface to the Orchid Pavilion*, calligraphy painting

Zhu Yunming (1464–1526)
Ming dynasty (1368–1644)
Hand scroll, ink and colour on paper
Length 20.8 cm, Width 77.8 cm

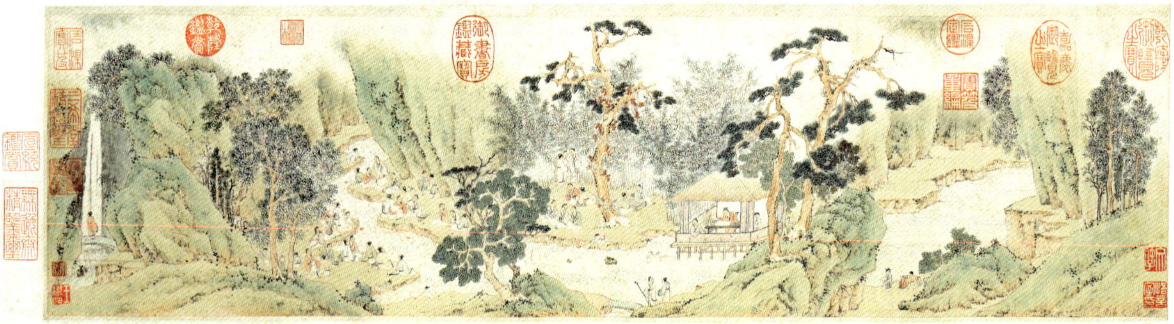

29

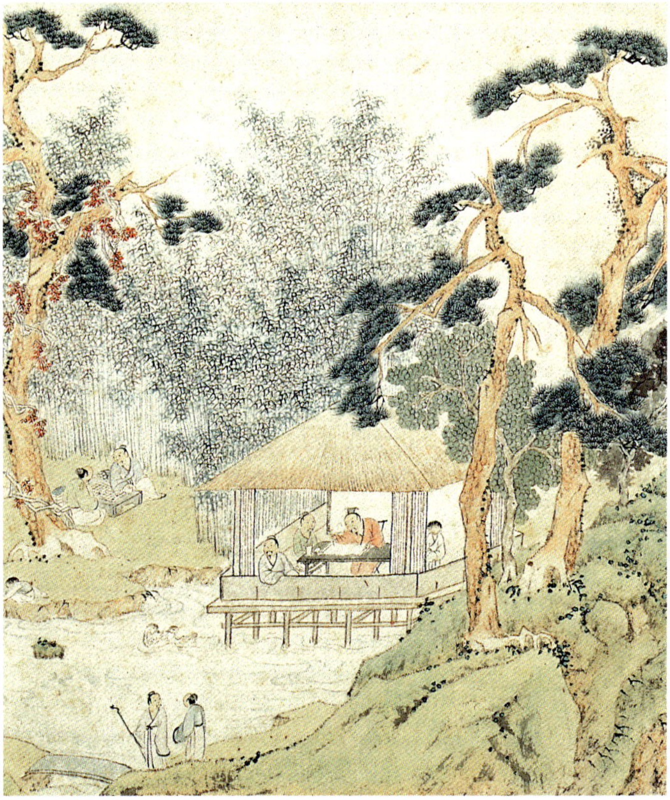

30 *Wu Yangzi in Meditation*

Tang Yin (1470–1523)
Ming dynasty (1368–1644)
Hand scroll, ink on paper
Length 29.5 cm, Width 103.5 cm

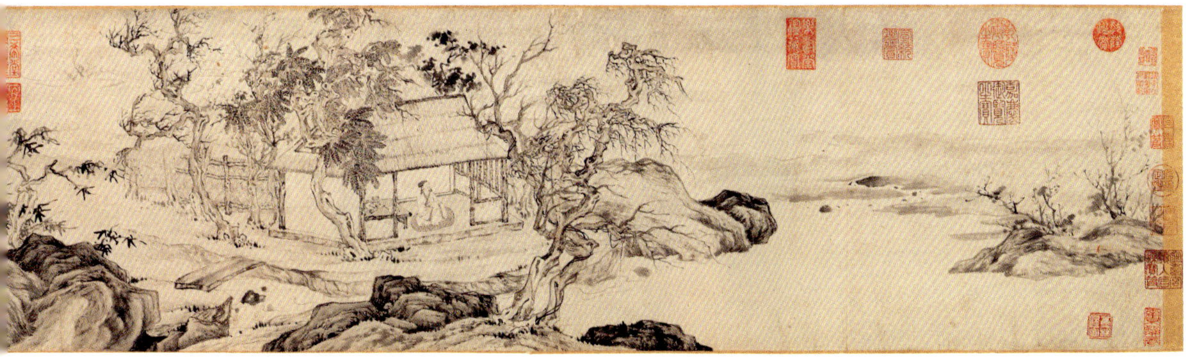

30

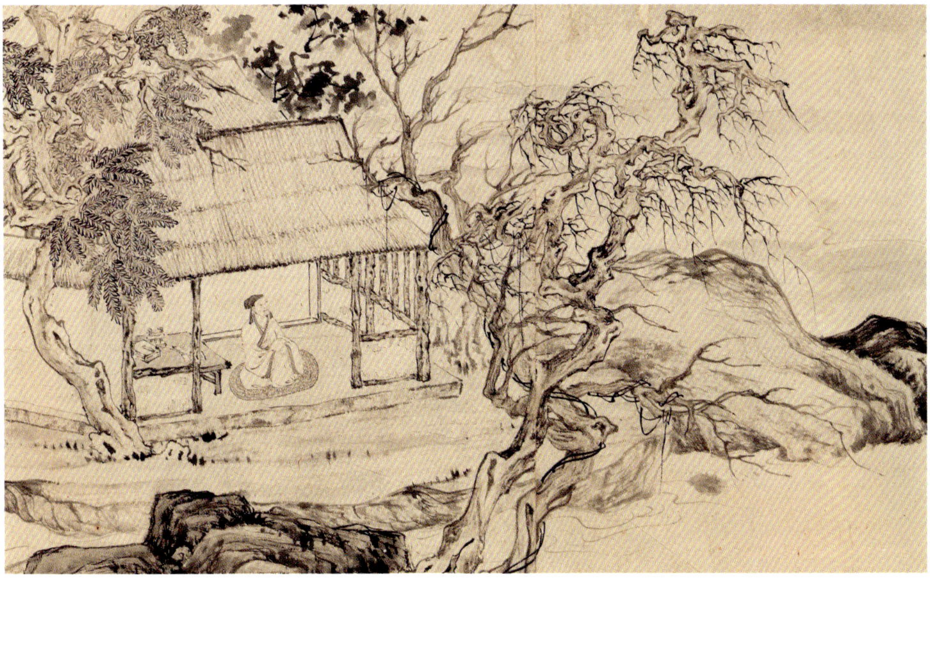

31 *Along The River During Qingming Festival*

Qiu Ying (dates unknown)
Ming dynasty (1368–1644)
Hand scroll, ink and colour on silk
Length 30.5 cm, Width 987 cm

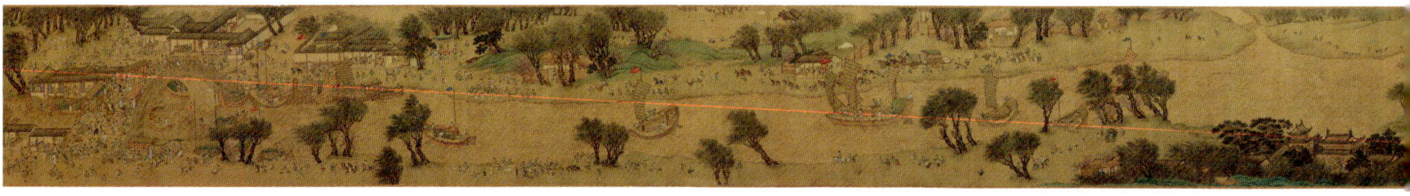

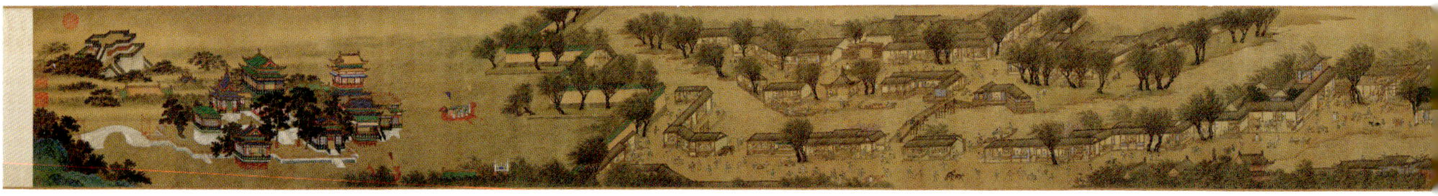

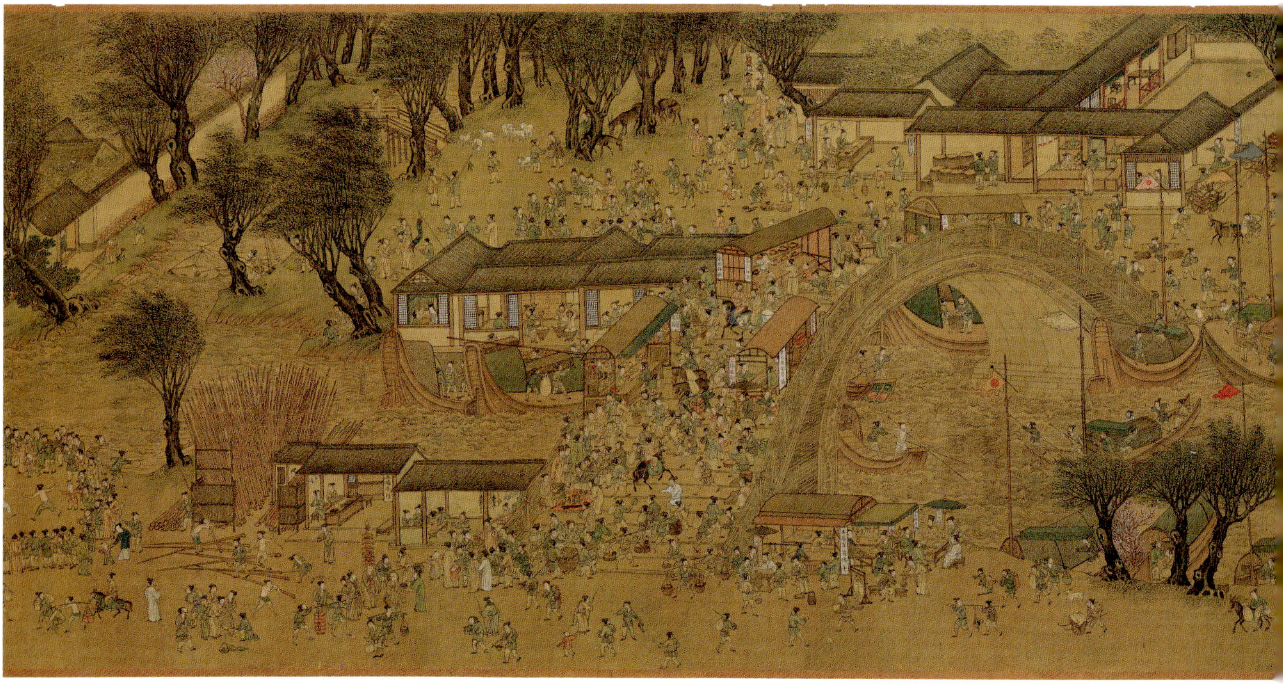

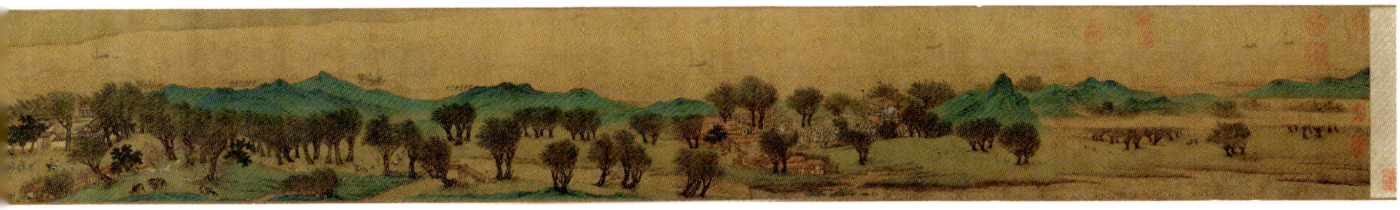

31

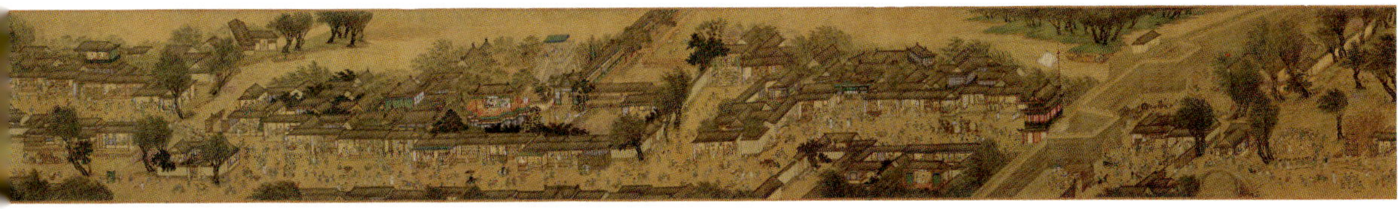

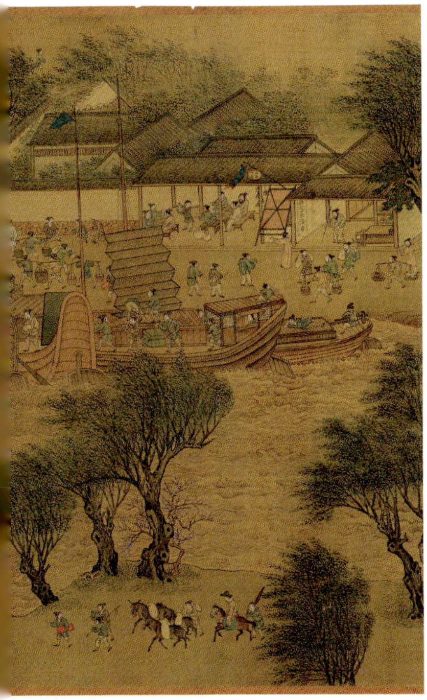

Qiu Ying was from Taiqiang in Suzhou. He was one of the 'four great masters of Wu', good at depicting people, landscape, flowers and birds and buildings. He was especially good at copying.

This painting depicts a prosperous scene in a southern Chinese city during the Qingming festival, with buildings and pavilions, people, horses, boats and carts representing a real scene. The painting begins with a scene of green mountains and water in the outskirts of Suzhou, with a rainbow bridge in the centre, with a river between two banks, shops set out, with all kinds of people bustling with activity, a lively city scene, and is a realistic depiction of social life in south China. This scroll is signed at the end with 'Qiu Ying Shi Fu Zhi'.

The painting has seals including 'Treasure viewed by Qianlong' and 'Records of Treasures at the Stone Canal'. Wang Xiaoliang

32 *Rustic Villa in the Forest*

Matteo Ricci (1552–1610)
Ming dynasty (1368–1644)
Hanging scroll, ink and colour on silk
Length 218.2 cm, Width 273.2 cm

33 *Ten Views of the West Lake*

Wang Yuanqi (1642–1715)
Qing dynasty (1644–1911)
Hand scroll, ink and colour on silk
Length 62 cm, Width 656.5 cm

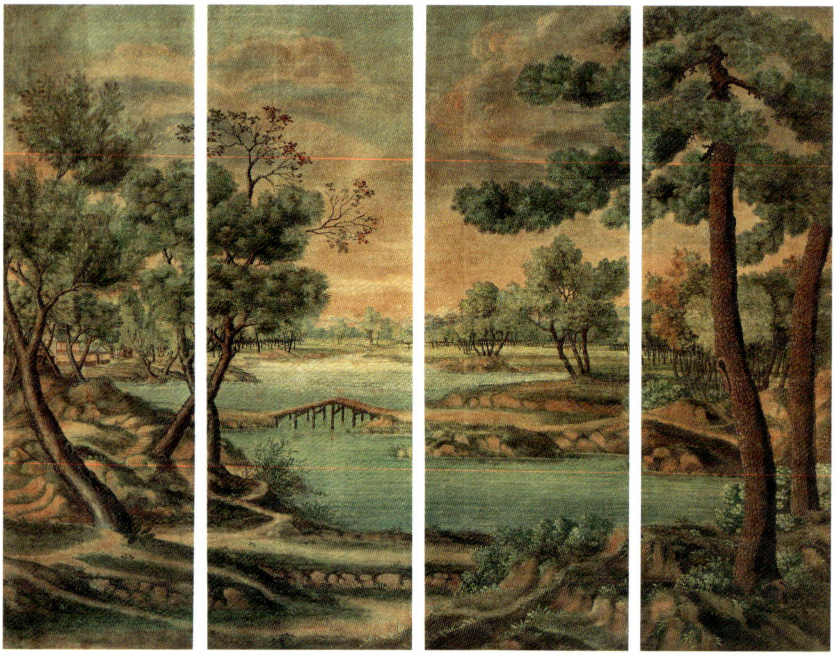

32

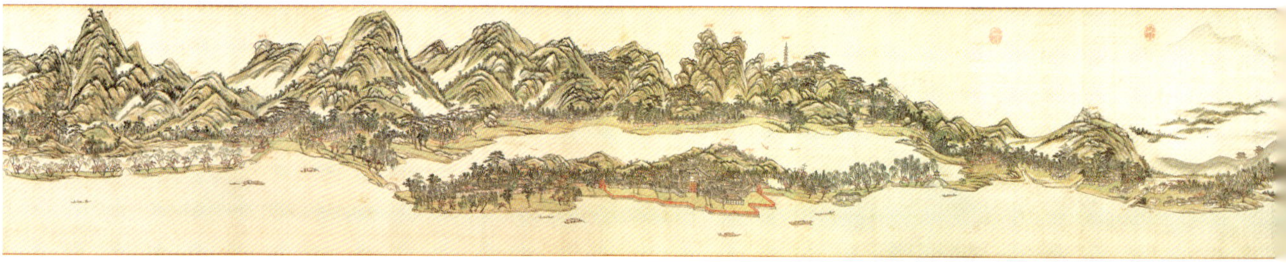

33

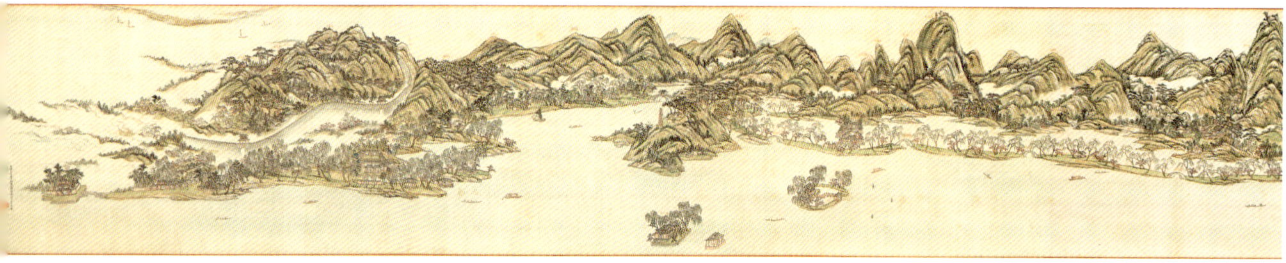

34 *Ancient Wood*

Shi Tao (1642–1707)
Qing dynasty (1644–1911)
Hanging scroll, ink and colour on paper
Length 175 cm, Width 50.7 cm

35 *Zhongkui with Angry Expression*

Gao Qipei (1660–1734)
Qing dynasty (1644–1911)
Hanging scroll, ink and colour on paper
Length 148 cm, Width 67 cm

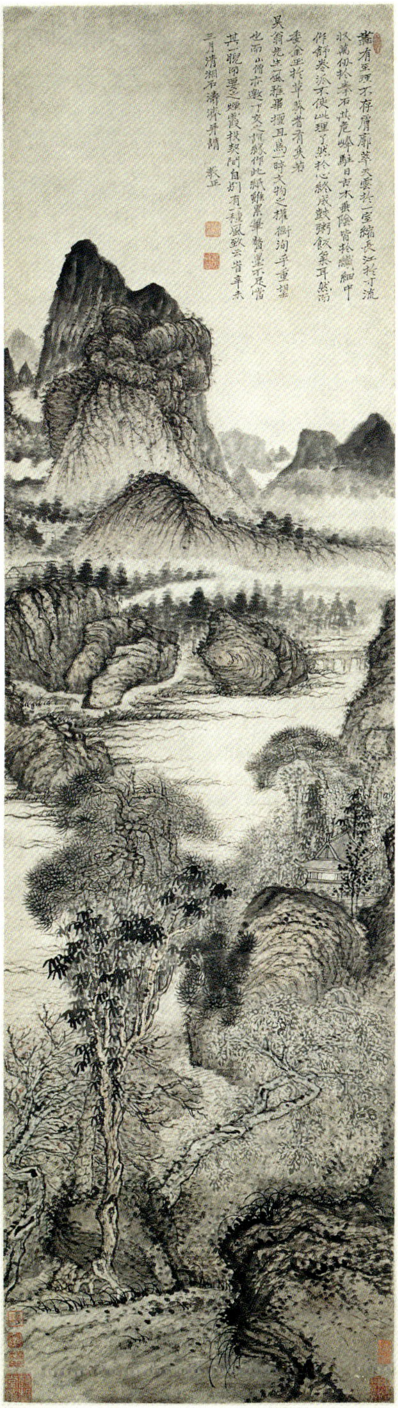

34

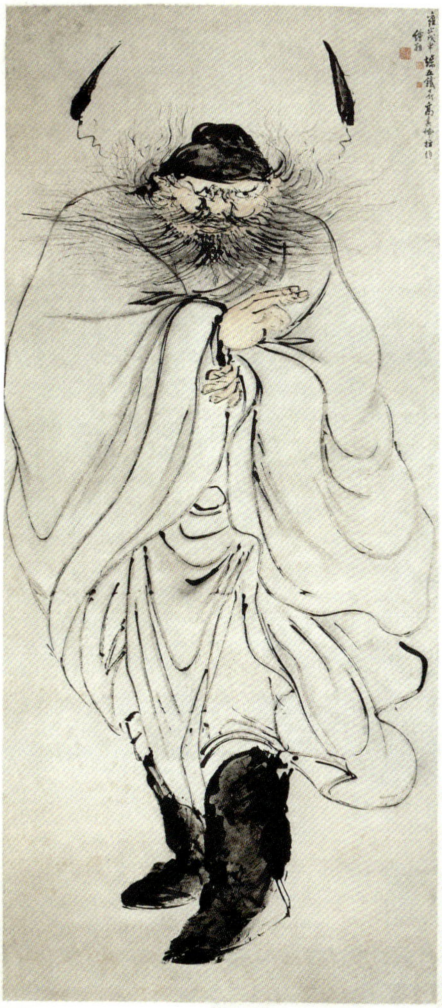

35

36 *Suzhou Prosperity*

Xu Yang
Qing dynasty (1644–1911)
Hand scroll, ink and colour on paper
Length 36.5 cm, Width 1,241 cm

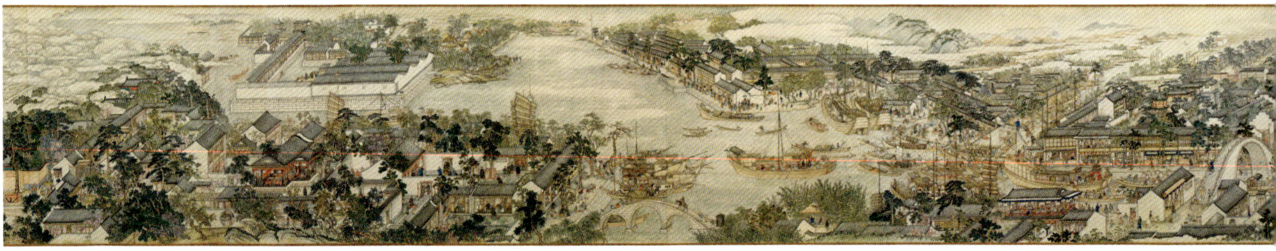

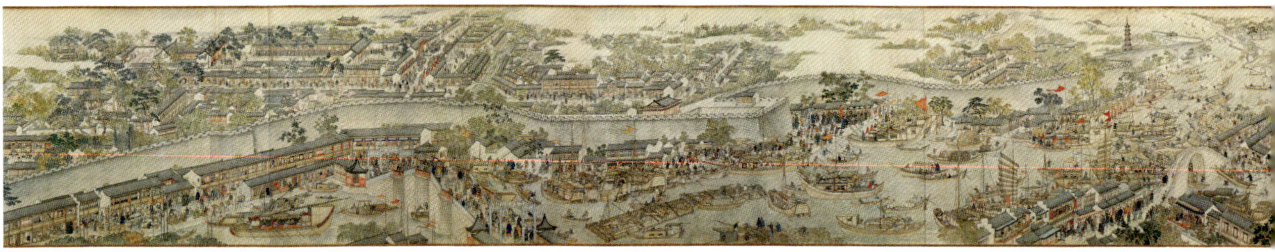

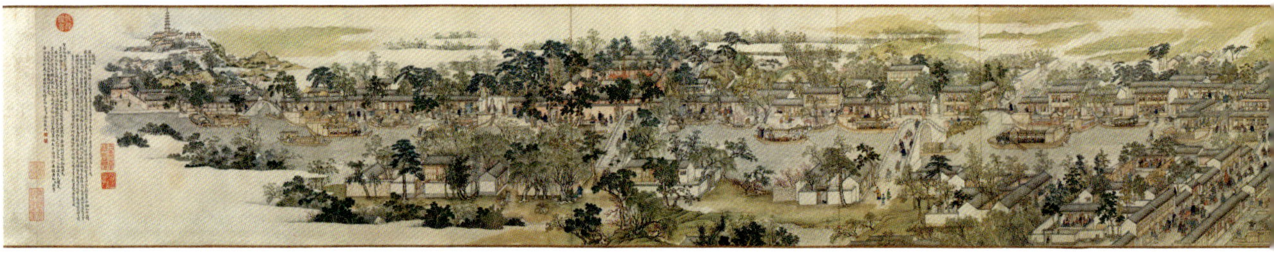

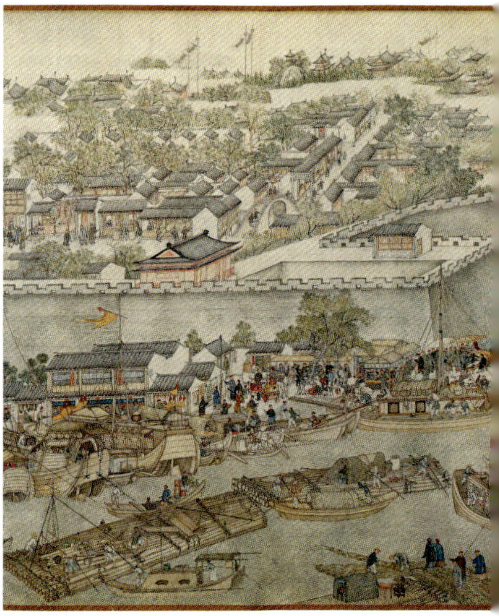

Xu Yang was from Suzhou in Jiangsu, and was in charge of painting in the inner palace. This painting was produced in Qianlong year 24, 1759 – its original name was *Propagating Prosperous Times Painting* – and depicts scenes of prosperity in and around the old city of Suzhou during Qianlong's reign. The painting begins from Lingyan Mountain and stops at the Huqiu mountain, shows work scenes, boats, ships, carts, ploughing and fishing, commercial transport, wedding and birthday banquet celebrations, halls for dancing and singing, government office and imperial examination halls. The life of the educated and merchant classes is on display in every form, with a total of four thousand eight hundred people, more than two hundred buildings, and three hundred boats. The people are lifelike, the scene is fresh and original, and can be seen as an illustrated gazette of Suzhou in the Qianlong period. The painting thus has important historical and artistic value. DONG BAOHOU

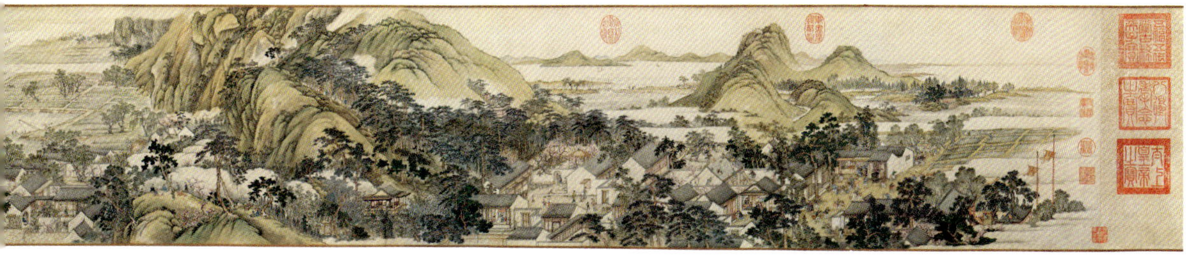

36

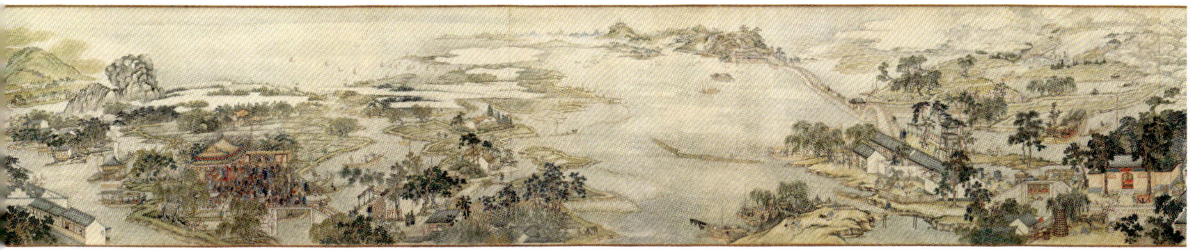

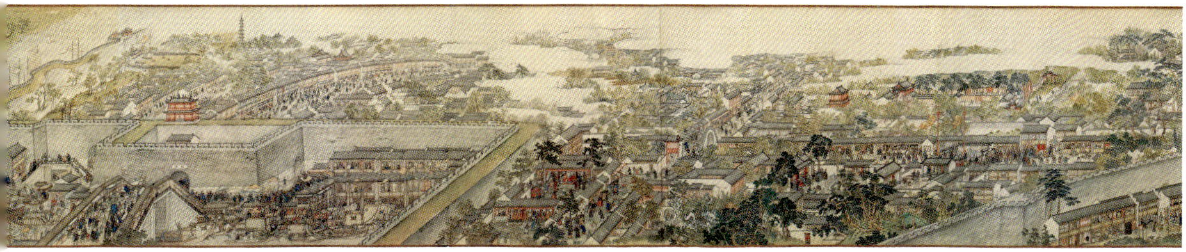

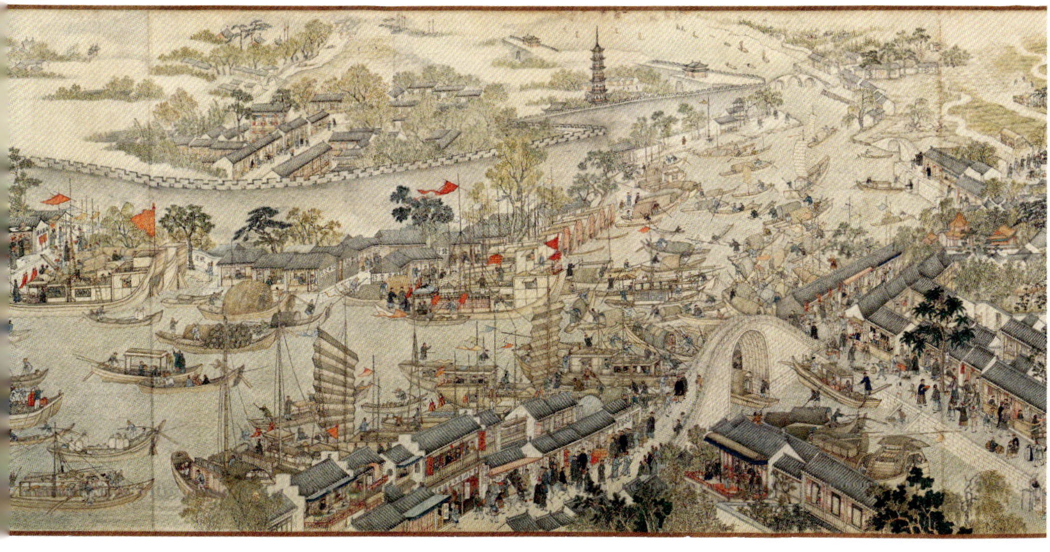

3

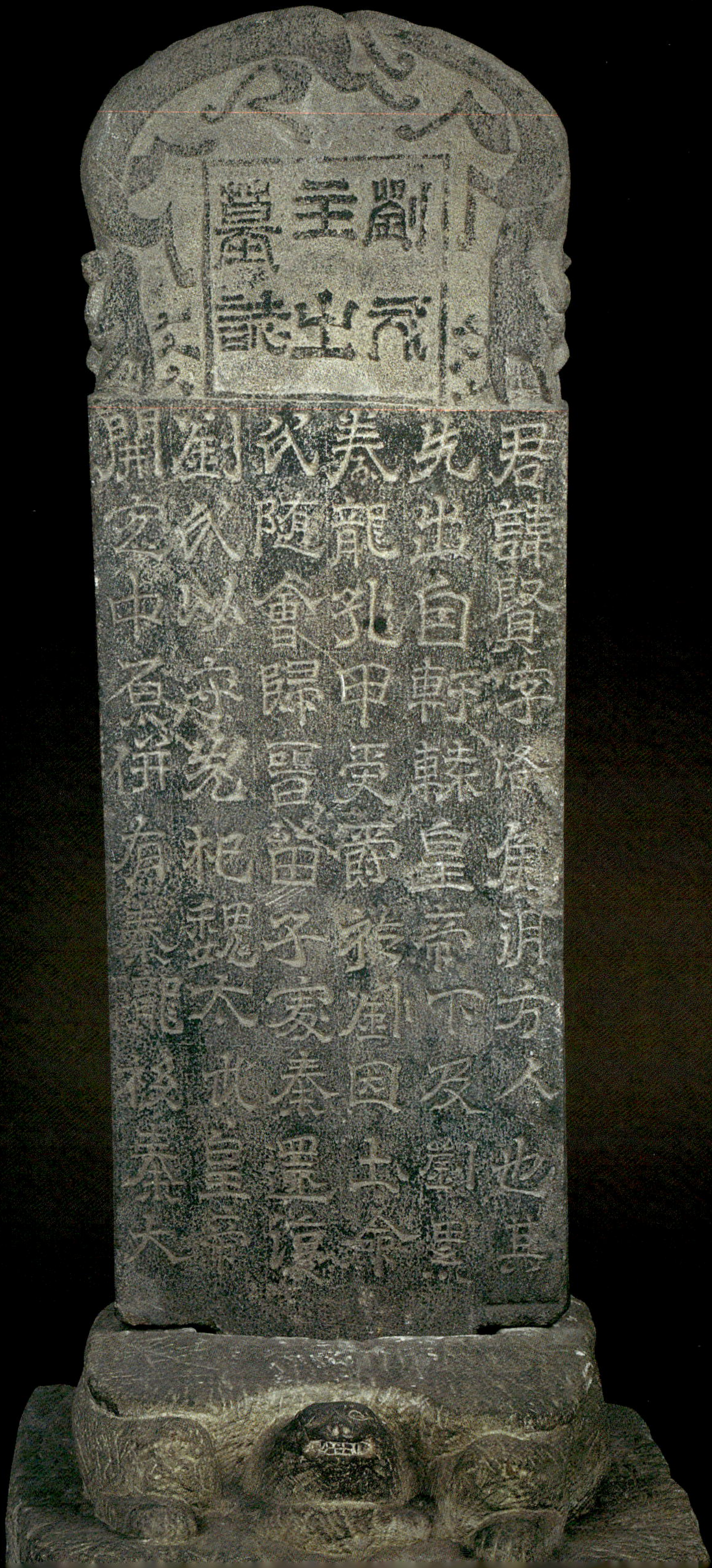
劉戍主之墓誌
君諱賢字洛侯朔方人也其
先出自軒轅黃帝下及劉累
豢龍孔甲受爵於劉因土命
氏隨會歸晉留子處秦還復
劉氏以守先祀魏大武皇帝
開定中原有秦部移秦大

Stele and Memorial tablets

Stele and memorial tablets are an important part of the Chinese historical and cultural record, and show how the ancients recorded history, commemorated their ancestors and transmitted culture.

They contain large amounts of written information, and constitute an important resource for researching ancient language, script and history. Scholars have always given them high regard. Epitaphs are mostly written by famous people, and contain the names of the principle occupant of the tomb, their native place, birth dates, position, biography, including information on current events of the time. They are important supplementary resources for official history, and are significant historical sources. At the same time, they are also a record of Chinese calligraphy, including the development and evolution of all kinds of styles of all periods, as well as the skilled carving techniques. Thus, apart from their value as historical or literary sources, Stele Inscriptions and memorial tablets are also valuable works of calligraphy.

The collection of stele inscriptions and memorial tablets at the Liaoning Provincial Museum spans a wide range of historical periods, back to the Han and Wei, and up to the Ming and Qing, with a total of more than two hundred pieces. They are rich in content and varied in form. The Eastern Han Yuanchu Fourth Year *Sikong Yuan Chang* stele excavated in 1923 in Yanshi in Henan Province is the oldest Han stele in the museum collection. The *Xiping Stone Classic* for which carving started in Han Lingdi's fourth year, and the later *Zheng Shi Stone Classic* re-erected in Cao Wei Zhengshi period in Luoyang Taixue are all fine examples of work of their time, and their fragments are part of the rare collections of the Liaoning Museum. The former is the earliest example of an official Confucian classic carved on stone, the latter was written in pre-Qin ancient script, seal script and clerical script, and are unique among ancient Chinese stone carvings. From the excavation of the Linquan memorial tablet of Liu Xian, we can see that this early form of stele was originally placed on the tomb. There are more than fifty memorial tablets from the Northern Wei. They belong to the royal family of Yuan, and aristocrats and important ministers of Eastern Wei, Northern Qi and Northern Zhou. These provide extra information to that contained in the *Weishu* and *Beiqishu* histories.

Although there are only a limited number of Sui and Tang memorial tablets, their historical value is significant. They have mostly been excavated since 1949 in the Liaoning area. The most important examples are the memorial tablets of Sui Governor Han Ji, of Sima Zuocai of Weizhou in the Tang, and of Zhang Xiu and Han Zhen. The mourning booklets and several memorial tablets of Liao Emperors' tombs are important pieces in the Liaoning Museum collection, providing primary sources for deciphering the Khitan script and language. The fifteen mourning booklets for the Liao Emperors Shengzong, Xingzong, Daozong and their Queens are all graded as national treasure items. Ming and Qing memorial tablets record the historical Liaodong nine-frontier garrison of the Ming dynasty and record the rising of the Manchu people and the fall of the Ming and rise of the Qing. LIU YUN

1 Yuan Chang Stele

Eastern Han Yuanchu 4th year (117)
Existing Height 77.5 cm, Existing Width 72 cm
Excavated in 1923 in Yanshi City in Henan Province

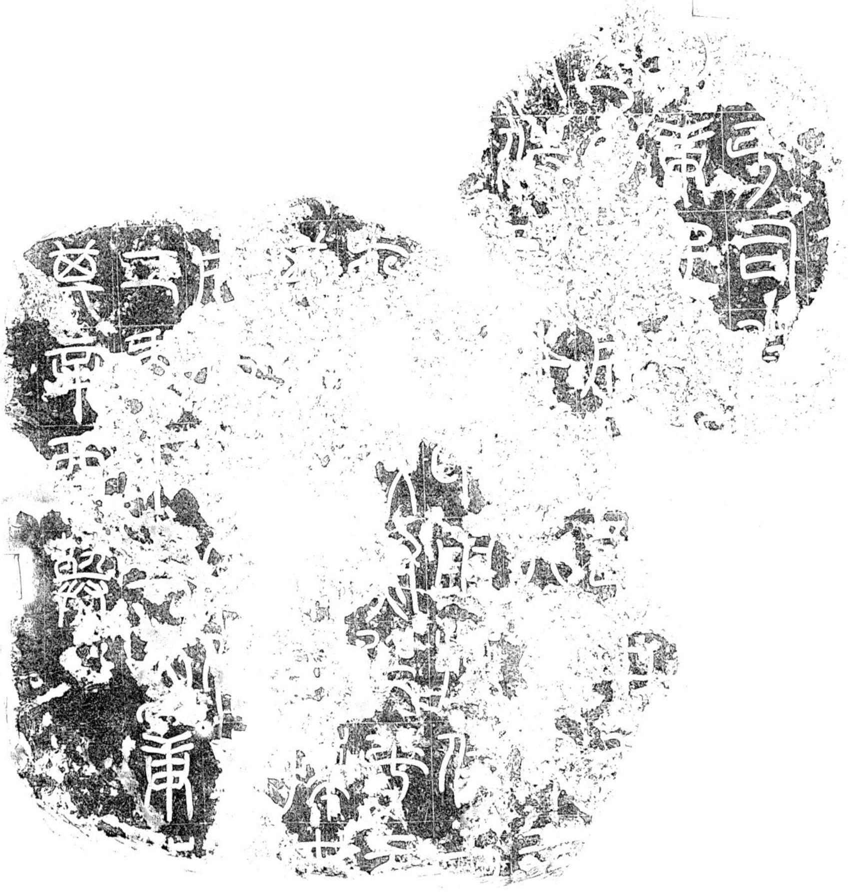

1

The full name of the *Yuan Chang Stele* is *Han Sikong Yuan Chang Stele*, and it was carved in the Eastern Han Yuanchu 4th year (117). It is the earliest stone carving in the Liaoning Museum collection. The stone is grey-white, upright in shape and is already fragmented. There are ten lines of seal characters on the body of the stele, of which now around four to eight characters remain in each line, making a total of seventy characters. The middle part of the stele has been pierced and is evidence of the development of the production of ancient Chinese steles. The stele is for Yuan Chang, courtesy name Shuping, of the Eastern Han, with an entry in the *Book of the Later Han*.

Extant Han dynasty carved steles in seal characters are extremely rare, and apart from the famous *Shao shi shen dao que ming*, the *Tianmu miaoshi que ming*, the *Qi san gong shan Stele*, and the *Yuan An Stele*, there is only the *Yuan Chang Stele*. The characters are clearly outlined on this stele, the traces of the characters are as sharp as if new, the space between each character is clearly marked, the strokes are square and forceful, strong and resilient, the character form is close in style to the Qin clerical script. This stele clearly shows the special liveliness and force of Han dynasty seal characters, and is a treasure among Han steles. LIU YUN

2 Xiping Stone Classic

Eastern Han Xiping 4th year (171)
Fragments of different sizes

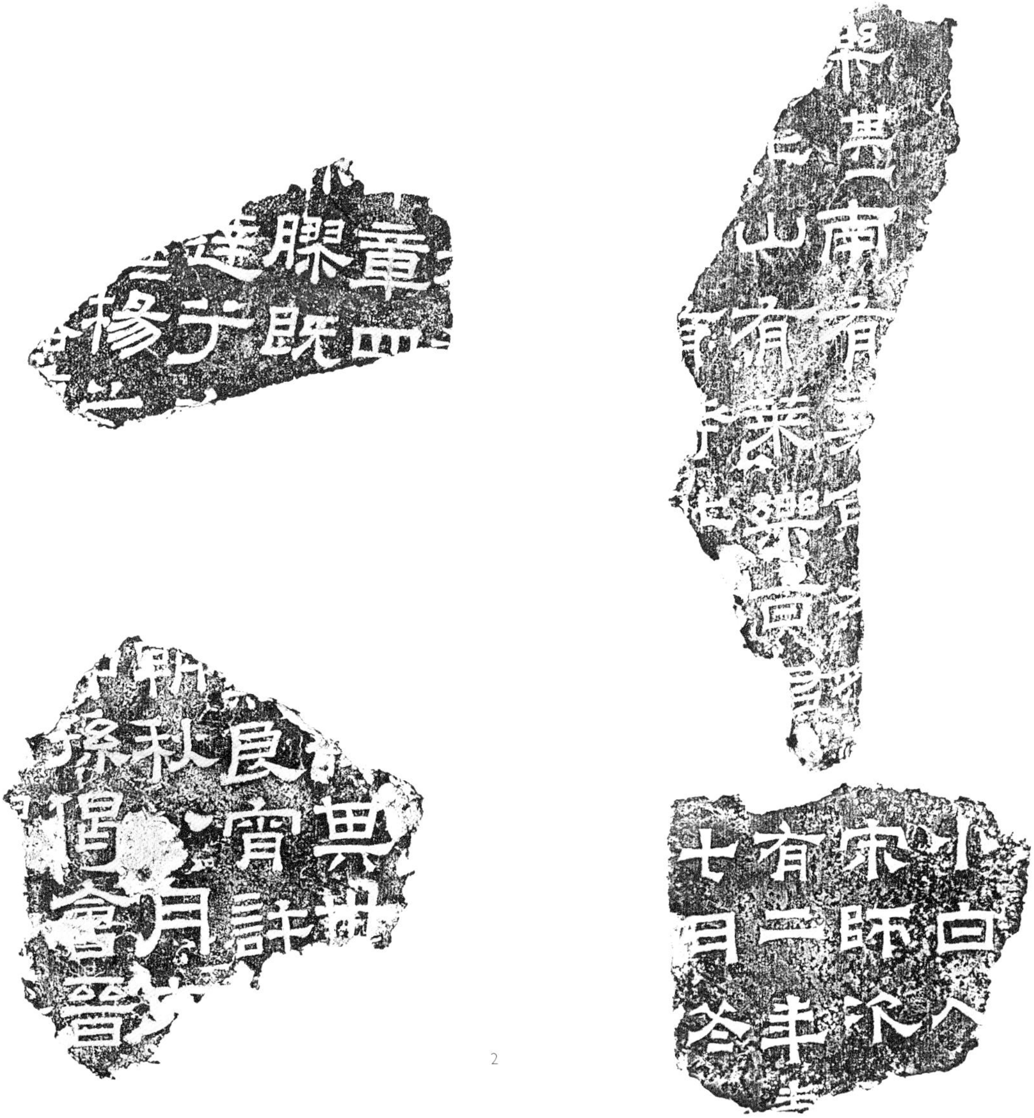

2

3 Zheng Shi Stone Classic

Three Kingdoms Wei Zhengshi 2nd year (241)
Existing Length 12.3 cm, Existing Width 2.9 cm

4 Celebration of General Wuqiujian at Wandu Mountain City

Three Kingdoms Wei Zhengshi 6th year (245)
Existing Height 38.9 cm, Existing Width 29.9 cm
Excavated in the 1930s at Xibancha Mountain, in Ji'an City, Jilin Province

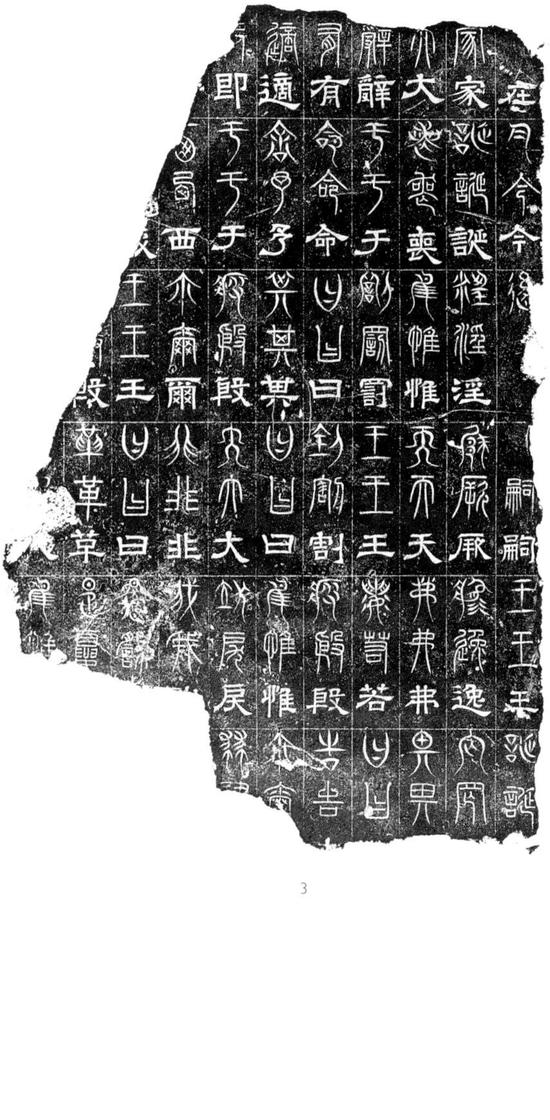

3

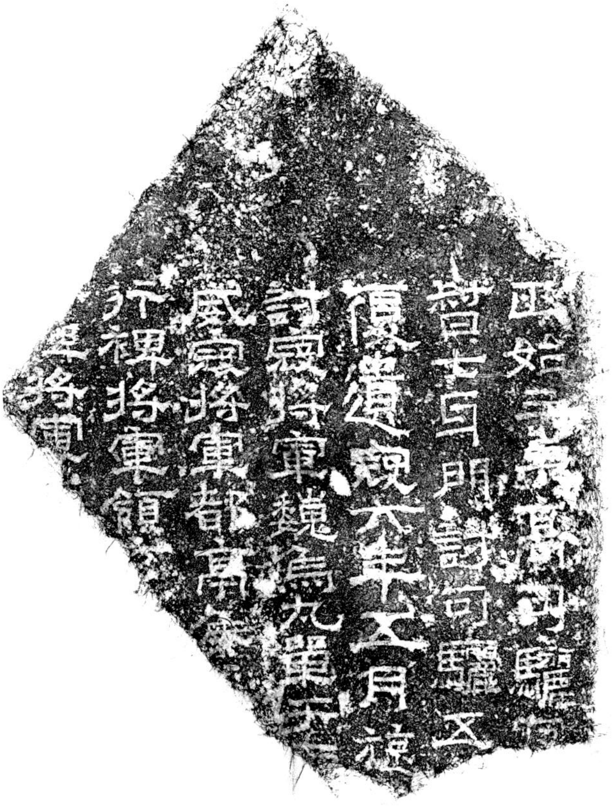

4

5 Liu Xian memorial tablet

Early Northern Wei (386–534)
Total Height 103.5 cm, Width 30.3 cm, Thickness 12 cm
Excavated in 1963 at North Xishangtai tombs at Chaoyang City in Liaoning Province

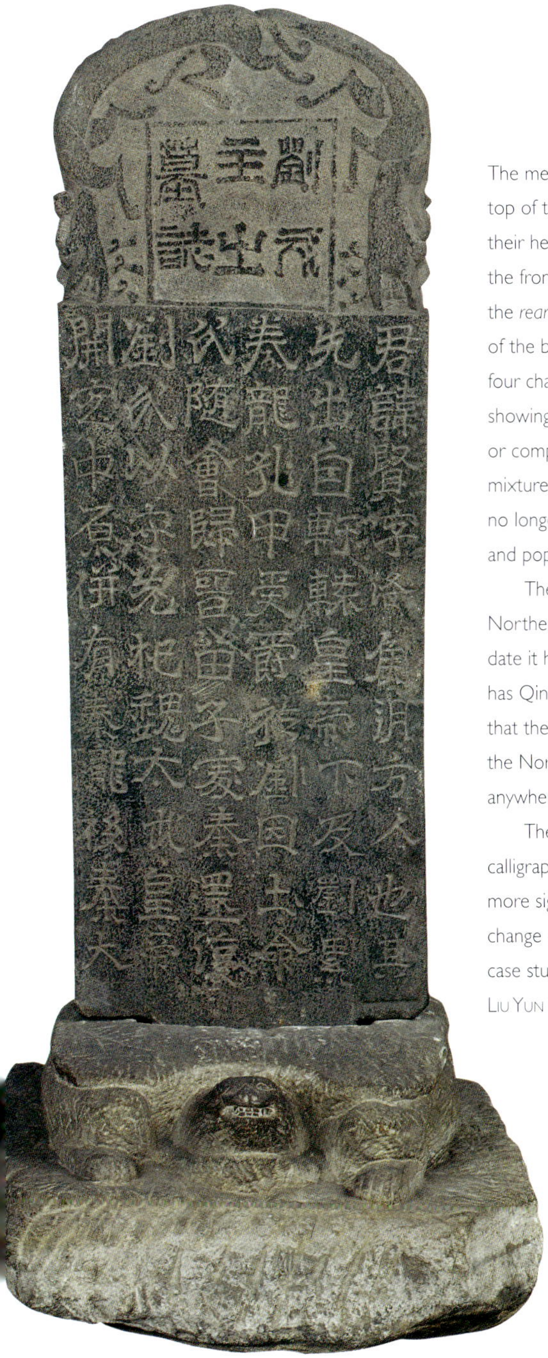

5

The memorial tablet has a tortoise-shaped base, a round top and a square body. The top of the stele has a relief of four hornless dragons. Their bodies and tails are coiled, their heads are hanging down. There are six seal script characters in three lines on the front of the top, 'Liu Mao Shu Zhu Zhi Mu Zhi', epitaph of garrison chief Liu; on the *rear* side of the top are carved twin *luan* birds crossed at the neck. On four sides of the body are round joined epitaph characters, altogether one hundred and ninety-four characters. The epitaph characters are basically in clerical script, but are already showing elements of regular script, the shape of the characters is not strictly formed or complete, the strokes are written quite casually, and have the unordered strange mixture of seal and cursive scripts. The characters are simple, forceful and natural, and no longer have the elegance of typical Han clerical characters, with several simplified and popular characters.

The deceased is Liu Xian, garrison chief of Linquan in Yingzhou during the Northern Wei. He was a local official of low rank. Although the text contains no clear date it has the following information: 'Wei Taiwu Emperor controls central China, and has Qinlong, and the big families moved from Qin to Yanqi.' From this we can estimate that the stele was raised before the move of the capital by the Xiaowen Emperor of the Northern Wei (493). It is the earliest example of a Northern Wei memorial tablet anywhere in China.

The excavation of this tablet has provided an important resource for researching calligraphy in the north of China before the maturity of Northern Wei calligraphy. Even more significant is the fact that it has preserved the grave stele form, reflecting the change during this period from grave steles to memorial tablet, providing an important case study for researching the origins and evolution of ancient Chinese memorial tablet.

Liu Yun

6 Memorial tablet of the first ranking concubine of the Xianwen Emperor in the Northern Wei

Northern Wei Jingming 4th year (503)
Length 41 cm, Width 40 cm
Excavated in 1923 at Mang mountain in Bei'anjia gou, Luoyang, Henan Province

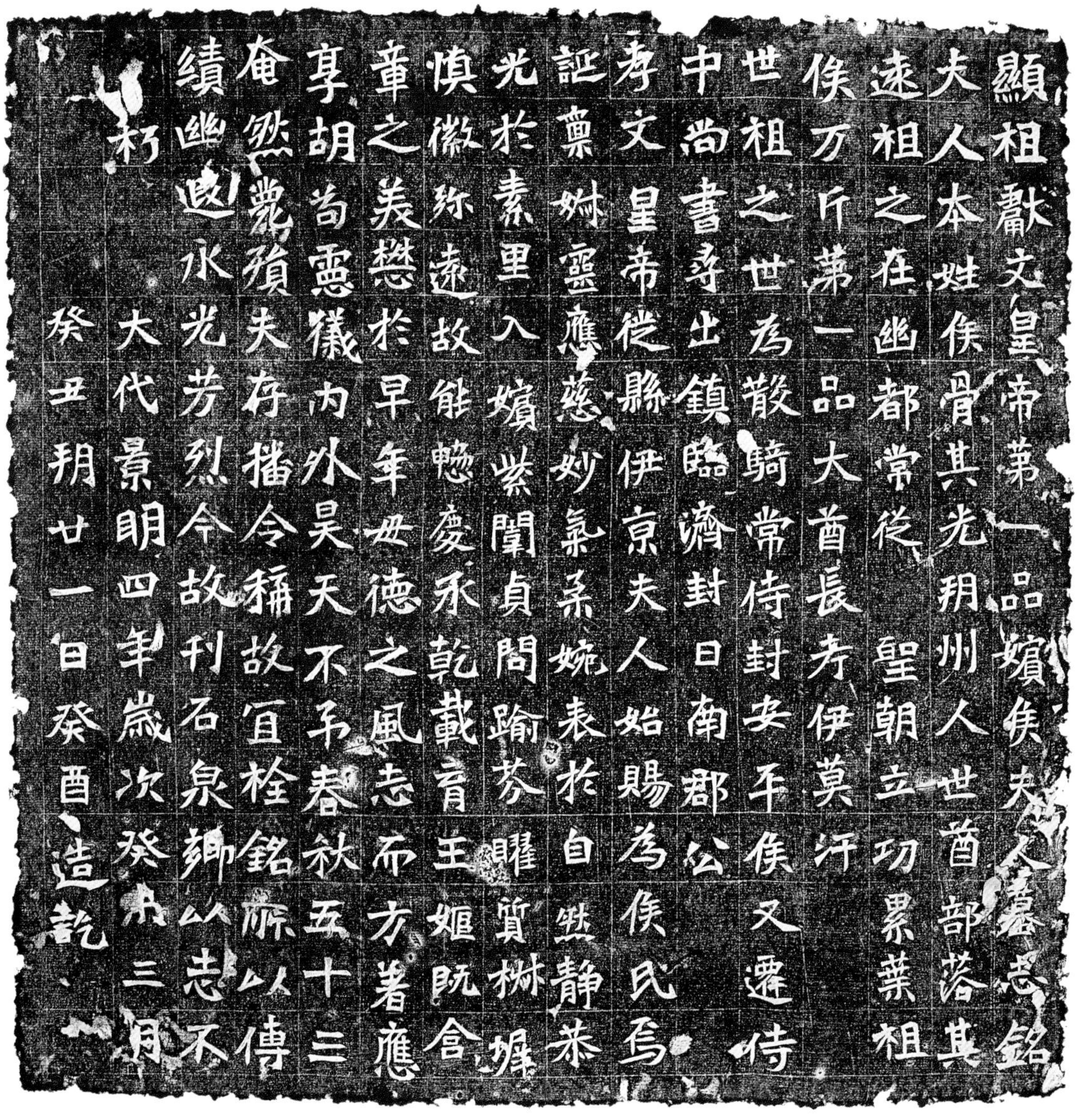

7 Memorial tablet of the concubine Lu to the King of Leling

Northern Qi Heqing 3rd year (564)
Length 68.2 cm, Width 67.2 cm
Excavated in 1912 in Nanxiang Bali, Cixian, Hebei

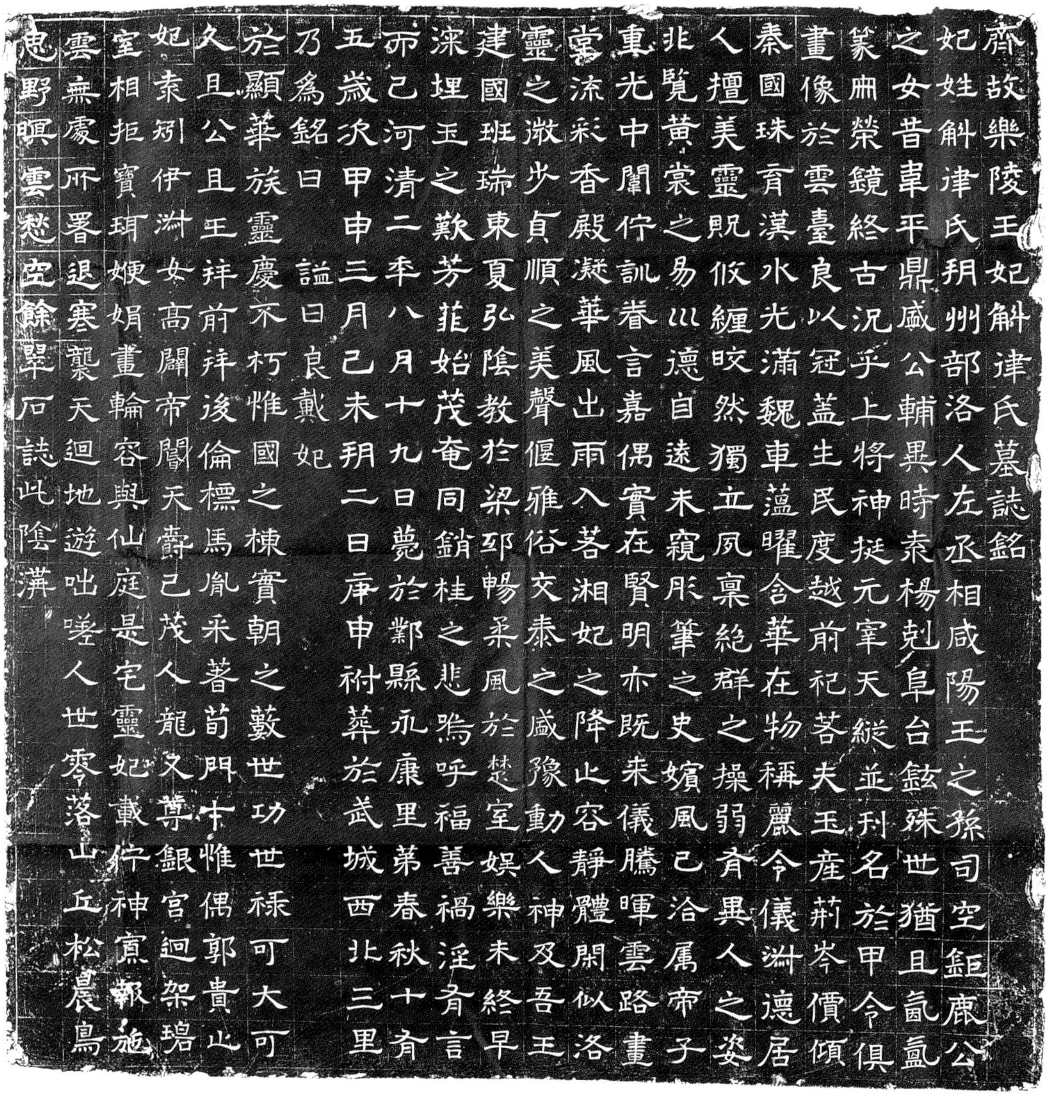

7

8 Han Ji memorial tablet

Tianbao 3rd year (744)
Length 55.4 cm, Width 56.4 cm
Excavated in 1977 at Langshan to the north of Chaoyang City in Liaoning Province

9 Yulü Yanning memorial tablet

Liao Tonghe 4th year (986)
Length 82.9 cm, Width 82.2 cm
Excavated in 1964 in Boshugou village in Wujiaxiang, Chaoyang City, Liaoning Province

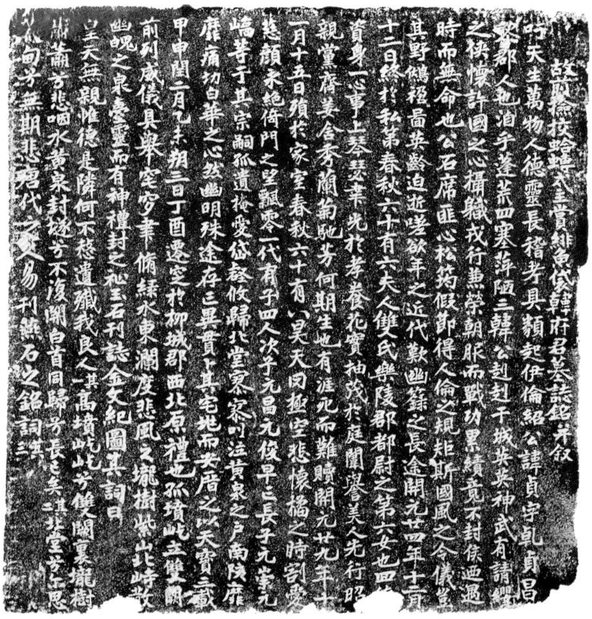

8

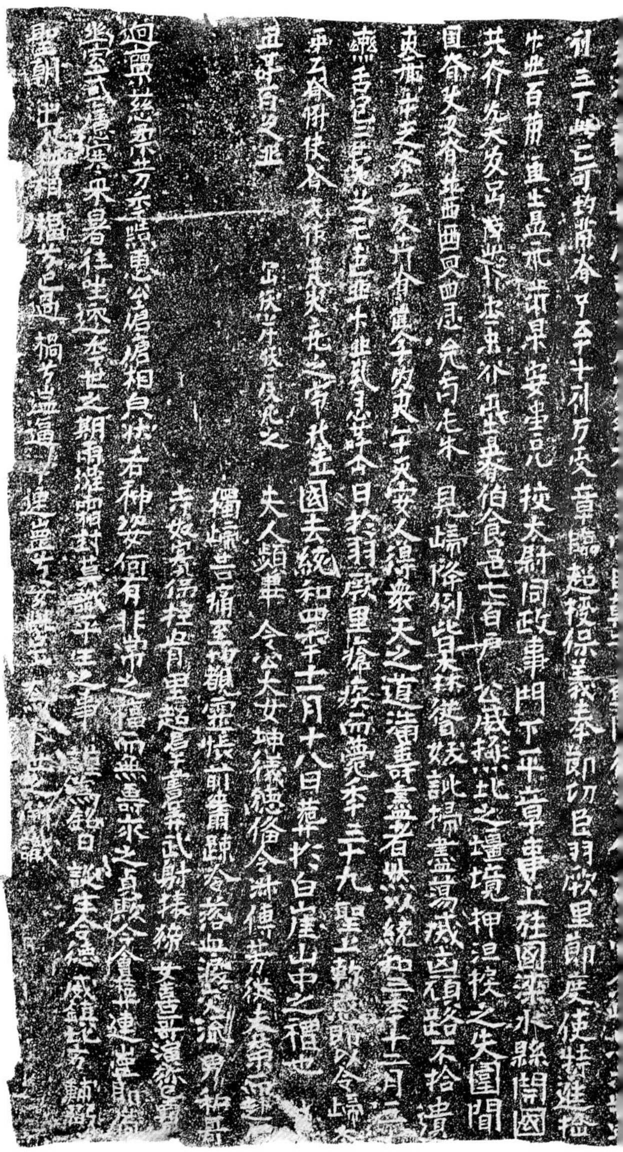

9

A grey-white stone, square-shaped, the cover stone is no longer extant. The text has been intaglio carved, divided into an upper and lower section. The upper section has nineteen lines in large Khitan script, the lower section has twenty-four lines of Chinese characters. The epitaph is to Yulü Yanning, whose ancestor was related to the emperor and was the governor of Yujueli, in present-day north Heilongjiang.

The square stone is not only an important resource for researching the northern border area of the Liao dynasty, it is also a primary source for researching the large Khitan script. Currently, out of the extant six examples of large Khitan script, the *Yulü Yanning memorial tablet* is the only tablet with matching inscriptions in Khitan script and Chinese characters. Liu Yun

10 Yulü Renxian memorial tablet

Liao Xianyong 8th year (1072)
Length 119 cm, Width 119 cm
Excavated in 1983 from the Yulü Renxian family tomb in Lianhua Mountain, Beipiao City, Liaoning Province

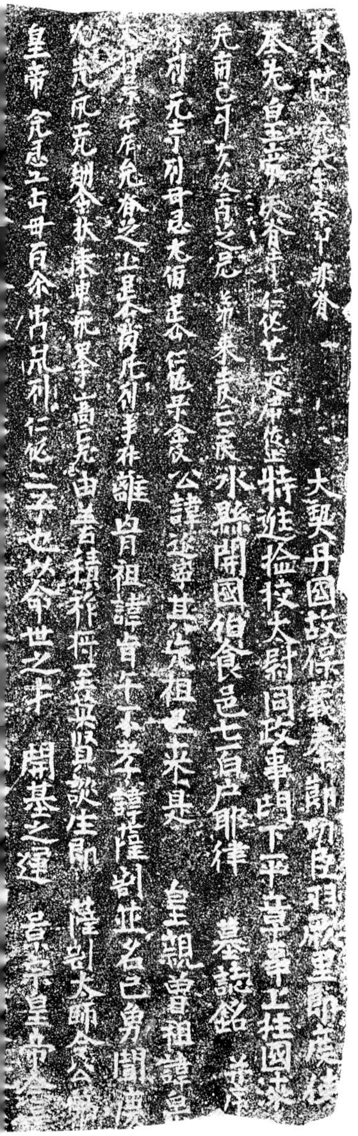

10

11 Liao Daozong Emperor, Queen, Mourning booklets in Khitan script and Chinese characters, and cover stones and rubbings

Liao Qiantong 1st year (1101)
Daozong Emperor Mourning booklet and cover stone in Chinese characters
Length and Width 130.7 cm, Thickness 28.8 cm
Daozong Emperor Mourning booklet and cover stone in Khitan script
Length and Width 134.6 cm, Thickness 27.6 cm

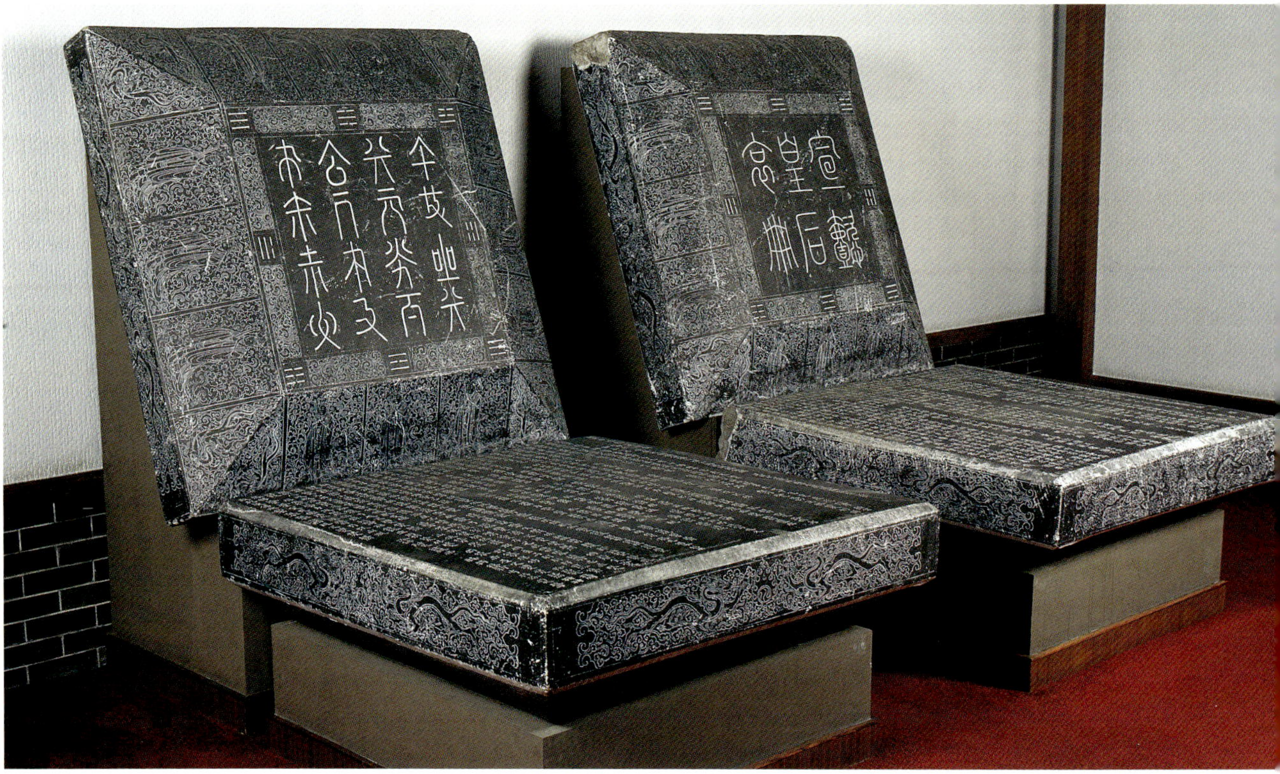

Xuanyi Queen Mourning booklets in Khitan script and Chinese characters and cover stones

The famous mourning booklets of Emperor Daozong and his Queen in Khitan script and Chinese characters is a national treasure. It comprises four pieces, all white Han jade stone, each stone weighing about 1.5 tonnes, carved in both Khitan and Chinese scripts, with around two thousand characters on each piece. The owners of the booklets are Liao Emperor Daozong Yulü Hongji (reign 1055–1101), posthumous title is Ren Sheng Da Xiao Emperor, who was fond of Chinese culture; and Queen Xuanyi of Daozong who was called Xiao Guanyin, and was accomplished in poetry and music. The mourning stones carved in Khitan and Chinese scripts to Emperor Daozong and Queen Xuanyi were found in the Yongfu tomb of Liao Qin tomb in 1930 and have been preserved in good condition.

In ancient China after emperors and empresses died, the new emperor's memorial speech would be carved onto jade slips. Gold or silver thread would then be used to tie them into a booklet. They would then be put into a stone box and placed in the emperor's tomb. Such a booklet was called a mourning booklet. In the Yongfu tomb, the mourning booklets had changed into carved memorial tablets, the first mourning booklets in the form of memorial tablets in the Liao dynasty.

The four pieces are high and majestic, the calligraphy is powerful and attractive, with

Xuanyi Queen Mourning booklet and cover stone in Chinese characters
Length and Width 130.5 cm, Thickness 30.8 cm
Xuanyi Queen Mourning booklet and cover stone in Khitan script
Length and Width 131 cm, Thickness 32 cm
Excavated in 1930 the Liao Qin tomb in Baitazi, Balinshi banner, Inner Mongolia Autonomous Region

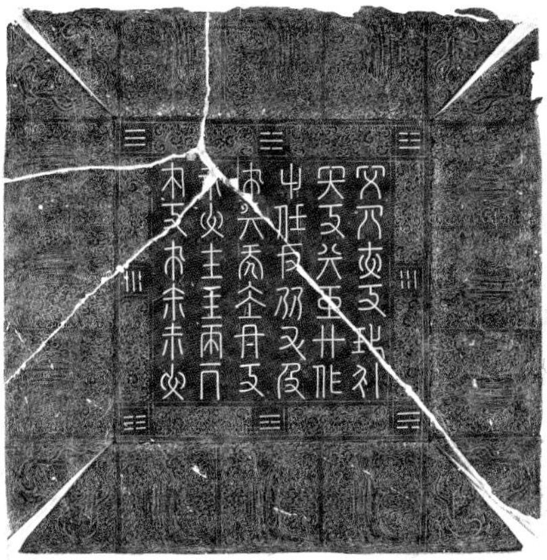

Liao Daozong Emperor Mourning booklet cover stone rubbing in Khitan script

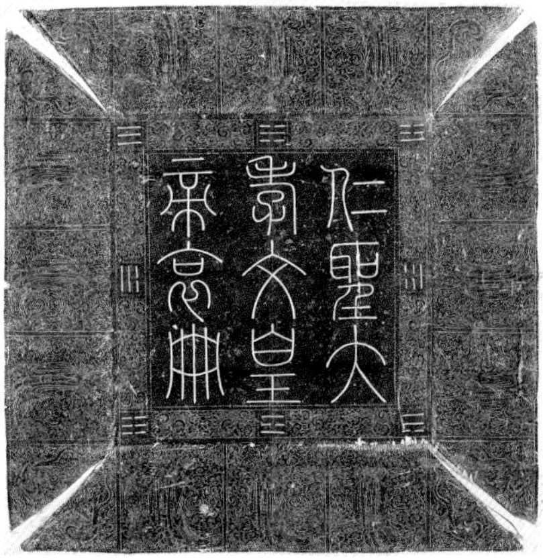

Liao Daozong Emperor Mourning booklet cover stone rubbing in Chinese characters

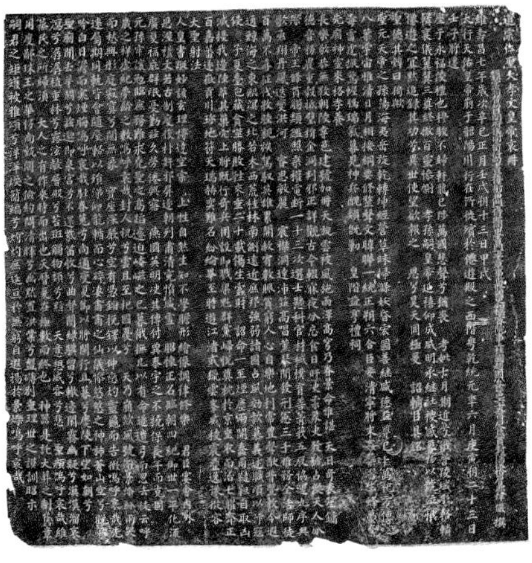

Liao Daozong Emperor Mourning booklet rubbing in Chinese characters

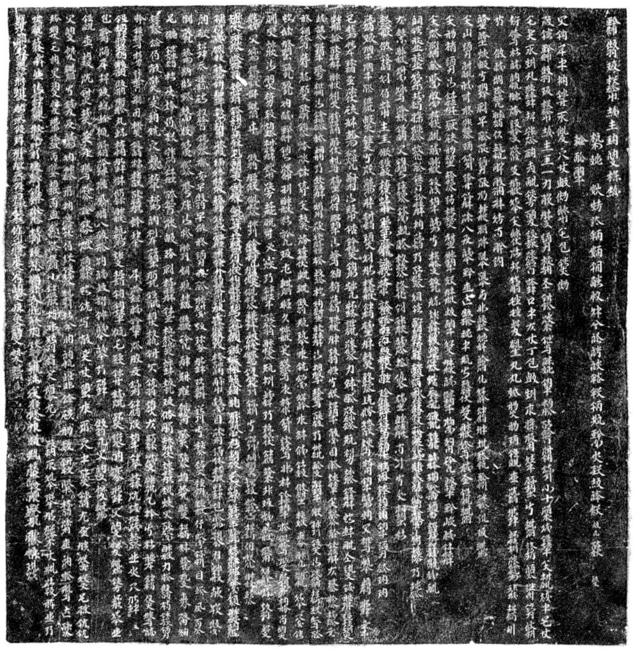

Liao Daozong Emperor Mourning booklet rubbing in Khitan script

fine carving work, and can be considered masterpieces of Liao dynasty carving. The four square stone covers have the booklet's title carved in seal script. The four slanting sides are linear carved with *bagua* hexagram and peony pattern. The carving is dignified; there are twelve elegant figures of the Chinese zodiac, with twin dragons and clouds in the four corners and two dragons playing and clouds on the sides. On the sides of the four epitaph stones two dragons playing and clouds are also carved, the epitaph on the front of the booklet is written into Khitan and Chinese. The two booklets in Chinese use the regular *Outi* script current in the Liao dynasty. The Chinese characters written to the Queen are powerful and similar in style to Tang calligrapher Liu Gongquan, although the name of this calligrapher remains unknown. The calligraphy is rich in changing strokes, and is of a very high standard, and is a rare example of a masterpiece of Liao Chinese calligraphy. The two pieces of Khitan text are carved in small Khitan script, and apart from a few examples of one Khitan character being represented as one original character, most are composed from two to seven original characters which makes the writing difficult. The calligraphy is a good standard and can be considered a fine example of Khitan calligraphy. The calligraphy technique of the epigraph to Queen Xuanyi is of a particularly high standard. The two texts in small Khitan characters are the earliest example of Khitan small script to be discovered, thus confirming their historical existence and offering a primary source of great scholarly value for researching Liao history, culture and Khitan script. Liu Yun

12 Song Guozhong memorial tablet

Ming Jiajing 37th year (1558)
Body stone Height 62 cm, Width 62 cm, Thickness 6 cm
Excavated in 1964 from Ming dynasty Song Guozhong's grave in Efang village, Liaoyang City, Liaoning Province

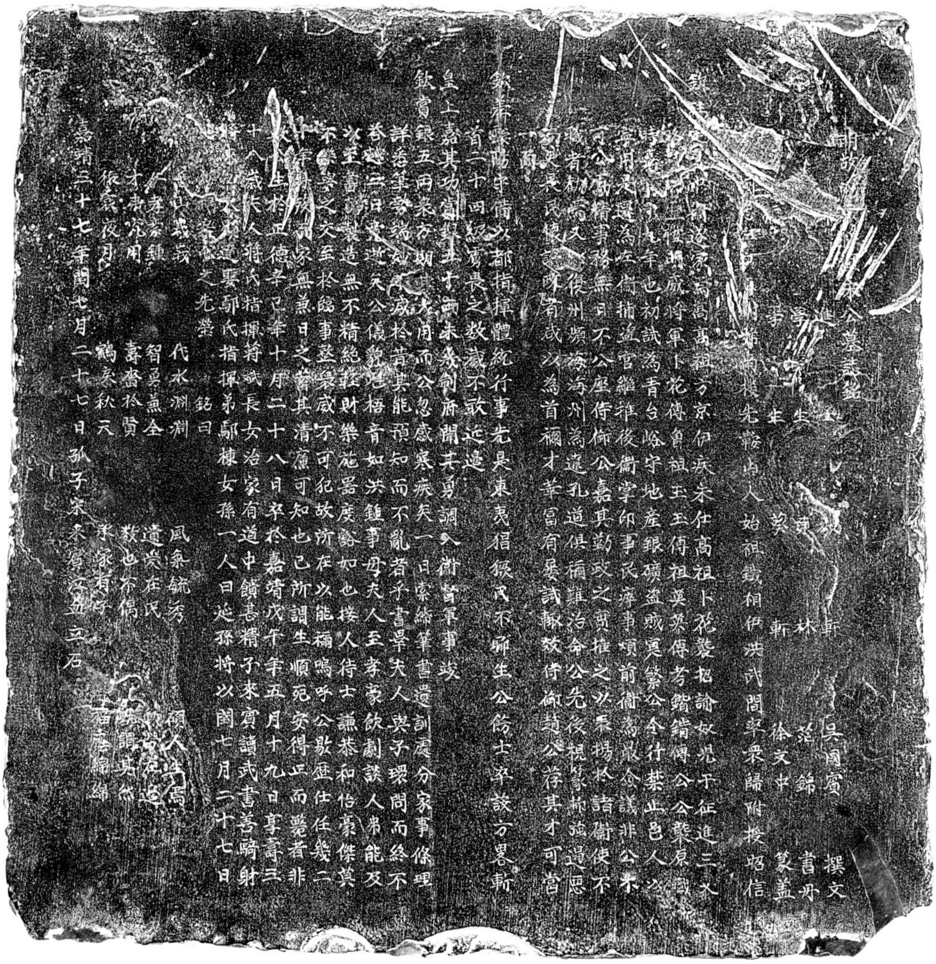

13 Princess Wen Zhuangchang grave pit tablet

Qing Kangxi 2nd year (1663)

Body stone Height 70.5 cm, Width 70.5 cm, Thickness 16 cm

Excavated in 1949 from the Princess Tomb at Beimiao'er gou, Yixian City, Liaoning Province

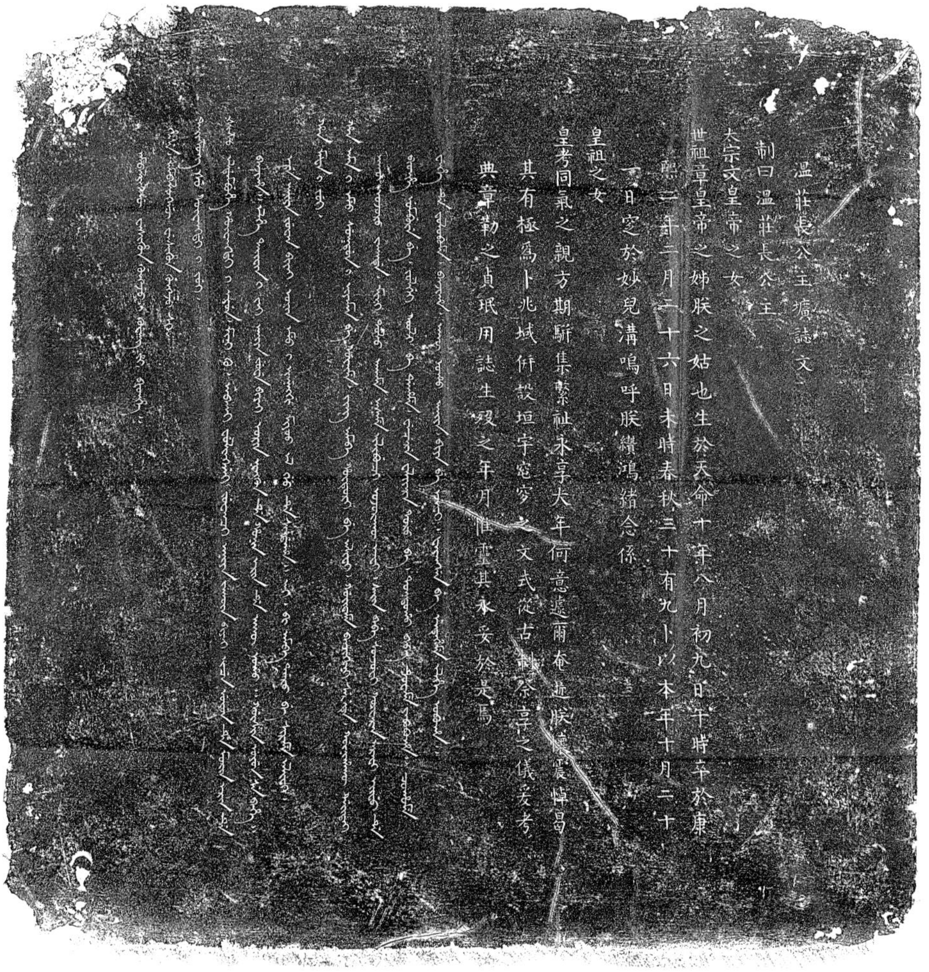

溫莊長公主壙誌文
制曰溫莊長公主
太宗文皇帝之女
世祖章皇帝之姊朕之姑也生於天命十年八月初九日午時卒於康
熙二年二月二十六日未時春秋三十有九卜以本年十月二十
一日窆於妙兒溝嗚呼朕纘鴻緒念係
皇祖之女
皇考同氣之親方期駢集繁祉永享大年何意遽爾奄逝朕懷震悼曷
其有極爰卜兆域仟設垣宇窀穸之文式從古制祭葬之儀爰考
典章勒之貞珉用誌生歿之年月惟靈其永妥於是焉

13

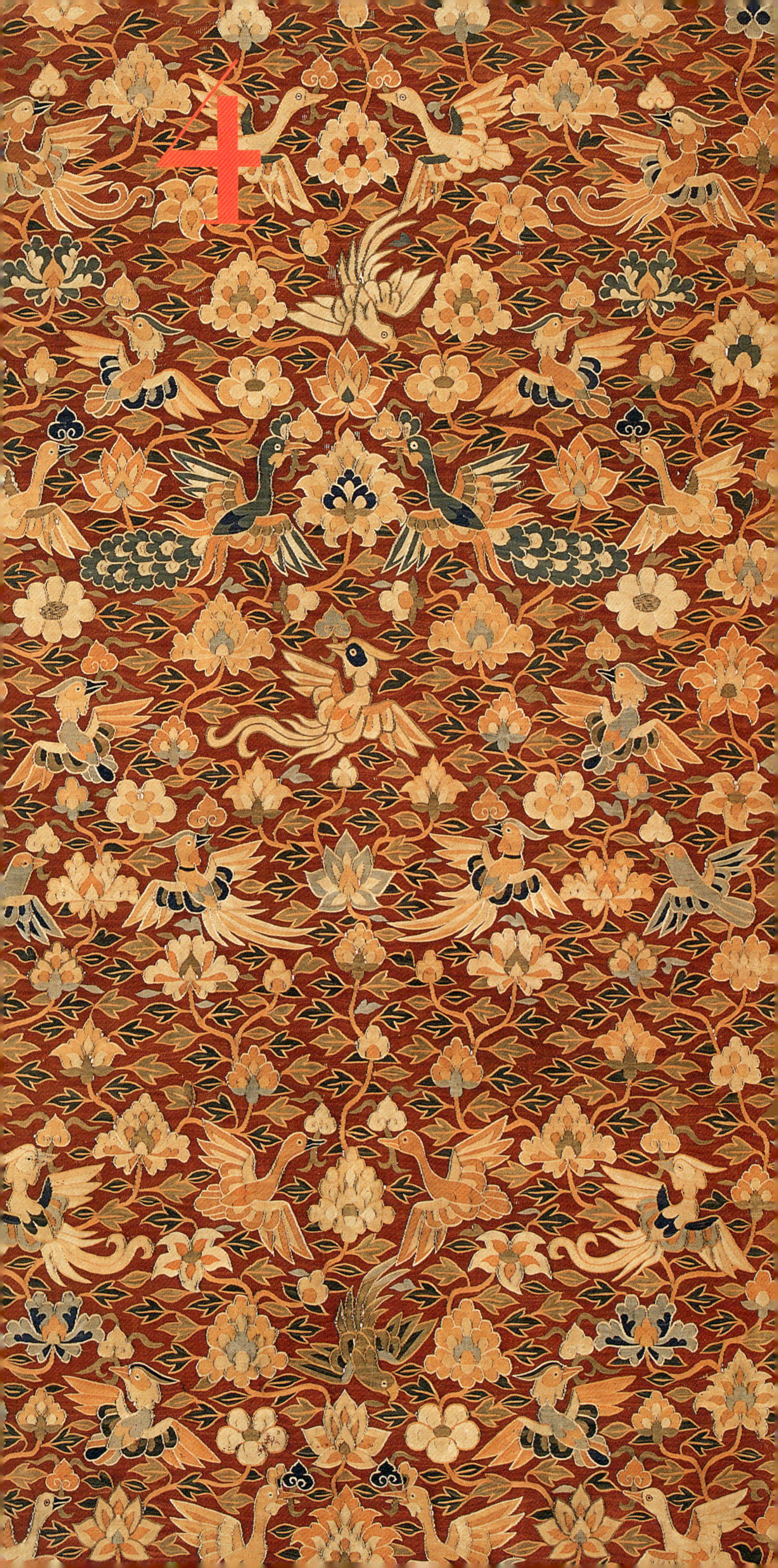
4

Tapestry and Embroidery

Most of the silk tapestries and embroidery in the Liaoning Provincial Museum collection once belonged to the collection of Zhu Qiqian, a famous politician and collector of textiles in the early Republican period. Zhu Qiqian became interested in ancient textiles at a young age. After several decades of concerted effort he built up a large collection of valuable objects, among which are rare examples of works from the Song and Yuan periods that are famous nationally and internationally.

Chinese *kesi* is a uniquely Chinese silk tapestry which is made from a beige silk warp, and a mixture of colours for the weft, using a weaving technique called 'full warp and partial weft' resulting in a hand-made finely woven silk textile where threads of different colours and lengths are shuttled and attached to create a pattern which is the same from both sides. Tapestries appeared in the Tang dynasty and developed from Central Asian textiles. In the early period they were mostly small and practical. Tapestries developed quickly in the Song dynasty with excellent technique and fine elegant colours, and were used mostly on the backing of valuable scrolls. A typical painting that uses cut tapestry is the *Purple Luan and Magpie*, and is the best-preserved extant Northern Song tapestry. Starting from the Northern Song and receiving inspiration from painting, the appreciation of tapestries that were copies of paintings became popular, reaching a peak during the Southern Song. The area around Suzhou produced famous artists like Zhu Kerou and Shen Zifan. *Painting of Camellia with Butterfly* is a representative work by Zhu Kerou. Furthermore tapestries that were both practical and for aesthetic enjoyment with subjects wishing luck or long life appeared, such as *Group of Spirits Wishing Long Life* and *Immortality Peach Flower*. Silk tapestry techniques developed further in the Ming and Qing periods, treating a wider range of subjects and increasing in production, combining silk tapestry with embroidery and painting. Suzhou became an important centre for tapestry as it already had a strong tradition of painting and textile skills. *Sounds of the Lute in Water Pavilion by Qiu Ying* and *Li Bai Evening Banquet in Garden of Peaches and Plums* are typical works of this period. Silk tapestries became more commercial in the middle to late Qing period. To save time and reduce the amount of labour required, paint was used instead of textiles, which lost the original interest of silk tapestries.

Embroidery appeared during the Western Zhou, and had matured by the period between the Warring States and the two Han dynasties. Significant improvements in materials, use and technique were made in the Tang period. Embroideries in the Song dynasty were influenced by the development of advanced painting techniques, and embroideries that were copies of paintings by famous artists began to appear. From this period two sorts of embroidery were produced, one for practical purposes and another for aesthetic enjoyment. Techniques for producing embroidery for aesthetic enjoyment were honed under the Southern Song with famous works being produced, with a great influence on later generations. The *Riding a Crane over Yaotai* is a classic example of combining painting and embroidery. *Cranes over Yaotai* are also popular subjects for paintings in the Song period. The Yuan dynasty inherited the techniques of the two Song dynasties, specialising in Buddhist figures and scriptures, continuing the great tradition of embroidery.

Embroidery became more widespread following the development of cities and a commercial economy in the Ming dynasty. Skilled women emerged, passed on their knowledge to apprentices, and operated on a local scale, embracing a more commercialised society. The Gu school of embroidery emerged in the Shanghai area, represented by Han Ximeng, inheriting the tradition of painting embroidery from the Song period, refining the technique and making an important contribution to embroidery in the Qing dynasty. Embroidery for practical purposes in the Qing was popular in clothing accessories among the noble and wealthy classes. In aesthetic embroidery regional schools of embroidery emerged: Su embroidery from Suzhou; Yue embroidery from Guangzhou; Shu embroidery from Chengdu, Sichuan; Xiang embroidery from Changsha, Hunan, and Peking embroidery from the capital. Piao Wenying

1 *Purple Luan and Magpie scroll*, silk tapestry

Northern Song dynasty (960–1127)
Length 132 cm, Width 55.6 cm

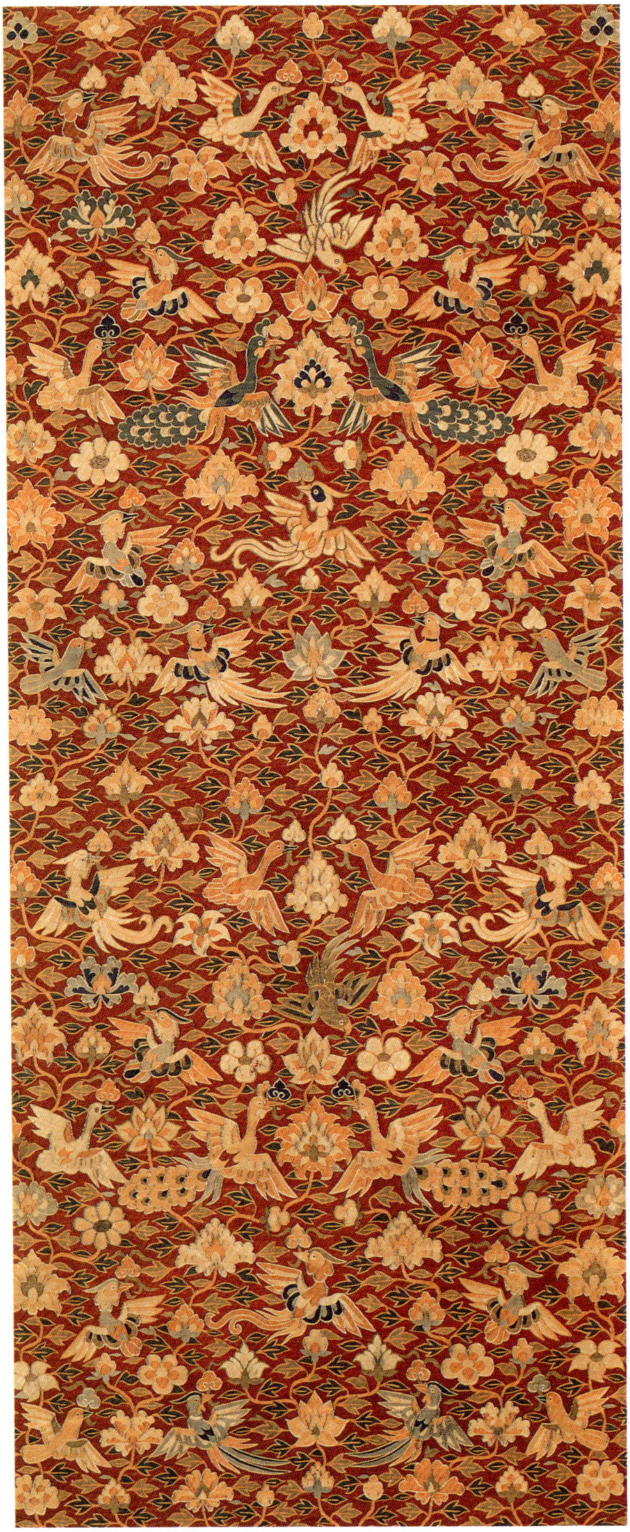

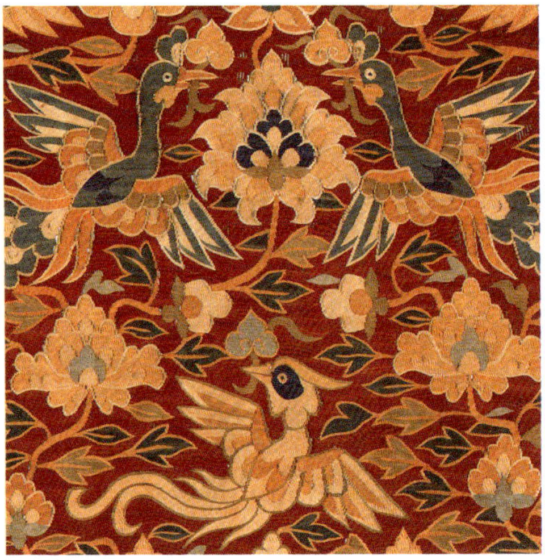

This is a typical tapestry from the northern Song, used as material for a painting backing. It has completely preserved two groups of patterns, each group is made up of five horizontal coloured birds and flowers, with leaves and branches connecting peonies and lotuses without break. Luan, a mythical bird like a phoenix, cranes, brocaded hens and peacocks are vividly depicted, in pairs or in rows, flying amongst the flowers. The matching round pattern popular in the Tang changed into a continuous row in the Northern Song period, although it retained the decorative style, and was still different from the naturalistic style of the Southern Song.

This item has rich colour with bold arrangement with yellow browns and blue greens of different depth, either in fading layers, or growing intensity. A purple background was a symbol of a noble position in the Northern Song. The bold decoration on a deep-coloured background shows the aesthetic awareness of colour in this period.

The weaving is plain and simple, mainly using flat shuttle, hanging shuttle, and crochet methods. Apart from the branches and flowers, the rest is outlined using pale yellow, blue or green crochet, emphasising the decoration of the lines. The waft uses strong silk thread, quite thick, but since the weaving is tight, a corrugated effect is the result. The centre of the sunflowers is woven in mixed white and blue, giving the effect of a fused colour. PIAO WENYING

1

2 *Painting of Camellia with Butterfly*, silk tapestry

Zhu Kerou
Southern Song dynasty (1127–1279)
Length 25.6 cm, Width 25.3 cm

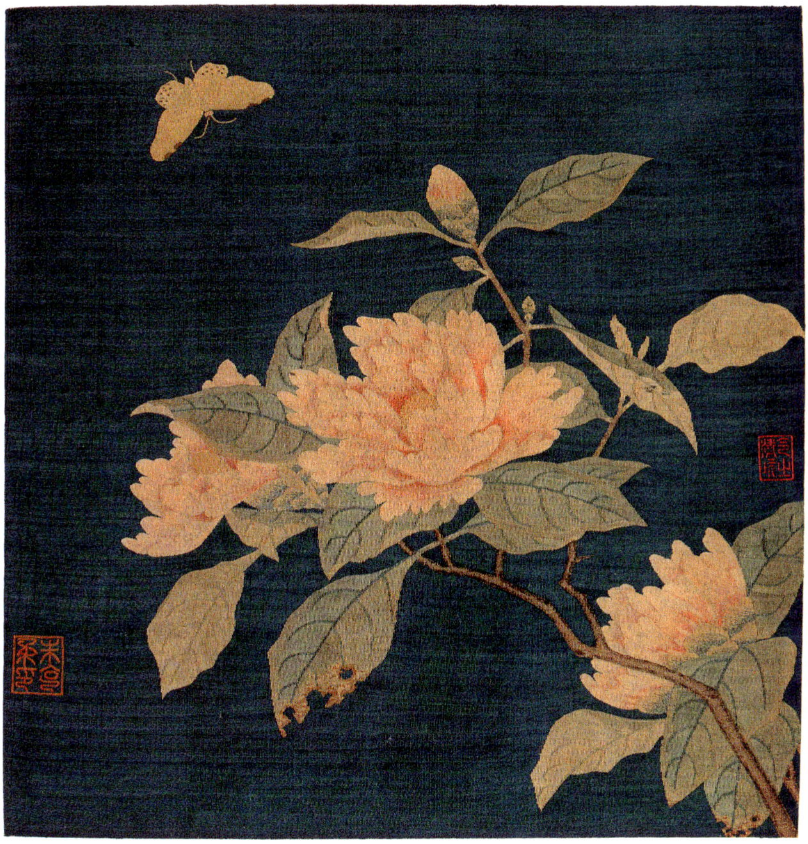

2

Silk tapestry enjoyed a period of prosperity during the Southern Song, making embroideries of famous paintings fashionable. During the process of making tapestry copies of famous paintings, weaving technique improved, and many famous weavers emerged in south China. Zhu Kerou, from Yunjian (present-day Shanghai), learnt the technique of tapestry from a young age, and enjoyed great fame from her skill in copying famous paintings of the time. She made fine tapestry of lively and vivid effect, and was not only successful in accurately reproducing the essence of the original, but also managed to add artistic merit to the original, almost achieving perfection. She was one of the artists who took the tapestry of the Southern Song to new heights. This tapestry of a bird and flower is a typical work by Zhu Kerou. The open flowers of the camellia are attracting the fluttering butterfly, in the left corner the characters 'Zhu Kerou's seal' are woven. The depth of colour of the flower's petals and sepals are represented by lines in different directions and of different length. The hanging shuttle technique is mature, and there are very few jagged lines, and no gaps between the weft. The surface of the tapestry is flat. Mixed coloured threads are mostly used, such as the dry brown and cream colour of the tree, with some brush strokes added above. The stamens protrude slightly in yellow and cream-coloured thread. The leaves of the tree are done in green and mixed green and yellow threads. The holes bitten by insects on the leaves are delicately woven with cream and brown thread, giving a natural effect. This was a special technique of Zhu Kerou. PIAO WENYING

3 *Group of Spirits Wishing Long Life*, silk tapestry

Southern Song dynasty (1127–1279)
Length 38.3 cm, Width 22.8 cm

4 *Round Fan with Peony Pattern*, silk tapestry

Yuan dynasty (1171–1368)
Length 22.6 cm, Width 26.3 cm

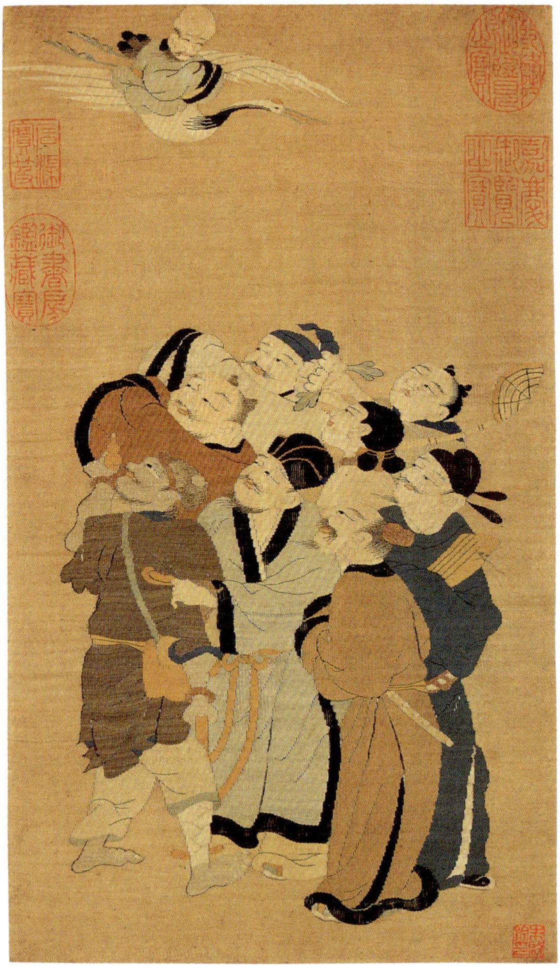

3

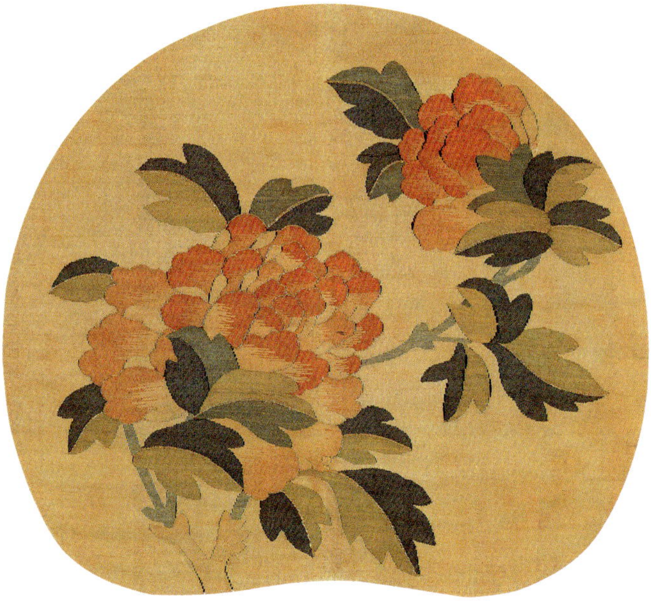

4

5 *Quilt with Golden Dragon Pattern*, silk tapestry

Liao (916–1125)
Existing Length 200 cm, Existing Width 150 cm
Excavated in the 1974 at Yemaotai, in Faku County, Liaoning Province

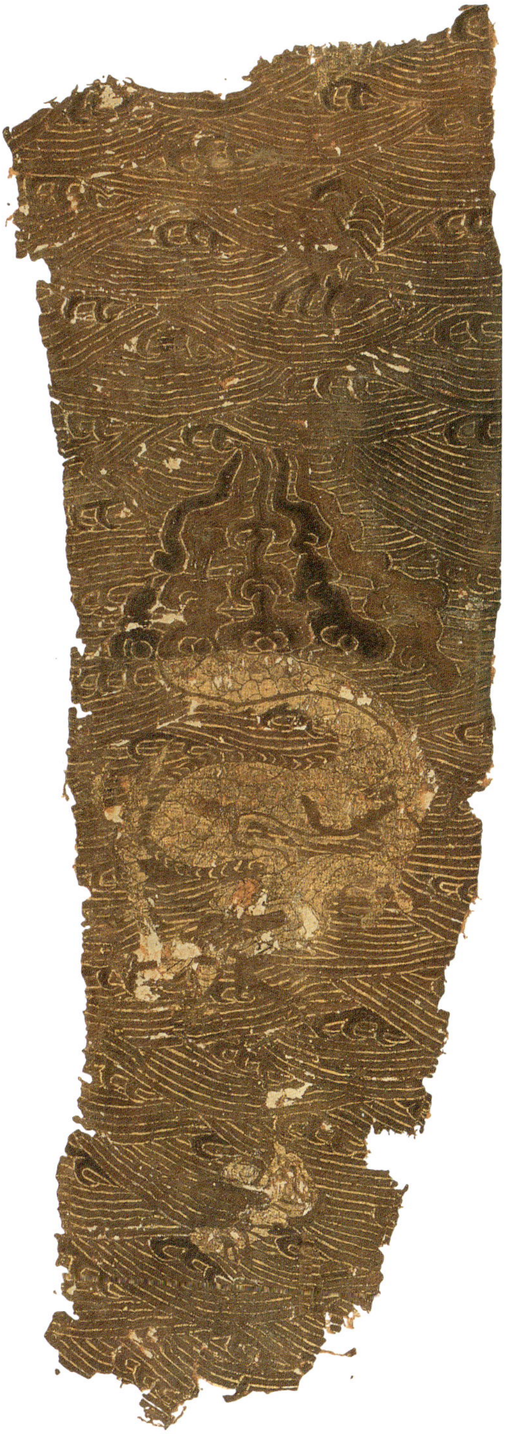

5

6 *Viburnum*

Yuan dynasty (1171–1368)
Length 203 cm, Width 46.5 cm

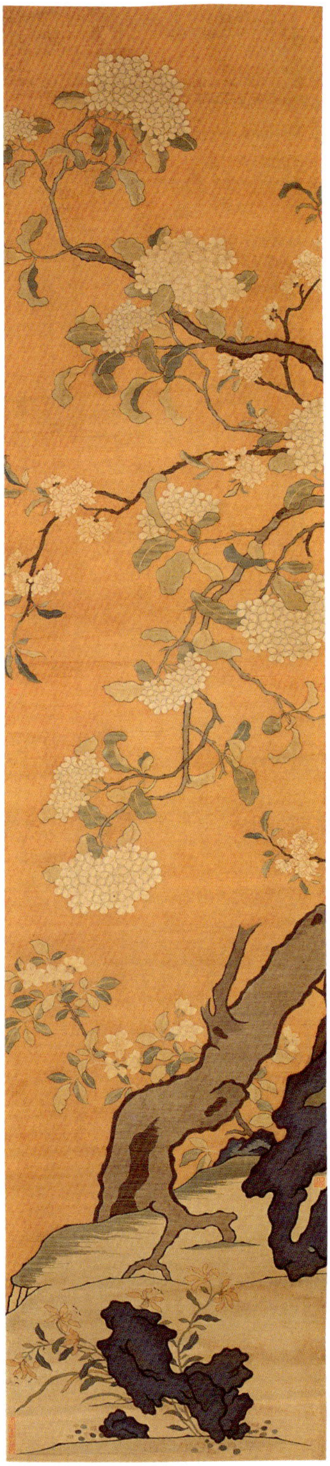

6

7 *Armillary Sphere Bo Gu Tu*, silk tapestry

Ming dynasty (1368–1644)
Length 138 cm, Width 44.8 cm

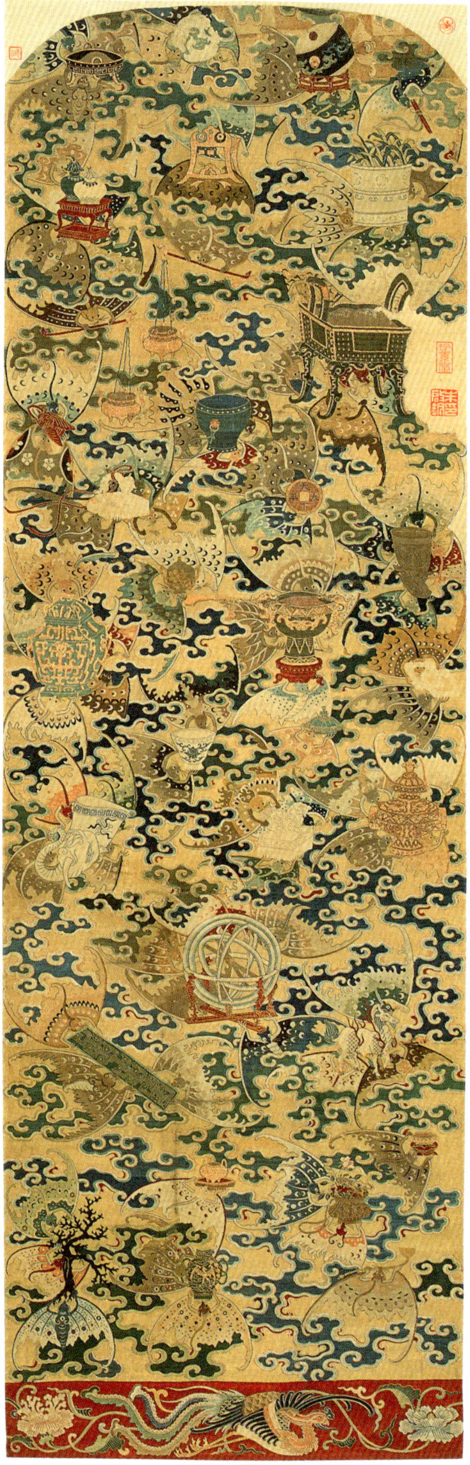

7

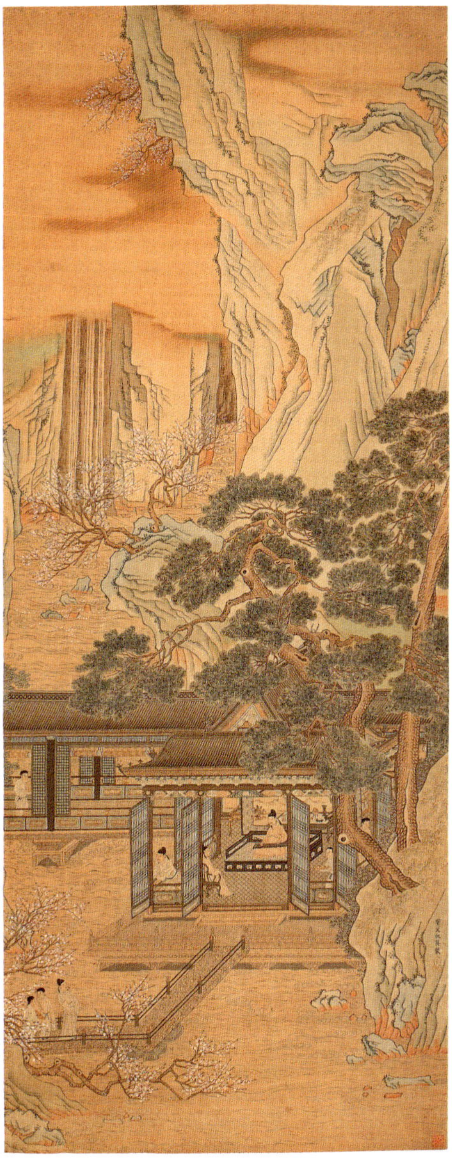

8

8 *Sounds of the Lute in Water Pavilion by Qiu Ying*, silk tapestry

Ming dynasty (1368–1644)
Length 138 cm, Width 55.4 cm

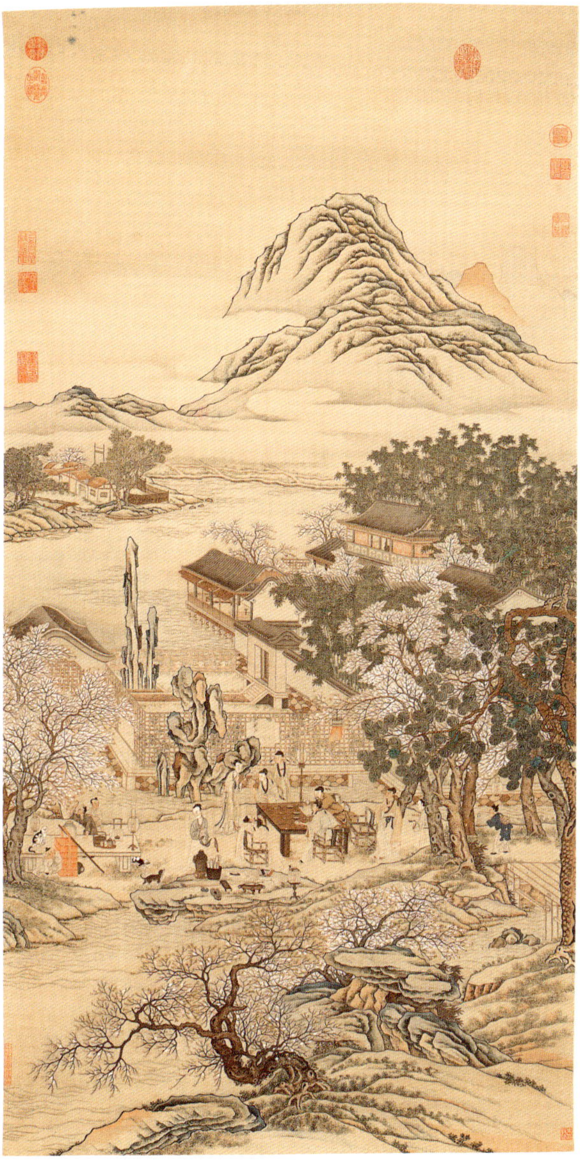

9

9 *Li Bai Evening Banquet in Garden of Peaches and Plums*, silk tapestry

Qing dynasty (1644–1911)
Length 136 cm, Width 70.8 cm

10 *Riding a Crane over Yaotai*, embroidery

Southern Song dynasty (1127–1279)
Length 25.2 cm, Width 27.1 cm

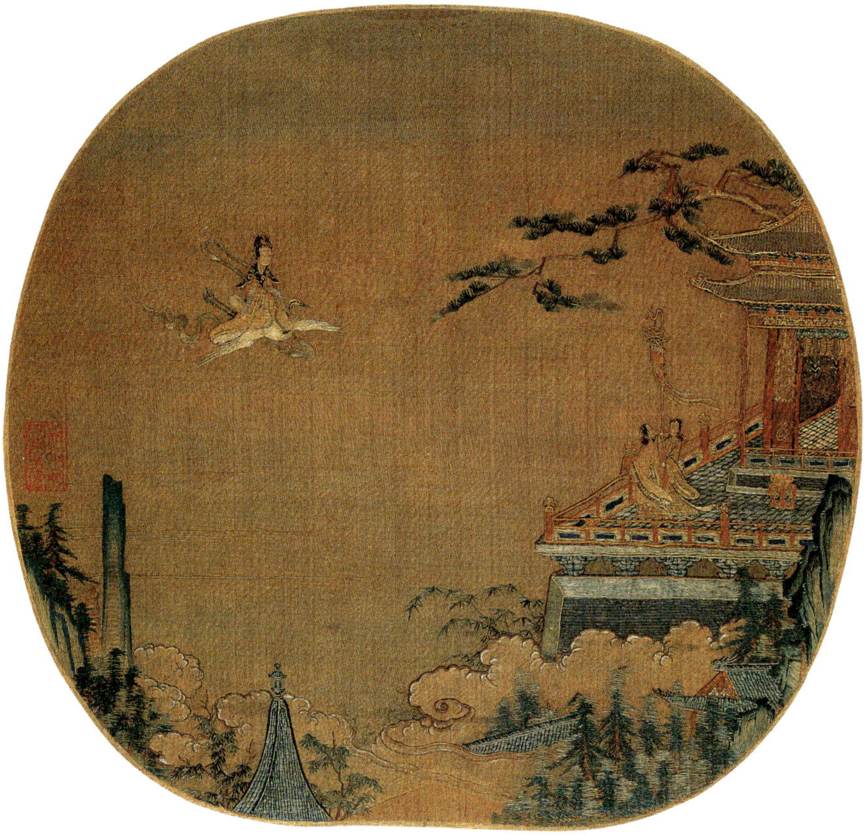

10

This Daoist figure and landscape is a classic Southern Song embroidery. The embroidery shows a fairy scene among the clouds. The mother of the Western King flies over sitting on a crane, two people hold a banner in welcome on the terrace of a pavilion below, surrounded by clouds and pine trees. This work is composed of several materials including fine thread split from silk, double-stranded thick twisted thread, flat gold thread, and twisted gold thread. The needlework is rich and varied, as if representing all the embroidery needlework of the Southern Song. The embroidery is delicate and is supplemented by extra brush work adding colour to the work. The most animated colourful part is the pavilion terrace, patterned layers have been embroidered on top of the needlework. For example the brickwork and building brackets and columns, windows and hanging screen have been embroidered in delicate patterns on top of the underlying needlework. The roof tiles have been embroidered in twisted gold thread and the eaves and top have been embroidered in flat gold thread. The figures are only 2.5 cm tall, but their expressions and clothes are clearly depicted. The walls of the pavilion have painted dragons on them, and a slight wash of colour has been added to the blue sky. The conception of this work is original and the technique exceptional. Piao Wenying

11 *Plum, Bamboo and Parrot*, thread embroidery

Song dynasty (960–1279)
Length 27.2 cm, Width 27.7 cm

12 *Perfection of Wisdom Sutras*, thread embroidery

Yuan dynasty (1279–1368)
Length 31.1 cm, Width 27 cm

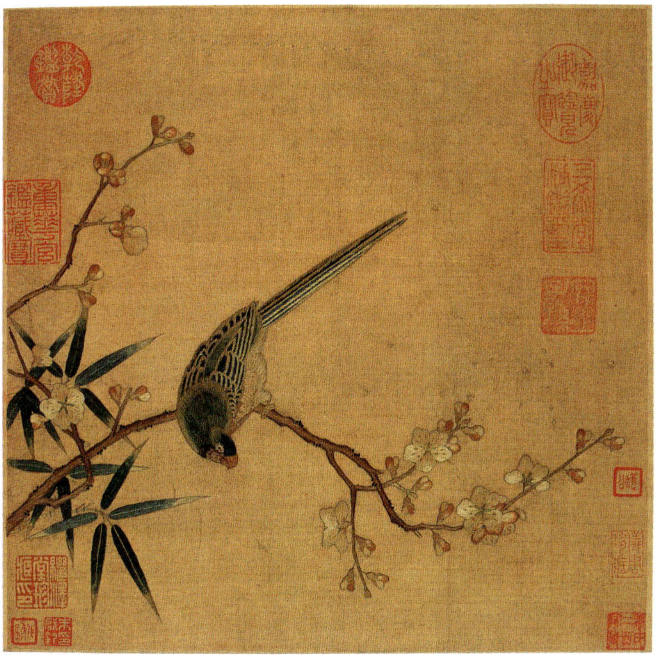

11

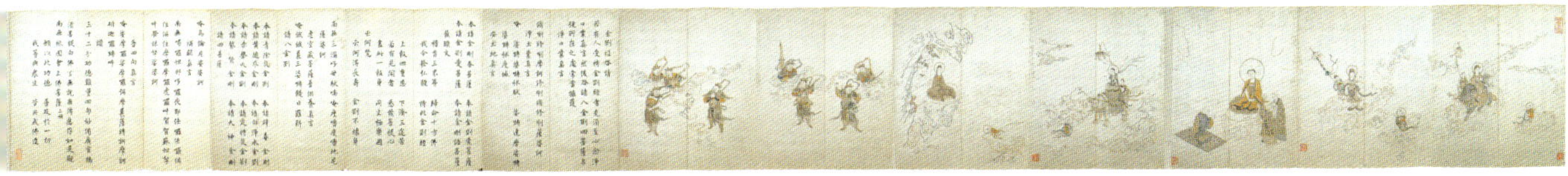

12

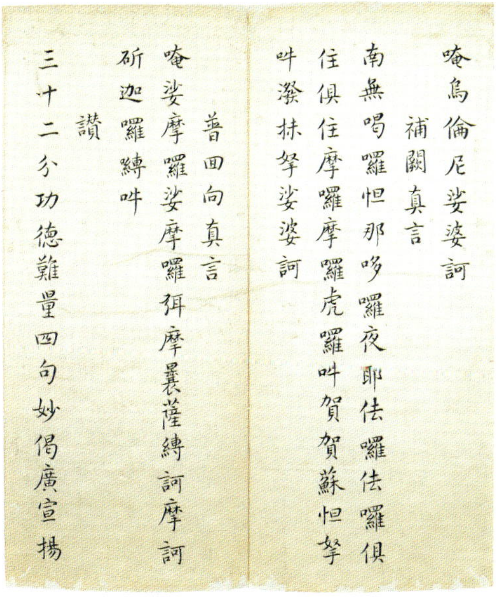

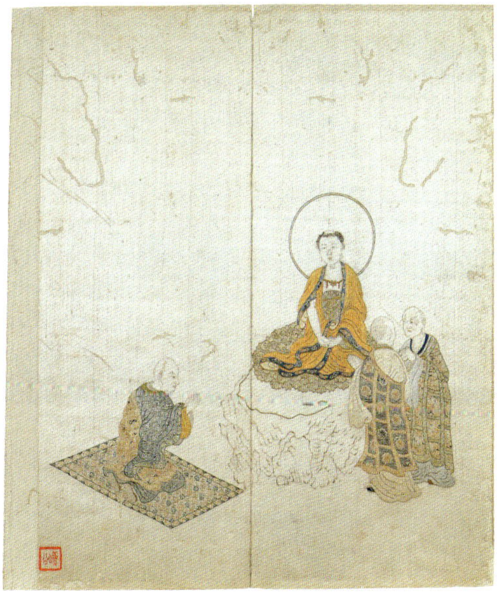

13 *Maitreya Buddha Scroll*, Gu Embroidery

Ming (1368–1644)
Length 54.5 cm, Width 26.7 cm

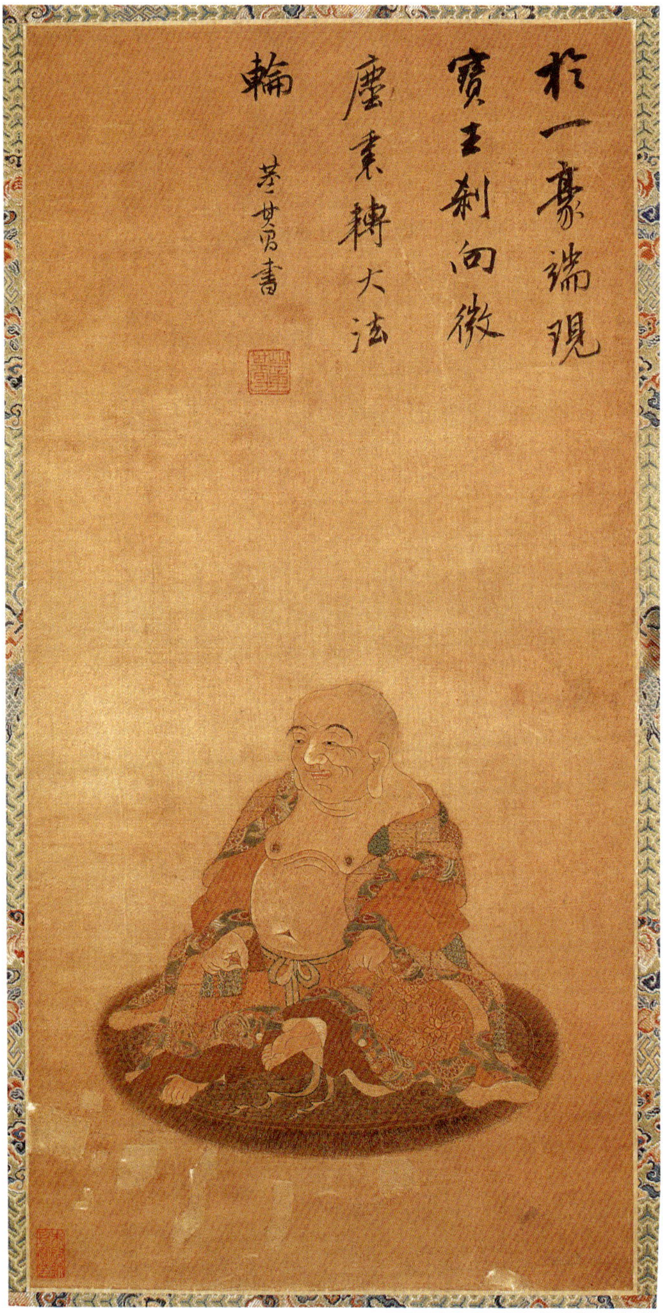

13

Gu Embroidery, also called 'Luxiang garden Gu Embroidery' was a Ming-period style from the Gu family in Shanghai. Gu Xiu inherited the embroidery painting art of the Song period, and explored many kinds of embroidery needlework, combining painting and embroidery, and occupies an important position in aesthetic embroidery, having a deep influence on later generations. This Maitreya Buddha has an inscription of Dong Qichang embroidered at the top. The embroidery needlework is rich and varied, using techniques such as fine thread from split silk, double-stranded twisted thread, split thread and twisted gold thread. For example the eyes and eyebrows of the Maitreya Buddha are outlined with split silk thread, and the Buddha's clothes are made from double-stranded twisted thread. The patch *kasaya* has a complex needlework, first using single-strand or double-stranded twisted thread for the background. On top of this twisted gold thread is used to embroider clouds and dragons in various patterns. Different colours are used in double-stranded firmly twisted silk to make horizontal patterns for the straw mat. The work achieves a three-dimensional, realistic effect. Piao Wenying

14 *Flower and Bird*, embroidery

Ming dynasty (1368–1644)
Length 25.1 cm, Width 23.7 cm

15 *Qixiang Building Figures Scroll*, hair embroidery

Gu family
Ming (1368–1644)
Length 64.1 cm, Width 22.4 cm

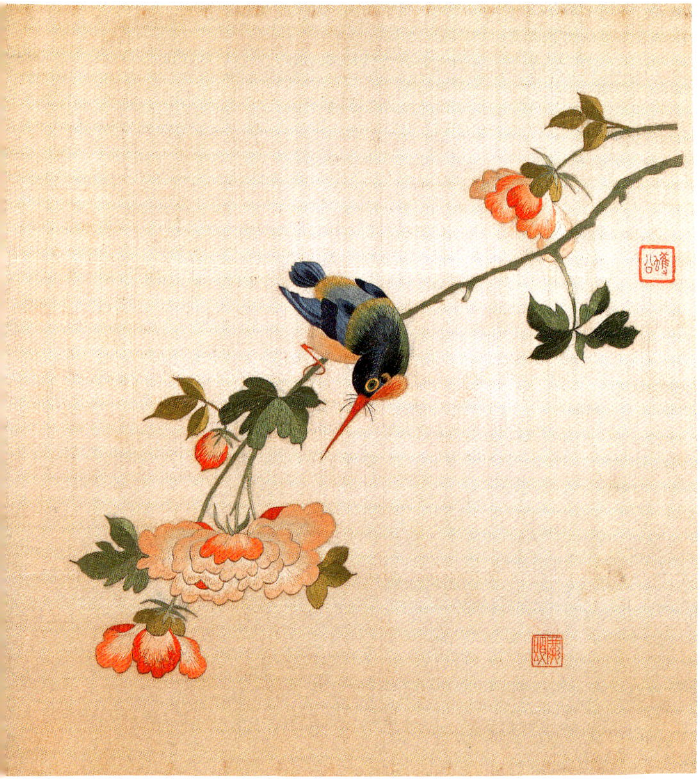

14

15

Hair embroidery uses the natural human hair, and is smooth and soft, aiming for simple purity, resulting in an effect similar to line drawing. Hair embroidery was already fashionable in the Tang and Song periods, and was developed further in the Ming and Qing periods. This work has a figure embroidered in outline, wearing a robe with loose sleeves, with an elegant look, and a child next to him holding a zither, with his body turned and left arm pointing upwards, and a round moon visible in the sky. There are lines of five characters embroidered above. The characters 'Qixiang building seal' are embroidered in yellow silk. The sketch of this picture is exceptional, with fine embroidery work. The basic needlework uses thread, which is then held fast by human hair. Carried stitches are used making the embroidery both smooth and interrupted, and the embroidery outline is visible. The figures' features, hair and clothes are all finely executed. PIAO WENYING

16 *Perfection of Wisdom Sutras*, brocade

Five Dynasties, Hou Liang Zhenming 2nd year (916)
Length 29.3 cm, Width 713 cm

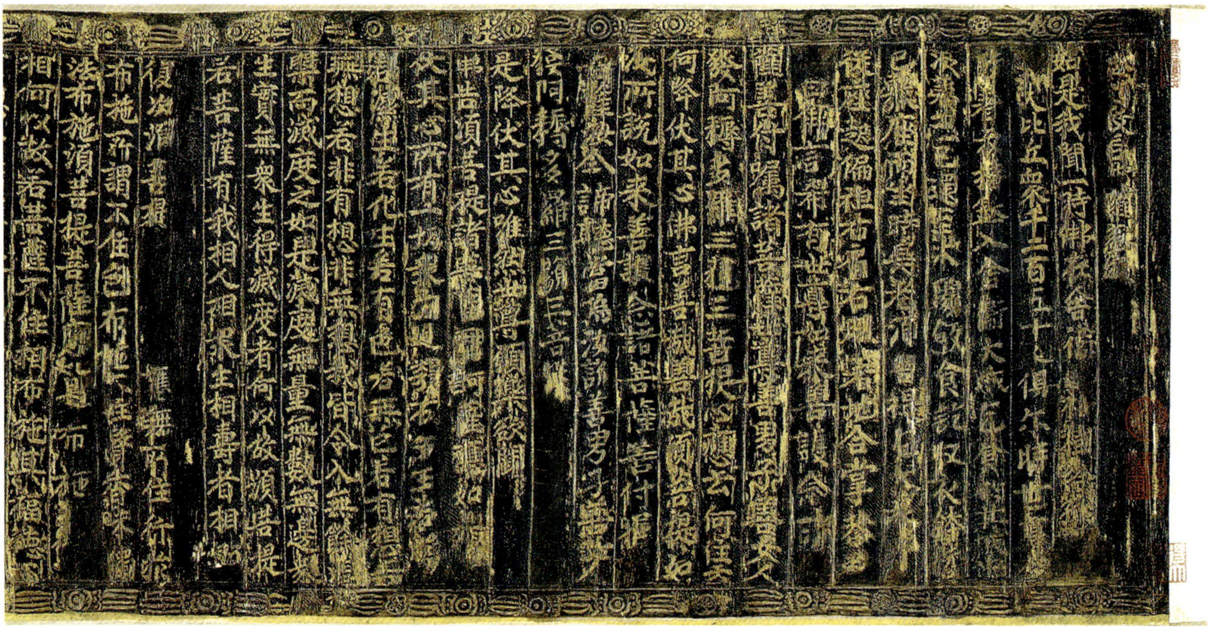

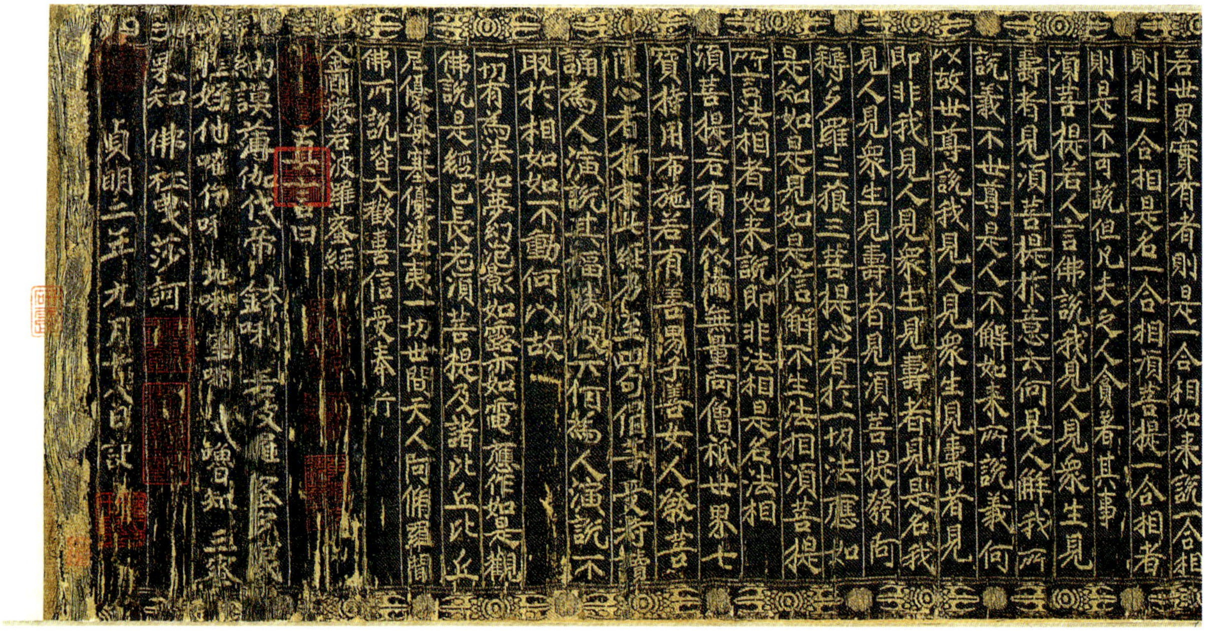

16

17 *Phoenix Brocade Scroll*

Yuan (1271–1368)
Length 53.5 cm, Width 548 cm

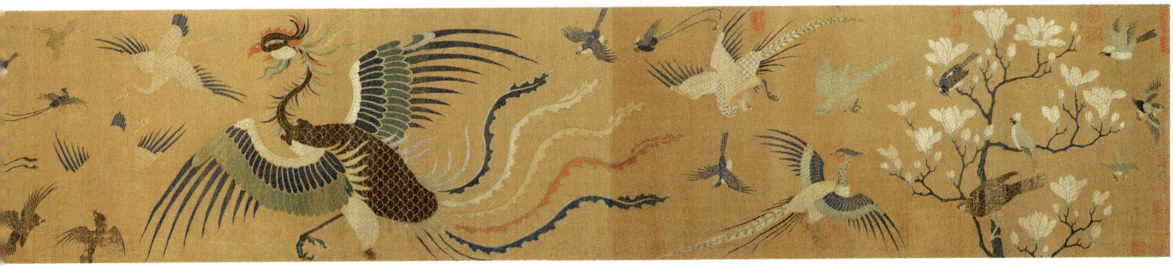

17

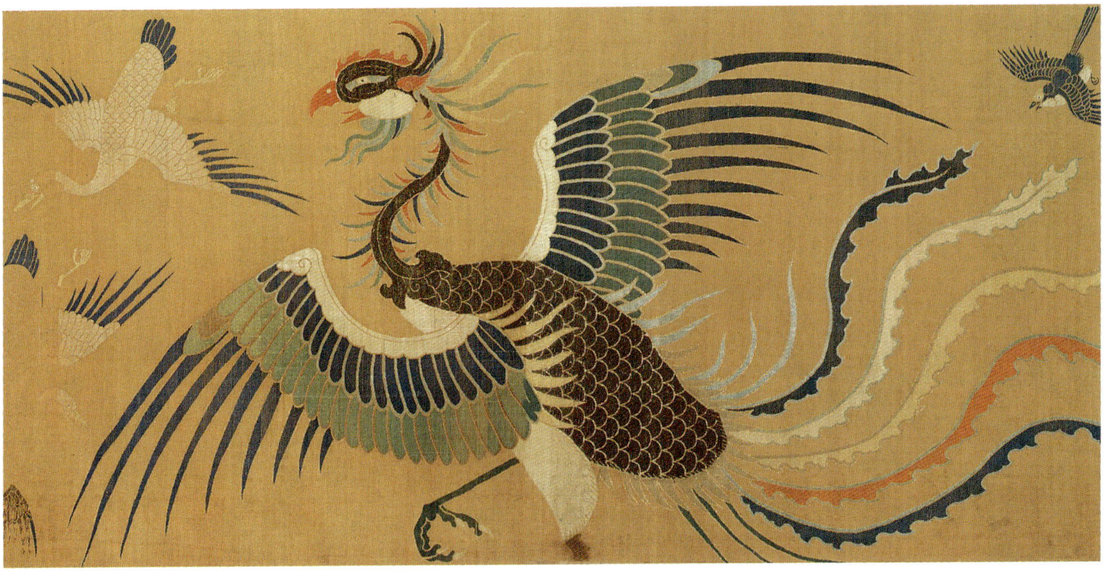

This hand scroll has a phoenix and series of birds embroidered. The phoenix is the largest, and is magnificent, making it the clear centre of the work. On the back of the embroidery is the stamp of Prince Sa Shizi of the Ming period (alive in Yongle's reign). Silk thread, flat gold thread and peacock feather thread are used. The whole work is composed of two joined sections with the same design, but with different coloured threads. The design is Chinese traditional brush painting of birds and animals, but the weaving technique is a special brocade style using flat gold thread for the outline. The two main phoenixes' heads, necks and bodies are woven from peacock feathers. This weaving method and structure was newly introduced in the Yuan period, showing that by this time new weaving methods were already being used on traditional paintings. PIAO WENYING

5

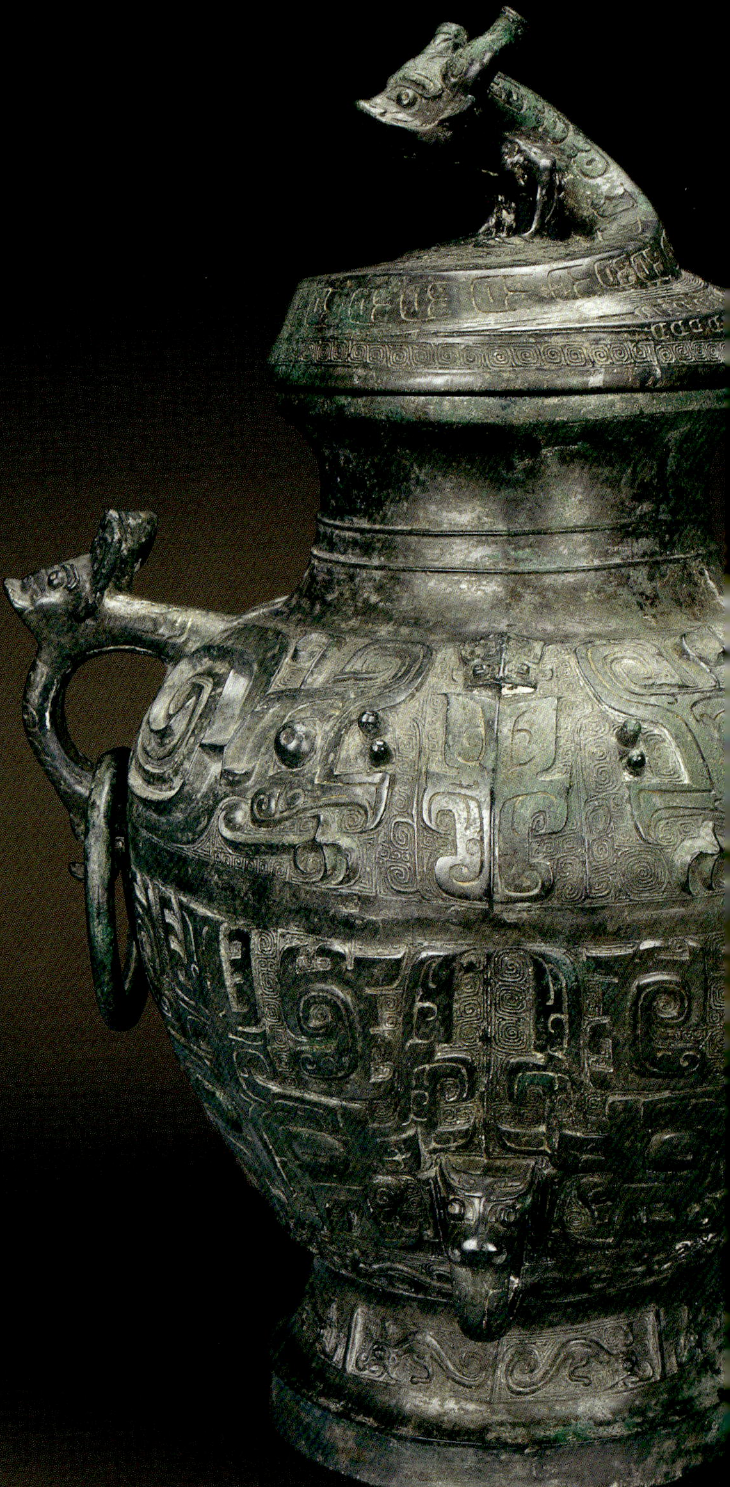

Bronzes

Bronzes were first cast in the Xia dynasty, maturing in style in the Shang and Zhou dynasties. Bronze production continued through the Ming and Qing periods. Artistic achievements in bronze ware have a four thousand year old history and are still appreciated today. The Liaoning Provincial Museum has a special collection of rare bronzes, with complex origins. Most of the bronzes are from former collections, including bronzes originally from the Fengtian Palace of the Puppet Manchu government's Central Museum, and from Luo Zhenyu's bronze collection. After 1949, a large number of bronzes came to the Liaoning Museum from the Palace Museum. In the late 1960s staff from the Museum selected a number of bronzes from the smeltery. After many years of sporadic purchases and private donations, the Museum's collection is quite sizeable. Some bronzes from former collections have no record of excavation site. Masterpieces from private collections include the *Three Daggers* from that of Luo Zhenyu. Apart from collection and research notes by Luo Zhenyu and Wang Guowei, other scholars such as Li Xueqin and Ma Chengyuan have also analysed them. For example, the Dacheng *Nanlü Chimes* represent the highest technology of the Northern Song.

Archaeological excavations since 1949 have also been a source of the museum's bronzes. The discoveries made from the 1950s to 1970s at Machang Gou, Xiaobotai Gou, Beidong village, Shanwanzi and Hua'erlou include a large number of late Shang and early Zhou bronzes. In pastures around Chaoyang Shi'ertai Ying, Kazuo Nandong Gou, Huludao Wujintang and Lingyuan Sanguan Dianzi curved short bronze swords, several bronze mirrors, and skate fish shaped ornaments dating from the Spring and Autumn and Warring States periods were excavated, all examples of specific local techniques. Decorative bronzes typical of the steppe with gold plating animal patterns were discovered in the tomb group at Tieling Xifeng Gorge. Exquisite Liao bronze mirrors were also discovered in Liao tombs and pagodas at places like Fuxin and Chaoyang. Each bronze piece contains a small piece of history, presenting aesthetic qualities for enjoyment as well as constituting an abundant historical resource. The three pulling daggers reflect the relationship between the clan system and religious law during the Shang dynasty. The Duke of Yan *yu* (receptacle for holding liquid) vessel reflects the historical event of the state of Yan invading the Liaoning area in the early Zhou period. The sword of the Yan king outlines the background of the state of Yan expanding its territory into the northeast region at the end of the Warring States period. The *lei* vessel with coiled dragon and *kui* design represents the culmination of high artistic bronze techniques in the early Zhou period. Tao Liang

1 Large round *ding* (food container) with *taotie* design

Late Shang period (early 13th – 11th century BC)
Height 86 cm, Diameter 61 cm
Excavated at Xiaobotai Gou, Kazuo County, Liaoning Province

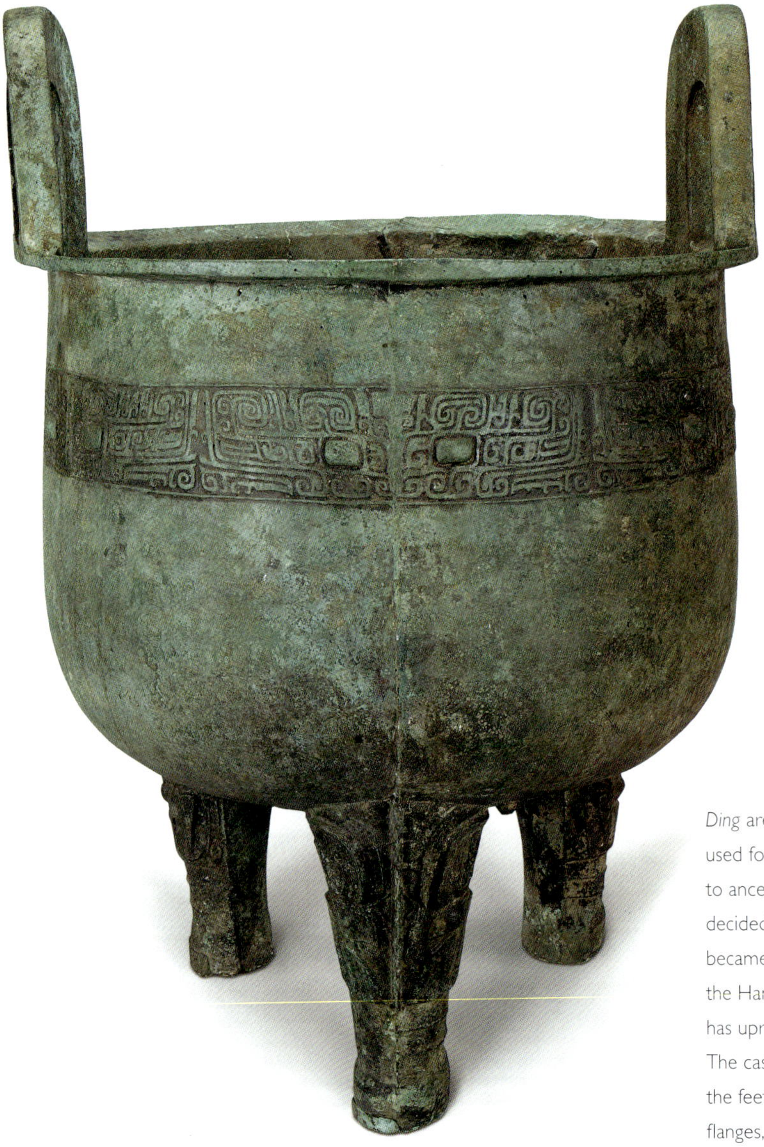

1

Ding are ancient Chinese cooking vessels, and were mainly used for cooking meat, as well as for cooking sacrifices offered to ancestors at ceremonies. Since all important matters were decided by rituals or on the battlefield in ancient China, *Ding* became a symbol of political power, and was used right up to the Han dynasty. It was the longest-used bronze vessel. This piece has upright handles, a deep body and columnar and hollow feet. The casting of the sides is thin. Underneath the rim and above the feet are single layers of animal designs. The feet have raised flanges, and the ears, body and feet all have soot marks on them. The vessel is 86 cm high, and weighs more than 50 kg, and is one of the largest Shang dynasty round *ding* vessels to be excavated in China, and is the largest bronze *ding* discovered up to the present day apart from that of the Shang king. TAO LIANG

2 Ni square *lei* vessel

Late Shang dynasty (early 13th century – 11th century BC)
Height 51.3 cm, Diameter 17.3 cm x 15.8 cm
Excavated at Xiaobotai Gou, Kazuo County, Liaoning Province

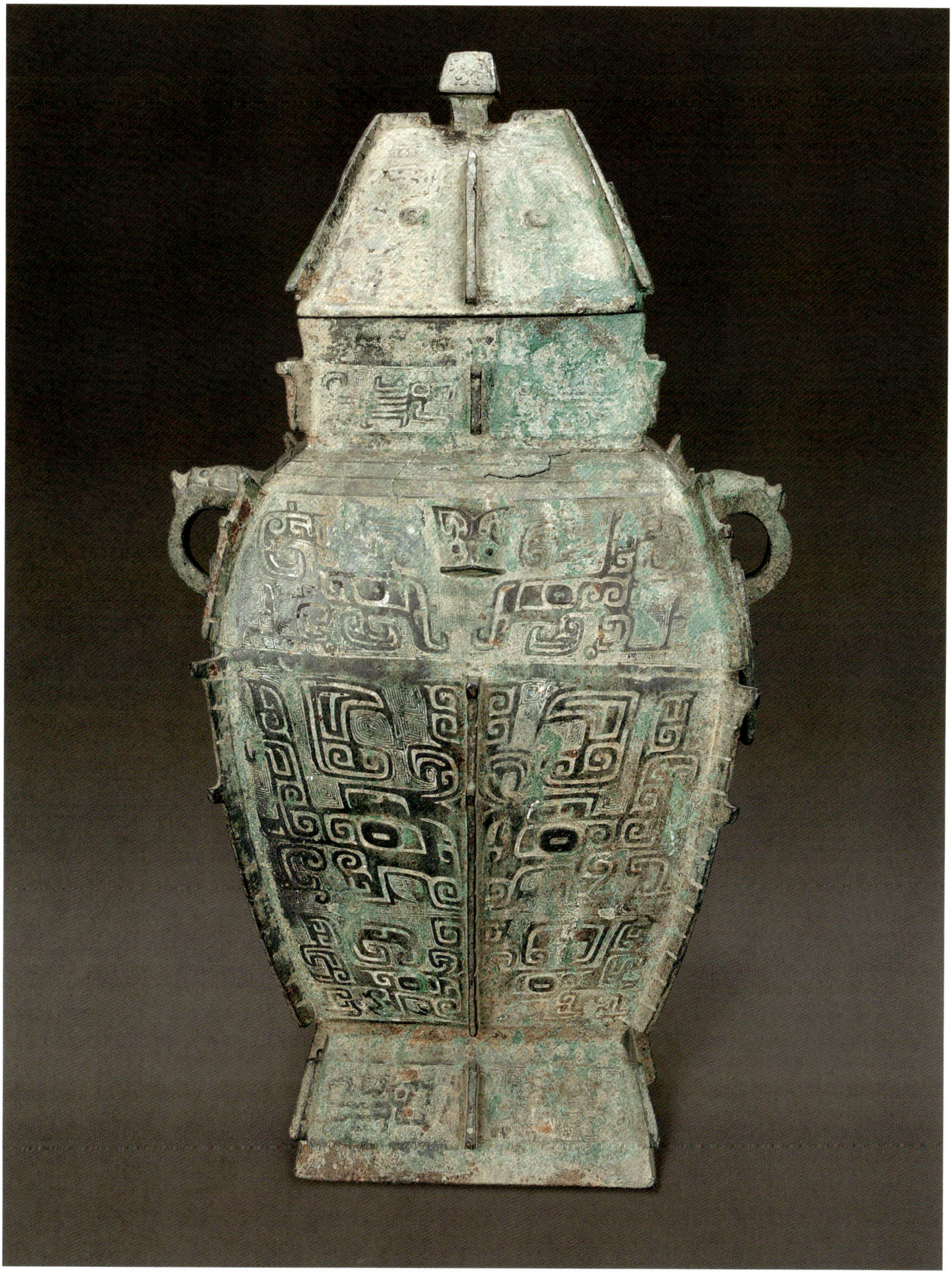

2

3 Three daggers

Shang (end of 17th century – 11th century BC)
Length 26–28 cm, Width 4–5 cm
Thought to be excavated at Yixian in Hebei Province

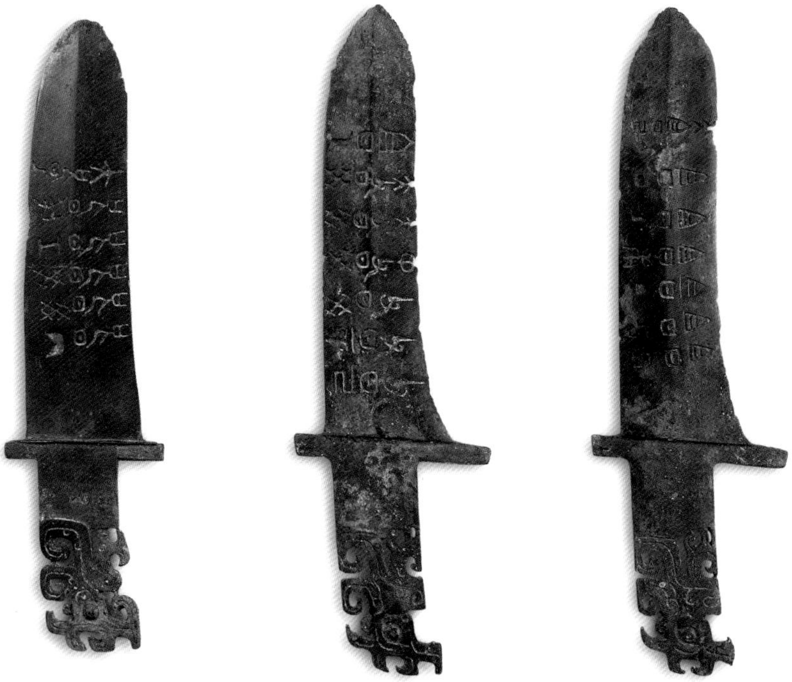

3

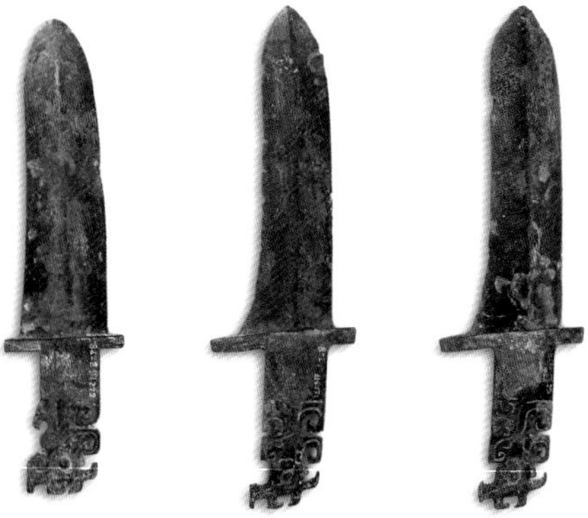

Luo Zhenyu records these daggers in books on his former collection such as *The Inscriptions on Bronze of the Three Dynasties* and *Guantang Jilin*. The three daggers are part of the same set, similar in shape with straight knife and short halberd. The inner part has been hollowed out and carved with phoenix patterns. There are inscriptions on the knife with the names of successive generations of the clan. The shapes of these daggers do not deviate from the usual style of Shang production, but there are small differences, for example the standing bird carved on the *nei* is the same size as the *nei*, or slightly bigger, and does not seem to be a typical beak from Yin ruins that would hang down crookedly. Wang Guowei wrote that 'it can be seen as a weapon of a northern principality during the Shang period'. Judging from the list of names carved on the knives, they were unlikely to be used in war, but as decoration in rituals and ceremonies in the ancestral hall. This group of daggers have the names of twenty people recorded on them, with four generations, great-grandfather, grandfather, father and brother, and as such are a very useful resource for researching clan and family system in the Shang dynasty. Luo Zhenyu's critical judgement that these are 'unparalleled handed-down ancient weapons' seems highly appropriate. Tao Liang

4 *Lei* (wine vessel) with looped animal handles with rings

Late Shang period (early 13th century – 11th century BC)
Height 41 cm, Diameter 17 cm, Base 16 cm
Excavated at Beidong village, Kazuo County, Liaoning Province

5 *Fuyi* bronze *jue* (ritual wine vessel)

Shang (late 17th century – 11th century BC)
Height 22.7 cm, Length from top to bottom 17 cm,
Body Diameter 6 cm

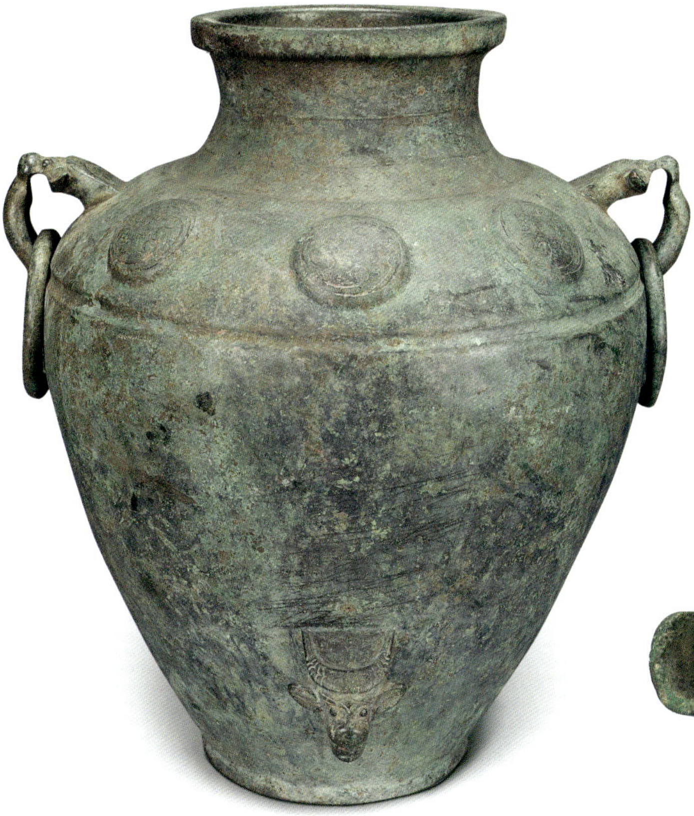

4

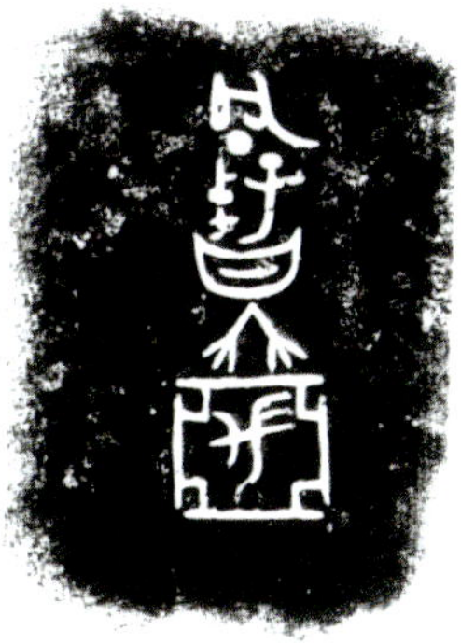

4 Inscription

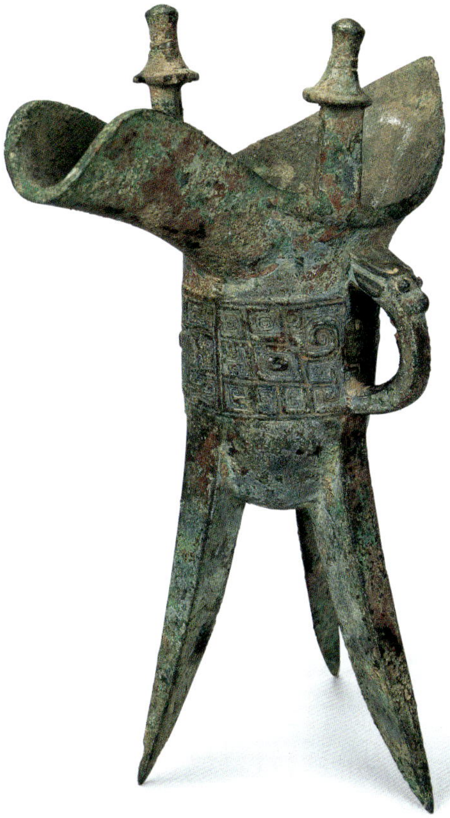

5

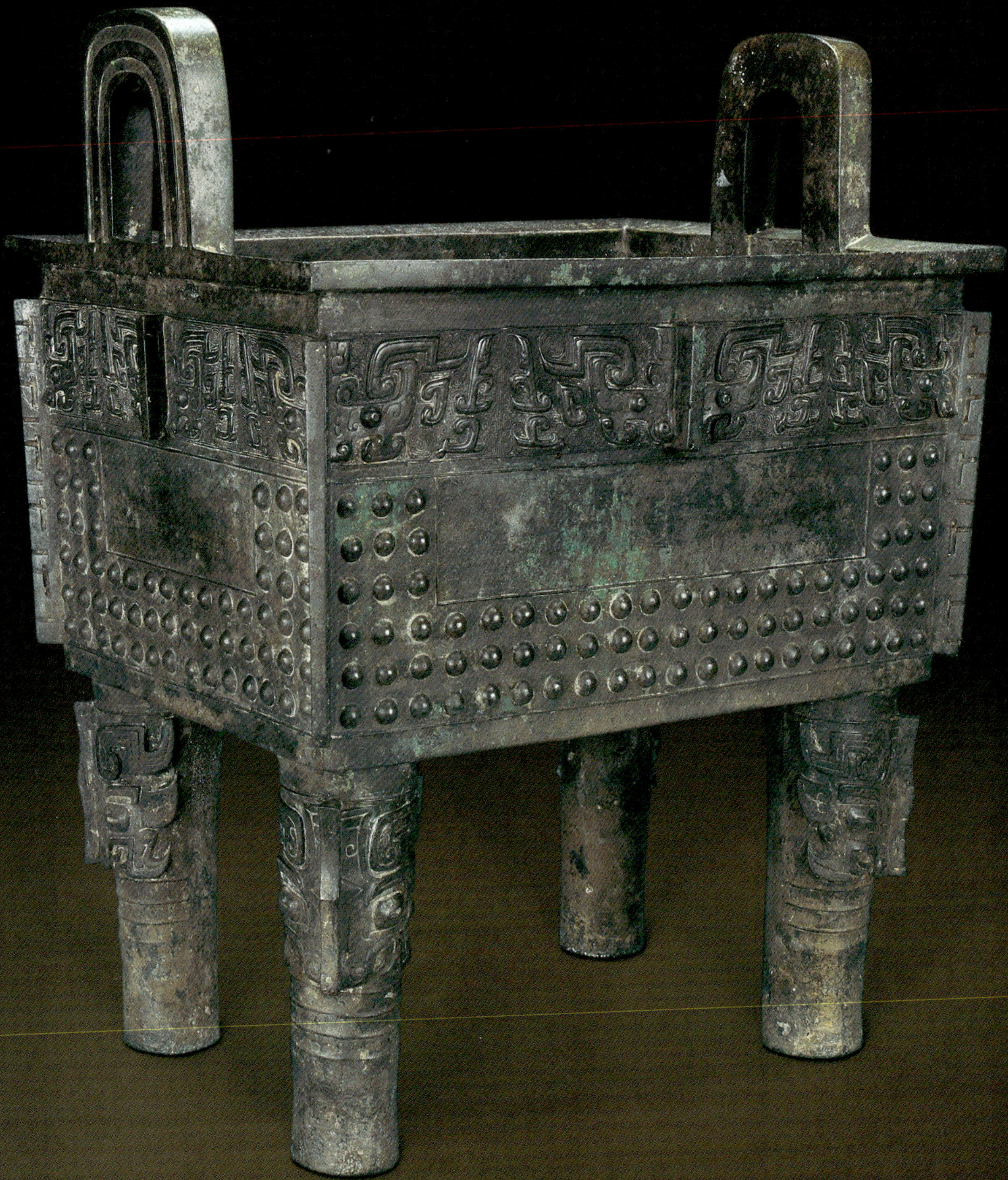

6 *Nie Fang ding* (food container)

Late Shang period (early 13th century – 11th century BC)
Length 40.8 cm, Width 30.5 cm, Height 51.7 cm
Excavated at Beidong village, Kazuo County, Liaoning Province

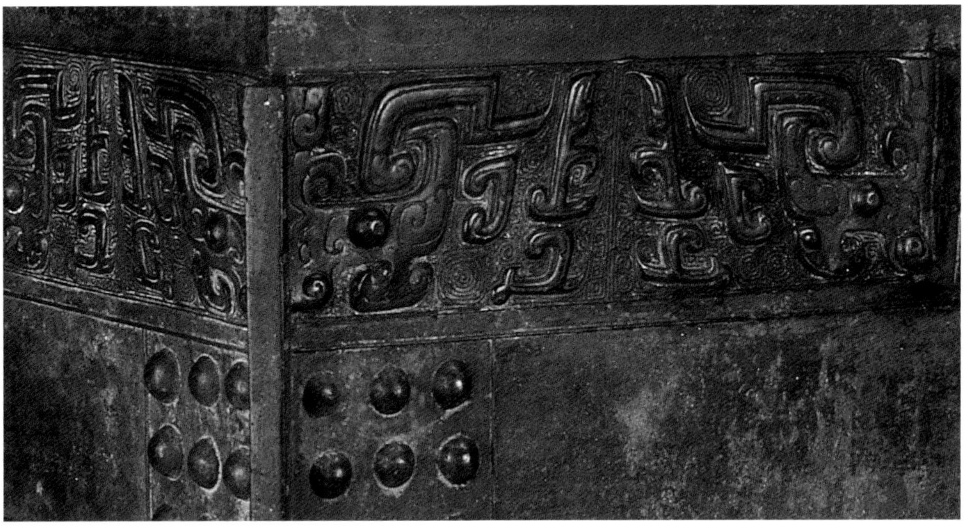

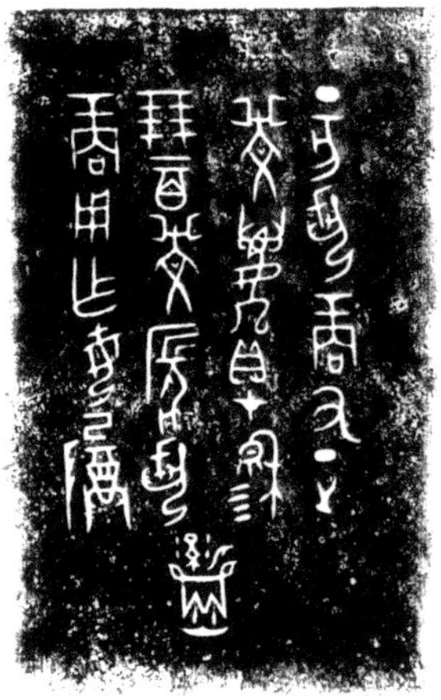

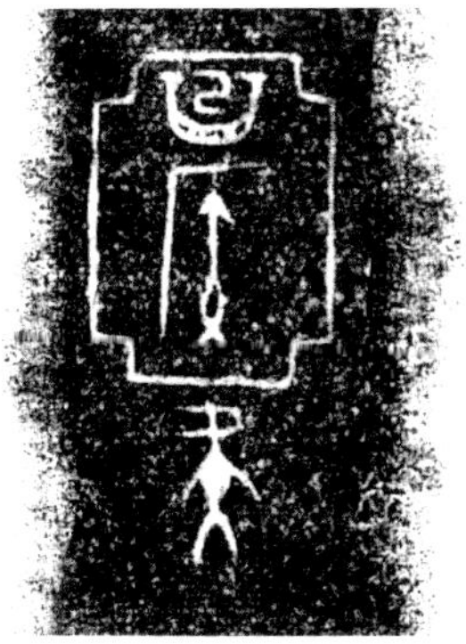

Inscription

The *Nie Fang ding* has upright handles, a square rim, a deep belly and columnar feet. There is a *taotie* design beneath the mouth rim, the body is decorated with a nipple pattern, the mouth is slightly bigger than the base and the columnar feet are thick and strong. The upper part of the feet has a faint *taotie* design, the four corners of the *ding* all have raised flanges. The pattern is exquisitely executed. The long wall of the inner body of this *ding* and its inner base have long inscriptions dedicated to the family. The discovery of the inscription has provided new information on the Shang official ranking system, revealing a previously unknown rank. Judging from the archaeological record, it seems that *fang ding* were all made for high-ranking nobles.

After the inscription on the square *ding* there is a *ji* character, which could be the crest of the Ji family. Ji family bronze ware has been excavated around the outskirts of Beijing among Yan bronzes around the time of Shang and Zhou. This kind of bronze ware has been excavated twice in the northern Yan territory area. It is all related to the Yan principality, and so one can conjecture that during the early Zhou period, the Ji clan worked for the Duke of Yan, that they were Shang refugees in the state of Yan after the collapse of the Shang by King Wu. The discovery of this bronze vessel in the Liaoning area proves the historical record that in the early Zhou period the Duke of Yan followed orders to pursue Wu Geng the Prince of Shang who was fleeing north.

Tao Liang

7 Fu Tian gu

Shang (late 17th century – 11th century BC)
Height 22 cm, Body Diameter 6.2 cm,
Rim Diameter 13.7 cm, Base 8.3 cm

8 *Jia* (wine vessel)

Shang (late 17th century – 11th century BC)
Height 30 cm, Body Diameter 17.4 cm, Rim Diameter 17.3 cm

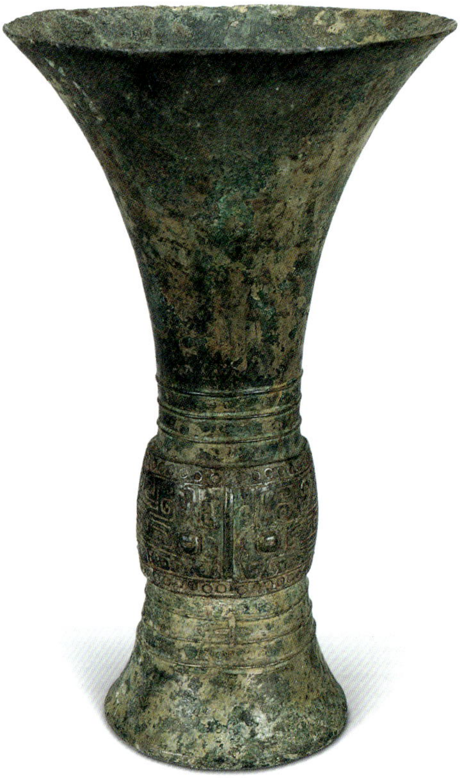

7

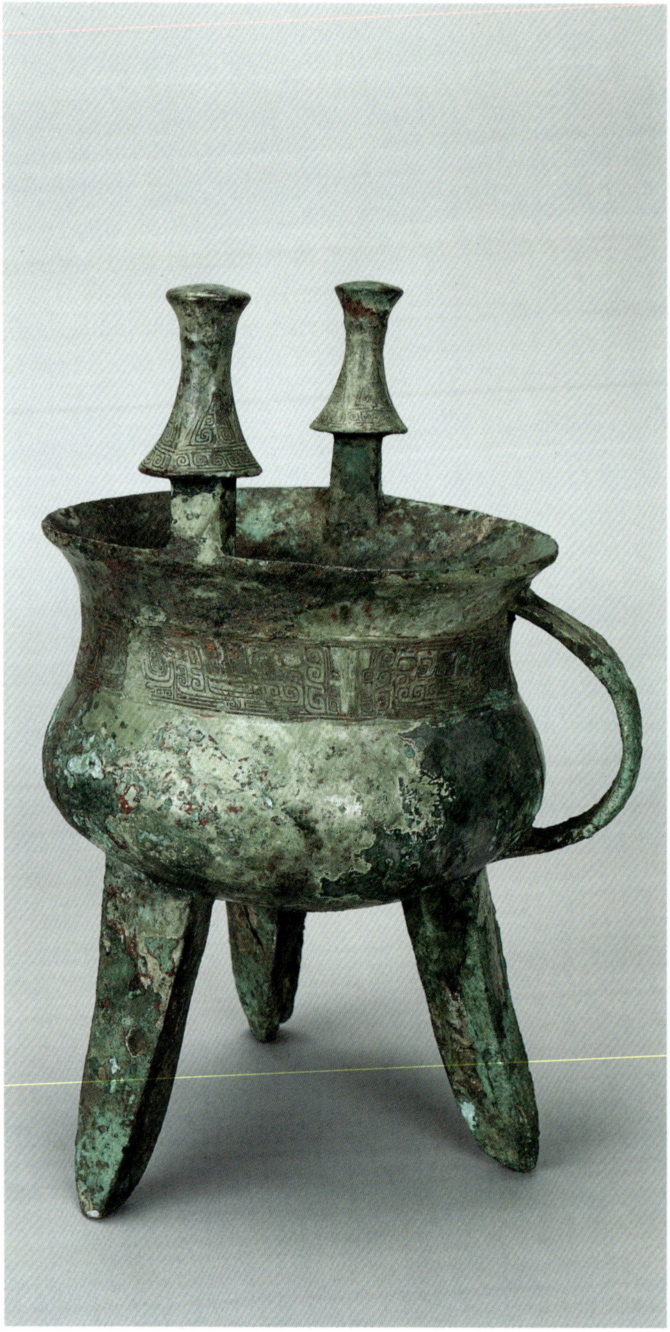

8

9 Cicada pattern dish

Late Shang period (early 13th century – 11th century BC)
Height 12.8 cm, Diameter 33.5 cm, Base 21.3 cm
Excavated at Machang gou, Kazuo County, Liaoning Province

10 *Shifa you* (wine vessel)

Western Zhou early period (11th century – 10th century BC)
Height 23.4 cm, Diameter 39 cm, Body Diameter 34.6 cm
Excavated at Machang gorge, Kazuo County, Liaoning Province

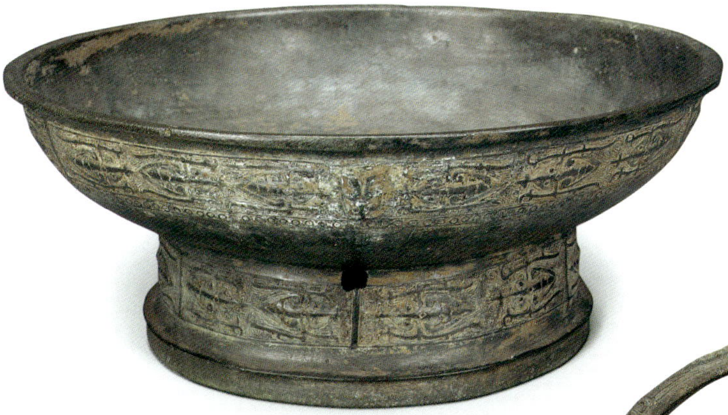

9

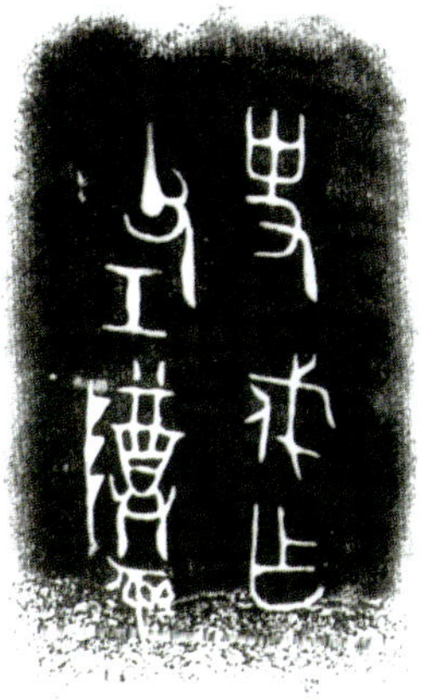

10 Inscription

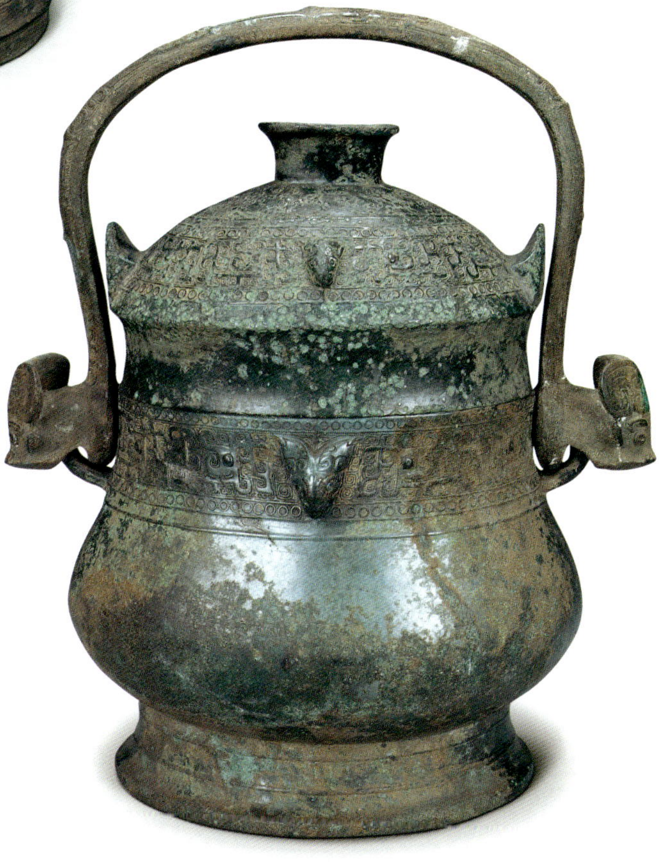

10

11 *Lei* (drinking vessel) with coiled dragon and *kui* design

Western Zhou early period (11th century BC)
Height 44.5 cm, Diameter 15.5 cm, Base Diameter 16.5 cm
Excavated at Beidong village, Kazuo County, Liaoning Province

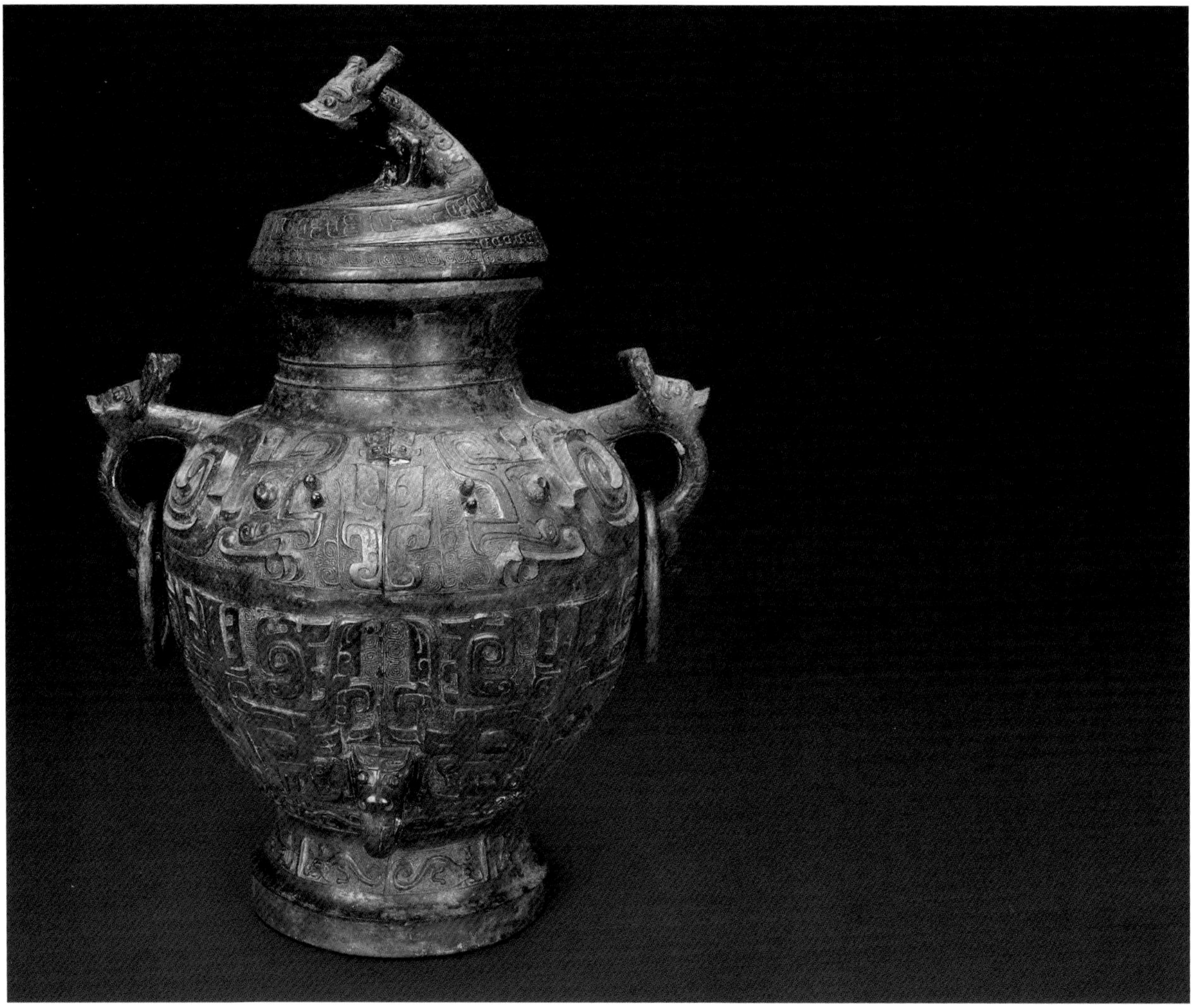

11

A *lei* was a drinking vessel used during the Shang and Zhou periods with a large capacity. This *lei* has been decorated with faint patterns, combining fine carving work, with a powerful three-dimensional effect. The decoration on the *lei* is divided across the shoulder and body sections, both with matching phoenix designs, with clouds and lightning around their bodies. The feet are decorated with a dragon pattern, or a *kui* pattern. The lid of the *lei* has a curled dragon carved on it, shaped like a lizard, with a pair of bottle-shaped horns. The dragon has a crouching body and tail, both feet on the ground, a curved elbow, as if about to pounce and burst into movement. It is very realistic. There are a few simple, lively cicada patterns on the dragon's chest and body. Exquisite pattern work and fluid casting along with a highly realistic effect are fine examples of the high artistic standards of the Zhou dynasty. TAO LIANG

12 Fish *zun* (wine vessel)

Western Zhou early period (11th century BC)
Height 37 cm, Diameter 25.3 cm, Base 15.3 cm
Excavated at Shanwanzi, Kazuo County,
Liaoning Province

13 Boju *yan* (food steamer)

Western Zhou early period (11th century BC)
Height 41 cm, Diameter 25.5 cm, Body Depth, 24 cm
Excavated at Shanwanzi, Kazuo County,
Liaoning Province

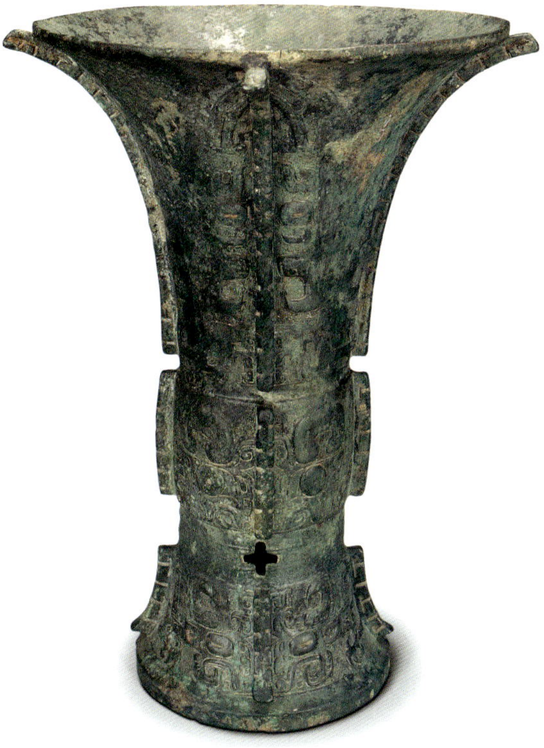

12

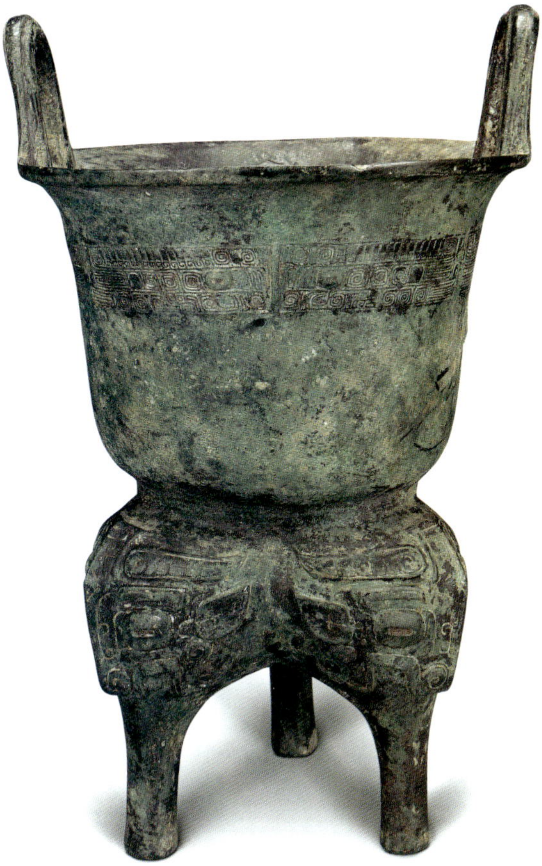

13

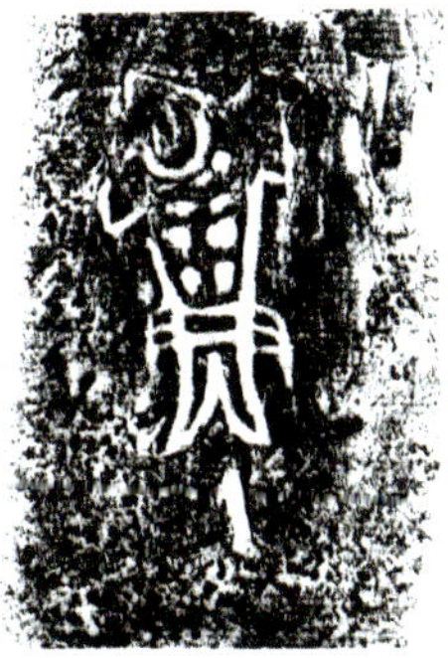

12 Inscription

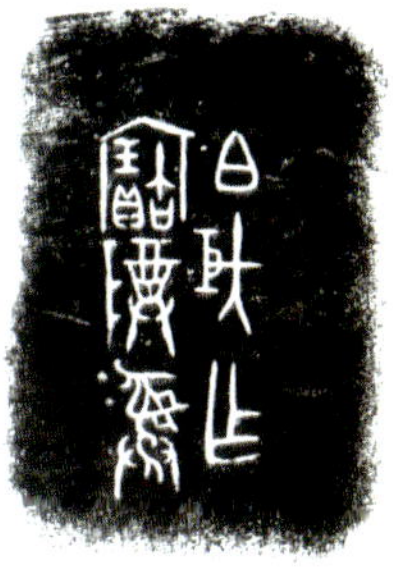

13 Inscription

14 *Yu gui* (food container)

Western Zhou early period (11th century BC)
Height 29.2 cm, Width 37.8 cm
Excavated at Xiaobotai Gou, Kazuo County, Liaoning Province

15 *Hu* with pierced handles (ritual vessel for holding wine with pierced handles)

Western Zhou early period (11th century BC)
Height 41.6 cm, Diameter 10 cm, Body Diameter 19.2 cm, Base 12 cm
Excavated at Machang gou, Kazuo County, Liaoning Province

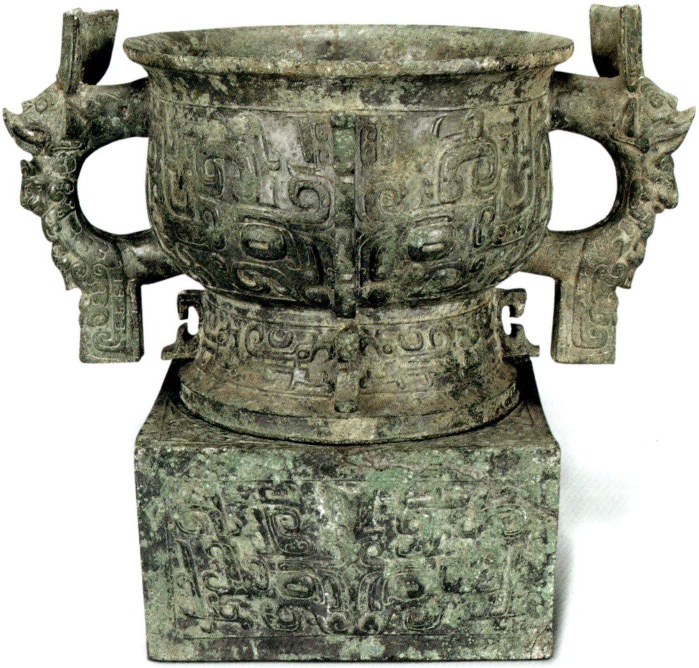

14

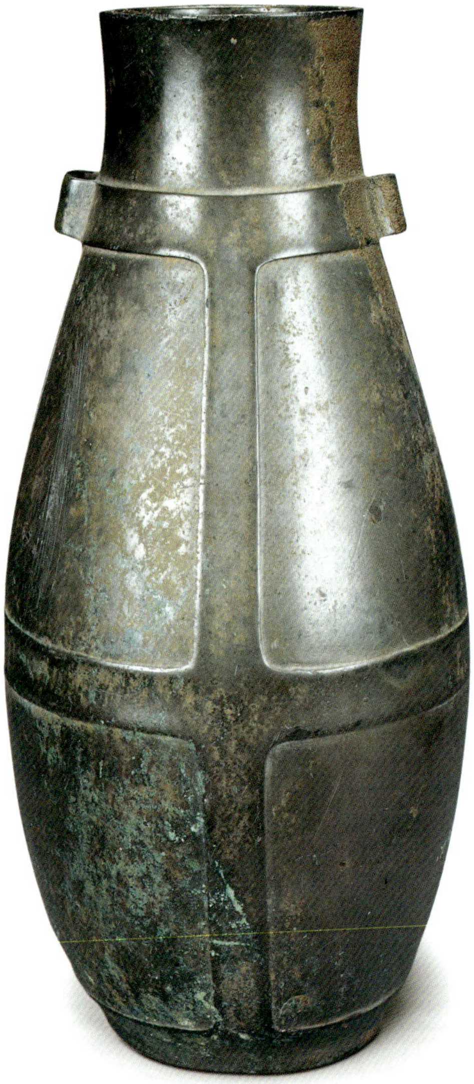

15

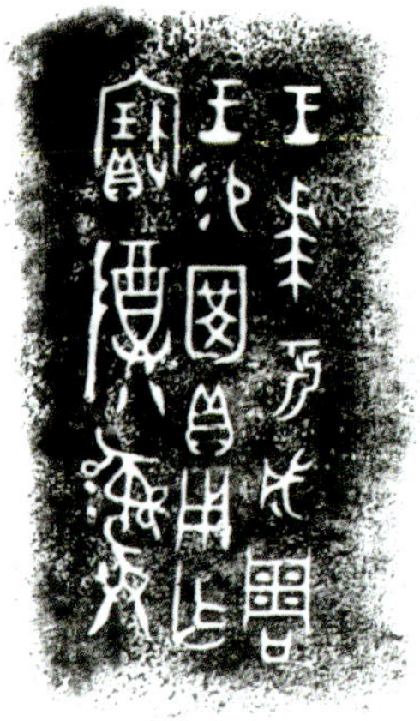

14 Inscription

16 Duke of Yan *yu*

Western Zhou early period (11th century BC)
Height 24 cm, Diameter 34 cm
Excavated at Machang gou, Kazuo County, Liaoning Province

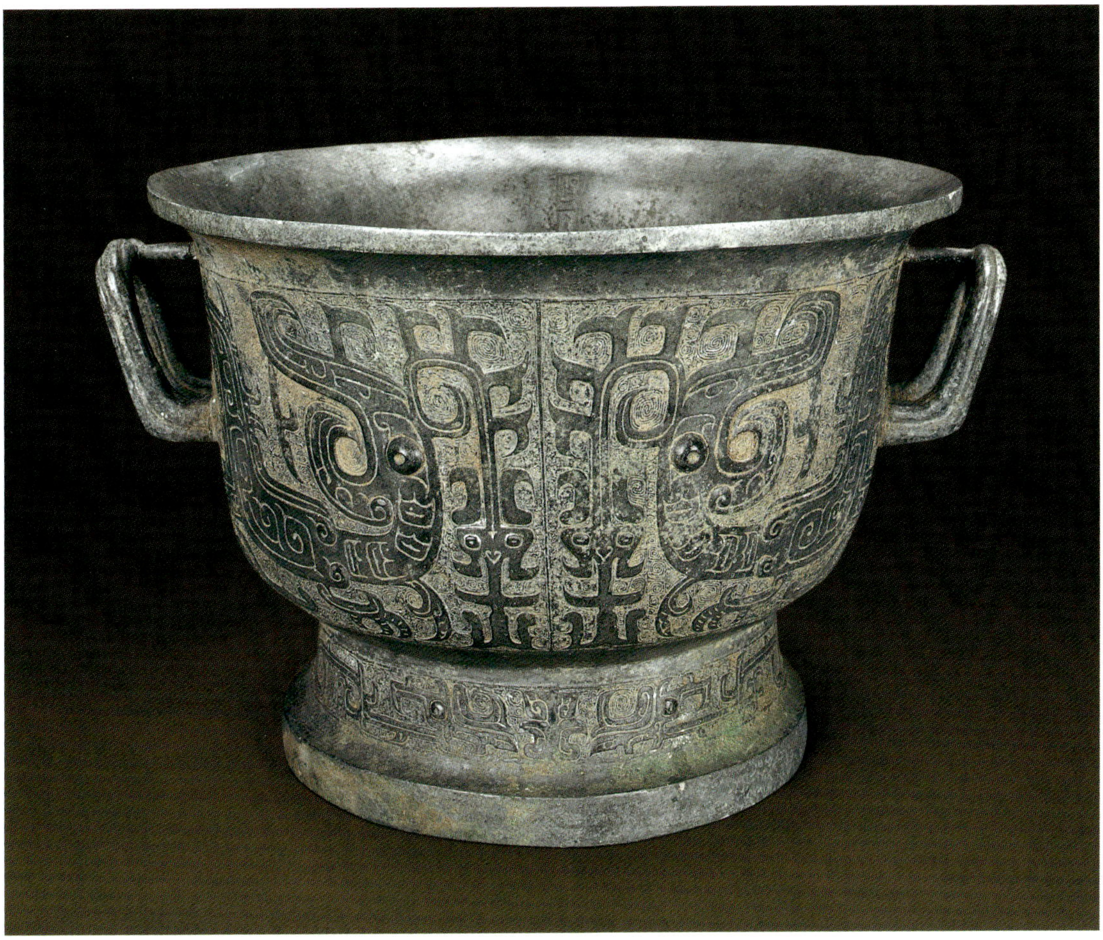

16

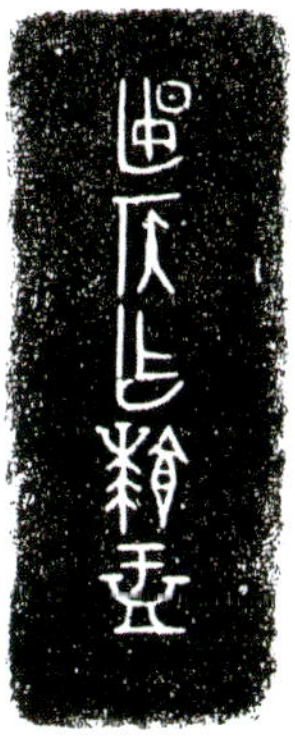

Inscription

A *Yu* is an ancient Chinese vessel used for holding cooked grain at rituals and ceremonies. This *yu* vessel has an open rim, attached handles, round feet. The main decoration is two symmetrical phoenixes, both plain and imposing. There is one line of characters carved inside the wall of the vessel, 'cooking vessel of Duke Yan'. The design of this vessel is early Western Zhou, and the inscription is similar to other *zhi* vessels excavated in the Hebei area. The *boju* vessel that was excavated around this vessel was also found in early Western Zhou tombs in Changping near Beijing. Thus it is highly likely that this *yu* vessel of the Duke of Yan was made for the second generation of Yan dukes. The discovery of a *yu* vessel belonging the Duke of Yan in the Liaoning area shows that in the early Western Zhou period, power from the Central Plains extended as far as Western Liaoning, which fits with the historical record of the Duke of Yan pursuing and attacking the Shang prince Wu Geng as he was fleeing north. Tao Liang

17 *Yu ding* ladle

Warring States period (475–221 BC)
Length 18.9 cm
Excavated at Hunyuan County, Shanxi Province

18 Inlaying silver goat-shaped *yu* vessel

Warring States period (475–221 BC)
Length 10.4 cm, Width 7.4 cm

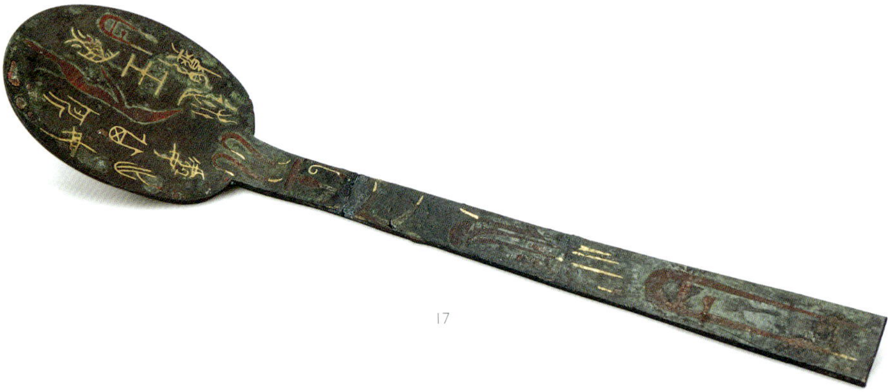

17

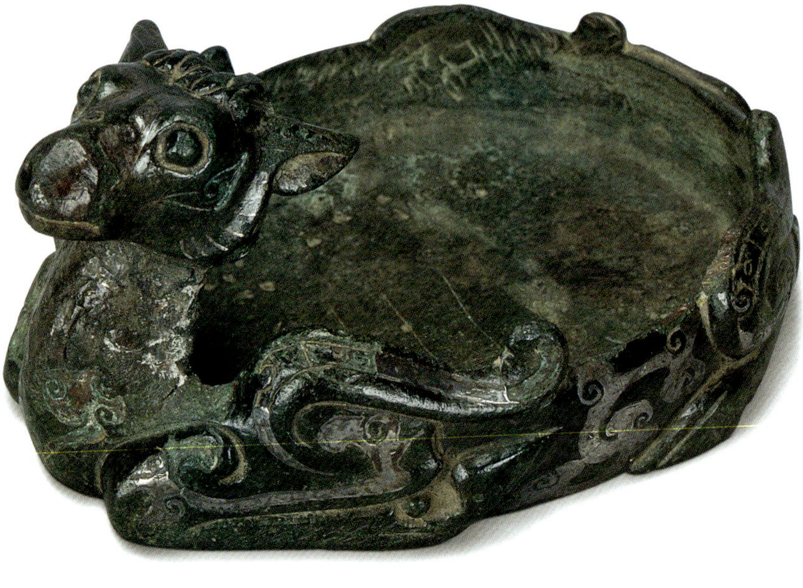

18

19 Bronze plate with human face

Late Spring and Autumn period, early Warring States (5th century BC)
Length 9.2 cm, Width 7.5 cm
Excavated at Shi'er taiyingzi, Chaoyang County, Liaoning Province

20 Large Bronze Mirror with Three Knobs

Late Spring and Autumn period, early Warring States (5th century BC)
Straight Diameter 22.8 cm, Thickness 0.8 cm
Excavated at Shi'er taiyingzi, Chaoyang County, Liaoning Province

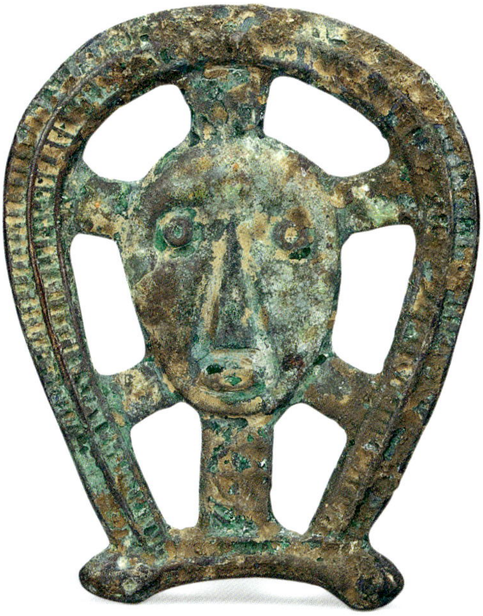

19

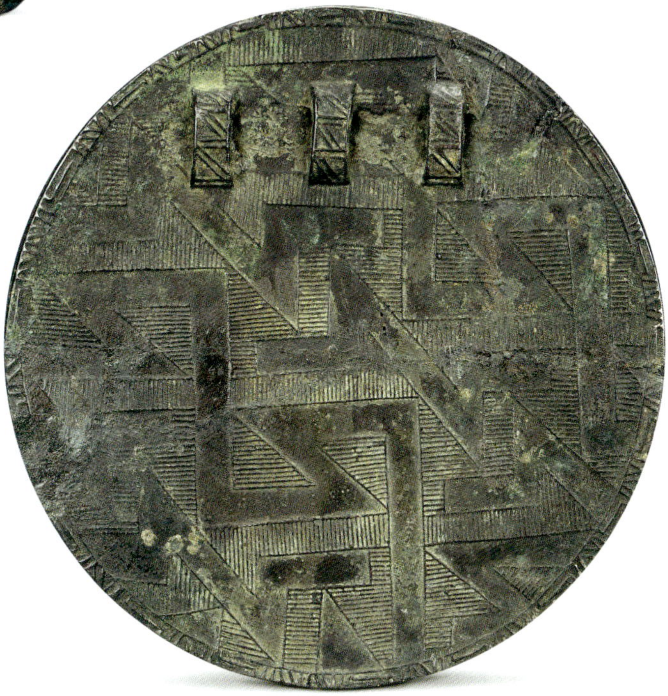

20

21 Yan King *zhi ge* (dagger-axe)

Late Warring States period
(3rd century BC)
Total Length 27.2 cm
Excavated at Dongguan yingzi, Beipiao City, Liaoning Province

22 Anguo King's Tiger fu

Warring States period (475–221 BC)
Height 1.55 cm, Length 7.8 cm, Width 2.78 cm, Weight 79.5 g

23 Second Emperor of Qin's Yuan Nian Minister *ge* dagger

Warring States period (475–221 BC)
Total Length 26.5 cm

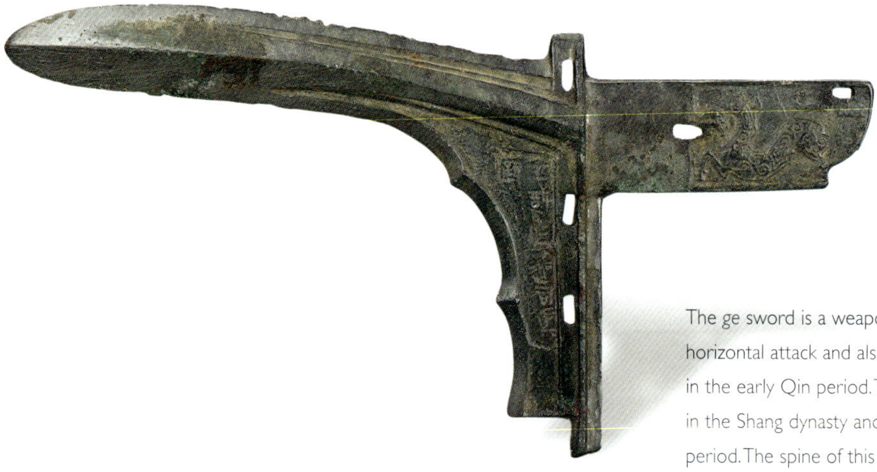

21

The ge sword is a weapon peculiar to ancient China. It can be used in horizontal attack and also for twisting; it was widely used by war chariots in the early Qin period. The origin of the ge is very early, it appeared in the Shang dynasty and was used down beyond the Warring States period. The spine of this weapon bulges slightly, both sides have a blood groove, and there are three curves on the blade. On the inside is a tiger design, done by exquisite craftsmanship. On the *hu* are seven characters, 'Yan Wang Zhi Zuo Yu Si Ma'. From the inscription it can be seen that the Zhi King of Yan ordered this weapon to be made for somebody. The inscription has been cast directly in to the weapon, different from the Warring States period convention of carving inscriptions after the weapon had been made. Some scholars believe that the Zhi King of Yan is the Zhao King of Yan recorded in history, the son of the Kuai King of Yan. Tao Liang

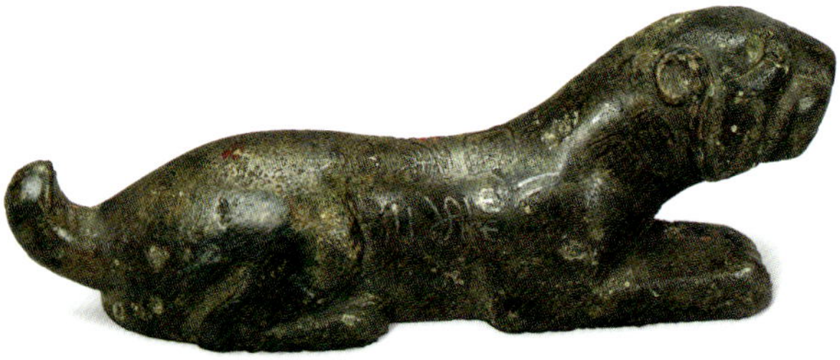

22

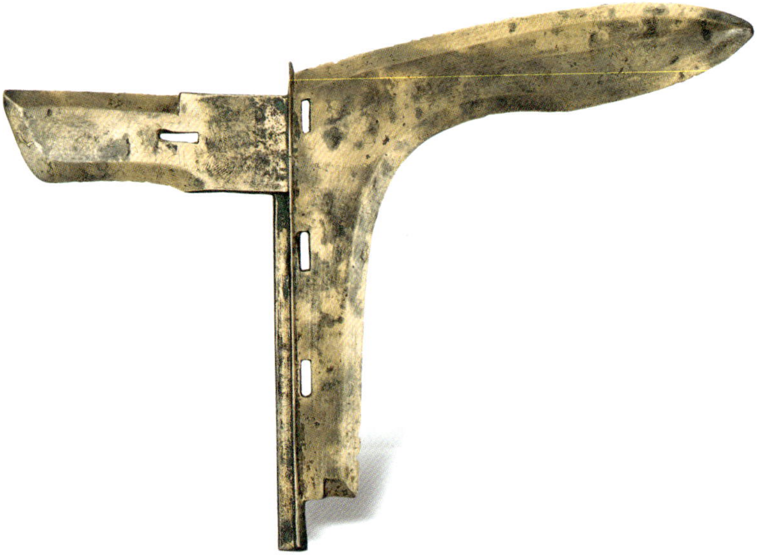

23

24 Curved-blade bronze short sword

Warring States (475–221 BC)
Total Length 46.8 cm
Excavated at Nandong gou in Kazuo County, Liaoning Province

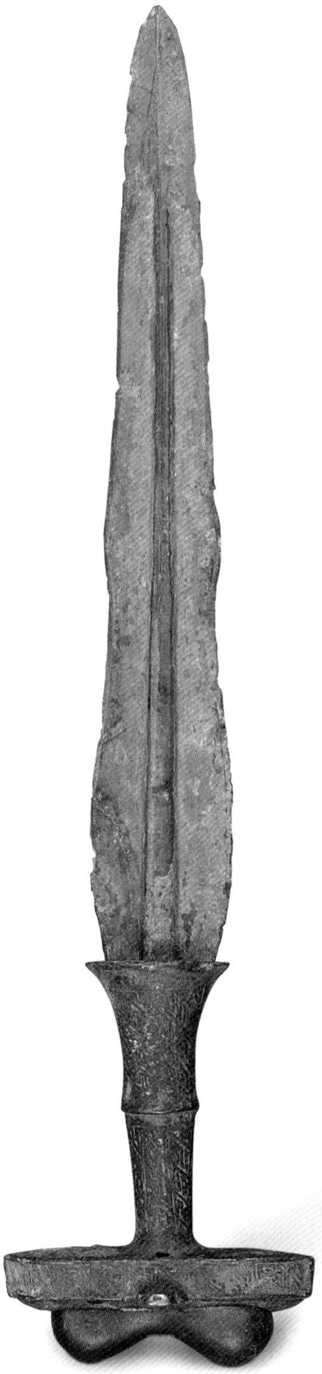

24

The sword is 'T'-shaped, the sword body has a round top and is jagged, at the centre of both sides of the blade a concave curve. The handle and body were cast separately, a short stem was inserted into a horn-shaped bronze handle, in the middle of the handle is a bamboo-shaped hoop, and a slender stone block has been added on the flat plate on the top of the handle to add weight, made from a strong black metal ore. This kind of sword with a curved blade is particular to ancient northeast Asia. The group of people who used a short sword of this shape was complex and varied, including many types of ancient races who might have used this weapon such as the Donghu, the Shanzei, Hui and Mo. TAO LIANG

25 Skate fish shaped ornament

Warring States period (475–221 BC)
Length 11 cm, Width 13 cm
Excavated at Nandong gou, Kazuo County, Liaoning Province

26 Bronze pieces decorated with snake holding frog in the mouth

Warring States period (475–221 BC)
Length 20 cm, Width 5.7 cm
Excavated at Sanguan dianzi, Lingyuan City, Liaoning Province

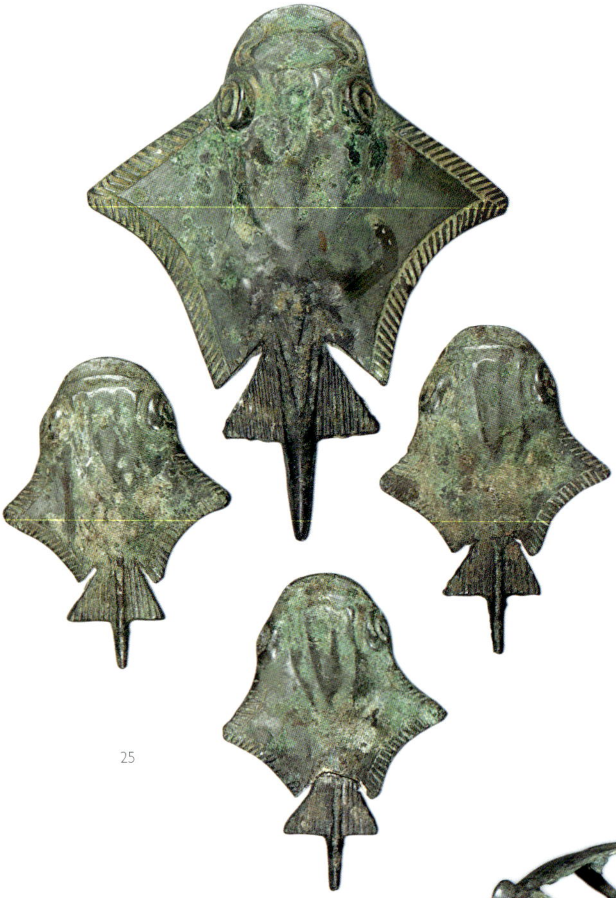

25

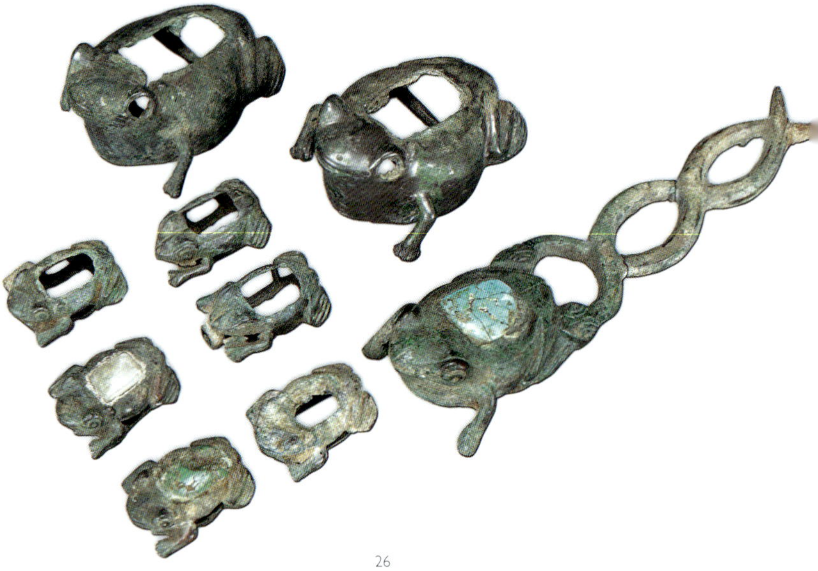

26

27 a: Gilded bronze decorative plaque with twin goat pattern
b: Bronze decorative plaque with tiger eating rabbit
c: Bronze plate decorated with a figure on horseback against a captive
d: Bronze decorative plaque with wolf and horse fighting

Western Han (206–8 BC)
Length 10~12 cm, Width 4~5 cm
Excavated at Xicha Gorge, Xifeng County, Liaoning Province

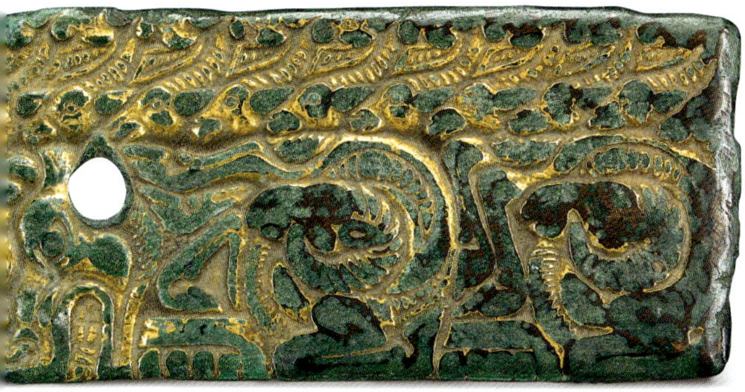

27 a

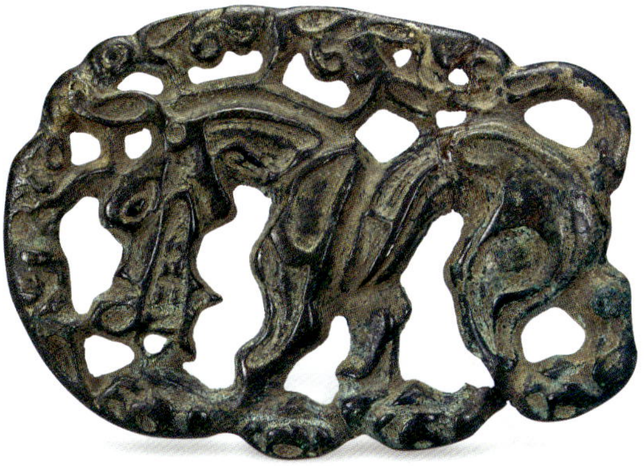

27 b

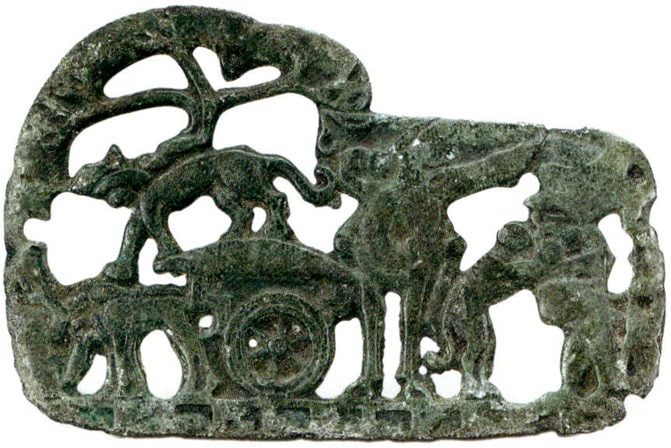

27 c

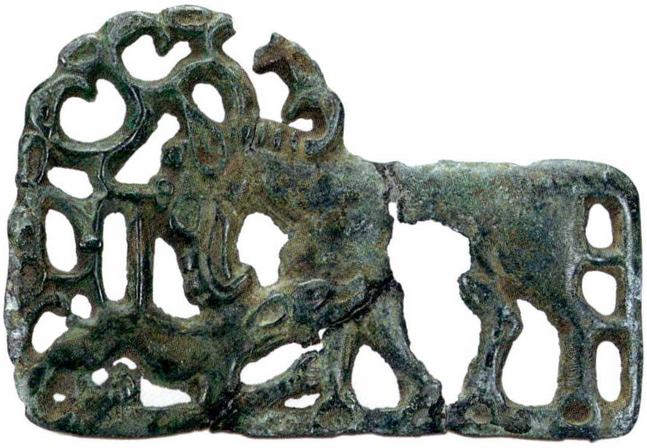

27 d

28 Yu Yang Palace bronze *shu dou*

Western Han (206–8 BC)
Length 36.6 cm, Width of spoon 4.5 cm.

29 *Zhonggong* goose-foot light

Western Han Jianzhao 3rd year (36 BC)
Height 69.4 cm, Base Diameter 21.4 cm, Light Diameter 19.9 cm

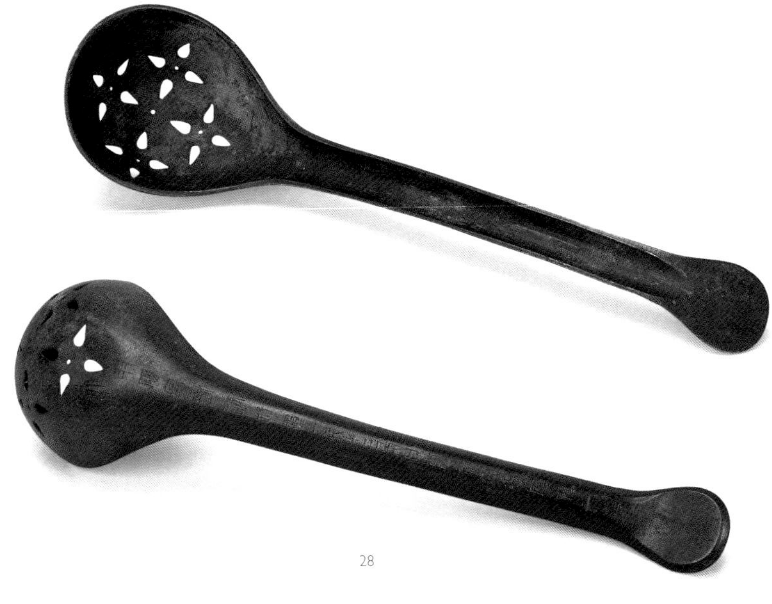

28

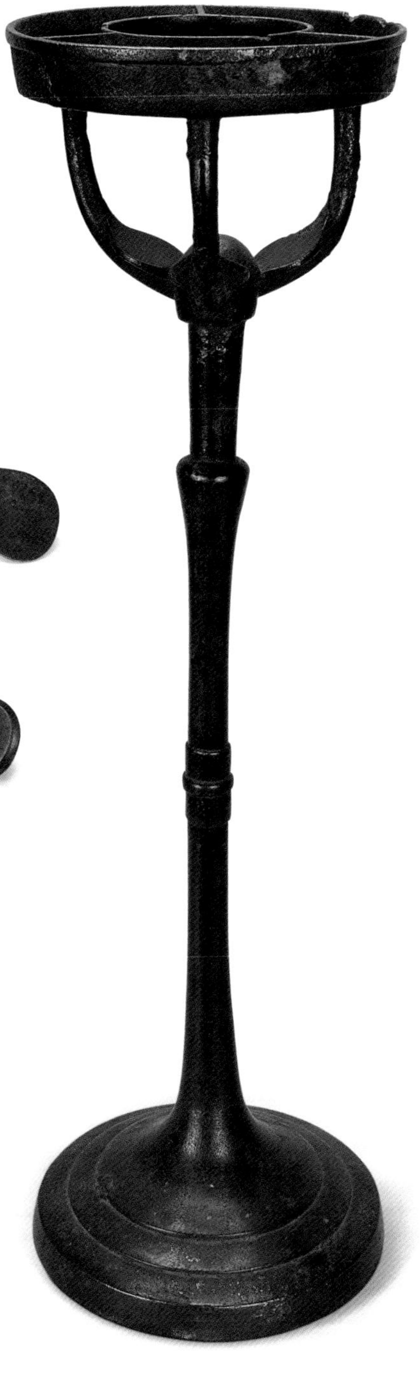

29

30 Yidao official measure

Eastern Han (23–220)
Height 24.5, Diameter 35 cm, Base Diameter 34 cm, Handle Length 8 cm

31 'Yongxing yuan year' fish and bird pattern washing utensil

Eastern Han Yongxing yuan year (153)
Height 22.3 cm, Diameter 47 cm, Body Diameter 40.4 cm, Base Diameter 27 cm

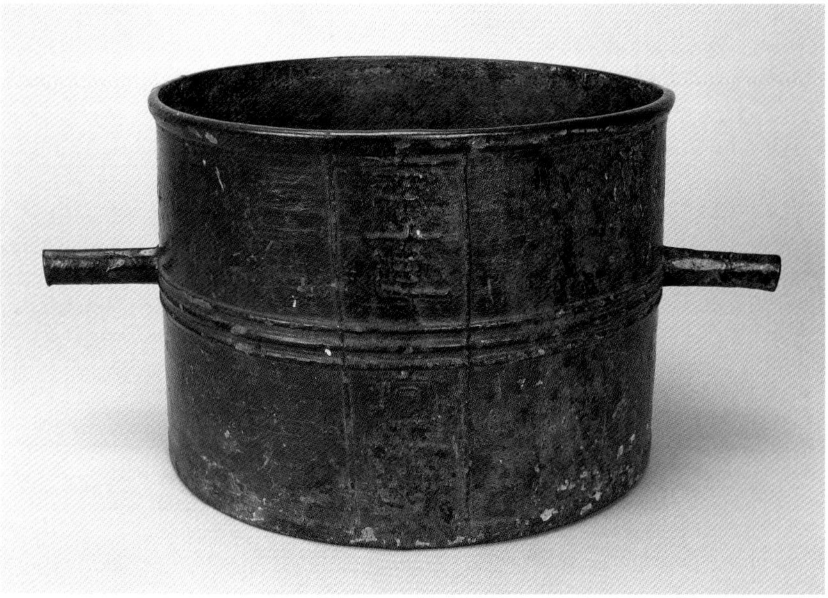

30

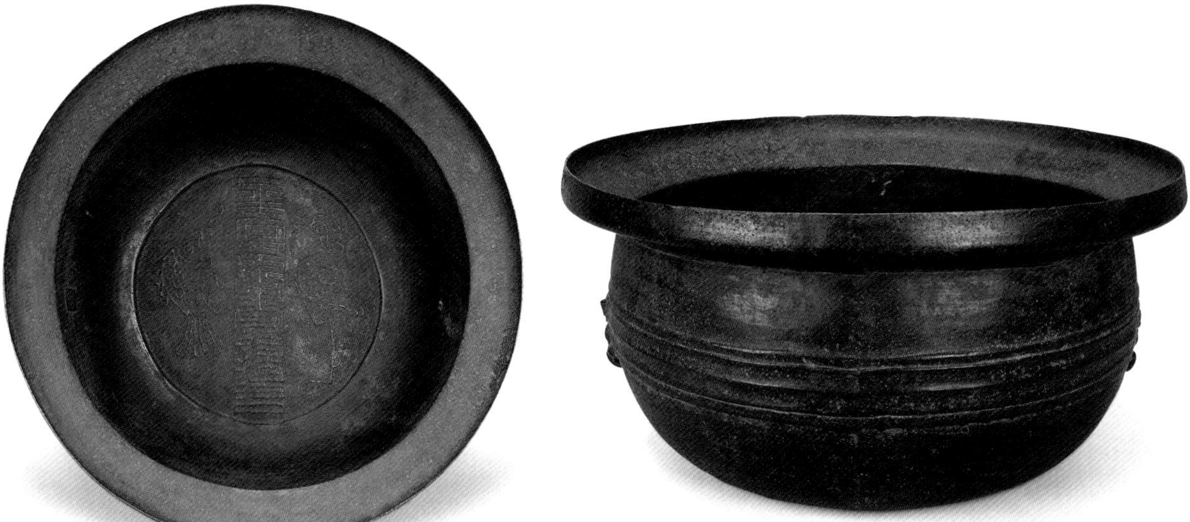

31

32 a: Gold-plated bronze crown
b: Gold-plated bronze shoe sole

Latter years of Western Han (1st century BC)
a: Height 38 cm, Width 57 cm
b: Length 33.4 cm
Excavated at Gaojuli tombs, Ji'an City, Jilin Province

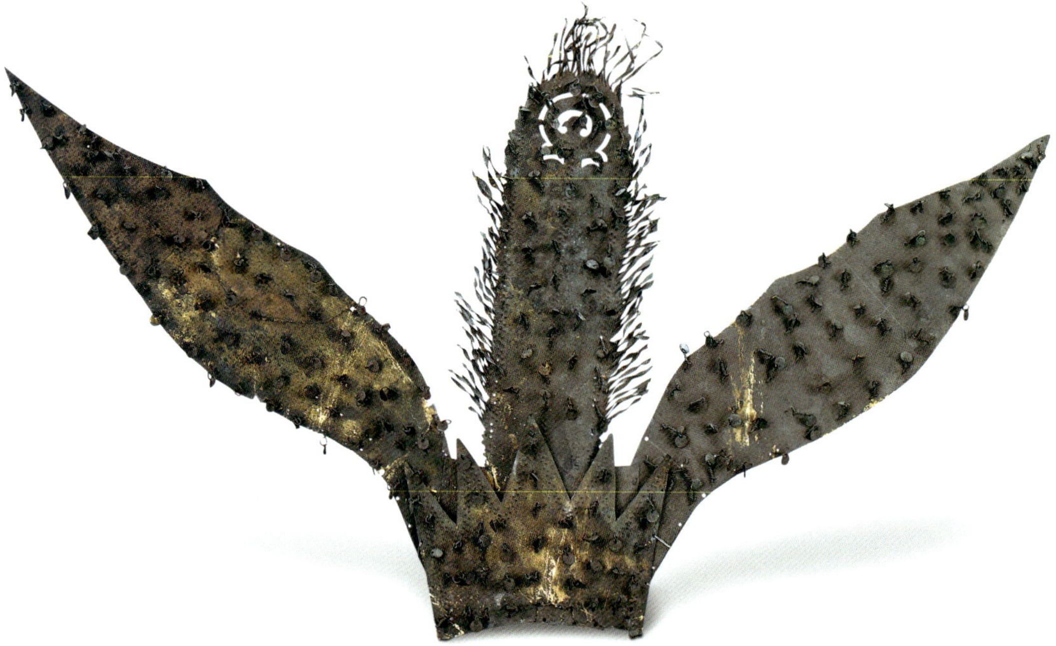

32 a

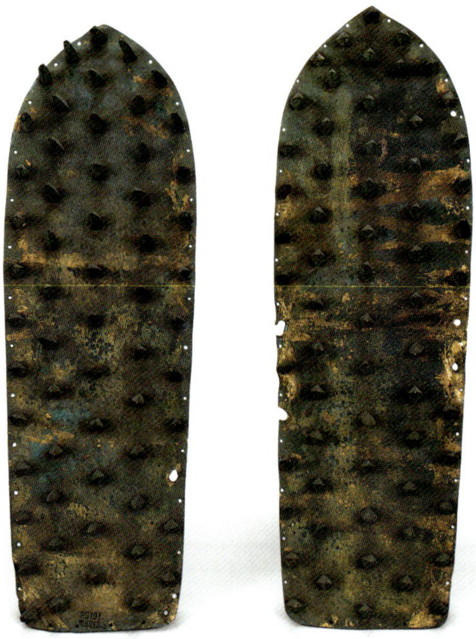

32 b

33 Bronze tiger

Northern Yan (409–436)
Length 36 cm
Excavated in 1965 at Fengsufu tomb, Beipiao City, Liaoning Province

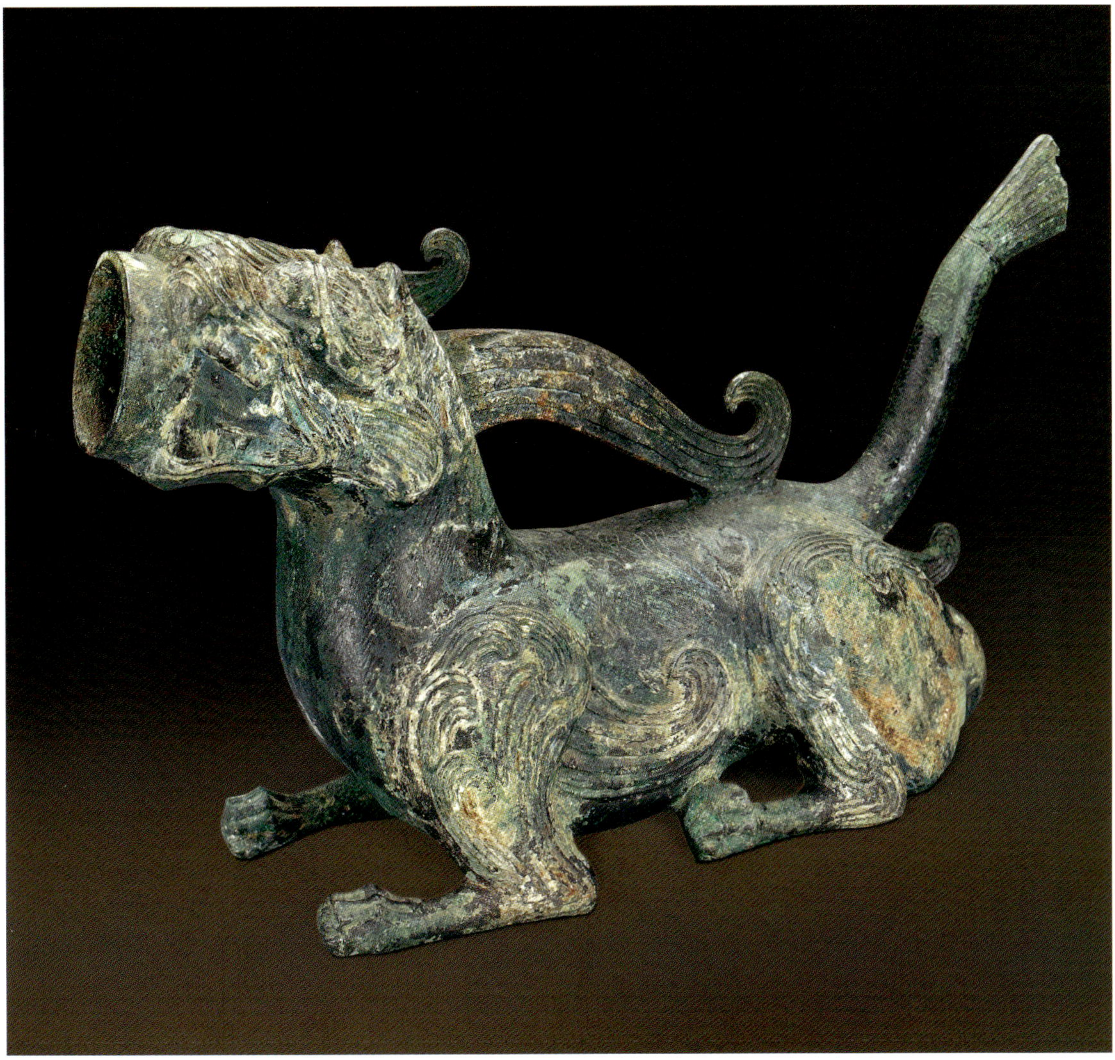

33

34 Large bronze mirror with dragon and cloud patterns

Liao (916–1125)
Diameter 38.5 cm, Thickness 1.9 cm
Excavated at Tazishan Liao stupas digongm, Fuxin City, Liaoning Province

35 Mirror with Kalavinka pattern

Liao (916–1125)
Diameter 22.8 cm, Thickness 0.2 cm
Excavated at Zhangjia yingzi, Jianping County, Liaoning Province

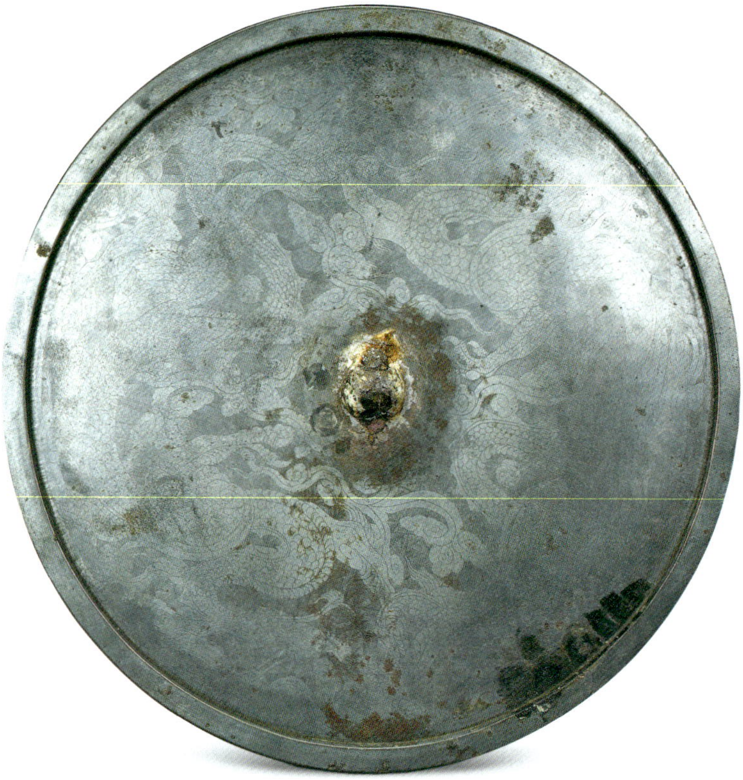

34

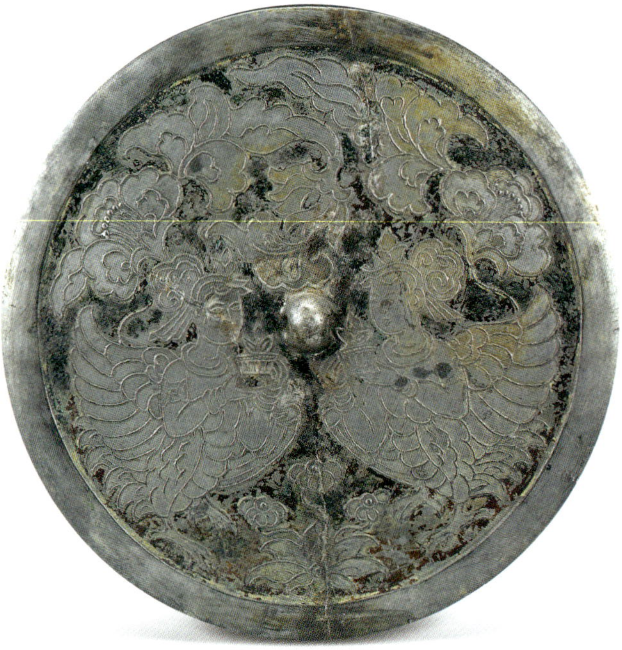

35

36 Lu Bu Bell

Northern Song (960–1127)
Height 180 cm, Diameter 81 cm

37 Large *sheng* southern Lü chiming bell

Northern Song Chongning 4th year (1105)
Total Height 28 cm, Diameter 18.4 cm x 15 cm

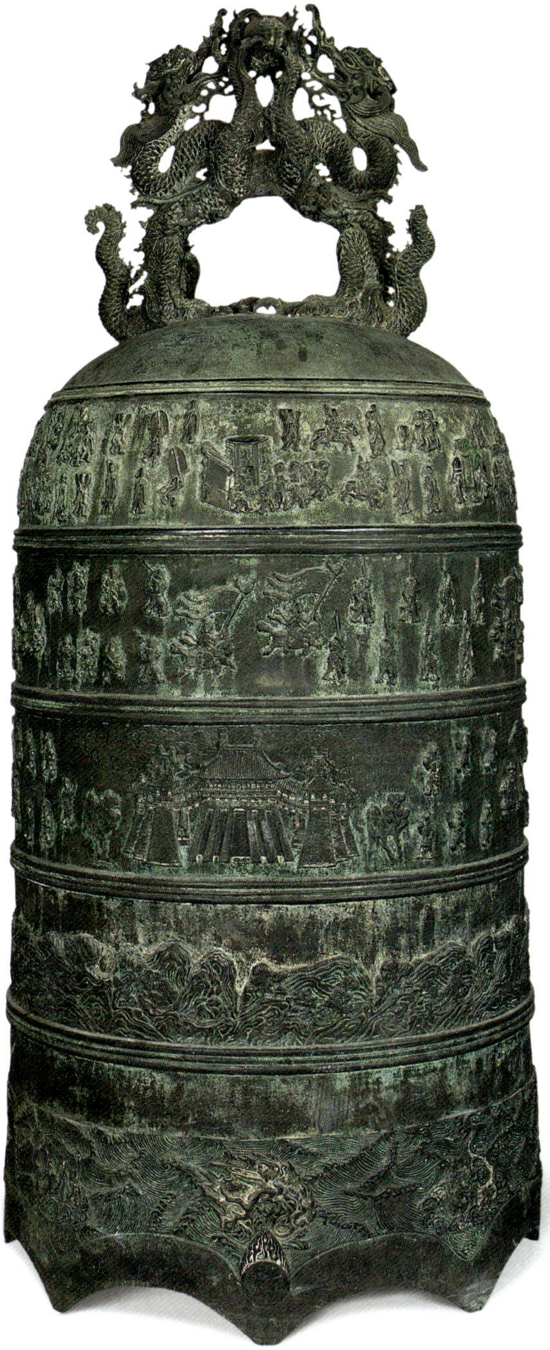

36

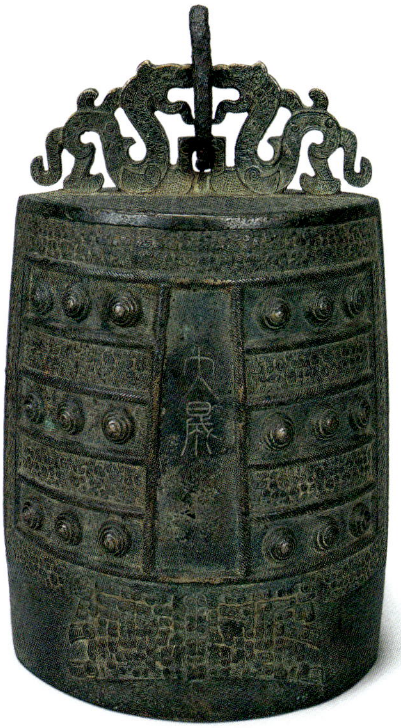

37

6

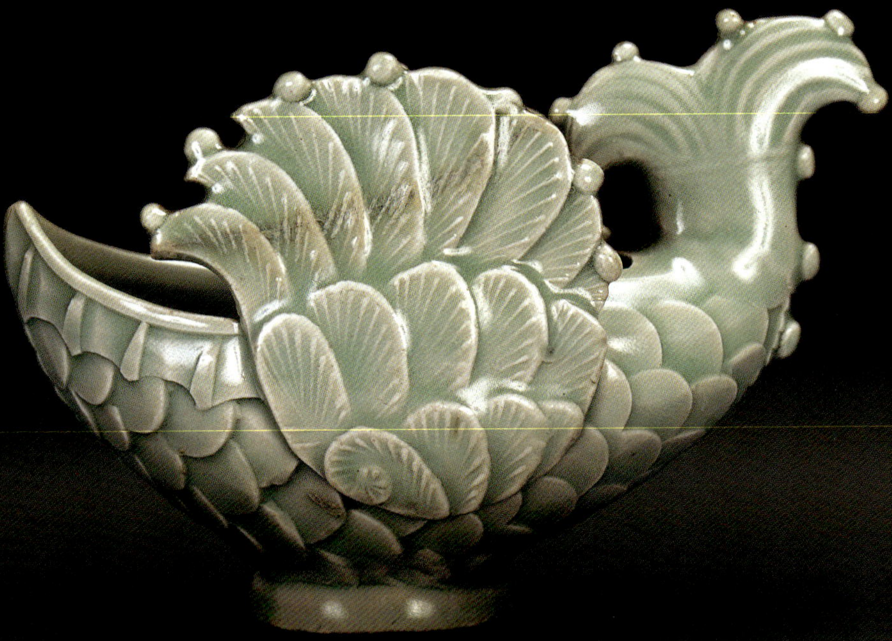

Ceramics

Ceramics play an important role in the story of Chinese art and culture. As objects to satisfy the needs of everyday life, or for aesthetic enjoyment, ceramics not only represent the scientific achievements of each period, but also contain rich cultural traditions, providing the beholder with great beauty and cultural depth. The ceramic collection at the Liaoning Provincial Museum encompasses the entire millennia-old history of ceramics in China. The collection includes coloured pottery from the Neolithic Age, ceramics from the Liao and Jin periods, and Jingdezhen ceramics from the Yuan, Ming and Qing periods.

The objects with the most local interest in the collection date from the Liao period, and occupy an important position among Liao-period ceramic collections in Chinese museums. Liao-period ceramics refer to objects produced by the northern nomadic Khitan people who founded the Liao dynasty, also called 'Liao pottery', which has a special position in the history of Chinese ceramics, and provides an important resource for researching Khitan Culture. Most of the ceramics in the Liaoning Museum have been handed down over the centuries, but there are also plenty of objects from recent archaeological excavations. There are many single-coloured glazed ceramics (white, yellow and green glazes), three-coloured *sancai*, white porcelain, dark reddish-brown porcelain, and white background black flowers. Common decorative techniques include carving, marking, painting, stamping, sticking. The design of certain objects was subject to influence from the Central Plains, such as bowls, dishes, jars, pots, whereas others have more local characteristics of the Khitan, such as the pilgrim bottle (called cockscomb-shaped kettle in Chinese), phoenix head bottles, long-neck bottles, chicken's-leg jar, oblong 'begonia' (*haitang*) dishes and square dishes. Among these, the cockscomb-shaped water vessels are most typical of Khitan design in Liao pottery. These were developed from leather skin objects, and the name comes from the cord tied through the top part that looks like a rooster's crest. With the development of Liao history, this style also underwent profound changes, reflecting the characteristics of each age. Such rich collections have provided a valuable resource for researching the evolution of the Liao cockscomb-shaped water vessel. Liao *sancai* are yellow, green and white low-temperature glaze, and developed from the basic Tang dynasty *sancai*. However, both the decorative technique and design of the object are considerably different from Tang *sancai*. Compared to the bright beauty of Tang *sancai*, Liao *sancai* has a clearer, more elegant style.

The production of ceramics in the Ming and Qing dynasties was mainly centred on Jingdezhen, and the quality and variety is superior to ceramics from other dynasties. Ming dynasty blue and white porcelain was most famous in the Yongle and Xuande reigns. The artistic techniques of Qing-dynasty coloured porcelain reached new heights during the Kangxi, Yongzheng and Qianlong periods. The Liaoning Provincial Museum has a rich and varied collection of Ming and Qing ceramics, a large proportion of which is from official kilns, ranging from Qing new elegant white and blue porcelain, red glaze and single glaze to brightly coloured pottery. This not only reflects the deep appreciation of ceramics of each generation of the Ming and Qing emperors and their palace lifestyles, but also the brilliance and creativity of the artists. Although there are only few ceramics in the museum collection from places other than Jingdezhen, those such as Dehua white porcelain, *guangcai* and *longquan* blue porcelain also reflect the brilliance of Chinese ancient ceramic art. Liu Li

1 Jar with coloured spout

Shang (16th–11th century BC)
Height 27.3 cm, Diameter 7.4 cm, Base Diameter 8 cm
Excavated in 1976 from early Bronze Culture tomb at Aohan Dadianzi, Inner Mongolia Autonomous Region

2 Coloured *li* with *taotie* design

Shang (16th–11th century BC)
Height 24.4 cm, Diameter 16 cm
Excavated in 1976 from early Bronze Culture tomb at Aohan Dadianzi, Inner Mongolia Autonomous Region

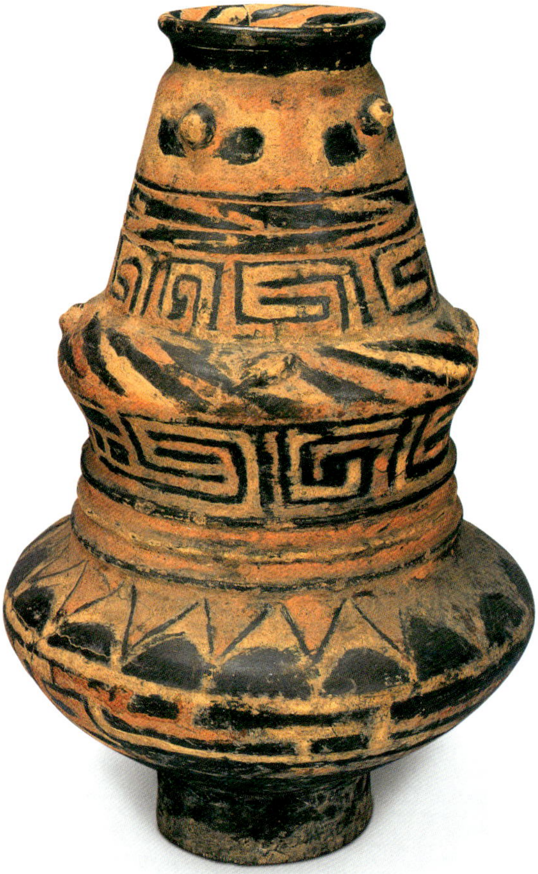

1

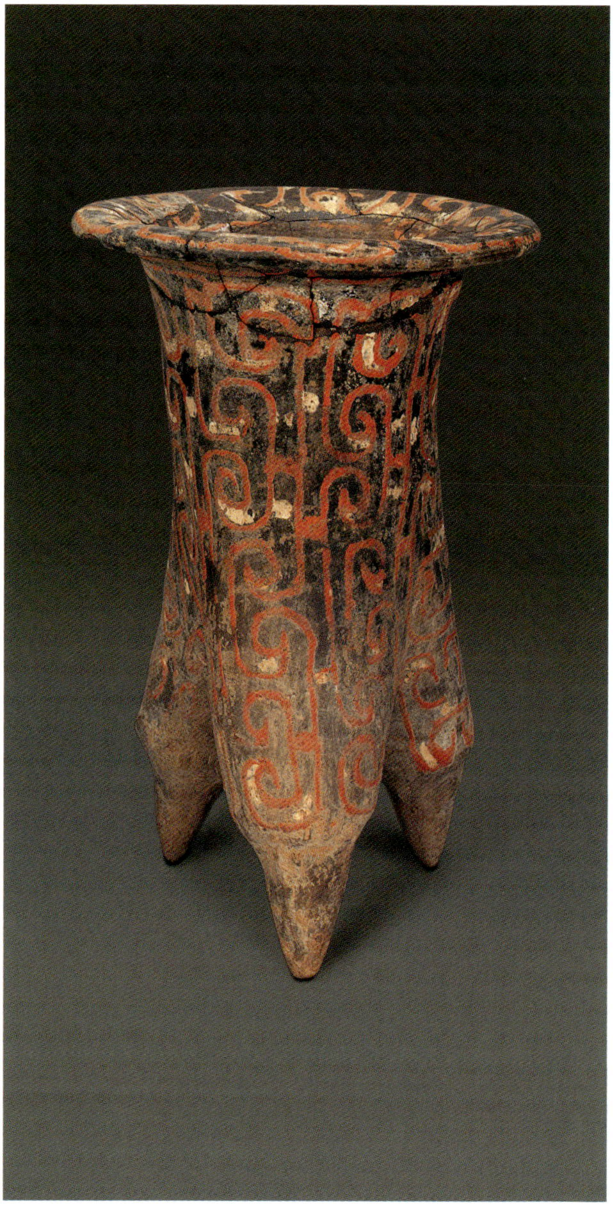

2

3 Green glazed pot dog

Eastern Han (AD 25–220)
Height 33.5 cm, Length 37 cm

4 Green ceramic animal pot

Three states (AD 220–265)
Height 19 cm, Length 25.4 cm, Diameter 7.4 cm

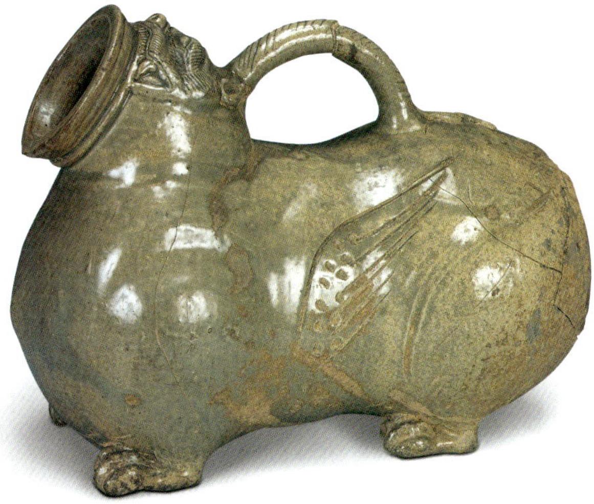

4

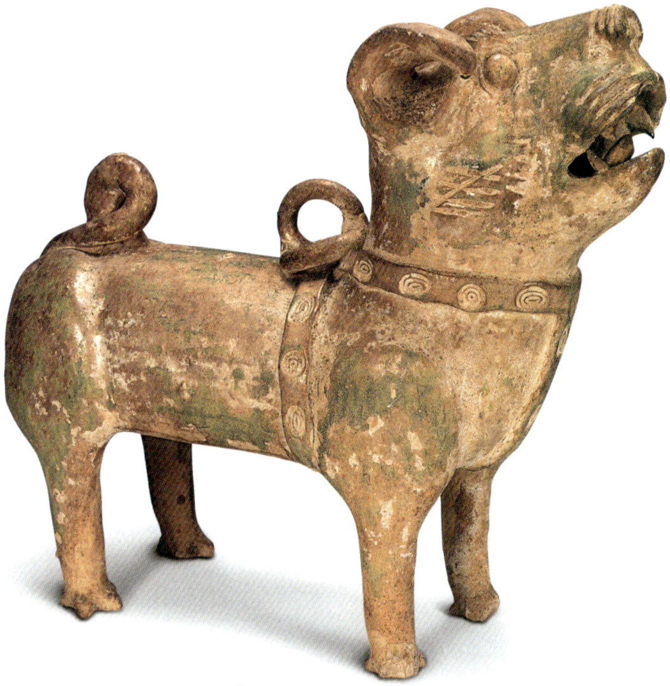

3

5 Colour-glazed jar tripod with cloud and dragon design

Tang (AD 618–907)
Height 17.8 cm, Rim Diameter 14.2 cm, Base Diameter 7 cm
Excavated in 1972 from Hanzhen tomb in Chaoyang City, Liaoning Province

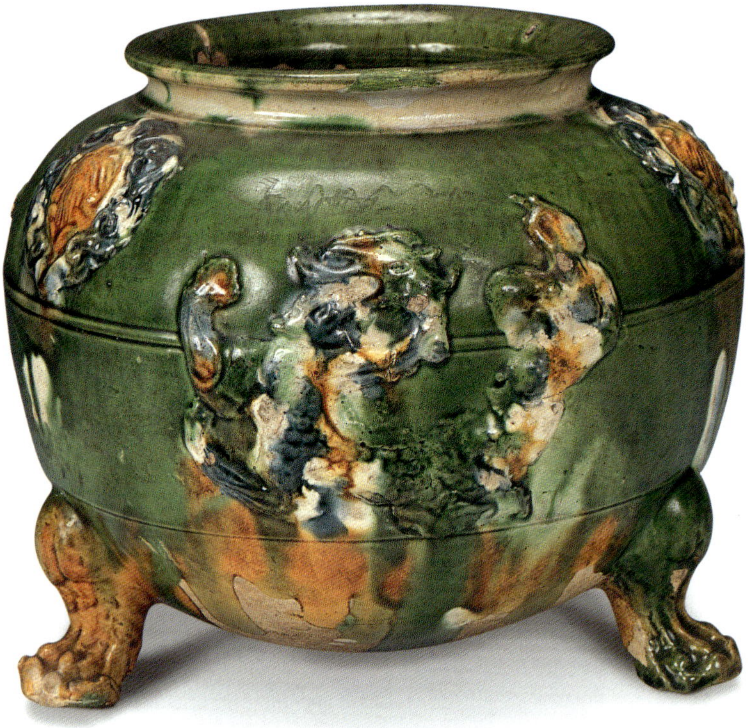

5

The rim of the tripod slightly protrudes outwards, with a rolled lip, a short neck, broad shoulders, round body and a small flat base to which are attached three feet in the shape of animal hooves. The pottery body is pink, with white slip coating on top, a green, yellow, white, blue *sancai* glaze applied, with no glaze on the inside of the object. The shoulder and body have protruding patterns. The whole vessel has been produced with an added mould technique. The shoulder has three equidistant groups of similar fire pearl designs. The body has three groups of identical dragon patterns. They have high heads, tails pointing upwards, completely upright, as if about to fly up to the sky, racing straight up with fire pearls and proud ferocious expression. The design of the whole object is ancient and simple, with a stable bearing, lively decoration, bright colours and precious glaze. It is a masterpiece of High Tang *sancai* art. Liu Li

6 Colour-glazed figure on horseback

Tang (AD 618–907)
Total Height 41.3 cm, Total Length 36 cm

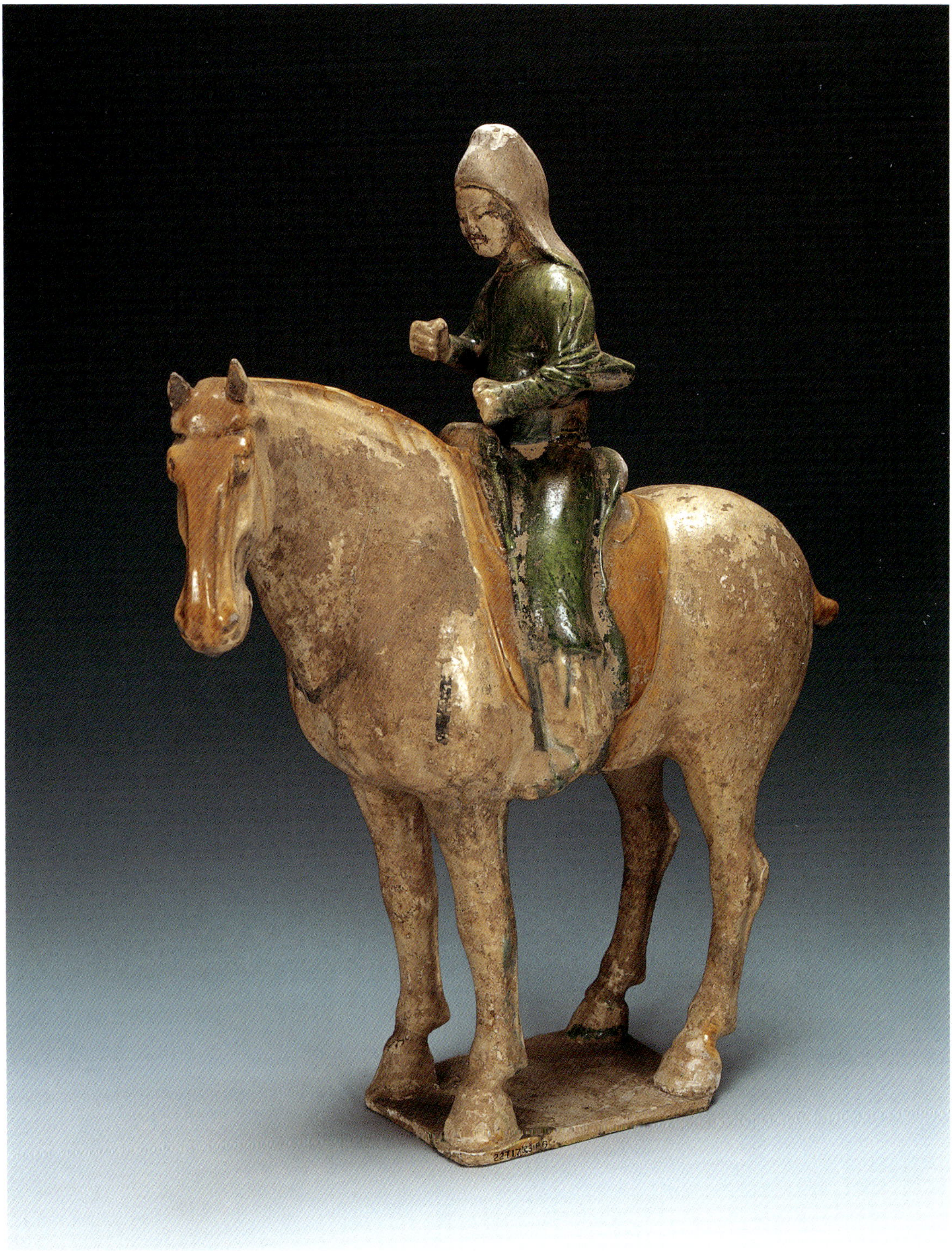

7 *Xing Kiln* white porcelain low-bodied horizontal bridge cockscomb-shaped water vessel

Late Tang to Five Dynasties (AD 618–960)
Height 17 cm, Diameter 2.9 cm, Body Diameter 15.3 x 15.1 cm

8 Yaozhou green *yu* (water vessel) in shape of flying fish

Five Dynasties (907–960)
Height 9.3 cm, Length 14 cm, Width 7.4 cm
Excavated in 1973 from Shuiquan Liao tombs at Beipiao City, Liaoning Province

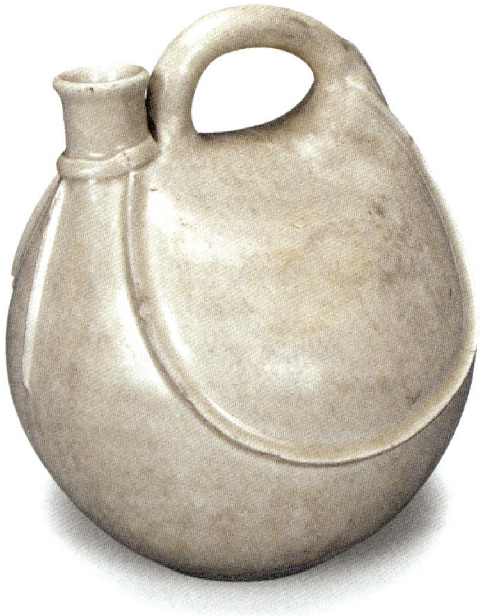

7

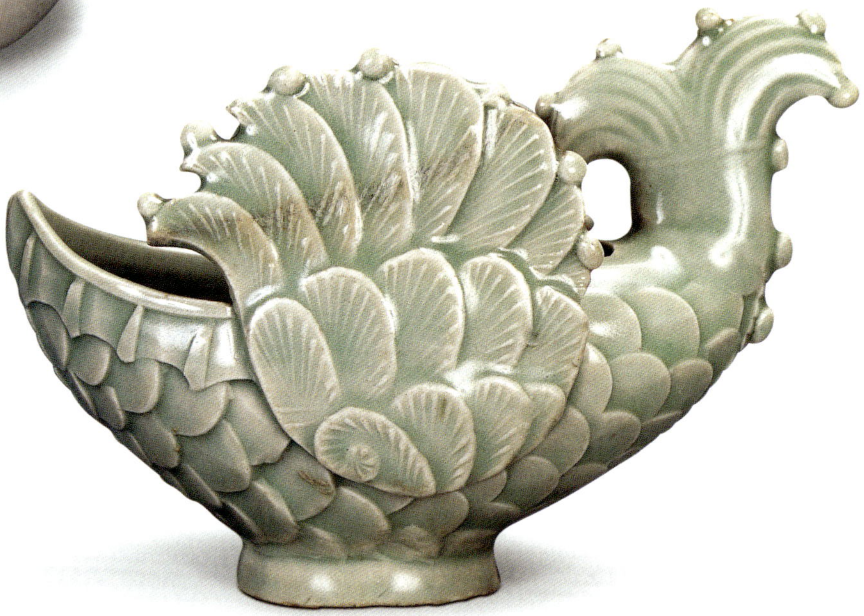

8

The design of the object is of a flying fish (dragon fish), turning upwards, with two wings flying upwards, the fish tail is the upper wing, making a U-shape, the inside of the vessel is divided into front and back sections, with a small round base on the bottom. It is white porcelain and the casting quality is fine and hard. The vessel is glazed in green on the inside and outside, the glaze colour is smooth and clear, with no glaze on the foot. The whole vessel has been produced from relief sculpture, the fish scales and wings are very realistic. Both wings and the tail have drops of water stuck on, showing that the fish is jumping out of the water. The shape of the vessel is beautiful and balanced, also with a realistic, lively effect. The vessel has a unique, refined design, showing off the skill and artistic flair of the artist. Liu Li

9 Jun kiln sky-blue photochromic glaze tripod censer with animal ears and ringed mouth

Song (AD 960–1279)
Height 17.7 cm, Body Diameter 20 cm, Rim Diameter 17.9 cm

10 Green glazed plum vase

Northern Song (AD 960–1127)
Height 39.7 cm, Base Diameter 10.6 cm, Rim Diameter 5.7 cm
Excavated in 1981 at Sanjiatun, Fengshan village, Heishuizhen, Jilin Province

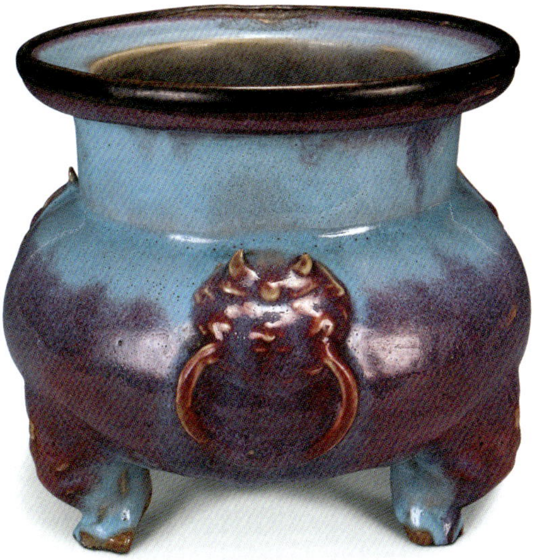

9

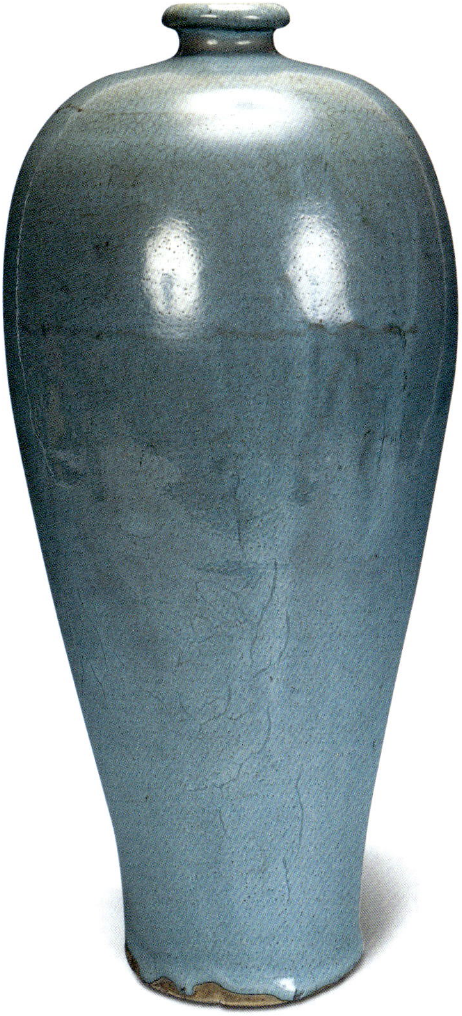

10

11 Green glazed cockscomb-shaped water vessel with round dragon and chrysanthemum design

Liao (AD 916–1125)
Height 29.5 cm, Diameter 5.9 cm, Base Diameter 9.5 x 8.9 cm

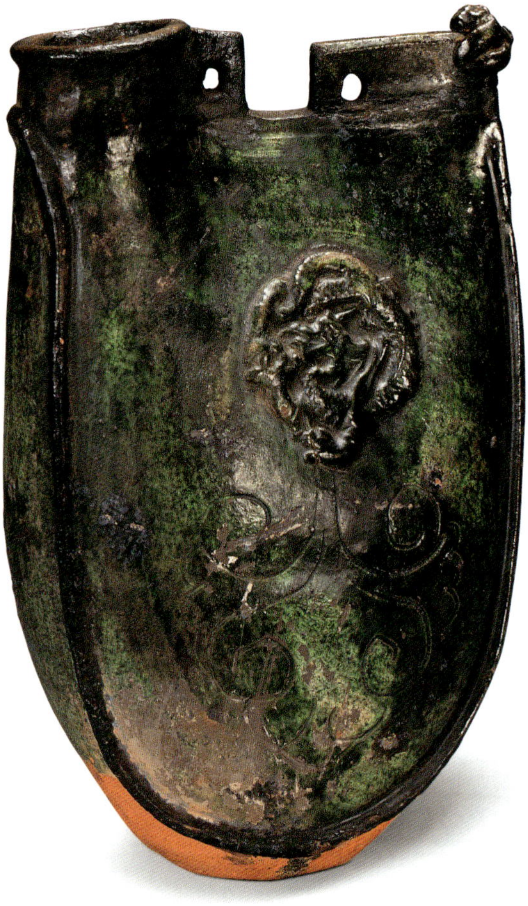

11

This pot has a flat, tall body, with a funnelled mouth, round lips, two holes for tying to a horse saddle, a red pottery casting, and an elliptical base with a slight inner curve, white coating, with green glazing. A decorative ridge has been stuck on both sides, one side has a round dragon design imprinted on it, the other side has a flowing chrysanthemum design and cloud patterns, the hole at the back has a figure attached to it. This vessel has been decorated with different techniques, including stamping, appliqué, incising and painting. The patterns are lively in a strong realistic style, and the artist has put decorations of people, animals and plants together. The design is fine, well arranged, showing the high level of skill of Liao ceramic artists. The rooster-crested pot is the most representative work of the Liao period, and best represents the objects made by steppe peoples. It gets its name from the holes on top through which string is tied that looks like the crest of a rooster, and it comes from the leather drinking flask that tribes on horseback would use. Over the course of Liao history, the style of the rooster-crest flask changed considerably in that there were ones with handles as well as string tied through. This cockscomb-shaped vessel is a treasure among such Liao period objects. LIU LI

12 Dark brown glazed single-hole cockscomb-shaped kettle

Liao (AD 916–1125)
Total Height 25.2 cm, Body Diameter 20.5 × 17.2 cm, Rim Diameter 5 cm
Excavated in 1974 from Liao tomb number 7, Yemaotai, Faku County, Liaoning Province

13 Three-coloured glaze round-handled cockscomb-shaped water vessel

Liao (AD 916–1125)
Height 39 cm, Body Diameter 13.6 cm, Base Diameter 8.4 cm

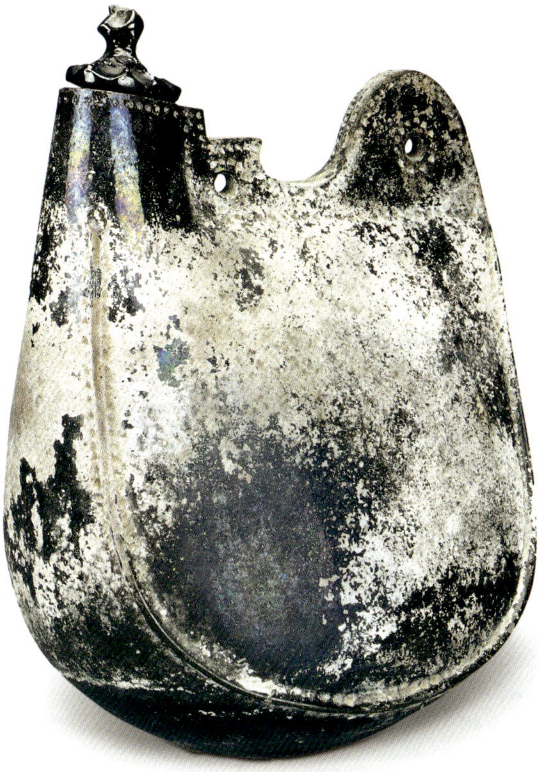

12

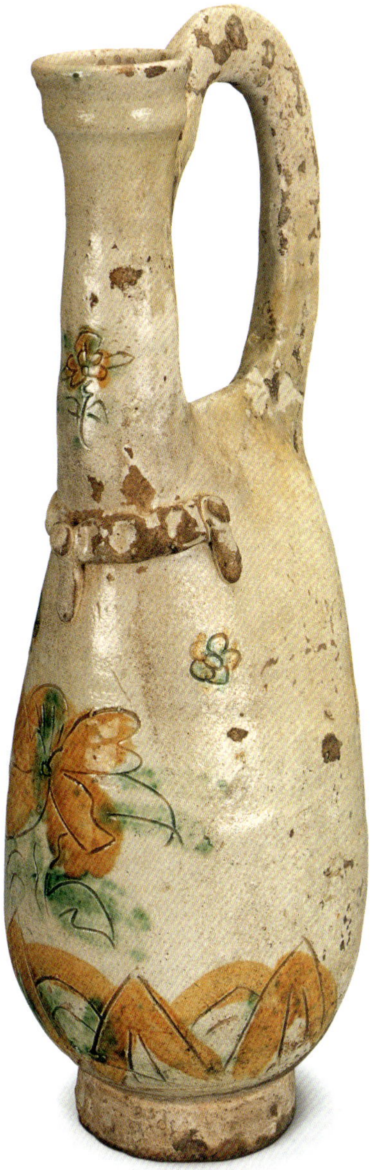

13

14 Gold rimmed white porcelain dish with *guan* character ('official')

Liao (AD 916–1125)
Height 4.6 cm, Rim Diameter 15.6 cm, Base Diameter 9.8 cm
Excavated in 1974 at Liao tomb number 7, Yamaotai, Faku County, Liaoning Province

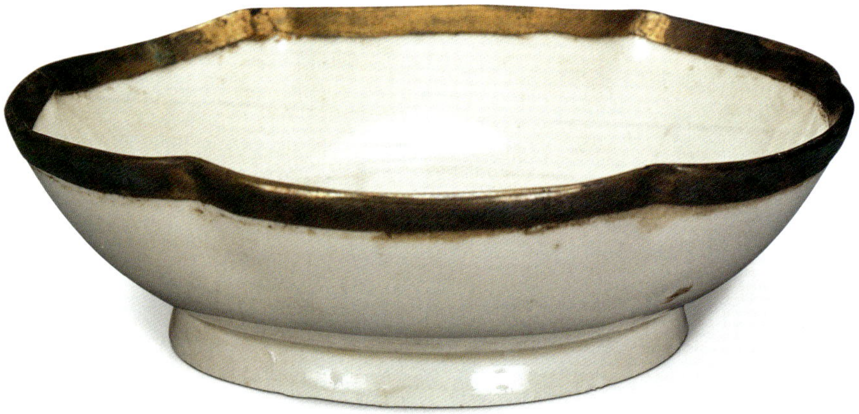

14

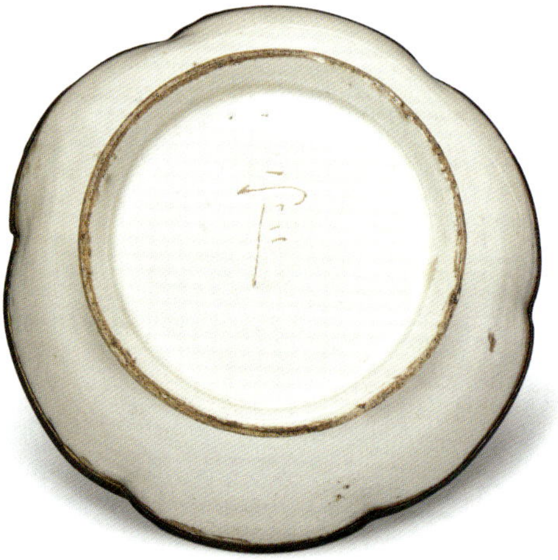

Inscription on base

15 Green glazed vase with phoenix head

Liao (AD 916–1125)
Height 52 cm, Base Diameter 10.4 cm,
Rim Diameter 11.6 cm
Excavated from Liao tomb number 2
Qinghemen, Fuxin City, Liaoning Province

16 White glazed vase with cut-decoration with peony design

Liao (AD 916–1125)
Height 45.6 cm, Rim Diameter 11.4 cm, Base Diameter 10.4 cm
Excavated in 1974 at Liao tomb number 7, Yamaotai, Faku County,
Liaoning Province

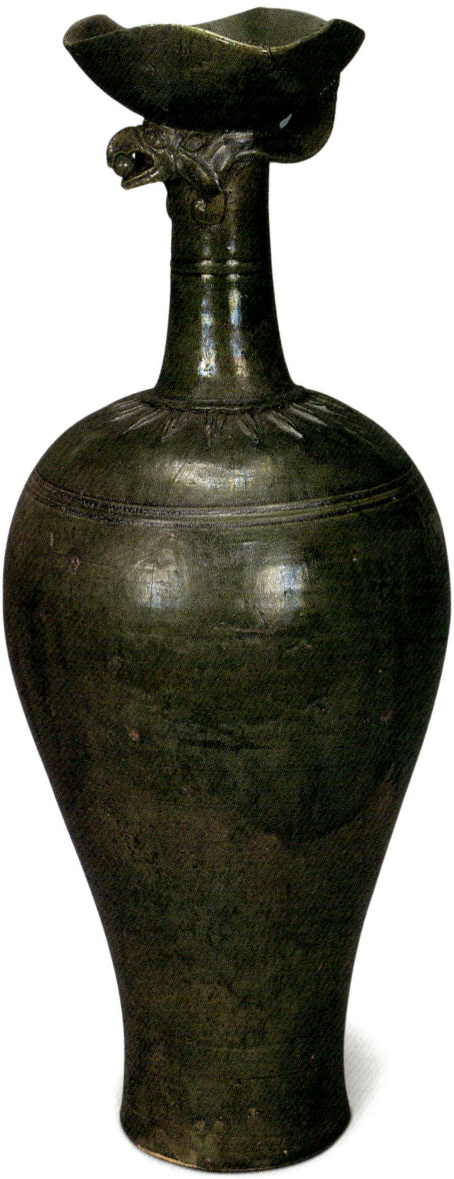

15

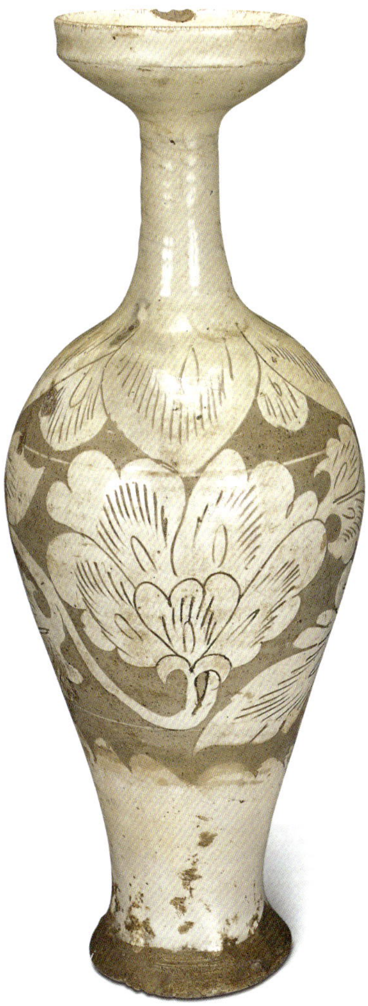

16

17 Yellow glazed gourd-shaped pot

Liao (AD 916–1125)
Height 25.6 cm, Rim Diameter 3.1 cm,
Base Diameter 7.8 cm

18 Yellow glazed long necked vase with peony design

Liao (AD 916–1125)
Height 36.6 cm, Rim Diameter 10.3 cm, Base Diameter 8.2 cm

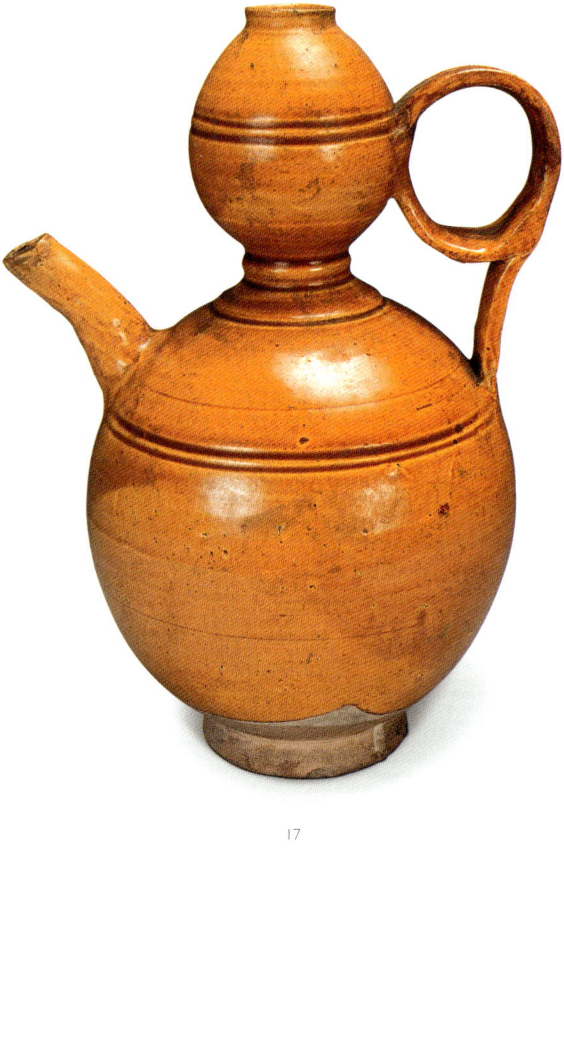

17

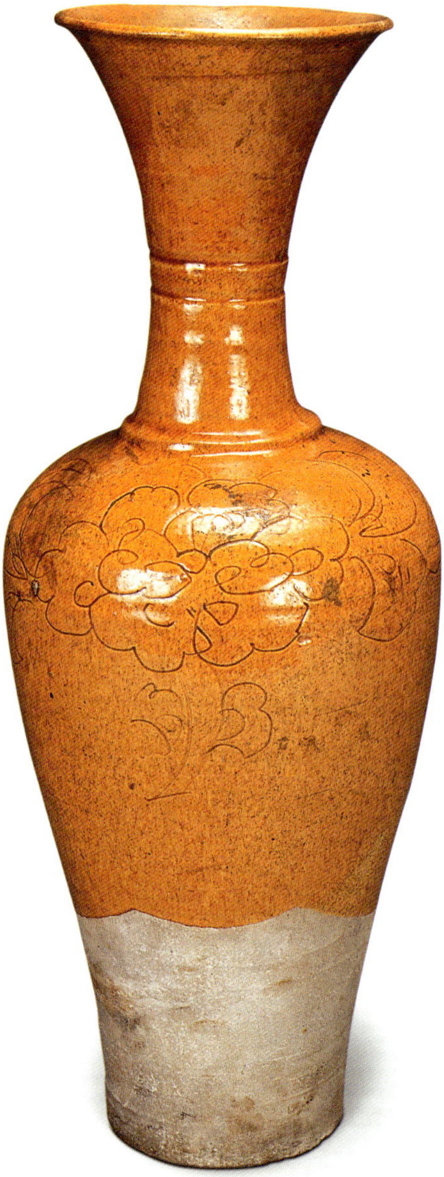

18

19 White porcelain iron-coloured crouching tiger shaped pillow

Liao (AD 916–1125)
Height 14 cm, Length 32 cm, Width 14 cm
Excavated in 1979 Guojia village Xida yingzixiang, Chaoyang County, Liaoning Province

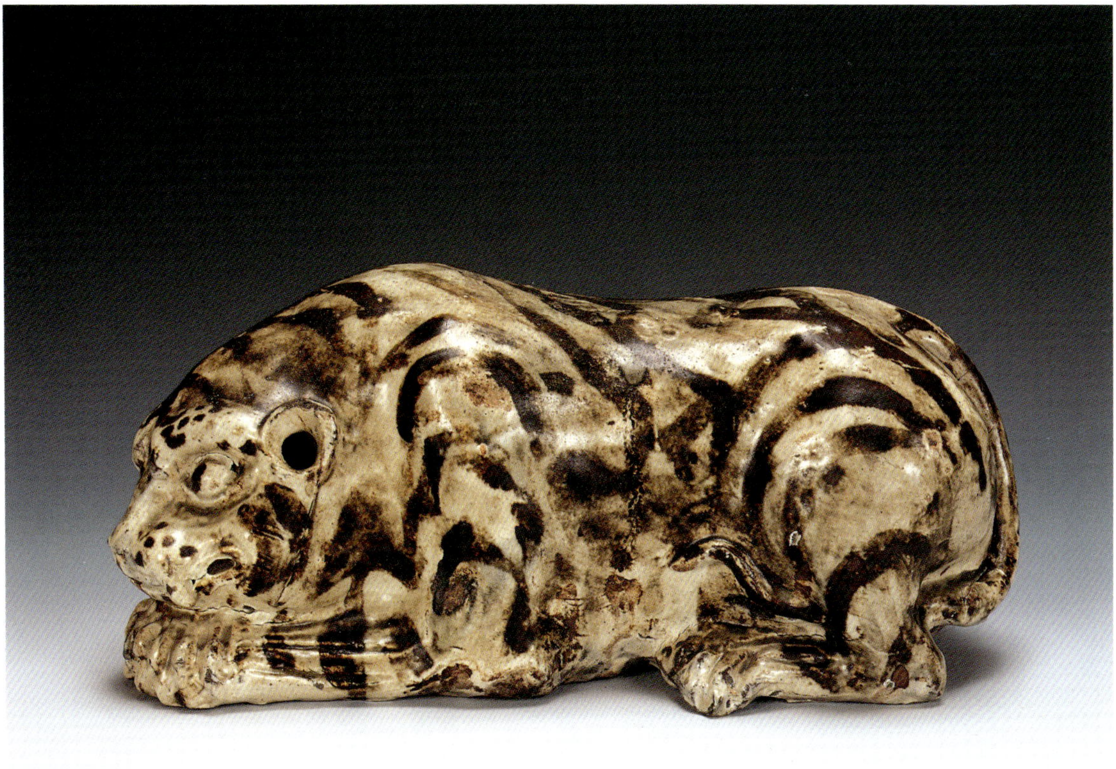

19

20 Three-coloured glazed, flat-handled pot with sea water and *tai ji* pattern

Liao (AD 916–1125)

Height 21 cm, Rim Diameter 3.7 cm, Base Diameter 10.8 x 8.9 cm

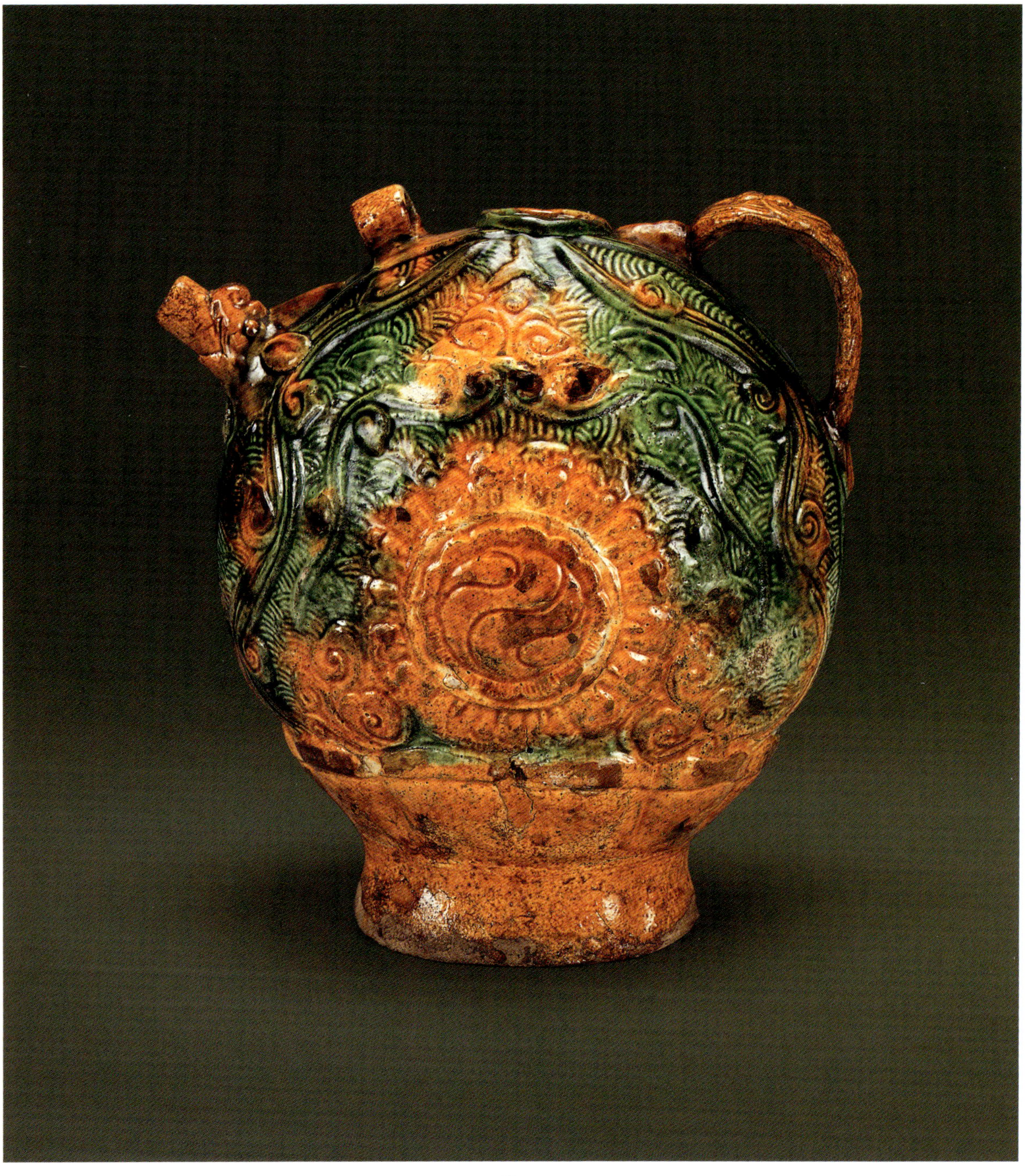

21 Long dish with three-coloured peony, pair of butterflies and begonia

Liao (AD 916–1125)
Height 2.1 cm, Rim Diameter 30.1 cm, Rim Width 17.9 cm
Excavated in 1956 from Liao tomb Batuyingzi, Xinmin City, Liaoning Province

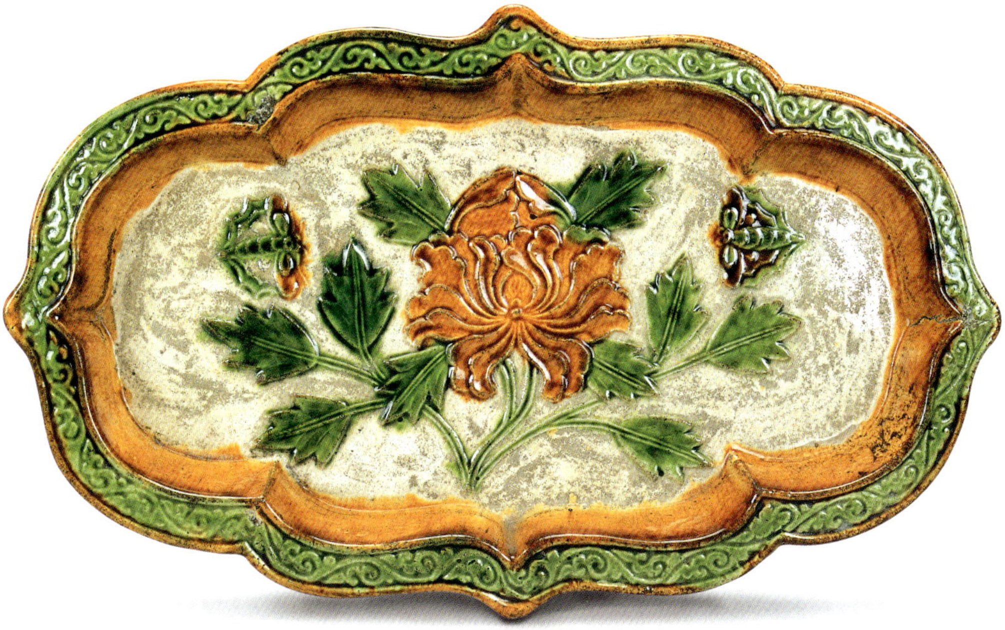

21

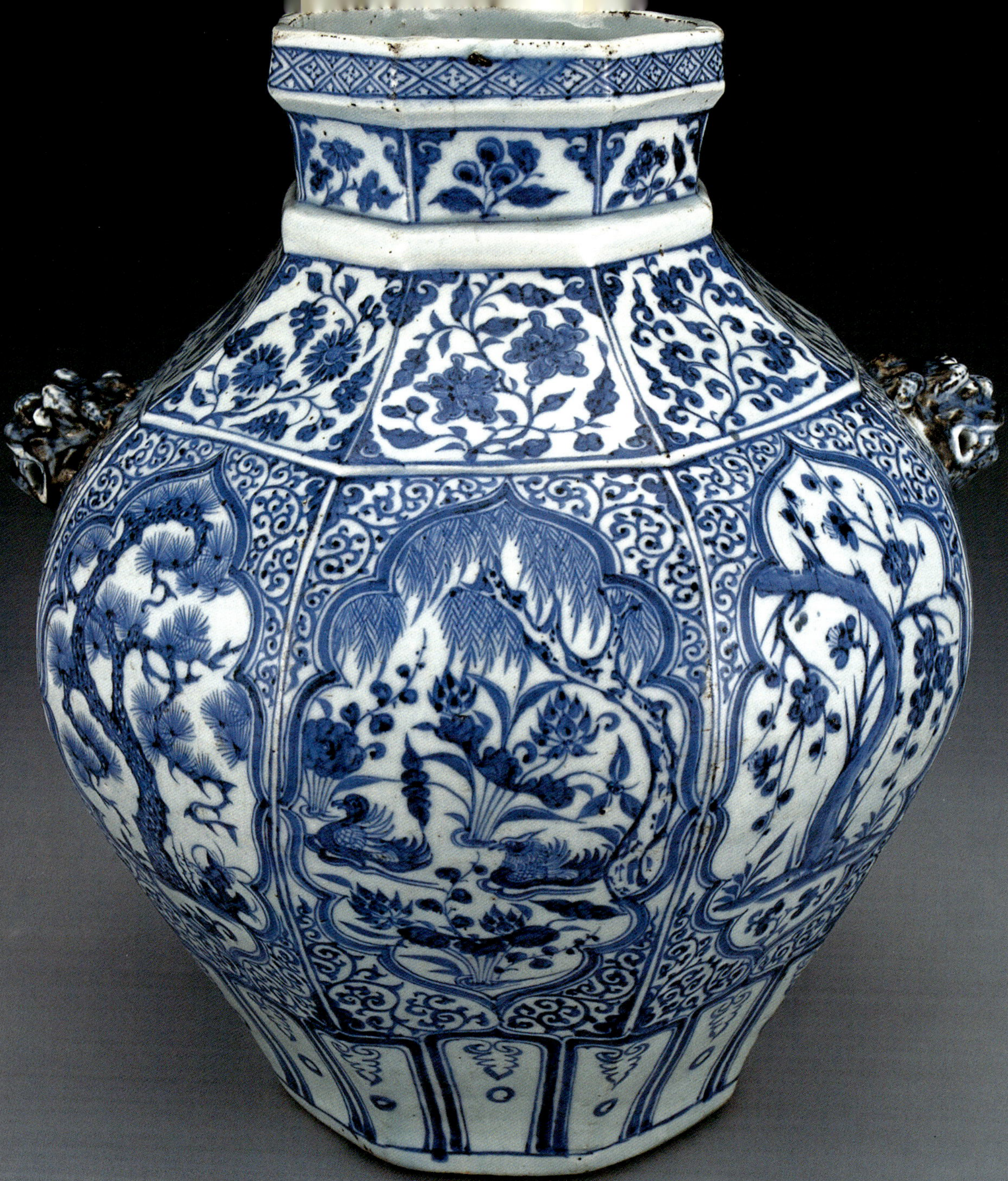

22 White and blue eight-ridged porcelain jar with pine, plum and bamboo

Yuan (1279–1381)
Height 39.7 cm, Diameter 15.3 cm

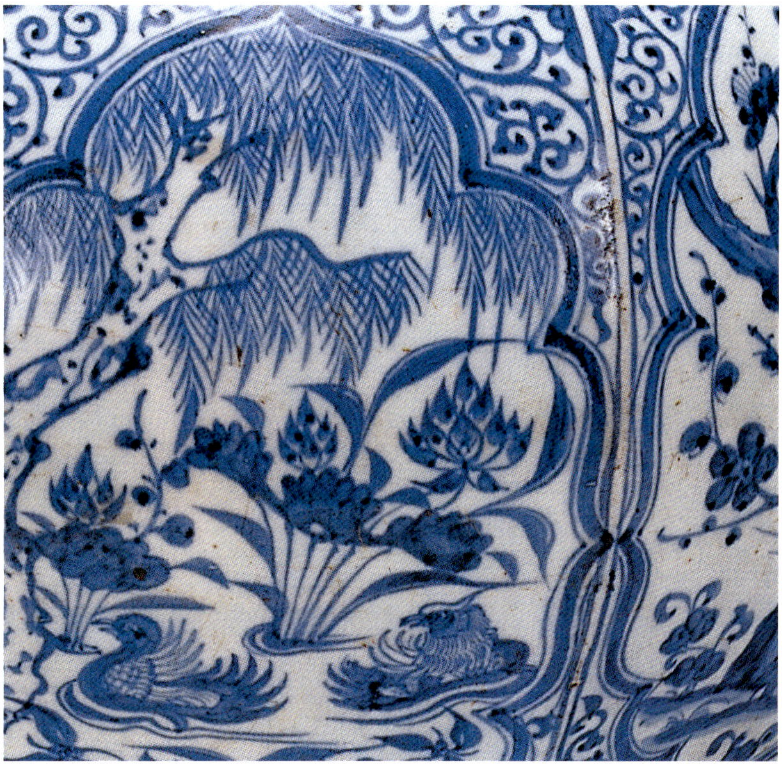

The whole object is shaped like eight ridges, with a short neck. The neck and shoulders are joined and have protruding ridges, running shoulders, swollen body and the shoulder area has matching animal ears stuck on to it, with a flat base. There is a white porcelain casting that is delicate but strong. The main body is made of transparent blue and white glaze. The underglaze is blue and white original materials, and is plain and elegant. The object is made up of five layers of decoration, and under the rim brocaded lines are painted. The neck and shoulders have flowers from the four seasons such as chrysanthemum flowers, pomegranate and peonies on the eight-faced reserved panel. The shin part is decorated in a changing-shape lotus petal pattern. The main body part has four groups of patterns including pine, bamboo, plum and mandarin duck in lotus pond decorated on the eight-faced reserved panel. Outside the reserved panel are rolled grass lines. The four groups of the neck and shoulders and body have similar, matching patterns, in symmetry.

The design of this object is simple and vigorous with intricate patterns, multi-layered, complex yet tidy, smoothly executed and artistically spaced. The artistic content has broken free of the confines of time and space, mixing plants and animals from different contexts and times, resulting in a picture that is clear and energetic showing the skilled technique of the craftsman. This is a masterpiece of Yuan blue and white porcelain. Liu Li

23 Blue and white bowl with high legs and dragon design

Yuan (1279–1368)
Height 11.4 cm, Rim Diameter 13.2 cm, Foot Diameter 3.9 cm

24 Large bowl with underglaze red with interlocking flower design

Ming Hongwu period (1368–1398)
Height 9.95 cm, Rim Diameter 20.6 cm, Foot Diameter 9.55 cm

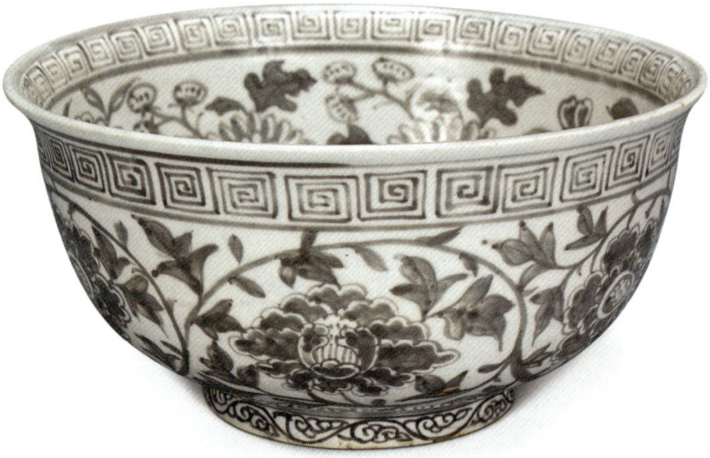

24

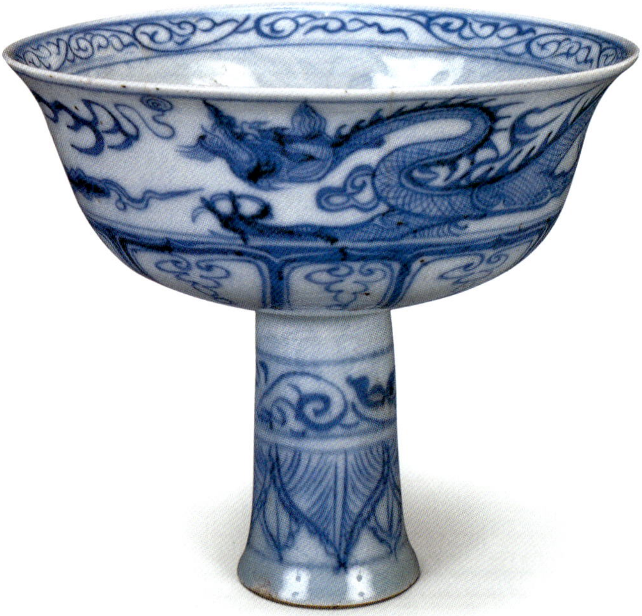

23

25 **Large blue and white dish with sea water and grape design**

Ming Yongle period (1403–1424)
Height 7 cm, Diameter 38.1 cm,
Base Diameter 24.3 cm

26 **Blue and white pot decorated with fruit and vegetables**

Ming Xuande period (1426–1435)
Height 29.5 cm, Rim Diameter 6.8 cm,
Base Diameter 9.7 cm

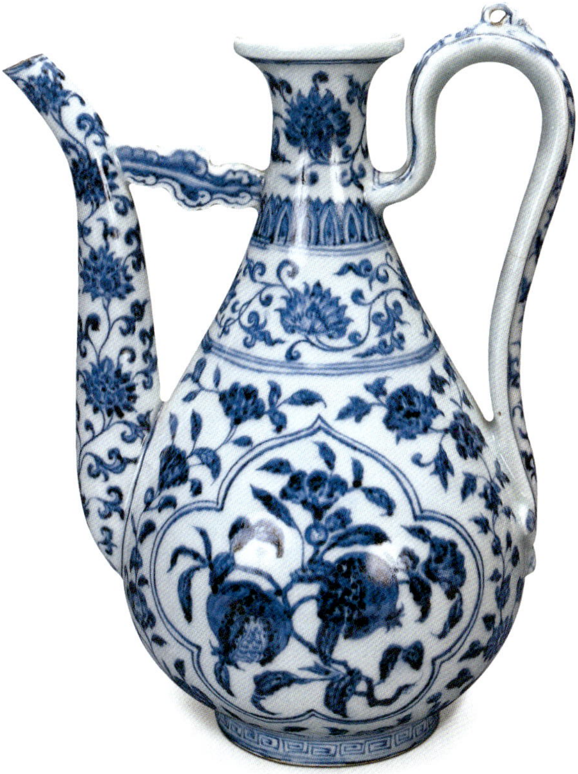

26

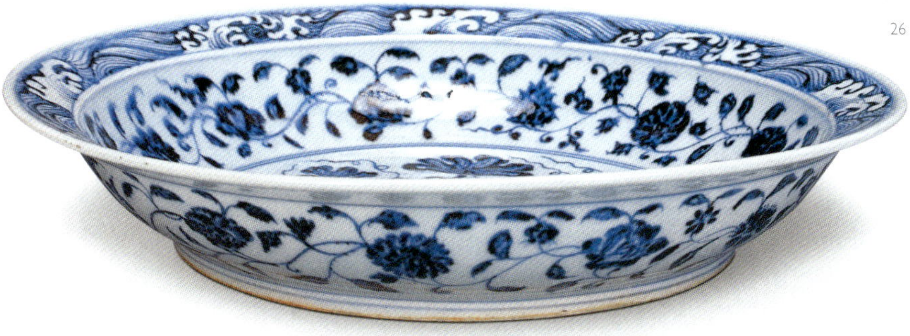

25

This dish has an uncovered top, wide curved rim, arched sides, round feet, sand base with no glaze and a white porcelain casting with slight yellow colour; greenish white glaze, with a blue and white underglaze as decoration, the inside base of the dish has grape patterns, the outside has two circles. On the inside and outside of the sides there is is an interlocking flower pattern. On the curved rim there are patterns of sea waves. The blue and white colour is elegant, and has rust spots. This object used imported blue and white materials called *suni boqing* as decoration. There is no year inscribed. It is hard and large in size, the design is neatly crafted, simple and vigorous, the glaze is smooth, and is a classic ceramic piece from the Yongle and Xuande periods. Liu Li

27 **Large bowl with white glaze and veiled pattern**

Ming Yongle period (1403–1424)
Height 10 cm, Rim Diameter 20.8 cm, Base Diameter 7.4 cm

28 **Ruby red glazed dish**

Ming Xuande period (1426–1435)
Height 6 cm, Rim Diameter 18.2 cm, Base Diameter 11.5 cm

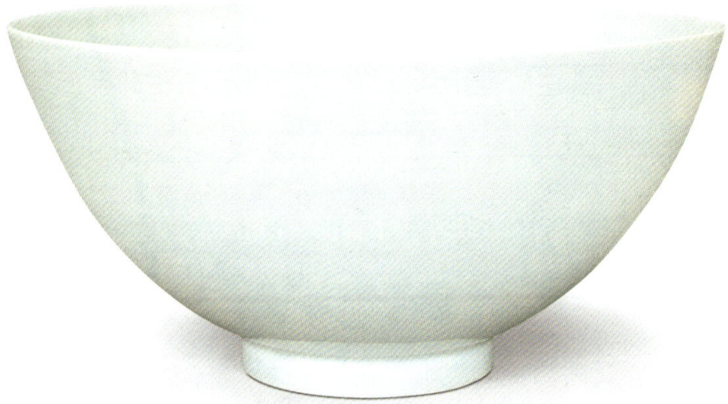

27

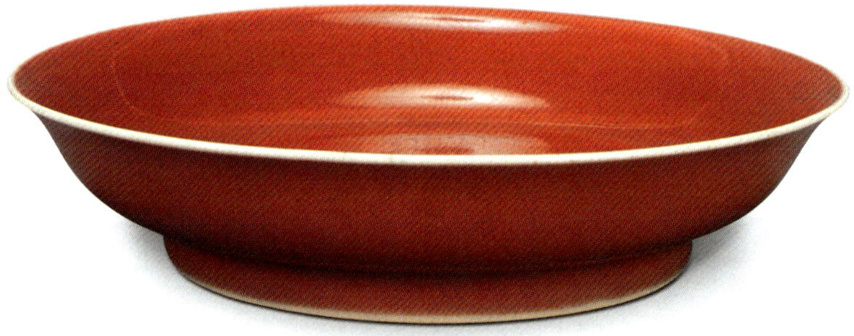

28

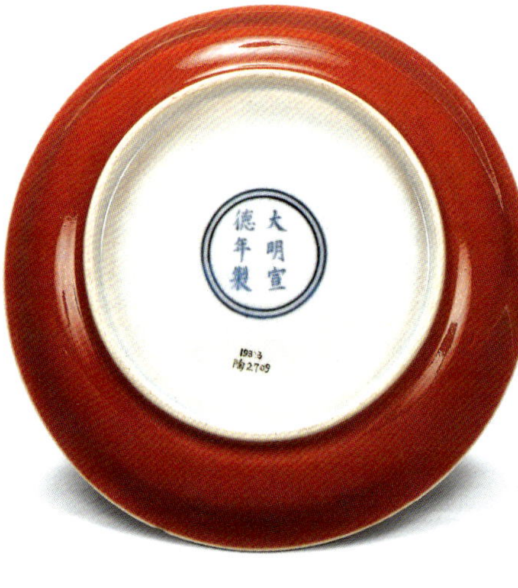

28 Inscription on base

29 Five-coloured covered jar with cloud and dragon design

Ming Wanli period (1573–1620)
Total Height 11.6 cm, Rim Diameter 8.9 cm, Base Diameter 9.3 cm

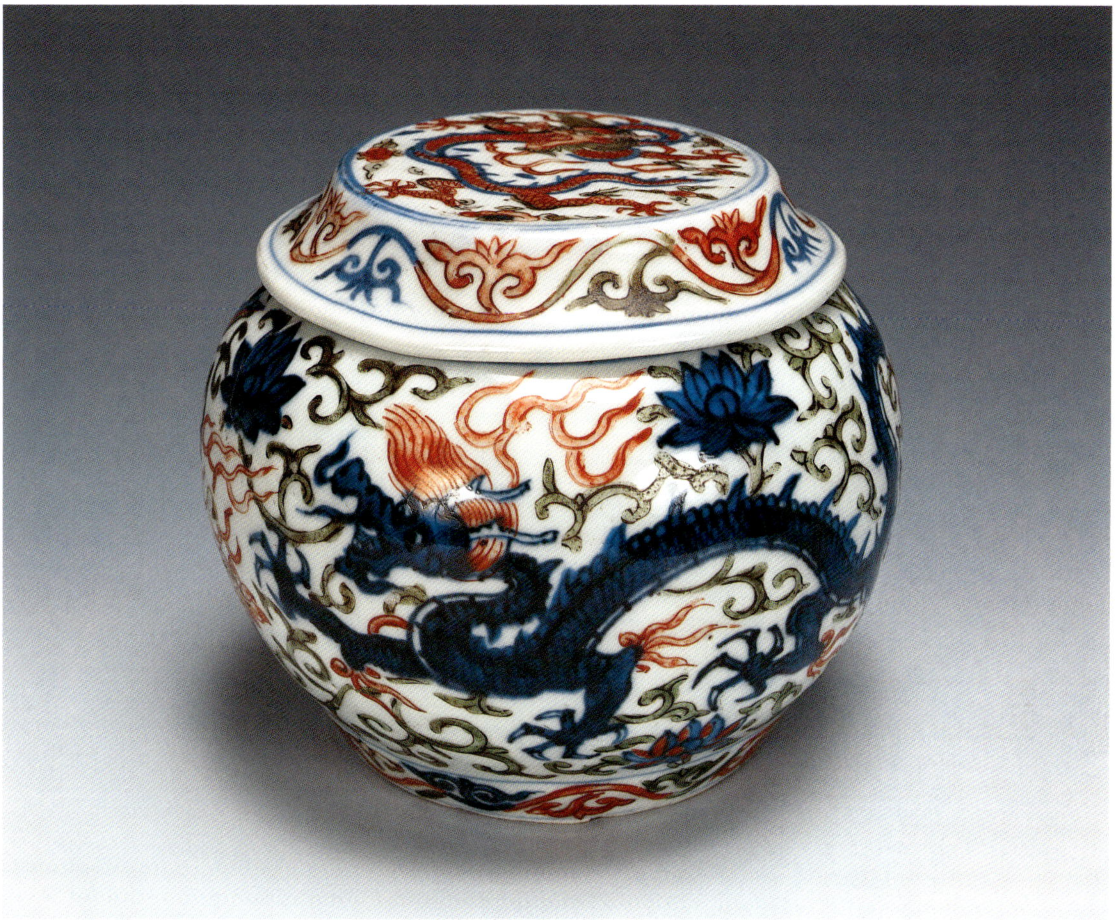

29

30 Five-coloured cups with twelve months' flower

Qing Kangxi period (1662–1722)
Height 4.9 cm, Rim Diameter 6.6 cm,
Base Diameter 2.7 cm

31 Yellow base three-coloured large dish with cloud and dragon design

Qing Kangxi period (1662–1722)
Height 7.3 cm, Rim Diameter 40.9 cm,
Base Diameter 26.1 cm

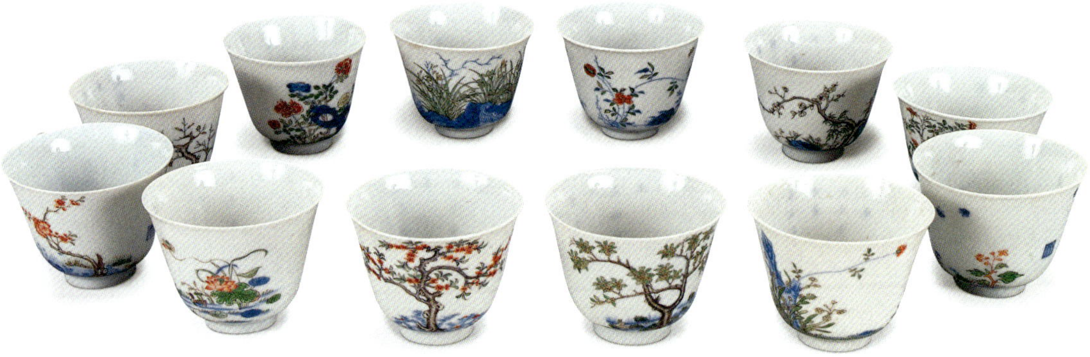

30

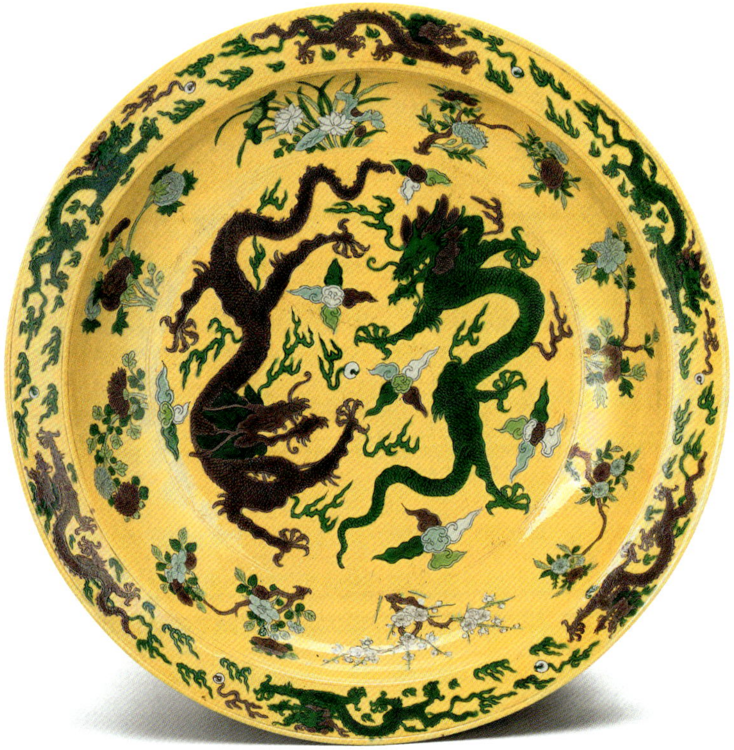

31

32 Cowpea red glazed *tai bai* zun with round hornless dragon design

Qing Kangxi period (1662–1722)
Height 8.8 cm, Rim Diameter 3.3 cm, Base Diameter 12.6 cm

33 Small enamel bowl with coloured peony design

Qing Yongzheng period (1723–1735)
Height 5.4 cm, Rim Diameter 10.9 cm, Base Diameter 4.3 cm

34 *Doucai* contrasting coloured round flower-covered jar

Qing Qianlong period (1736–1795)
Height 12.1 cm, Rim Diameter 5.7 cm, Base Diameter 6.6 cm

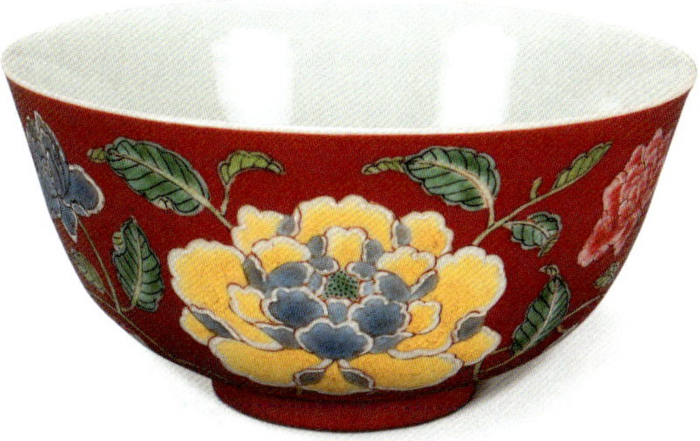

33

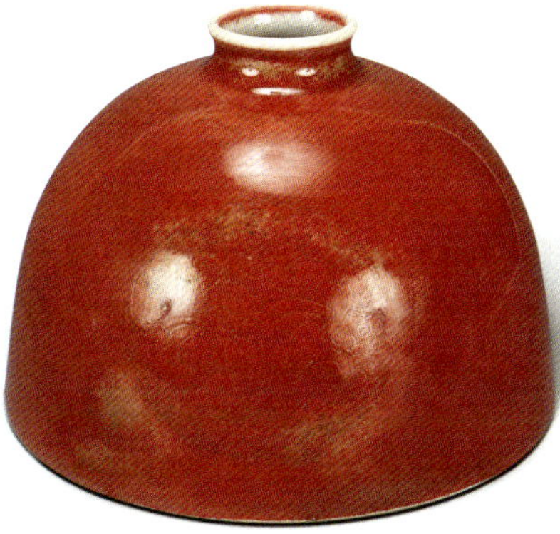

32

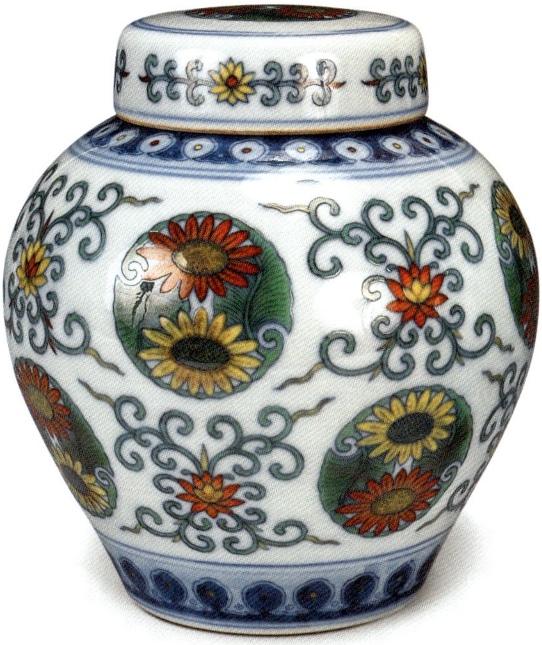

34

7

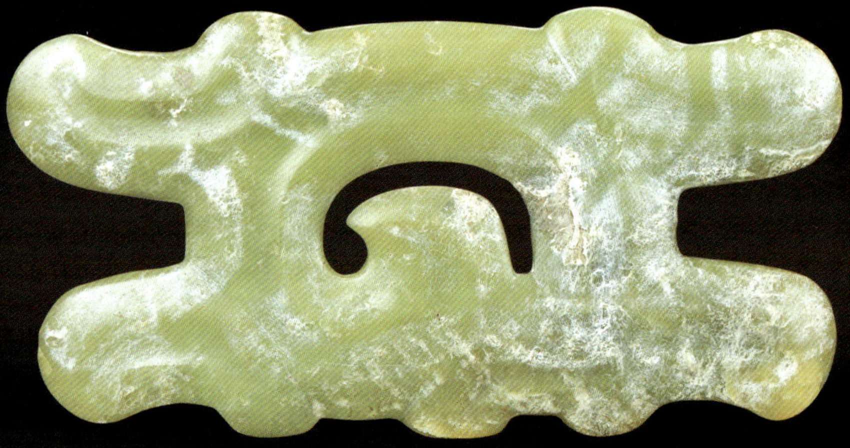

Jade

Chinese jade has an eight-thousand-year history. The jade collection at the Liaoning Provincial Museum features Hongshan Culture jade from the Neolithic period, Liao dynasty jade and Qing dynasty jade.

The collection divides between pieces from archaeological sites, and those that have been handed down through generations. Liaoning is in the northeast of China, which in the Neolithic era was divided between the Xinglongwa and Hongshan Cultures. In the Liao dynasty it was also an area of political power. Hence jade from archaeological discoveries is mostly either Hongshan or Liao. Pieces handed down mostly come from three sources: pieces from the original Ancient Objects department of the Committee of the National Shenyang Museum; objects moved from Ha'erbin during the Chinese Civil War by the Northeast Cultural Artefacts Committee; pieces acquired after 1949.

The design of jade from Xinglongwa Culture that dates from eight thousand years ago mainly includes *jue*, dagger-shaped objects, tubes and chisels, simple jades, quite small pieces with basic design and no decoration. Jade pieces from the early Hongshan Culture basically continued the style of Xinglongwa Culture down to the late Hongshan Culture (about 6000–5000 BC), which was an unprecedented period of jade prosperity in the west Liao area. Jades from this period developed much further in variety and quantity than those in the Xinglongwa period. Lingyuan Niuheliang, Kazuo Dongshanzui and Fuxin Hutougou are important sites for Hongshan Culture. The Liaoning Museum collection includes hooked-cloud shaped pieces, pipe-shaped pieces, C-shaped pieces, ring-shaped pig dragon, *bi* jade with blade, *bi* jade strung together, *bracelet*, birds and turtles – all typical of Hongshan jade.

The Liao kingdom was a powerful state established by the Khitan people in northern China in the early tenth century. Liao Culture was a mixture of the Central Plains, steppe and Buddhist Culture, all of which can be clearly seen in Liao dynasty jade work. Liao dynasty jade can be divided into three categories from these three cultures, all of which are represented in the Liaoning collection.

Jade of excellent quality was produced in large quantities during the Qing dynasty (especially the mid-Qing period), and constituted a peak in Chinese jade production. Jade handed down at the Liao Museum is mostly from the Ming and Qing dynasties. Apart from jade ware that was popular during the Qing dynasty such as vessels, aesthetic objects, stationery and decorative pieces, there were also many imitations of ancient jade. Many of these belonged to the Qing palace and reflect the high standard of jade production of the Qing dynasty. Zhou Xiaojing

1 Jade *jue*

Xinglongwa Culture (8000 years ago)
Straight Diameter 3.9 cm, Thickness 1.4 cm

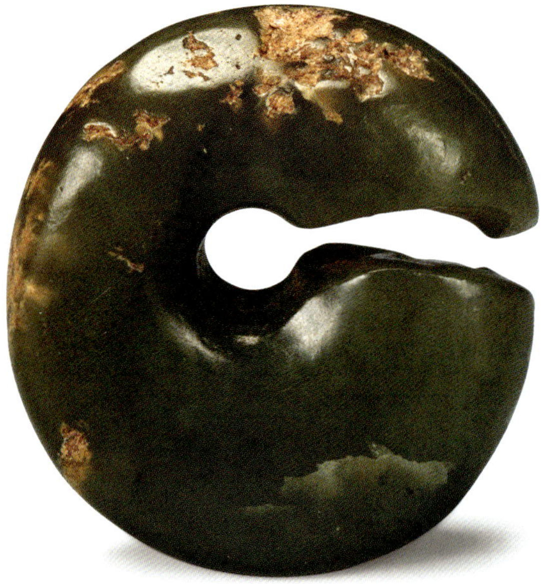

1

2 Jade pig dragon

Hongshan Culture (6000 to 5000 years ago)
Height 15 cm, Width 10.2 cm, Thickness 3.8 cm
Collected from Jianping County, Liaoning Province

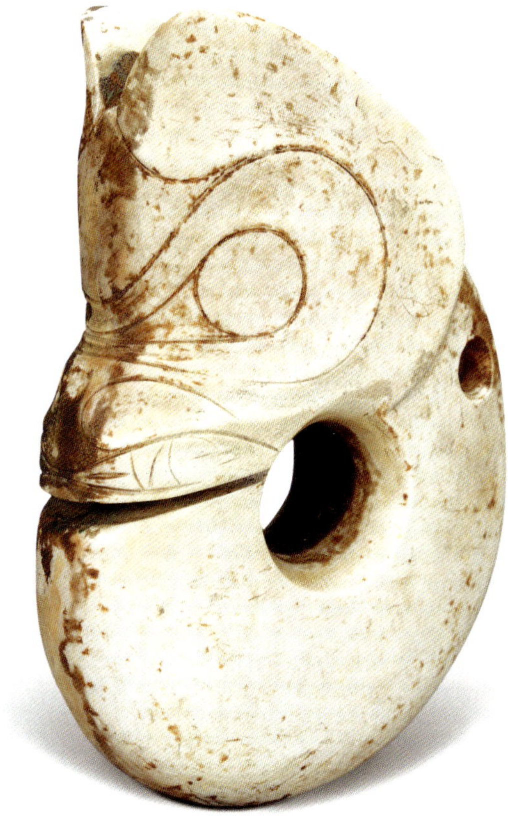

2

This piece is a typical design of Longshan Culture. It is white serpentinite. It has a large head, and short, fleshy ears, whilst the mouth has sharp protruding teeth and the hole between the head and tail has not completely broken. The production of the object is smooth and sturdy. All the painted lines are smooth, and the face has undulating earthenware ridges impressed on it, matching the carved lines, giving the effect of a protruding face. Since the face of the object is similar to the shape of a pig, with its coiled torso it is also similar to the shape of an ancient Chinese dragon, hence the name. This is the largest and the most regular-shaped extant object from the Hongshan Culture. Li Huijing

3 Hooked-cloud shaped jade pendant

Hongshan Culture (6000 to 5000 years ago)
Length 22.5 cm, Width 11.5 cm, Thickness 0.5 cm
Excavated at site 16, Niuheliang, Lingyuan City, Liaoning Province

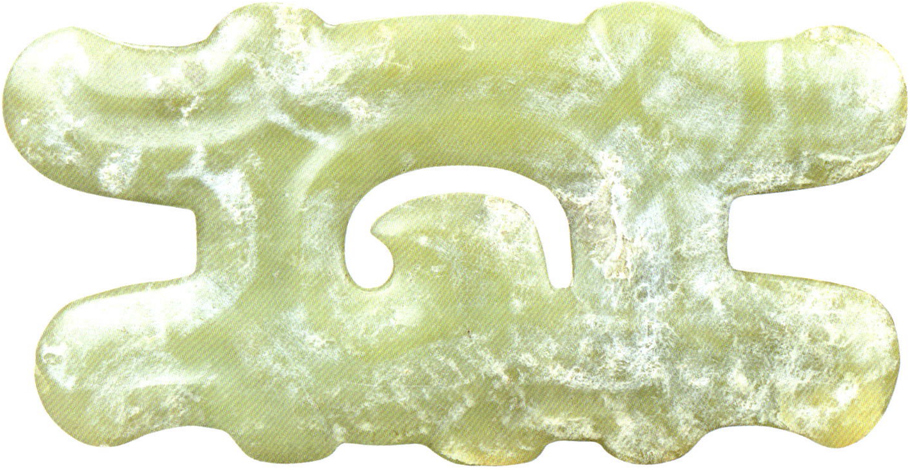

3

This piece of pale green jade is larger and more complete than other similar pieces. Each part of the object seems to be slightly wider. On the main face of the object rubbing lines are visible, on the reverse there are no lines visible. It is symmetric from top to bottom and left to right, apart from a round part protruding in the middle of the long side, which helps differentiate the front and back sides. Some scholars estimate that this is not the usual jade pendant, but was a separate object used with ceremonial axes. Li Huijing

4 Jade piece with three holes

Hongshan Culture (6000 to 5000 years ago)
Length 9.2 cm, Height 2.8 cm, Width 1.8 cm
Excavated at site 16, Niuheliang, Lingyuan City, Liaoning Province

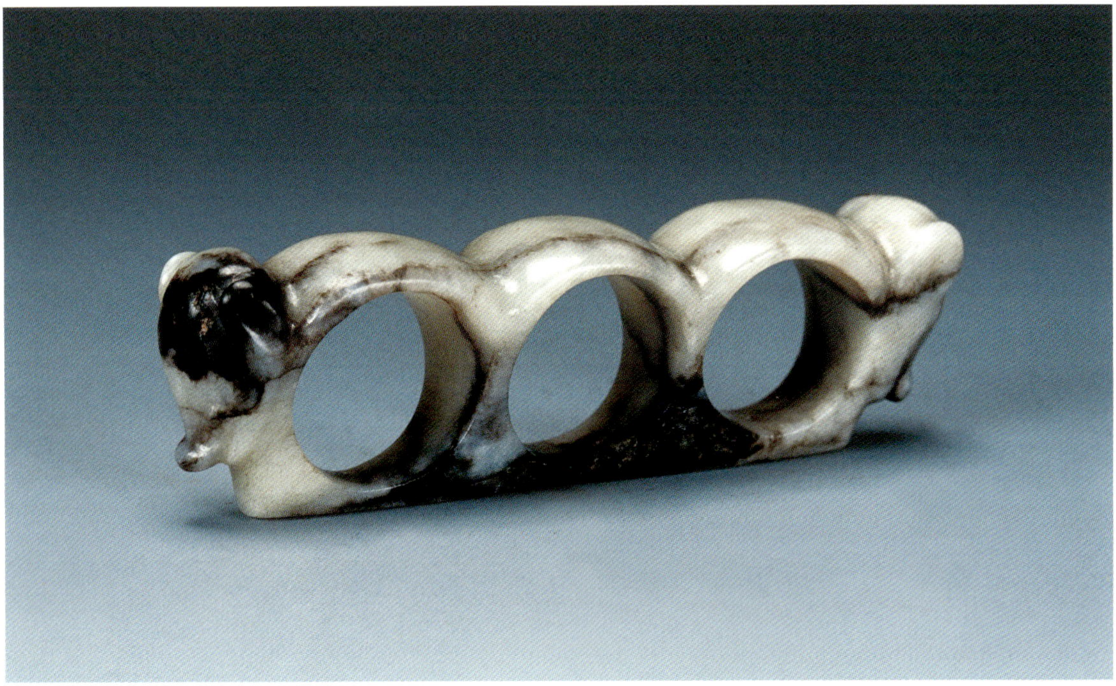

4

This is a piece of blue and green jade with black and brown markings. It has three round holes of the same size. Both extremities have an animal head carved on them, with a long face, large ears, and a protruding mouth, shaped like a pig's head. The top extremity of the object has a joined arc shape, the lower extremity is flat. The whole design of the object is highly original and of high craftsmanship. The three round holes can be pierced by fingers. Underneath the three holes are one to two small holes, showing that pendants could be hung from it. Li Huijing

5 Jade hoop in the shape of a horse's hoof

Hongshan Culture (6000 to 5000 years ago)
Length 18.6 cm, Widest point 10.7 cm, Thickness 0.3–0.7 cm
Excavated at site 2, Niuheliang, Lingyuan City, Liaoning Province

6 *Bi* (ritual disc)

Hongshan Culture (6000 to 5000 years ago)
Width 10.5–12.5 cm, Thickness 0.3 cm
Excavated at site 16, Niuheliang, Lingyuan City, Liaoning Province

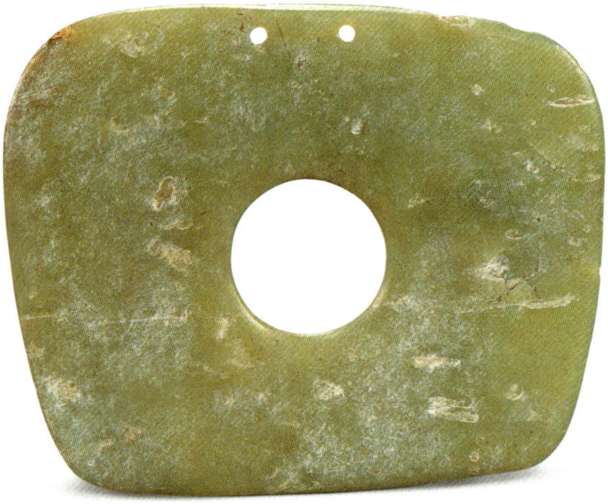

6

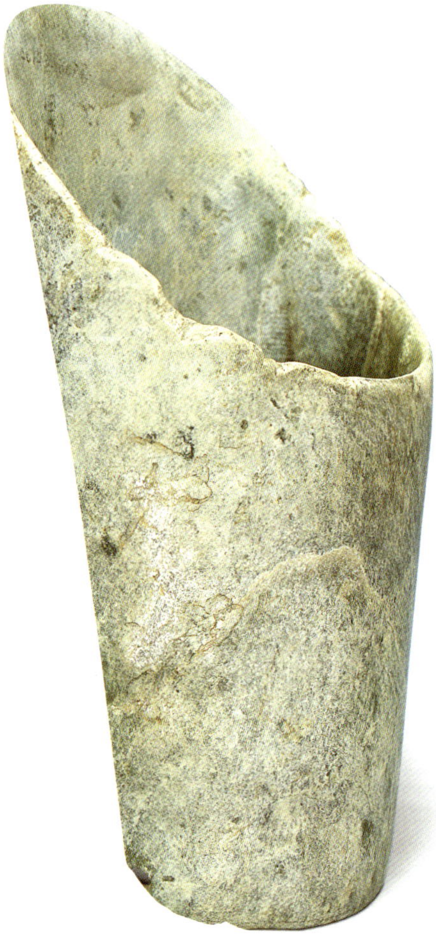

5

7 Three-ringed *bi* (ritual disc)

Hongshan Culture (6000 to 5000 years ago)
Height 6.4 cm, Width 3 cm
Excavated at Hutou gou, Fuxin City, Liaoning Province

8 Double dragon-head jade pendant

Hongshan Culture (6000 to 5000 years ago)
Length 4.1 cm
Excavated at Dongshan site, Kazuo County, Liaoning Province

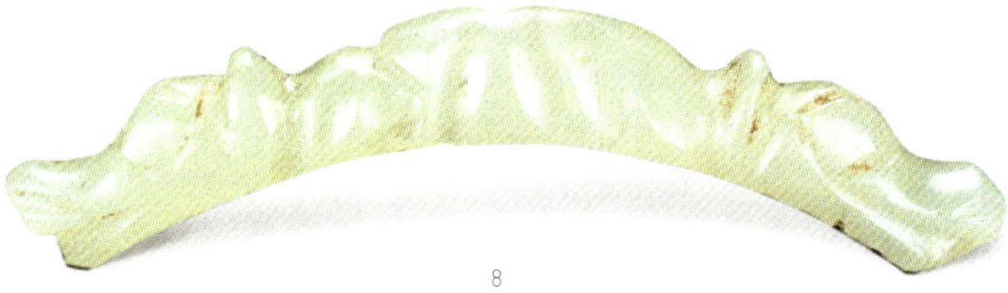

8

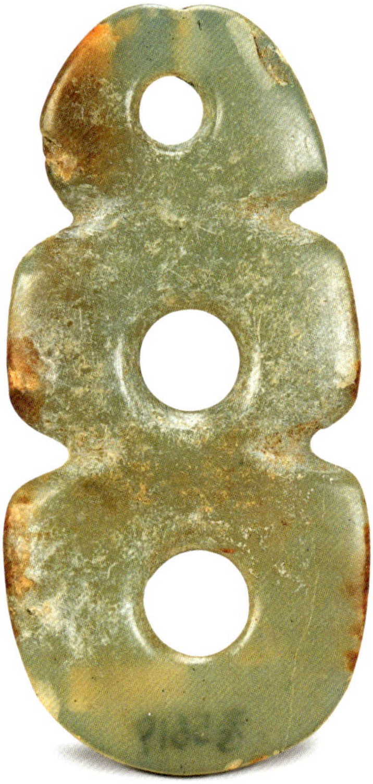

7

9 a: Tortoise; b: Bird; c and d: Owls

Hongshan Culture (6000 to 5000 years ago)
a: Length 4.8 cm, widest point 2.8 cm
b: Length 4.8 cm, widest point 4.9 cm
c: Length 3.1 cm, widest point 3 cm
d: Length 2.1 cm, widest point 5.3 cm
Excavated at Hutou gou, Fuxin City, Liaoning Province

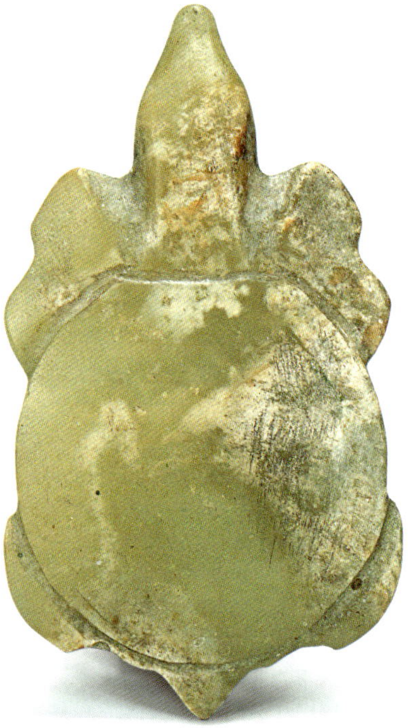

9 a

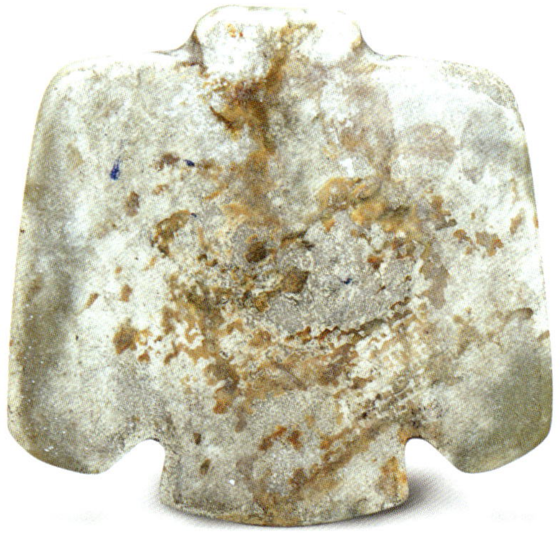

9 b

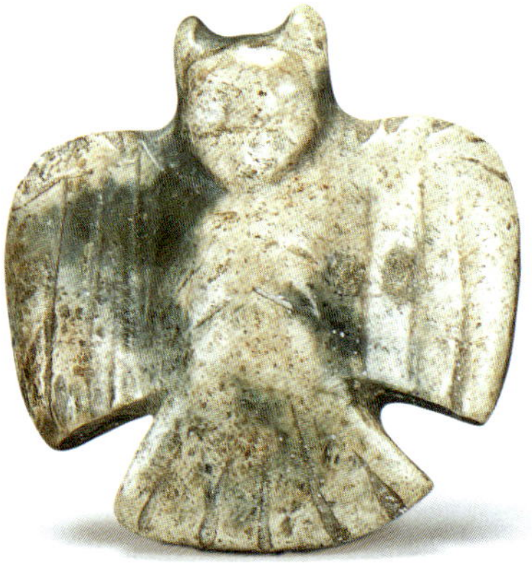

9 c

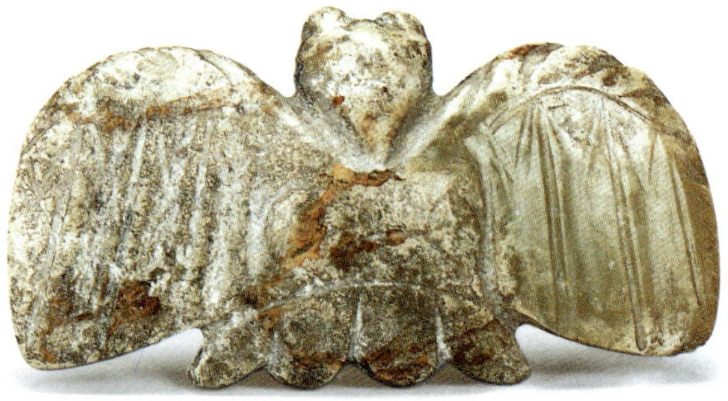

9 d

10 Turquoise owl

Hongshan Culture (6000 to 5000 years ago)
Length 2.5 cm, Width 2.8 cm, Thickness 0.4 cm
Excavated at Dongshanzui, Kazuo County,
Liaoning Province

11 Turquoise fish-shaped earrings (two pieces)

Hongshan Culture (6000 to 5000 years ago)
Left I ength 2.4 cm, Right Length 2.5 cm
Excavated at Hutou gou, Fuxin City,
Liaoning Province

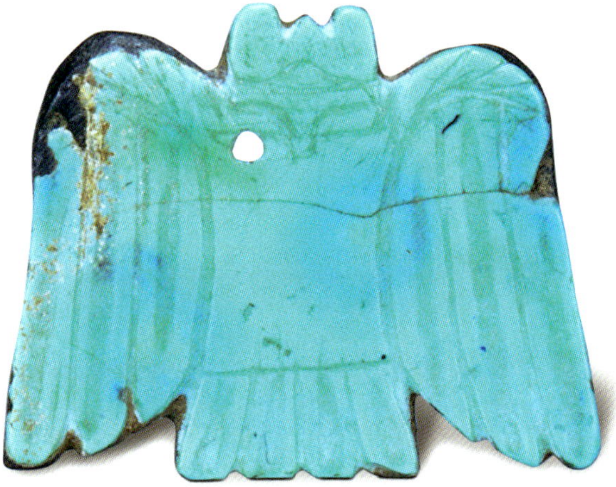

10

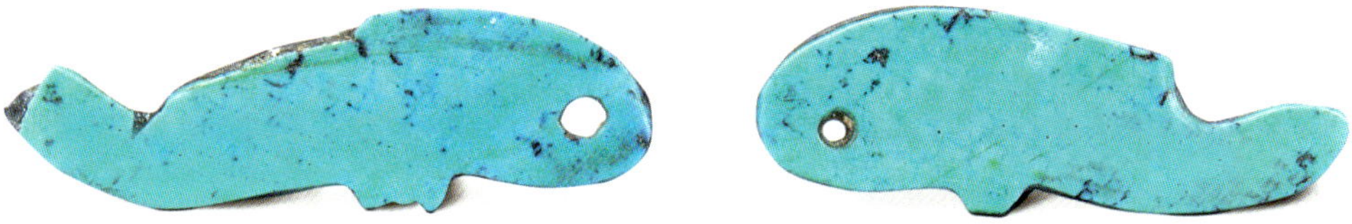

11

12 White jade sword head

Northern Yan (409–436)
Straight Diameter 4 cm, Thickness 1.4 cm
Excavated at northern Yan Fengsufei tomb, Xiguan yingzi, Beipiao County, Liaoning Province

13 Jade wine cup

Northern Yan (409–436)
Height 3.3 cm, Diameter 8.6 cm
Excavated at northern Yan Fengsufei tomb, Xiguan yingzi, Beipiao County, Liaoning Province

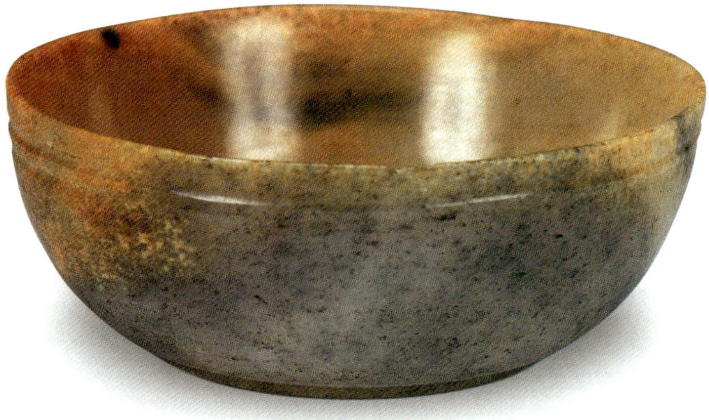

13

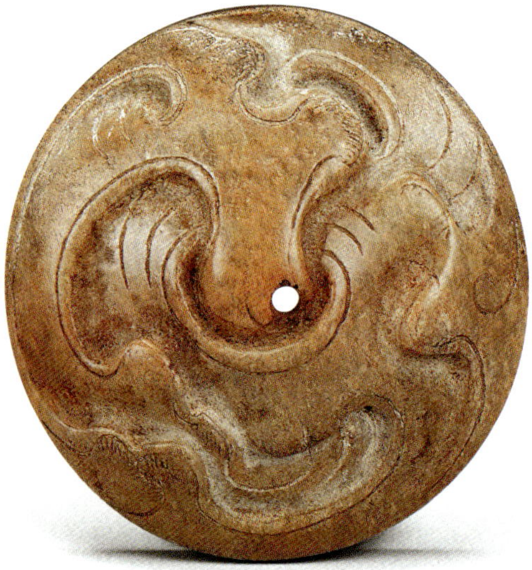

12

14 White jade *apsaras*

Liao (916–1125)
Height 4.6 cm, Width 3.5 cm
Excavated at white stupa tomb, Kazuo County, Liaoning Province

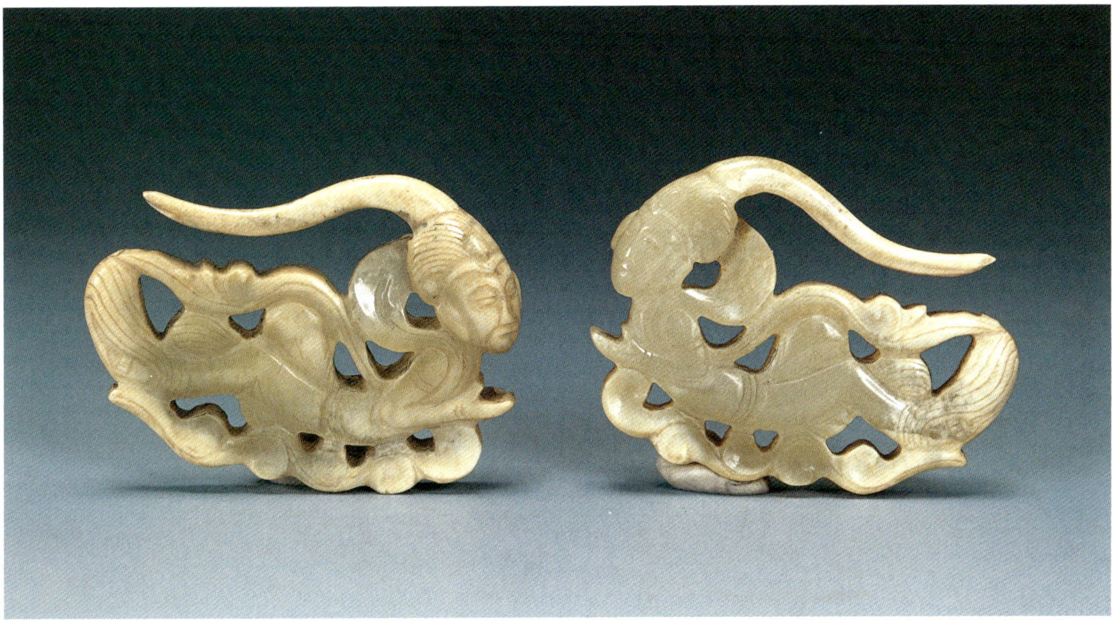

14

These two extremely rare blue white jade ear decorations are in the shape of flying *apsaras*. Especially interesting is that the flowing hair of the *apsaras* is used as the hook of the decoration. The design is meticulous, inspirational, amply showing off the developed level of Liao dynasty jade and the liveliness of its craftsmanship and design. This piece is exquisitely wrought, with finely carved *apsara* figures with their heads raised and chests out, both hands pressed together in front of the chest, with a garment floating off the shoulders, and an upper garment tightly fitting the body, long trousers covering the feet. The lower body has auspicious clouds. The *apsaras* have serene expressions, dignified and respectful, with a slight smile on their lips. LI HUIJING

15 Amber case inscribed '*die sheng*'

Liao (916–1125)
Height 9.8 cm, Width 5.6 cm
Excavated at Tayingzi Liao stupa palace,
Hongmaozi County, Fuxin City, Liaoning Province

16 Bamboo patterned white jade bottle on a gold chain

Liao (916–1125)
Total Height 17 cm, Case Width 4.4 cm
Excavated at Liao stupa underground palace,
Hongmaozi xiang, Fuxin City, Liaoning Province

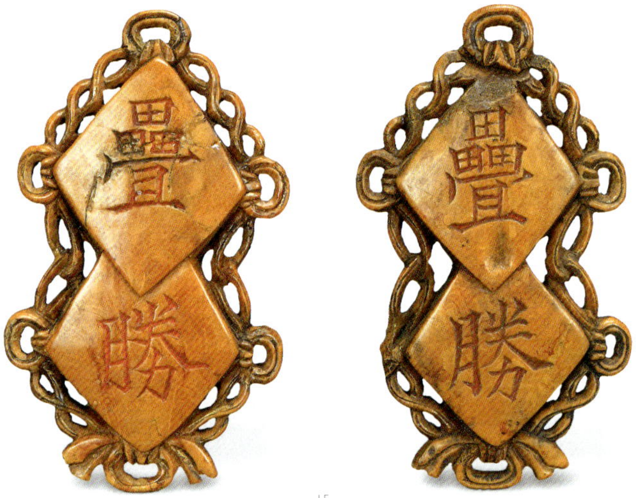

15

The case is made up of a lid and base, and the characters 'die sheng' are intaglio carved in regular script on the lid and base, meaning auspicious. The side of the case is decorated with a silk tie, indicating that it was used for hanging or as a pendant during festivals. Special festival objects can be placed inside the case, such as Dragon Boat Festival mugwort and realgar. Li Huijing

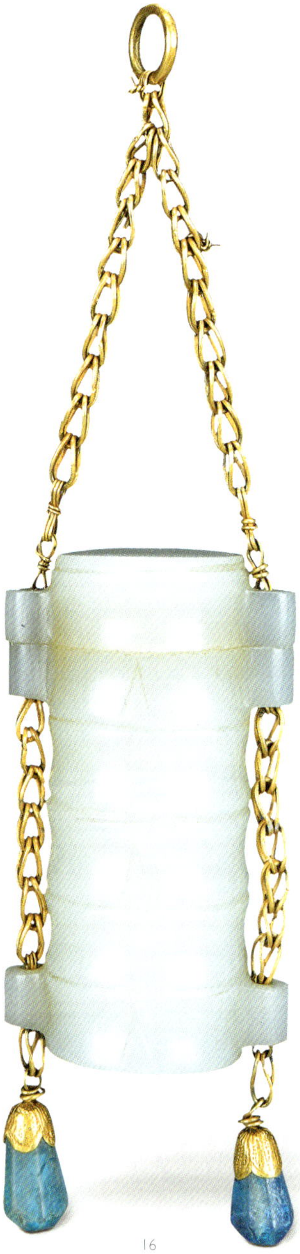

16

17 a: White jade wine cup with dragon design; b: White jade wine cup with lotus petal design

Liao (916–1125)
a: Height 3.4 cm, Diameter 6.2 cm
b: Height 3.5 cm, Diameter 6.1 cm
Excavated at Liao stupa underground palace, Hongmaozi xiang, Fuxin City, Liaoning Province

18 a: Small agate cup; b: Flower-shaped agate bowl

Liao (916–1125)
a: Height 2.6 cm, Diameter 4.9 cm
b: Height 5.3 cm, Diameter 14.4 cm
Excavated at tomb number 4, Qinghemen, Yixian, Liaoning Province

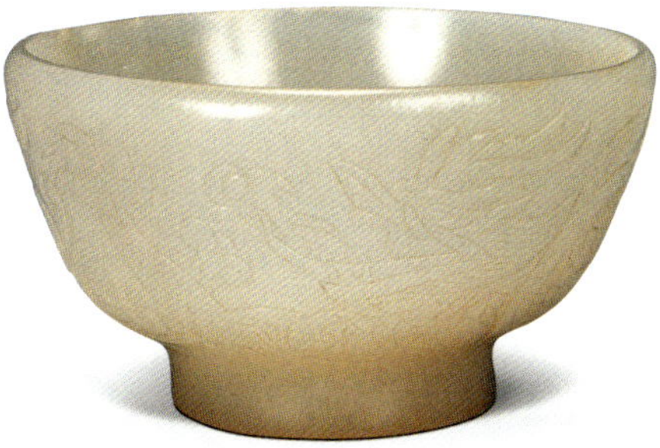

17 a

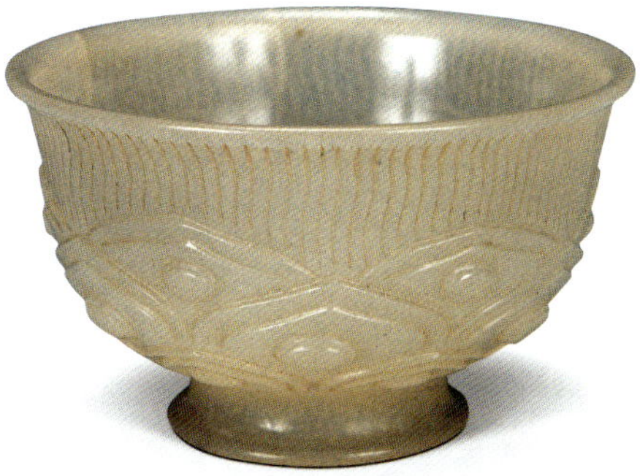

17 b

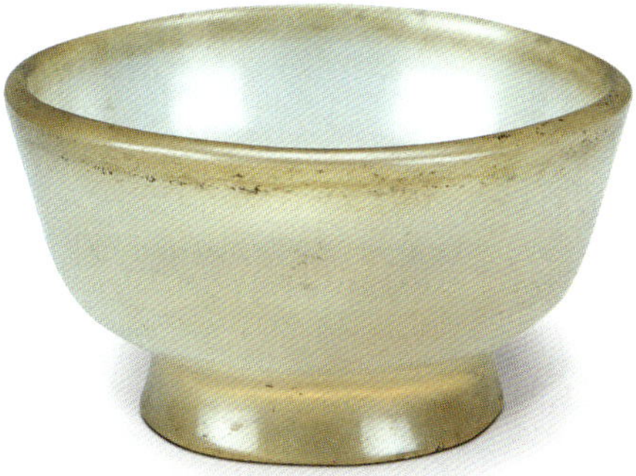

18 a

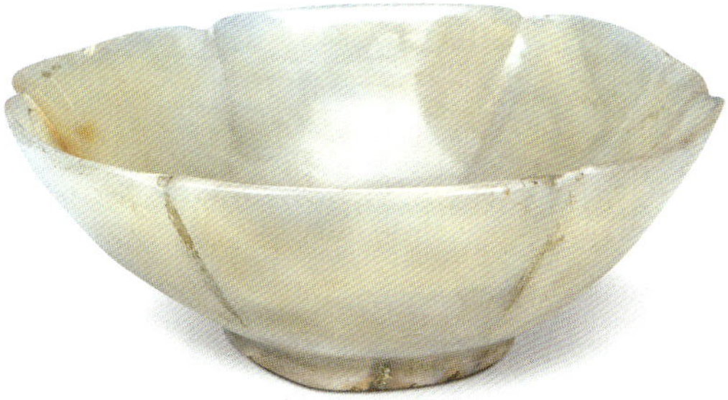

18 b

19 a: Amber ornament in the shape of a lotus leaf; b: Overturned leaf amber ornament

Liao (916–1125)
a: Width 8.6 cm, Height 6.8 cm, Thickness 2.4 cm
b: Width 9.4 cm, Height 3.1 cm, Thickness 2.9 cm
Excavated at Batu yingzi, Xinmin City, Liaoning Province

20 Green jade double geese small case with a lid

Liao (916–1125)
Height 9.3 cm, Width 3.8 cm
Excavated at Qinghemen, Fuxin City, Liaoning Province

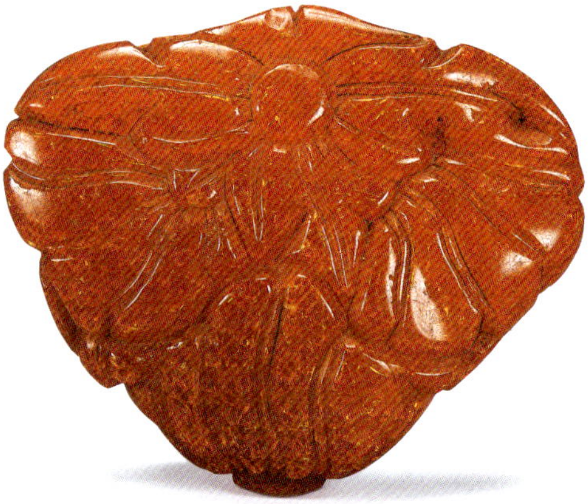

19 a

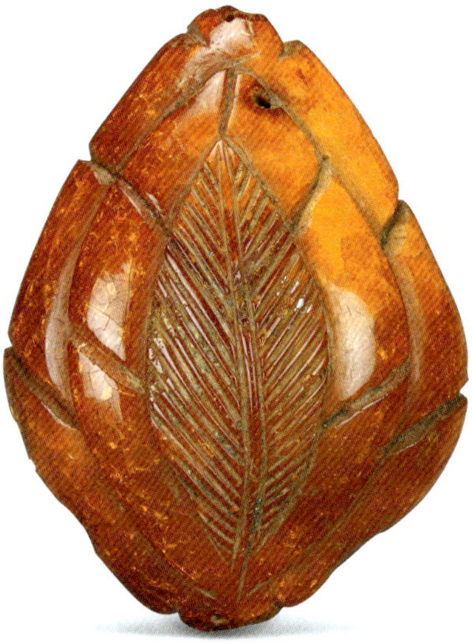

19 b

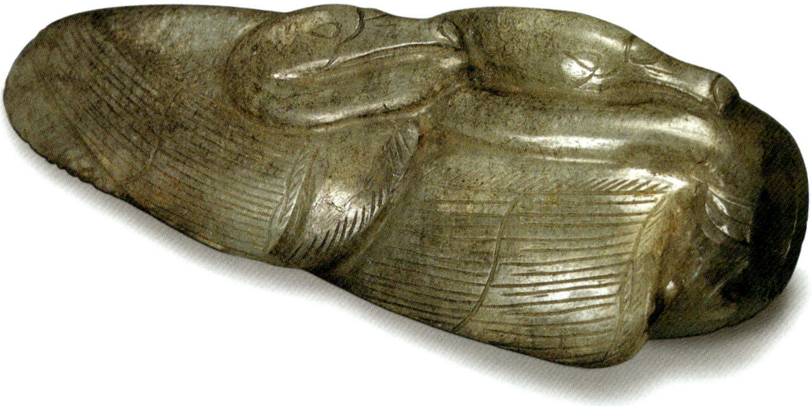

20

21 Green jade *gua*

Qing (1644–1911)
Height 18.1 cm, Width 5.65 cm

22 Cup with greenish white jade handles

Qing (1644–1911)
Height 2.9 cm, Length 10.45 cm, Total Width of Ears 8.1 cm

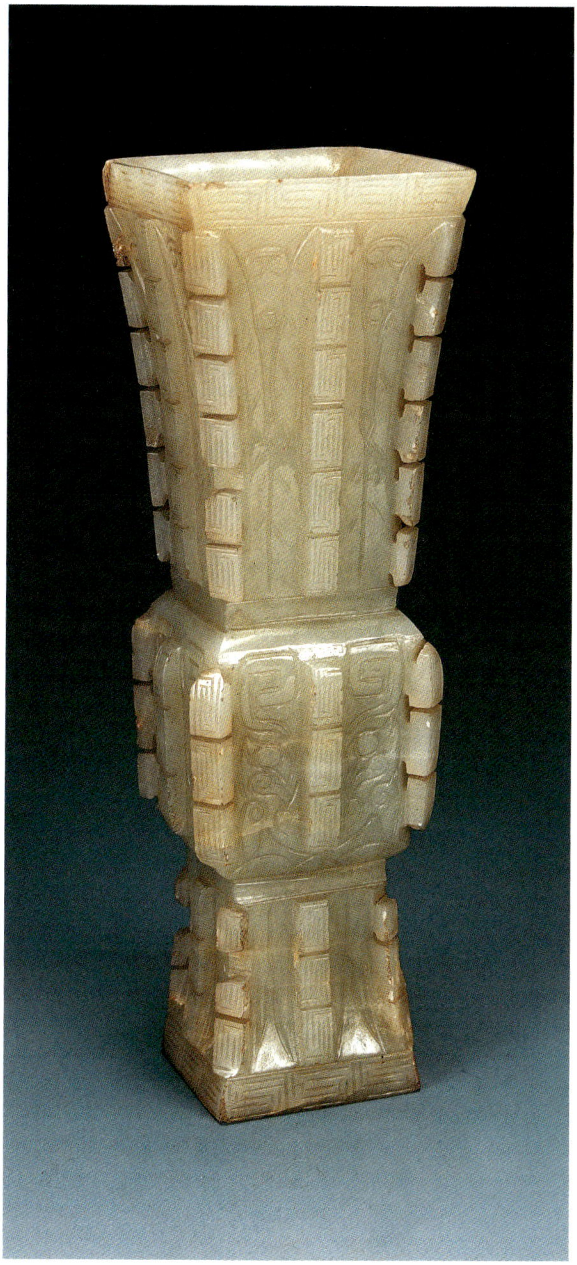

21

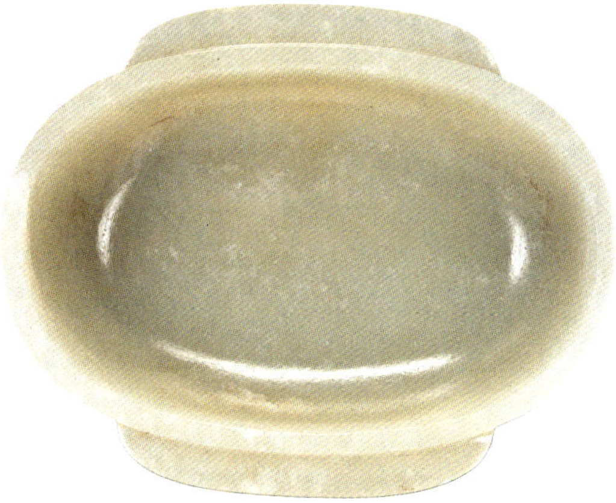

22

23 **Transparent carved pine deer monkey white jade ornament**

Ming (1368–1644)
a,b Length 6.8 cm, Width 5.8 cm, Thickness 0.85 cm

24 **Imperial seal with inscription of Qing Shizong, the Emperor Yongzheng, in Manchu and Chinese script**

Qing Yongzheng period (1723–1735)
Length 12.7 cm, Width 12.7 cm

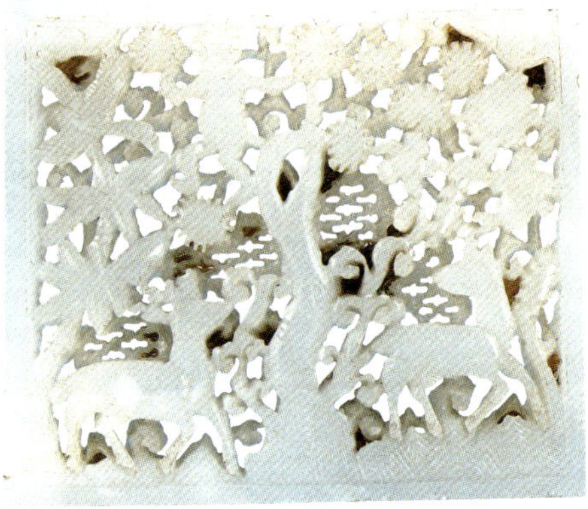

a

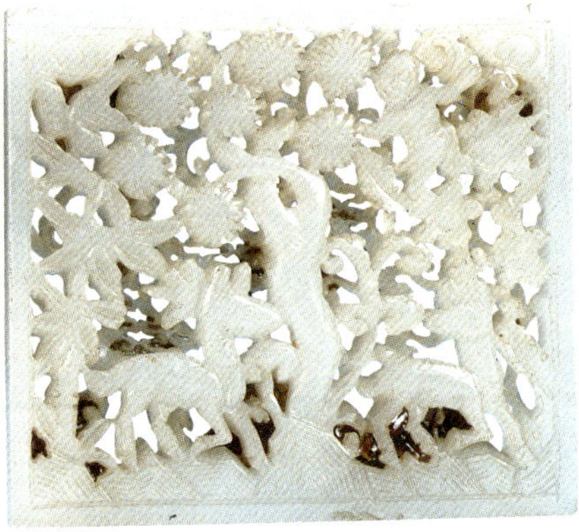

b

23

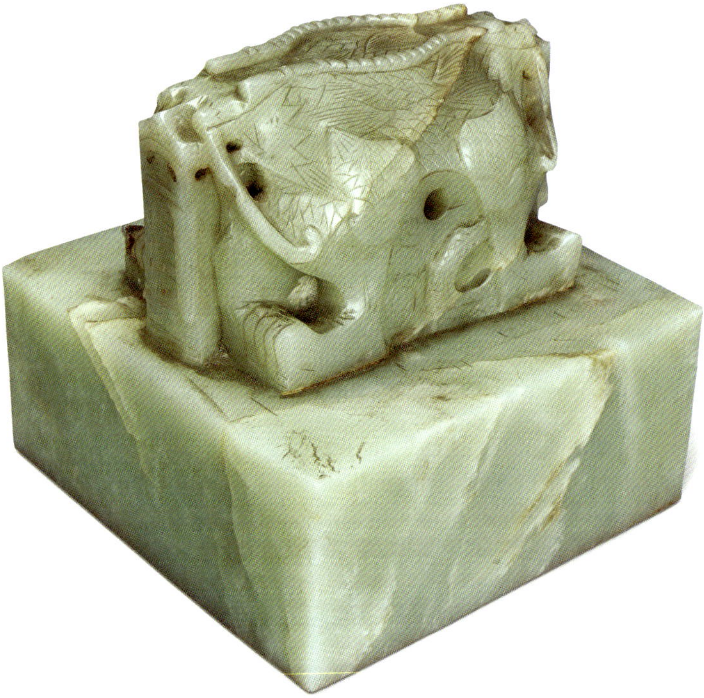

24

25 Painted gold green jade bowl with cloud and dragon pattern

Qing (1644–1911)
Height 5.2 cm, Diameter 11.5 cm, Base Diameter 5 cm

26 Green jade *gui* with animal with ringed ears

Qing (1644–1911)
Total Covered Height 11.1 cm, Total Ear Width 14.3 cm, Space Between Feet 3.8 cm

27 Green jade screen illustrated with seamstress

Qing (1644–1911)
Length 34 cm, Width 24.7 cm, Thickness 1.45 cm

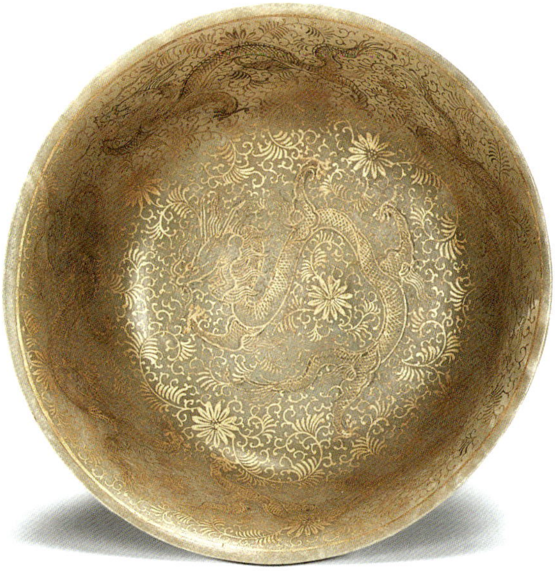

25

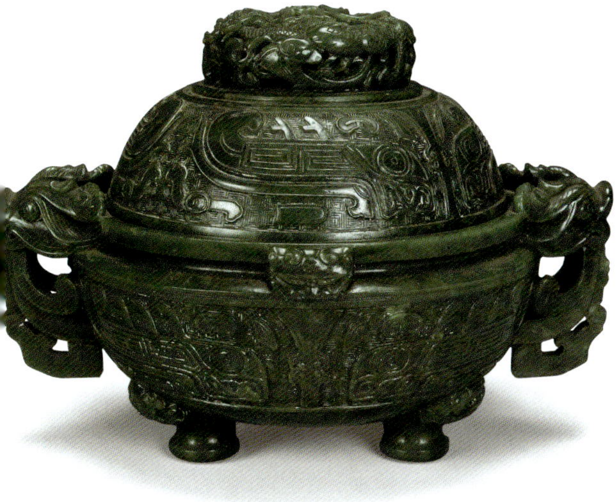

26

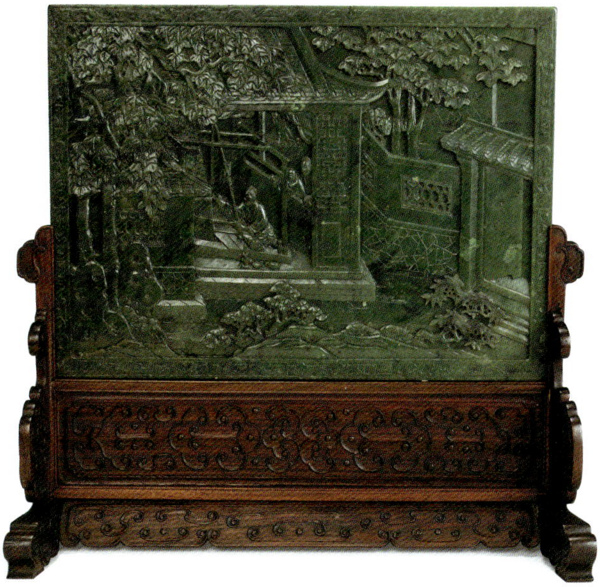

27

8

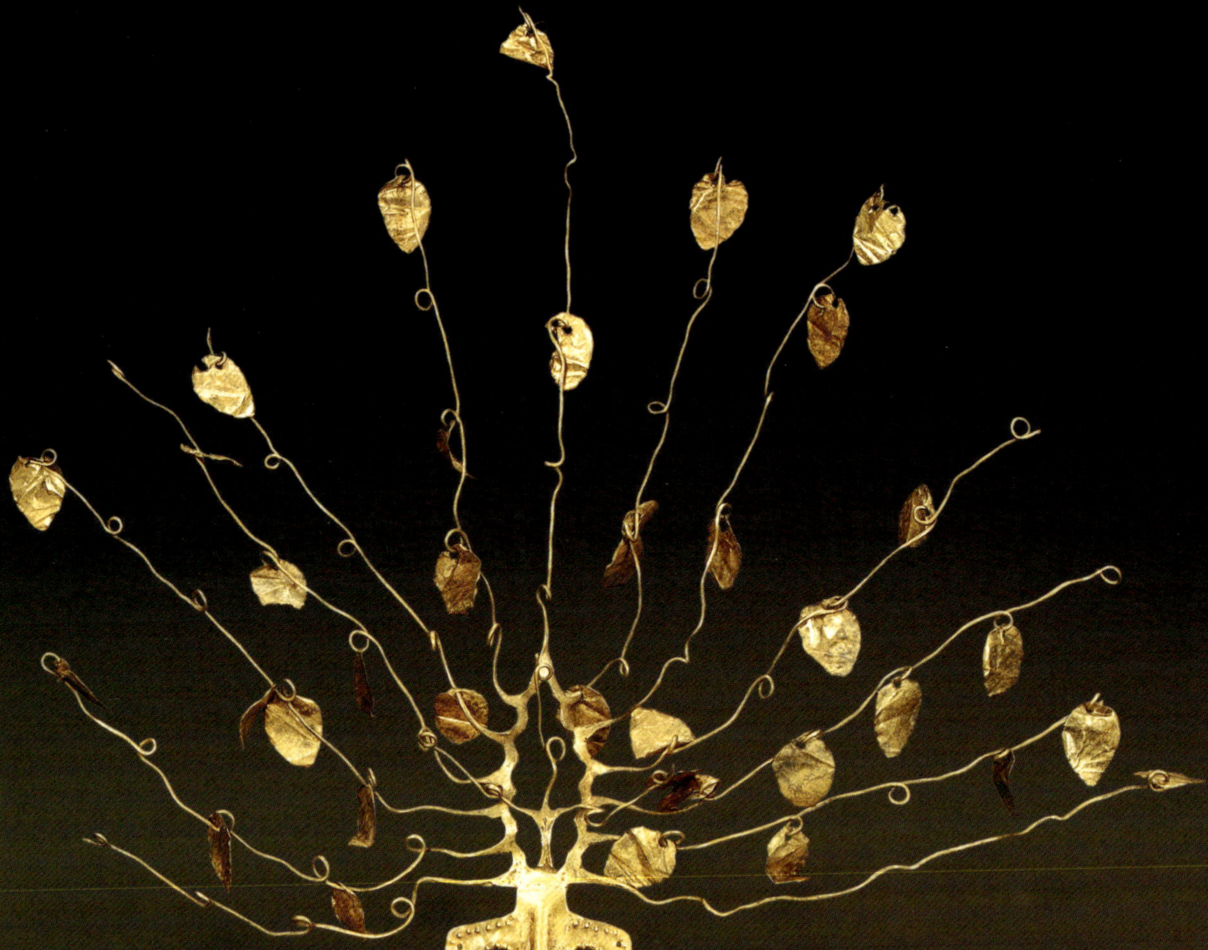

Gold and Silver ware

Gold and silver ware occupies an important position in the history of Chinese traditional culture and art. The collection of gold and silver ware at the Liaoning Provincial Museum mostly comes from the excavation of tombs of ancient northern peoples such as the Fuyu, Xianbei, Khitan and Manchus. From the Warring States period down to the Qing dynasty, the collection is varied, and includes objects from everyday life, decorative objects, imperial seals, horse accessories, burial goods and religious ritual items. The craftsmanship uses varied techniques such as carving, chiselling, engraving, painting, gold-plating, openwork, filigree and welding. Some gold and silver pieces contain precious jade, emerald, tourmaline and turquoise. Most of these objects are exquisitely made with brilliant technique, full of local characteristics, and have high artistic and historical value.

The deer and tiger-shaped decorations excavated from the Warring States tombs at Sanguan Dianzi at Lingyuan clearly show the artistic characteristics of a people from the northern steppe, and have a strong sense of local culture. In the 1950s, the tomb of a Han dynasty northern people was excavated at Xifeng Xicha Gou, yielding more than ten thousand objects, the golden ear decorations being the most striking among other gold and silverware. Tomb number 2 at Beipiao village yielded a set of pre-Yan gold pieces, including gold decorations shaped like flower trees, gold objects shaped like a new moon with inlaid jade, rings with inlaid jade and gold, and gold thimbles. Fengsufu tomb also yielded a large number of gold pieces, including golden pans, gold hair decoration, gold *buyao*, gold seals with tortoise-shaped knobs, and gold-plated wooden horse stirrups. All these are exquisite pieces and are representative of the gold ware used by the northern Yan ruling class, reflecting the high artistic achievements of the Xianbei people. The gold seal 'Fanyang official seal' confirmed the identity of the person buried in the tomb, and as such is very rare.

The Liao dynasty was established in north China by the Khitans, controlling the areas of present-day northern and western Liaoning Province. Gold and silver ware excavated from the Liao tombs of this area show local characteristics, with hair decorations, horse accessories, vessels for food and drink, and ornaments making up most of the collection. The Liaoning area is rich in stupas which have yielded large quantities of Liao cultural artefacts. Most representative are the Chaoyang north stupa and the Fuxin Hongmaozi Liao stupa, which contained several precious Buddhist artefacts.

Most gold and silver pieces from the Ming and Qing periods were court treasures, although use of fine quality gold and silver objects among wider sections of society had become fairly widespread. For example, the golden phoenix ornaments, silver hairpin, gold and jade inlaid necklaces and the pocket watches with gold cases excavated from a Qing official's tomb in Kazuo County are all fine examples of the high craftsmanship. Du Xiqing

1 Gold ornament with deer and tiger shape

Warring States period (475–221 BC)
Height of deer shape 3.8 cm, Length 4.9 cm;
Length of tiger shape 5.7 cm, Width 2.8 cm
Excavated from bronze short sword in tomb at Sanguandianzi, Lingyuan City, Liaoning Province

2 Golden ear ornament

Western Han (206BC-8AD)
Length 6.8–8 cm
Excavated at Xichagou tomb, Xifeng County, Liaoning Province

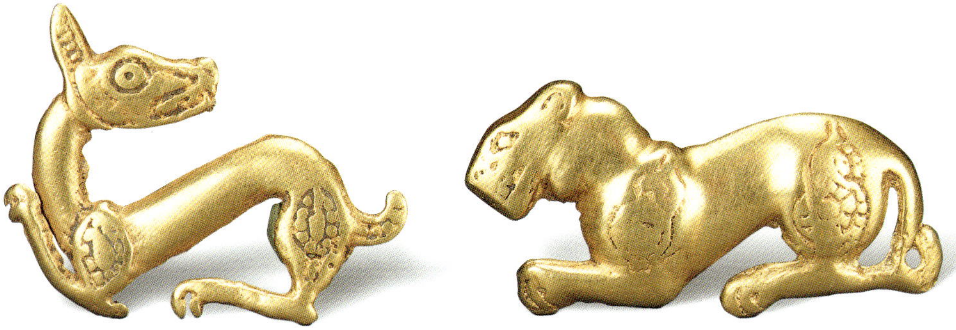

1

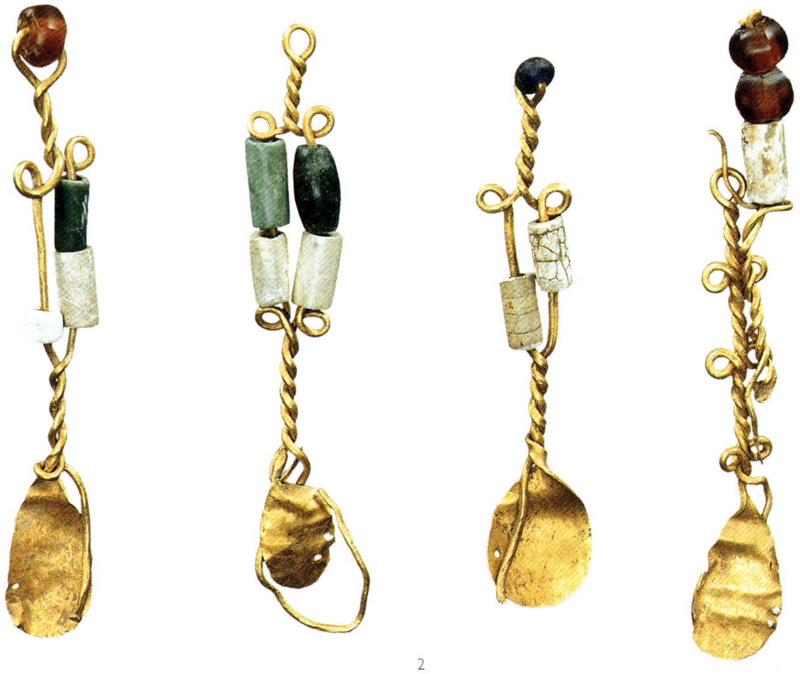

2

3 Golden ornament in shape of flower tree

Jin dynasties (265–420)
Height about 27.3 cm
Excavated at Fangshen village, Beipiao City, Liaoning Province

4 New moon shaped ornament with inlaid jade and phoenix pattern

Jin dynasties (265–420)
Width 14 cm, Height 5 cm
Excavated at Fangshen village, Beipiao City, Liaoning Province

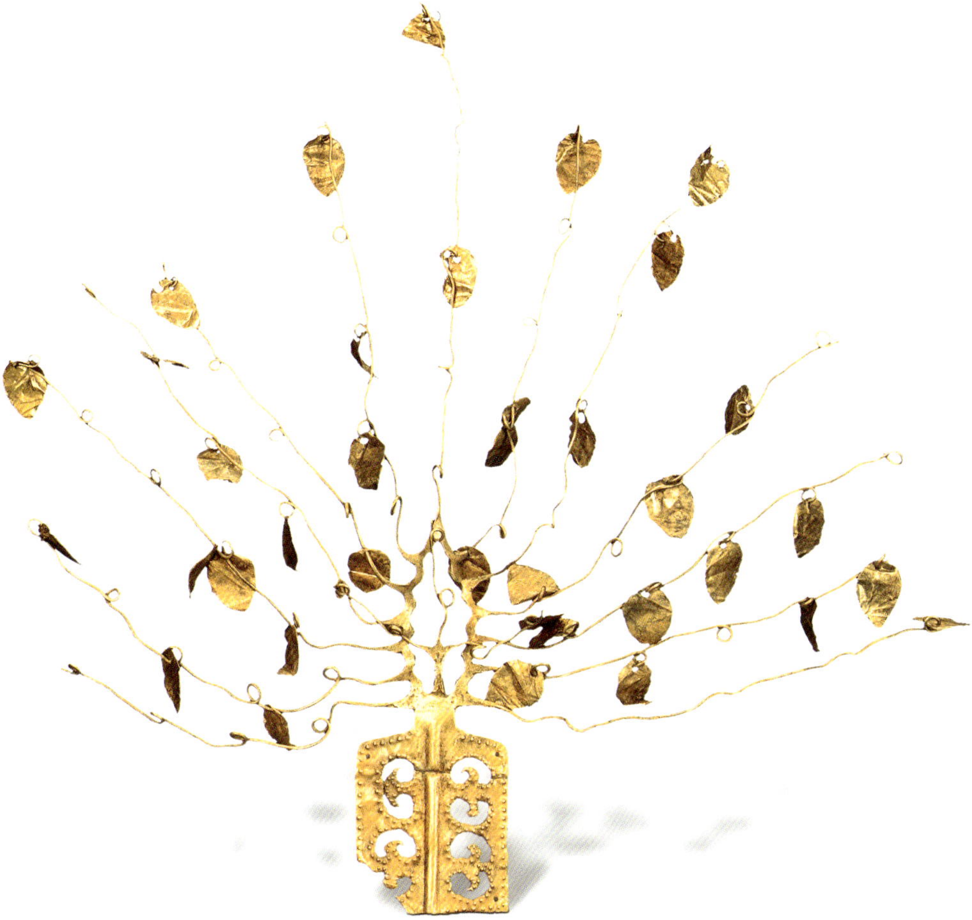

3

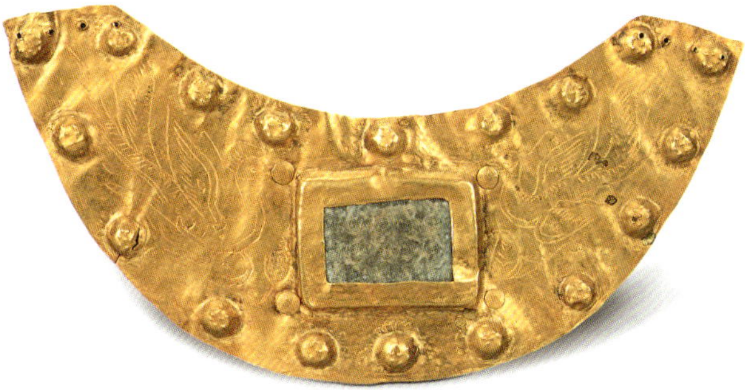

4

5 Gold plate with three-deer design

Jin dynasties (265–420)
Height 7.1 cm, Width 8.7 cm, Weight 34.2 cm
Excavated from Bao'an temple, Yixian, Liaoning Province

6 Gold earrings

Jin dynasties (265–420)
Total Length 8.9 cm, Diameter 0.3 cm
Excavated from Bao'an temple, Yixian, Liaoning Province

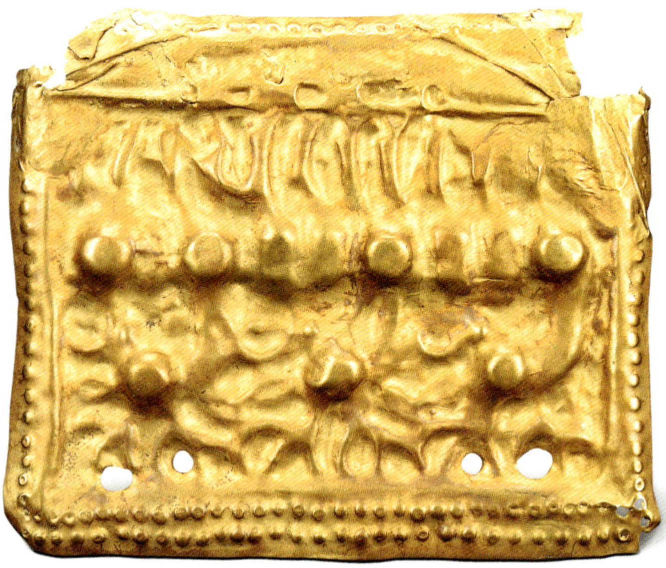

5

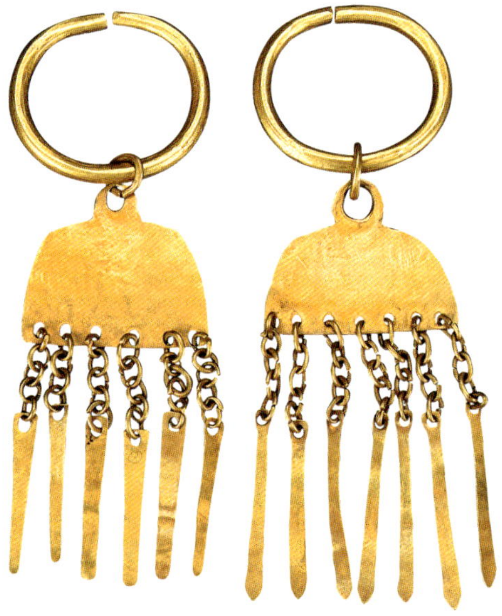

6

7 Gold headdress ornament in the shape of a mountain with Buddha design

Northern Yan (409–436)
Height 6.8 cm
Excavated in 1965 at a Fengsufu at Xiguanyingzi, Beipiao City, Liaoning Province

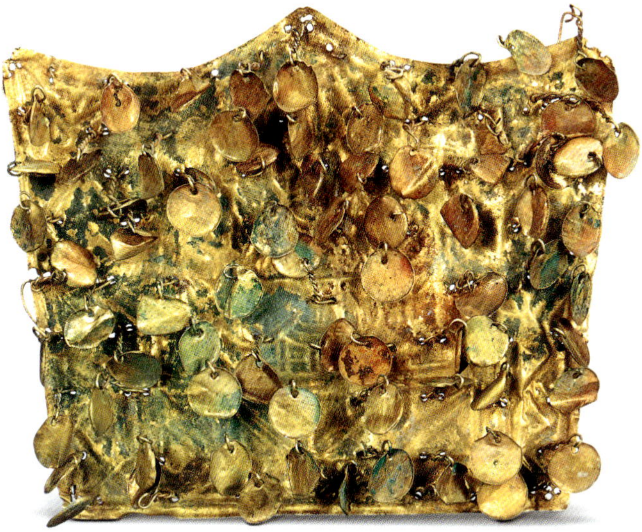

7

Gold crowns were used by high-level officials of the Han and Jin dynasties as status symbols. According to the historical record, golden earrings used both mountain shapes and cicadas as decoration. On one side of this earring there is a gold-plated seated Buddha and attendant, the other side has a gold leaf hair ornament, and shows the flourishing of Buddhism in the state of northern Yan. Also, this gold earring has decoration other than cicadas, showing the mixing of Chinese Culture, Buddhist Culture and Xianbei Northern Culture. Du Xiqing

8 Gold-plated wooden horse stirrups

Northern Yan (409–436)
Height 23 cm, Width 16.8 cm
Excavated in 1965 at a northern Yan Fengsufu Tomb at Xiguanyingzi, Beipiao City, Liaoning Province

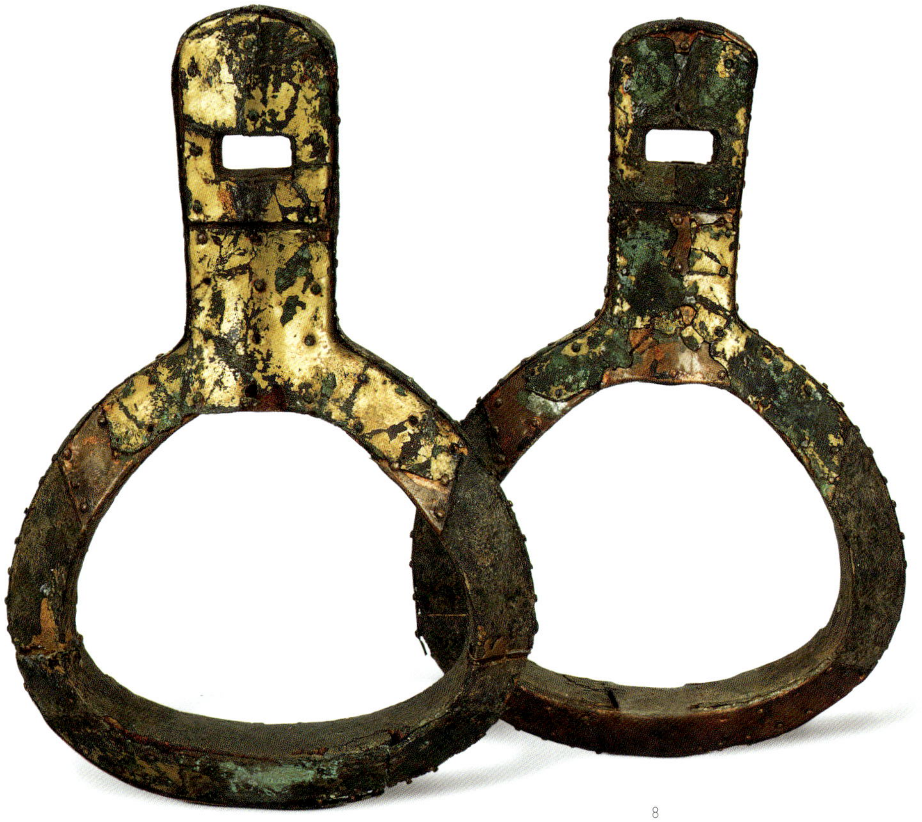

8

The wood on the inside of this pair of stirrups is made from mulberry wood, the surface is covered in gold plated bronze pieces, which are nailed to the wood by gold-plated bronze nails. In the stirrup holes are iron plates, with black lacquer applied on top. This is the only extant complete stirrup that has a proven date since the tomb from which it was excavated from dates from 415.

The horse stirrup is a Chinese invention. The earliest stirrup emerged around the third century, and was a triangular single stirrup which hung on the left flank of the horse, and was just used to help the rider mount and dismount in an emergency. Stirrups used as a pair developed in the fourth century, by which time the rider and the horse could ride together as one. Horse tack could only be considered complete when it reached this stage of development. After this the horse stirrup reached Europe, and was important in the development of medieval knightly chivalry. Early practical stirrups that have been excavated mostly belonged to the Murong Xianbei people. Although this stirrup has preserved the triangular shape, it had already developed to the paired stirrup stage, and is an important object for researching the development of ancient riding tack. Du Xiqing

9 a: *Fanyang gongzhang* golden seal; b: *Liaoxi gongzhang* gold-plated bronze seal; c: *Da Sima zhang* gold-plated bronze seal; d: *Cheqi da jiangjun* gold-plated bronze seal

Northern Yan (409–436)
a: Total Height 1.98 cm, Length of seal face 2.27 cm, Width 2.35 cm
b–d: 2.75 cm, Length of seal face 2.46 cm, Width 2.22 cm
Excavated in 1965 at a northern Yan Fengsufu Tomb at Xiguanyingzi, Beipiao City, Liaoning Province

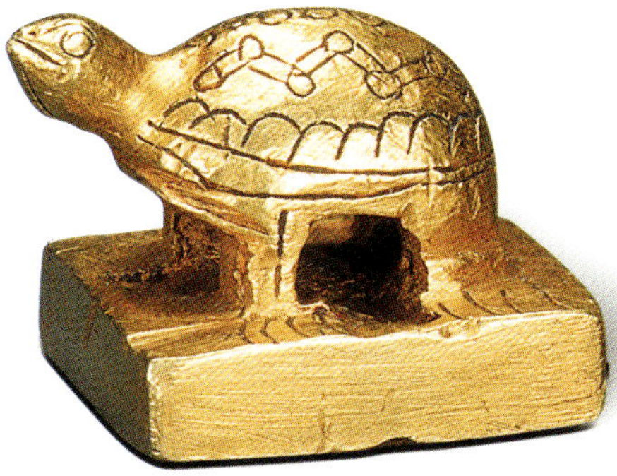

9 a

9 a Surface of the seal

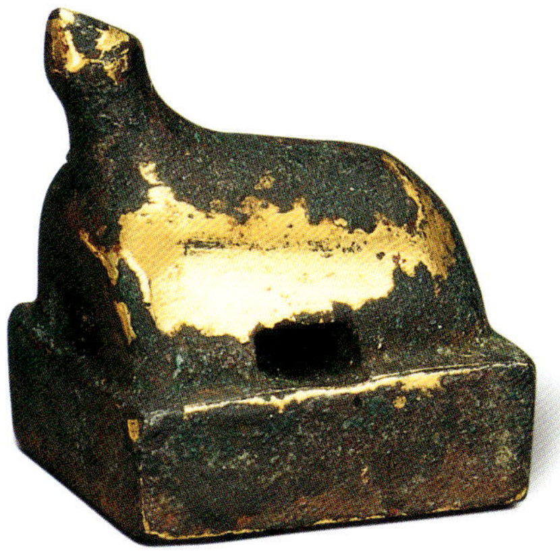

9 b

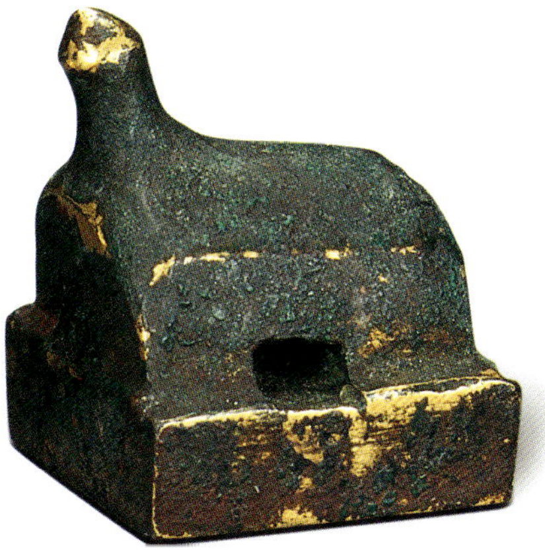

9 c

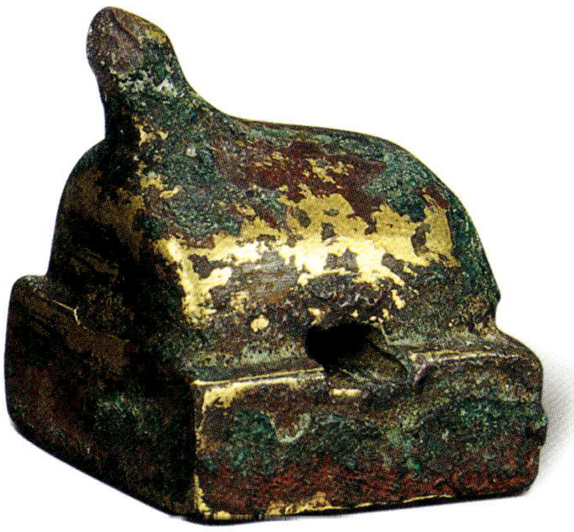

9 d

10 Gold headdress ornament

Northern Yan (409–436)
Total Height 26 cm
Excavated in 1965 at a northern Yan Fengsufu Tomb at Xiguanyingzi, Beipiao City, Liaoning Province

11 Gold headdress ornament with cicada design

Northern Yan (409–436)
Height 6.8 cm
Excavated in 1965 at a Fengsufu at Xiguanyingzi, Beipiao City, Liaoning Province

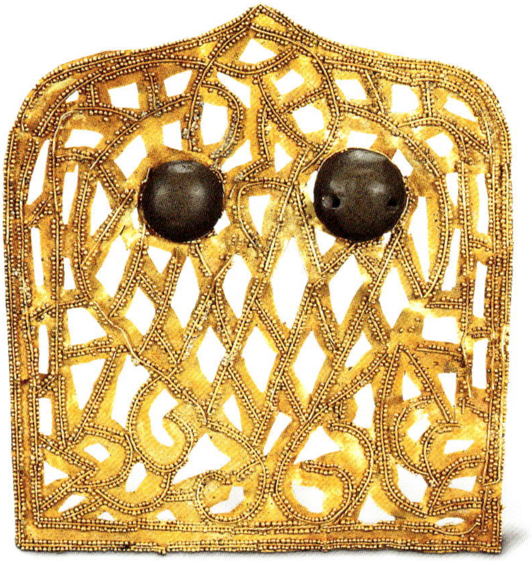

11

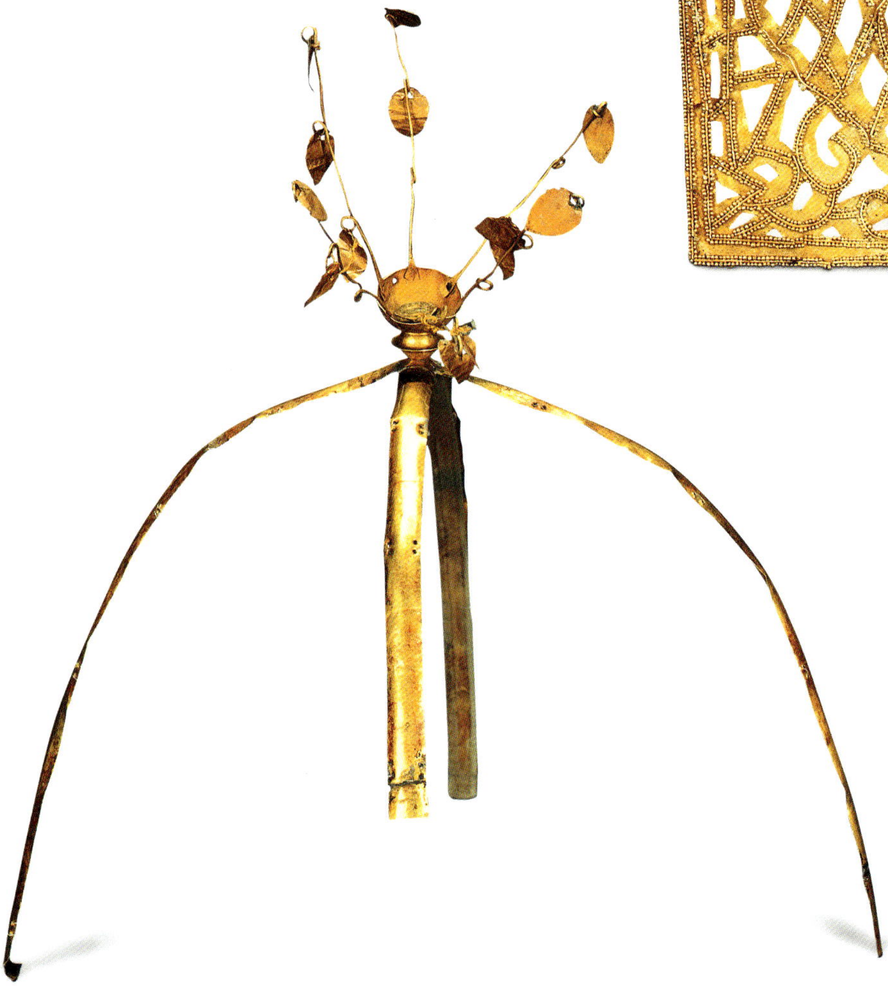

10

12 Gold-plated silver crown

Liao (916–1125)
Height 18.7 cm, Diameter 20.1 cm
Excavated in 1956 at Xintulu village, Jianping County, Liaoning Province

13 Gold ear ornament in the shape of a phoenix

Liao (916–1125)
Height 5.6 cm, Length 4.7 cm
Excavated in 1956 at Liao tomb at Zhangjiayingzi xiang, Jianping County, Liaoning Province

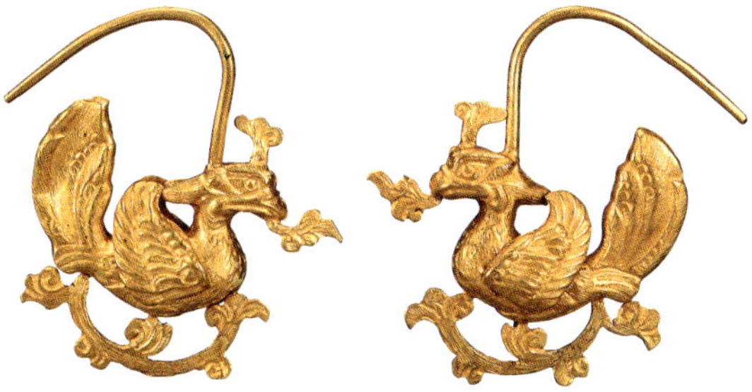

13

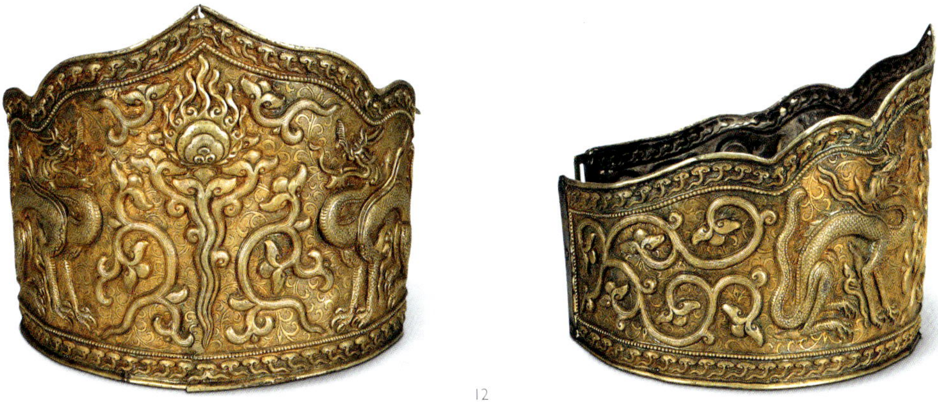

12

This crown has first had silver casting and been carved, and has then been gold plated. It has a circular tube shape, is high at the top and low at the back, both parts are tied with silk thread; there are three auspicious clouds covering volcanic pearls in the middle, with two seated dragons on the sides, with winged heads and raised tails. The base has a slender pearl pattern with curved grass lines, exquisitely made, showing the Liao skill for fine gold work. This piece has been reused and was already round when found, and so must have been a crown. Du Xiqing

14 a: Gold earrings in the shape of a fish; b: Gold bracelet with flower pattern

Liao (916–1125)
a: Width 3.7 cm
b: Length 6.5 cm, Width 1.4 cm
Excavated in 1956 at Liao tomb at Wangfugou village, Zhuluke xiang, Jianping County, Liaoning Province

15 Gold hairpin in dragon boat shape

Liao (916–1125)
Height of dragon boat 2.2 cm, Length 2.9 cm, Length of hairpin 5.3 cm
Excavated in 1956 at Liao tomb at Batuyingzi, Xinmin City, Liaoning Province

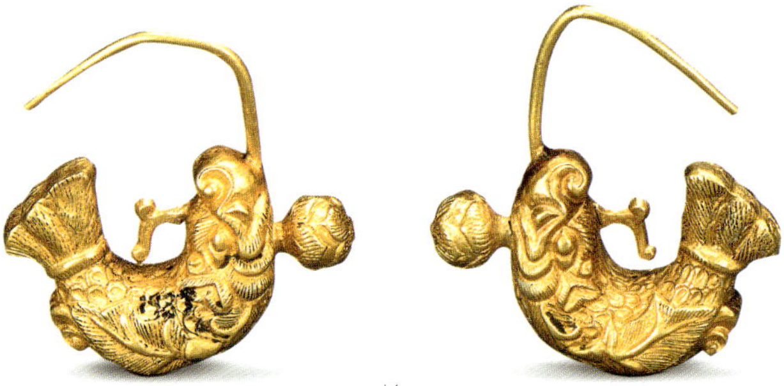

14 a

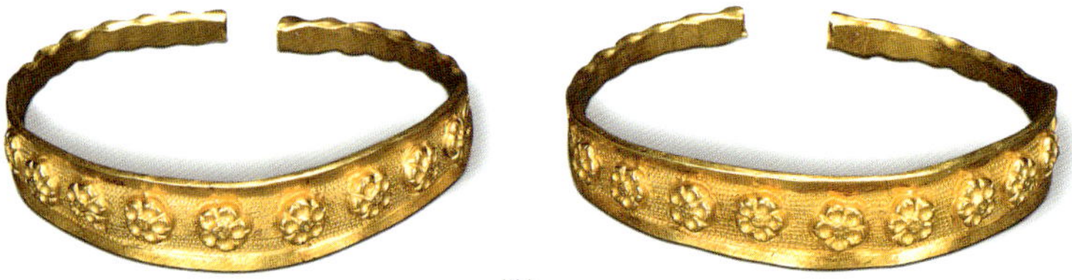

14 b

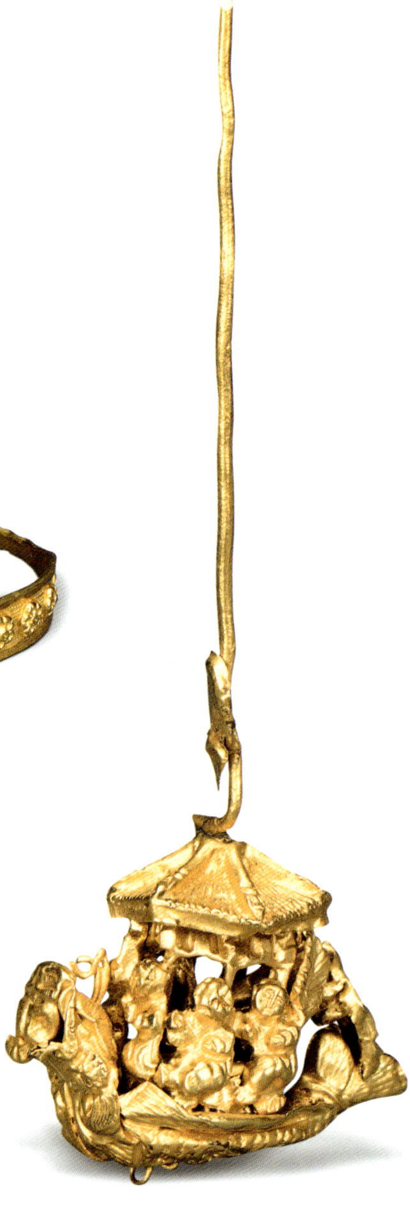

15

16 Gold-plated silver saddle bridge

Liao (AD 916–1125)
Width 39 cm
Excavated in 1956 from Liao tomb at
Xintulu village, Jianping County, Liaoning Province

17 Silver mask

Liao (916–1125)
Length 18 cm, Width 20 cm
Excavated at Liao tomb at Jiaominzhu shuiku,
Fuxin City, Liaoning Province

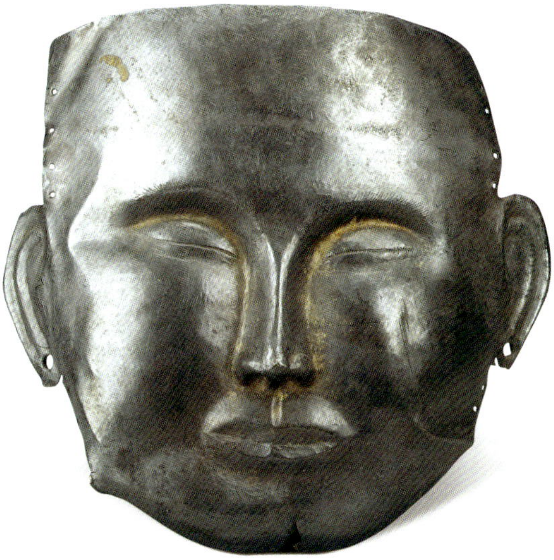

17

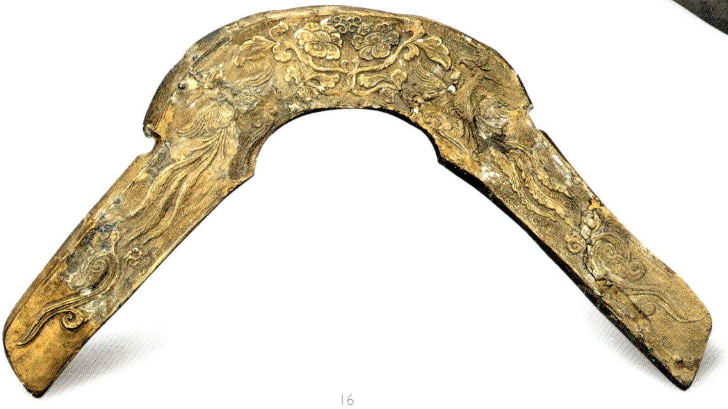

16

The saddle bridge has a design of three peony flowers on top with pearl pattern base. The main part has a pair of phoenixes, a large mouth, wings, a long tail. A saddle bridge is the high part of the two parts of the wooden saddle, the outside has been gold plated to protect the saddle wood, and is also a decoration. The Khitan people were experienced horsemen, and their traditional craftsmanship reached a very high level.
Du Xiqing

18 Golden stupa

Liao (916–1125)
Total Height 25 cm, Top Diameter 10 cm, Weight 360 g
Excavated in 1967 at a Liao palace stupa at Hongmaozi, Fuxin City, Liaoning Province

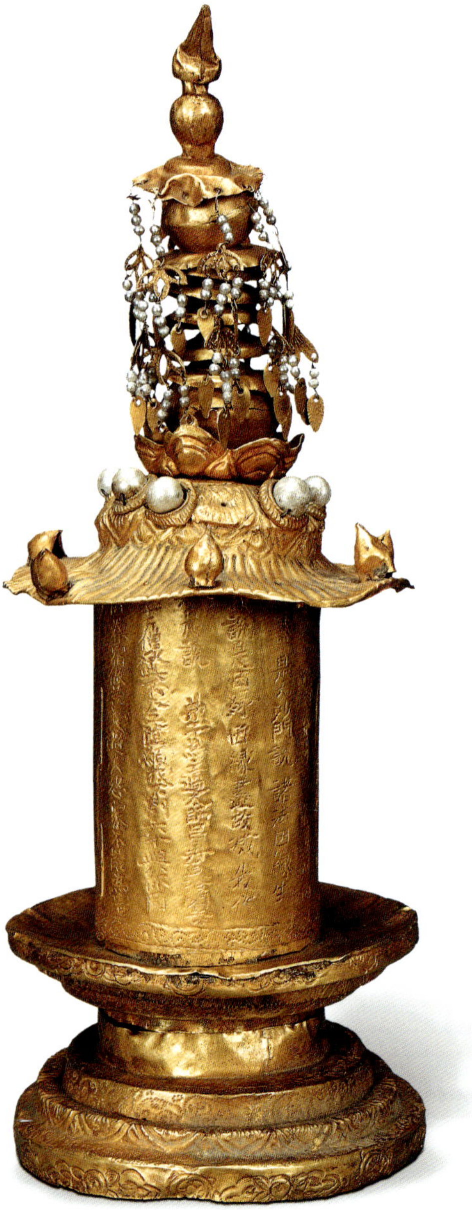

The stupa is made of gold plate, and is composed of a plinth, main body, eaves and top. The round plinth has three tiers from top to bottom, covered with lotus, grass and peony patterns. The stupa body is made from a round tube covered with gold leaf, the front has a high niche surrounded by inscriptions of eleven lines carved in gold. Reading from the right of the niche, the text goes all the way around the stupa with Buddhist prayers, stupa builder's wishes and mantras. The stupa eaves have been carved into tiles, decorated with fire pearls around the sides. Lotuses are carved on to the eaves with pearls on the inside, linking up with the seat. The top part is pierced with treasure pearls, has a wheel of law, and is gourd-shaped. The canopy has pearl and jade necklaces hanging around it, which are composed of little pearls and small gold leaf. Upon excavation there was a jade case inside the canopy containing Buddhist relics. The golden stupa was housed inside a large silver stupa. These three pieces were offered by those who made the stupa. Du Xiqing

19 Silver stupa

Liao (916–1125)
Total Height 46.3 cm, Base Diameter 14.4 cm
Excavated in 1967 at a Liao palace stupa, Fuxin City, Liaoning Province

20 Silver scroll with inlaid characters

Liao (916–1125)
Length 117 cm, Width 13 cm
Excavated in 1967 at a Liao palace stupa at Hongmaozi, Fuxin City, Liaoning Province

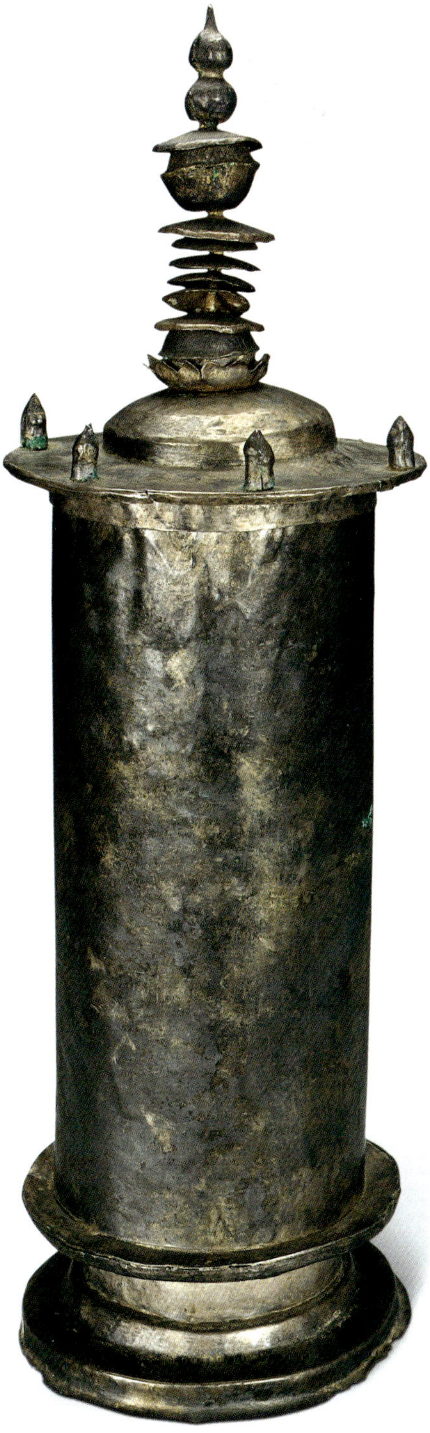

19

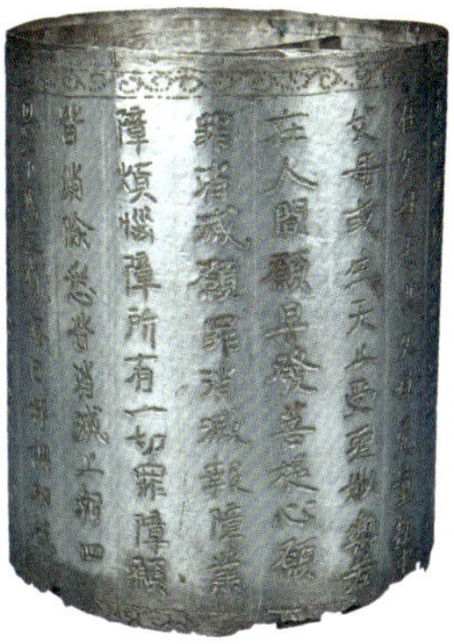

20

9

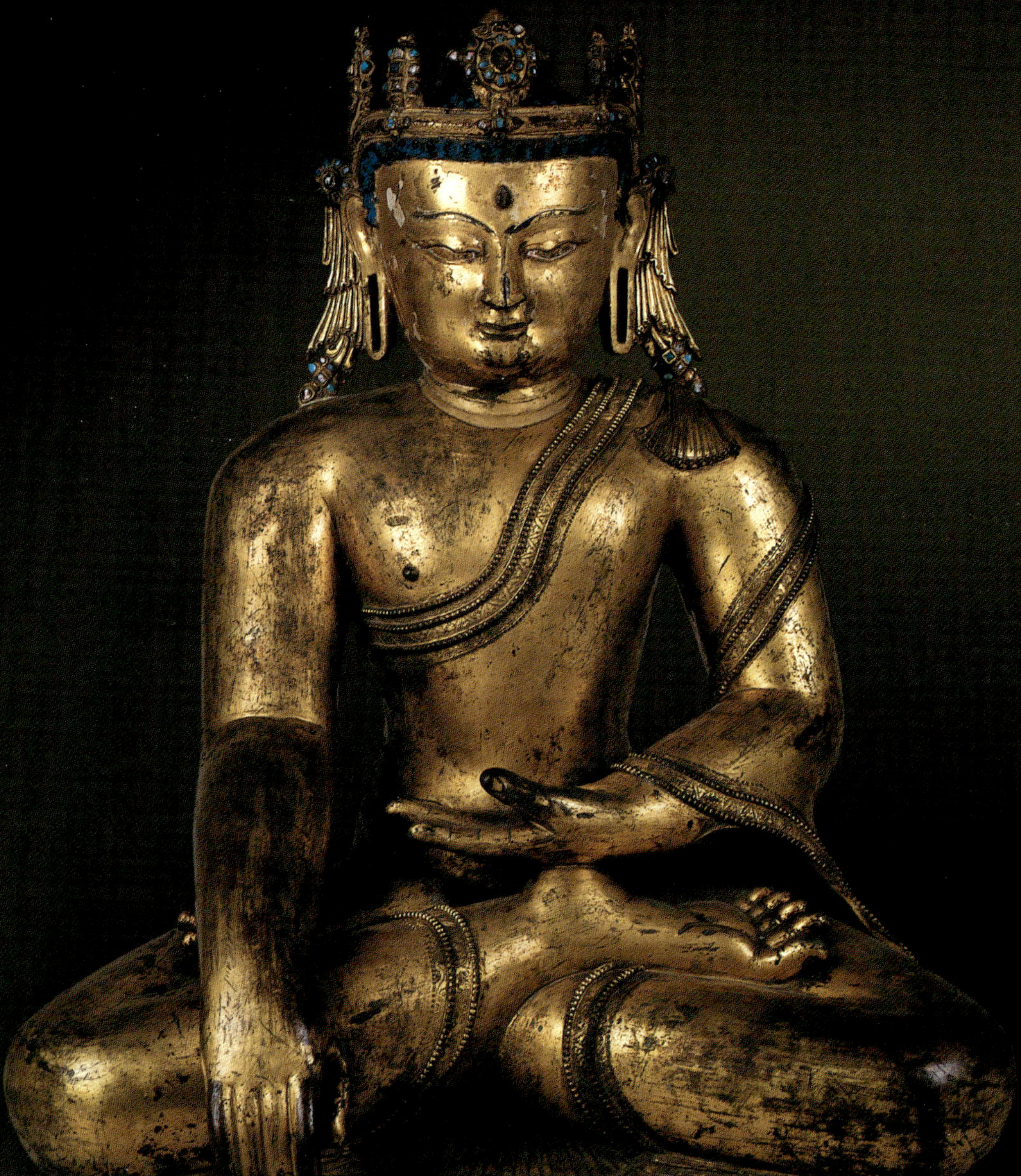

Buddhist Figure sculpture

Buddhism originated in ancient India founded by Shakyamuni at the end of the sixth century BC. Images of the Buddha played an important role in the transmission of Buddhist belief. The term 'Buddha' here refers to a range of images such as the historical Buddha, bodhisattvas, *arhats*, deities and heavenly beings.

The Liaoning Provincial Museum collection of Buddha figures can be divided into Chinese and Tibetan styles. Chinese figures of Buddha are mainly stone sculptures or gold-plated bronze statues. The stone sculptures mainly date from the Northern dynasties and Sui and Tang periods, some have dated inscriptions, and all have great artistic and historical value. The earliest Chinese bronze statue in the Liaoning Museum collection is a gold-plated seated Shakyamuni Buddha dating from the Sixteen Kingdoms period. Sui dynasty sculpture retained the rhythms of the Northern Qi and Zhou periods with a similar style. In the Tang dynasty the style reached its perfection. Generally speaking, the quality of Ming dynasty Chinese Buddhas seemed to decline, with quite static positions and gestures, lacking in vitality or natural rhythm. Wood carving from this period is plentiful, taking real people as its original subject matter, closing the gap between gods and people. The most striking of these carvings are of *arhats*, using simple and clear technique, full of vitality, weighty gestures, with calm expressions, and, with firm straight lines in their robes, they are important works in the history of sculpture.

The figure of the teaching Buddha is the earliest Tibetan bronze figure at the Liaoning Provincial Museum. It was carved in the ninth century, with expressions in the old style, wearing large garments over the shoulders with decorative U-shaped patterns on top. He is sitting in the lotus position, with a lotus seat, with full wide lotus petals linking top and bottom. Yuan dynasty sculpture mainly followed the Nepalese style, injecting new vitality into Chinese traditional sculptural art. The bronze gold-plated Akshobhya Buddha is a fine example of this period; wearing a five-leaf crown, with a jade stone at the top, and was exquisitely crafted. Most of the Ming dynasty gold bronze Buddhas are from the Yongle and Xuande palaces, and are finely made with dignified expressions and symmetrical bodies.

In esoteric Tibetan Buddhism, the mother of the Buddha is an important princess and was venerated. Tara, as Buddha's mother, mostly appears with a calm peaceful expression, often with a full beautiful face and fine hair, drooping shoulders and a slender waist, full breasts and arms, a curvaceous feminine body. The 15th-century Green Tara figure can be considered a fine example of this kind of bronze sculpture.

Guru images are an important variety in Tibetan bronze sculpture. Buddhist gurus usually refer to historical figures who made important contributions to the transmission of Buddhism. Their images were venerated by later generations and were popular, systematic and solemn in the tradition of Tibetan esoteric Buddhism. This is related to the importance ascribed to gurus in Tibetan practice. Realistic carving techniques are used in this variety to depict the master's real features, with spiritual vivid expressions. The Ming large silver and gold-plated sculpture is completely carved out of silver, with gold plating added. It is exquisitely crafted and extremely rare, and is a masterpiece of Tibetan figure of Buddha. Zhang Li

1 *Guanyin* statue in white stone

Northern Qi Tianbao 8th year (AD 557)
Height 56.4 cm

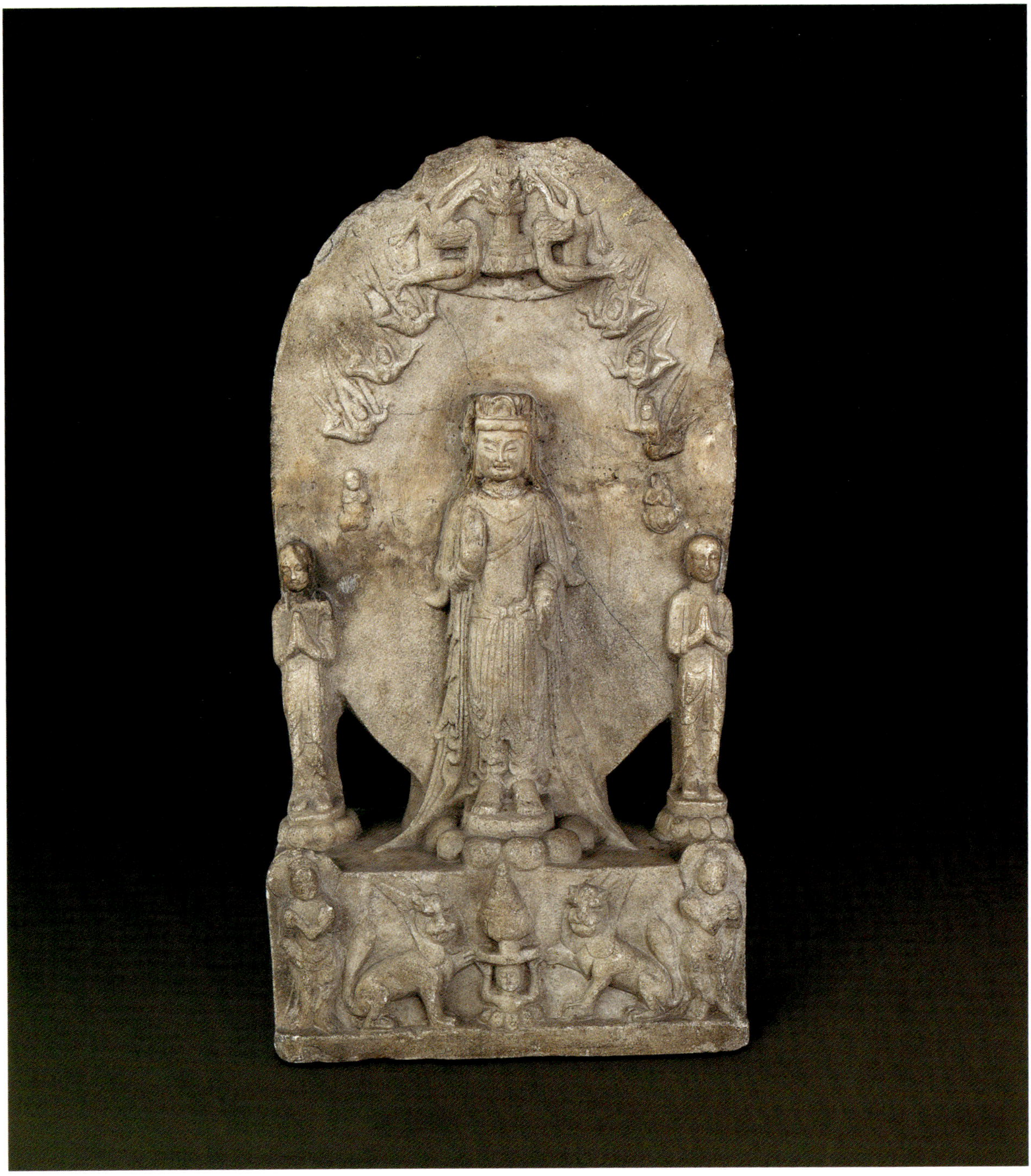

2 *Bodhisattva* statue carved in white stone

Northern Qi (AD 550–577)
Existing Height 43.9 cm

3 *Bodhisattva* statue carved in white stone

Sui (AD 581–618)
Existing Height 50 cm

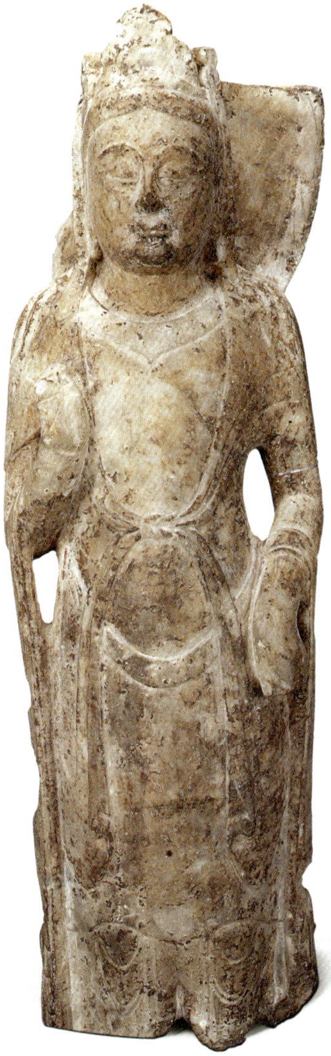

2

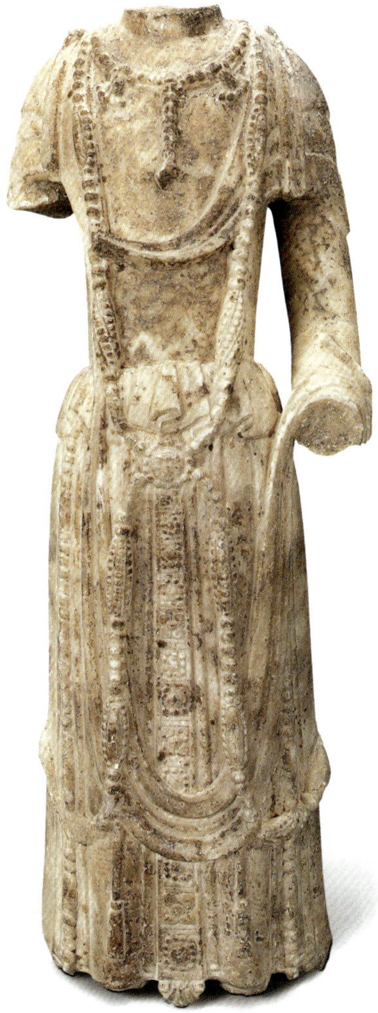

3

4 Bronze gold-plated Shakyamuni seated statue

Sixteen Kingdoms (AD 303–420)
Height 7.8 cm

5 Bronze gold-plated standing *Guanyin*

Sui (AD 581–618)
Height 13.3 cm

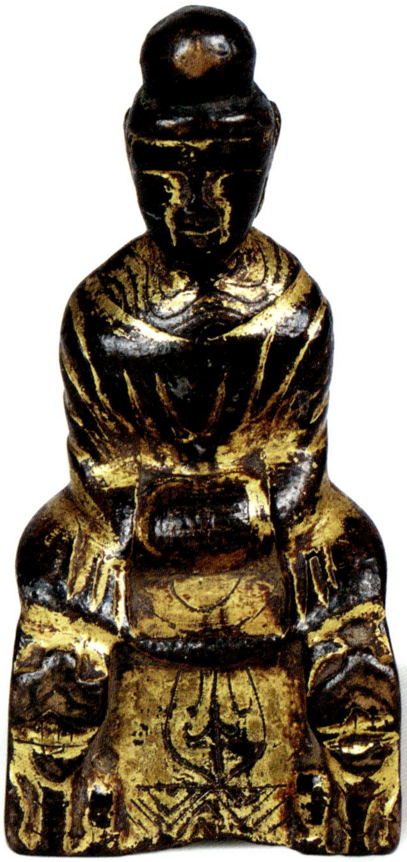

4

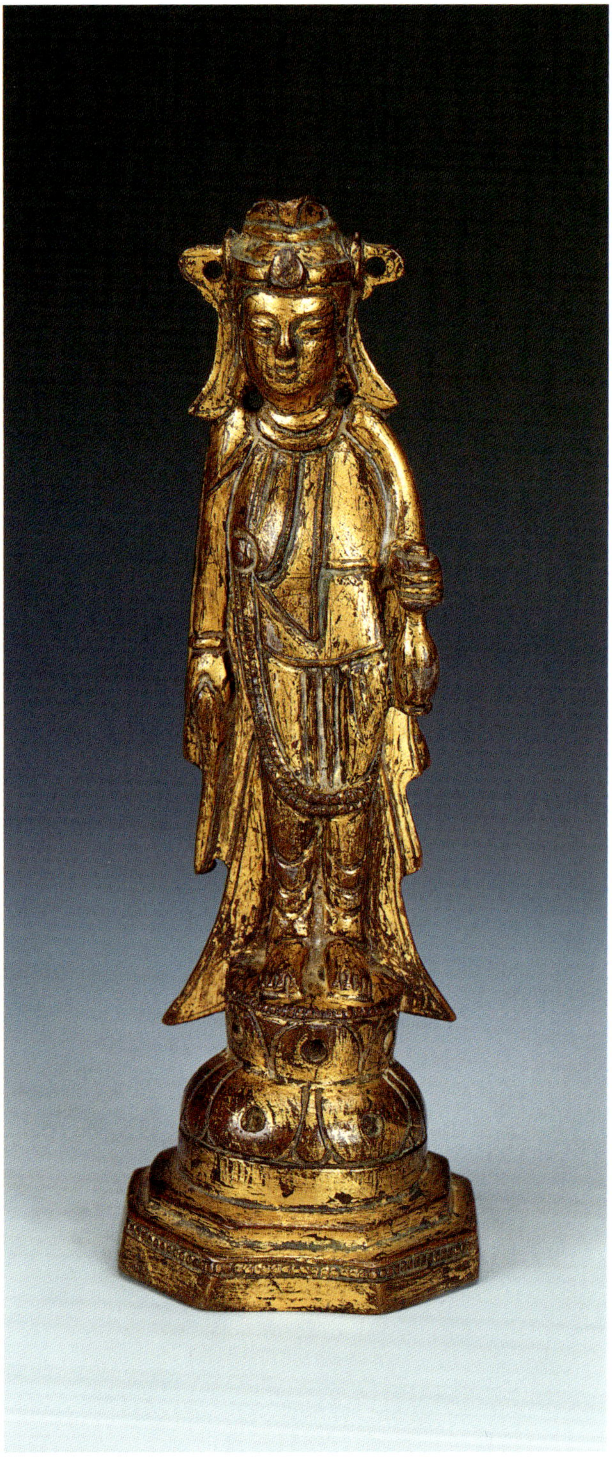

5

6 Bronze teaching Buddha

9th century
Height 13.8 cm

7 Gold-plated Shakyamuni seated statue

Five Dynasties (AD 907–960)
Height 13.5 cm

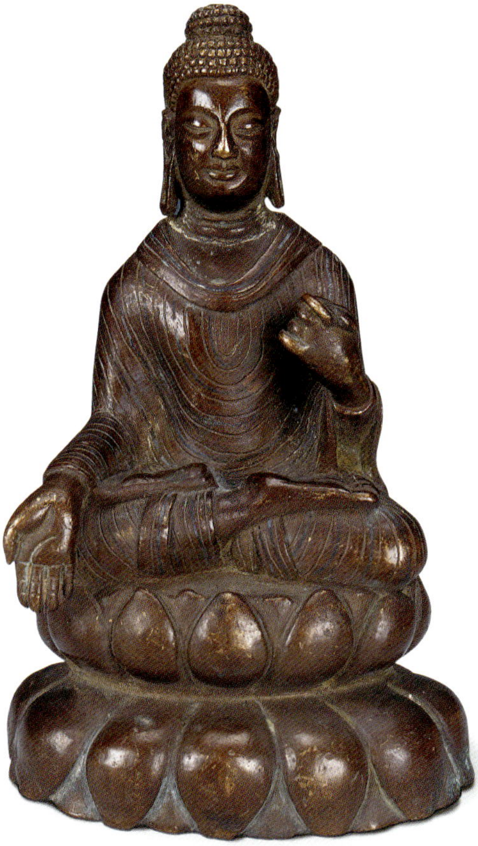

6

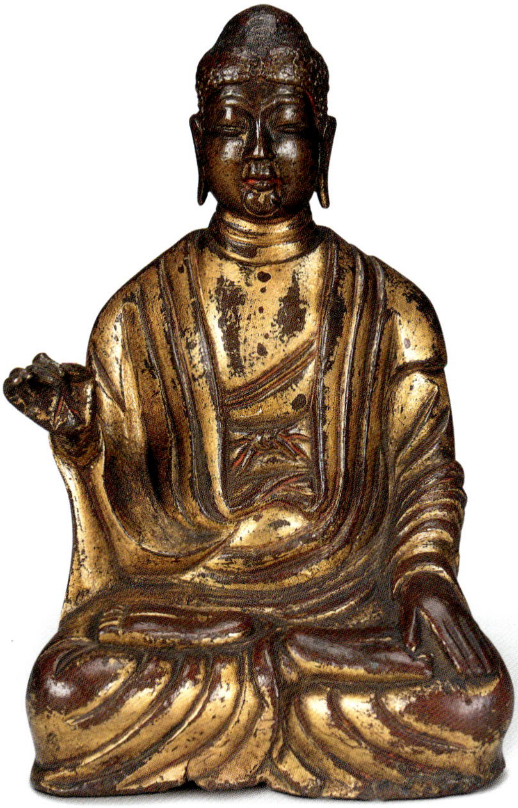

7

8 Bronze gold-plated Ajaya Guanyin

Dali Kingdom (AD 937–1253)
Height 46 cm

9 Bronze gold-plated Nepalese Aksobhya Buddha

Yuan (AD 1271–1368)
Height 58 cm

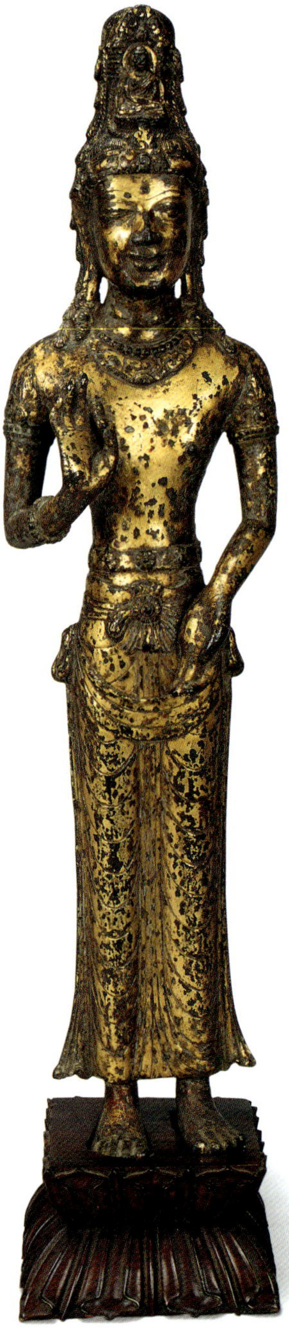

8

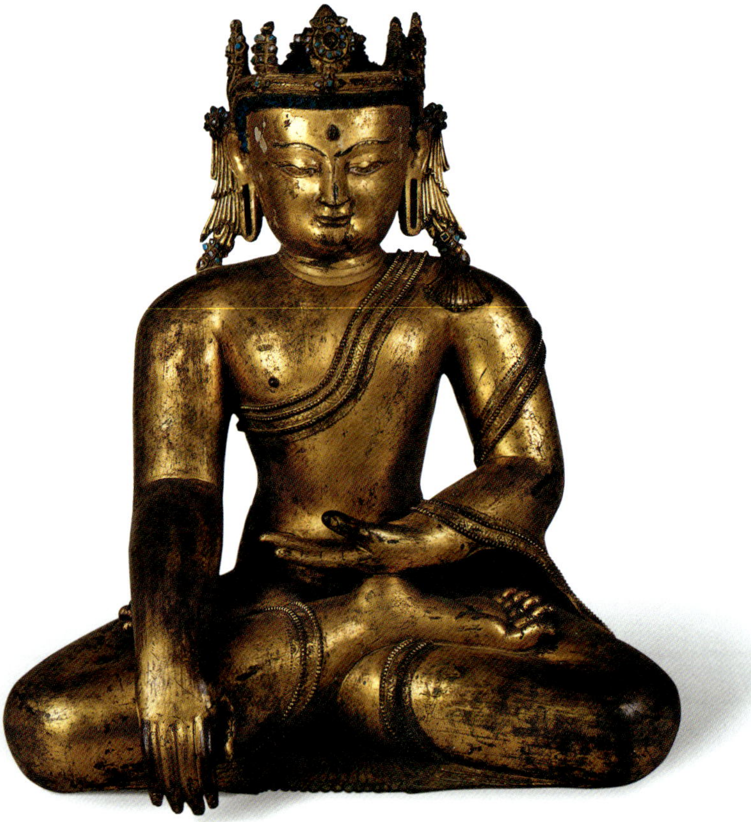

9

After Buddhism was transmitted to the Erhai region, it mixed with the original local religion, forming a local form of Yunnan tantric Azhali Buddhism. After the Dali kingdom was formed, the main god of Yunnan Azhali Buddhism, Ajaya Guanyin, became the main respected god. This Guanyin has a long slender body, with a bare upper body and bare feet, wearing a lotus treasure crown. An Amitabha Buddha in the lotus position is inlaid into the crown. Guanyin does not have clear gender characteristics and is popularly called the slender-waist Guanyin. This piece is a classic example of ancient Buddhist figure sculpture from the southern Dali kingdom in Yunnan, and is full of local cultural characteristics. Zhang Li

10 Bronze gold-plated Prince Siddhartha Gautama

Ming dynasty (1368–1644)
Height 33 cm

11 Bronze gold-plated *Guanyin* statue

Ming dynasty (1368–1644)
Height 74 cm

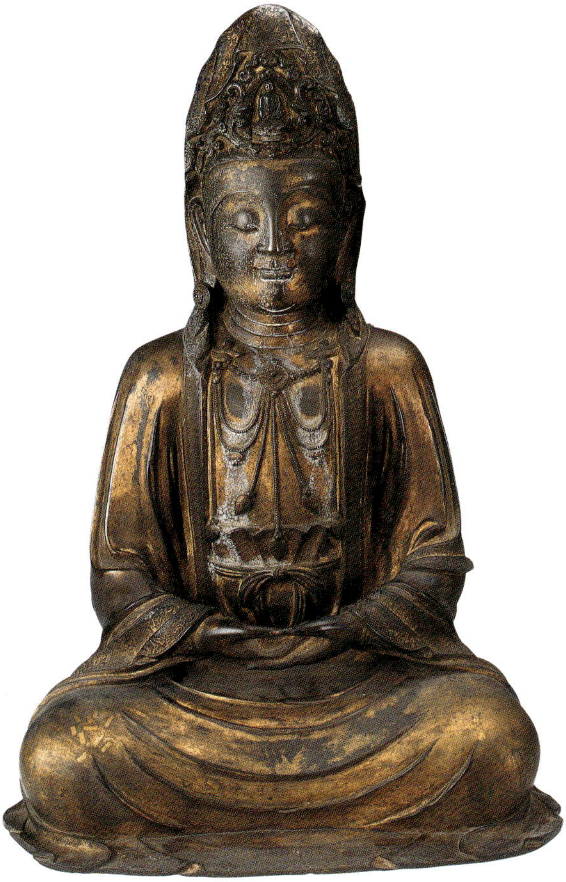

11

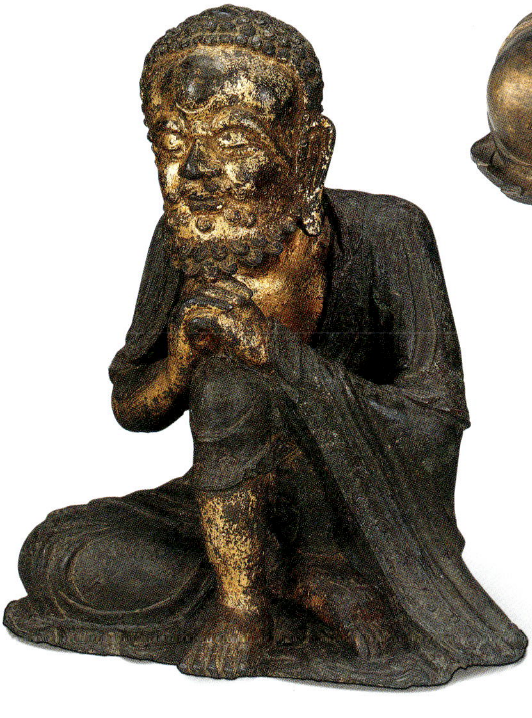

10

12 Bronze gold-plated Shakyamuni seated Buddha

Ming Yongle period (1403–1424)
Height 19.2 cm

13 Tibetan figure holding a diamond

14th century
Height 24.3 cm

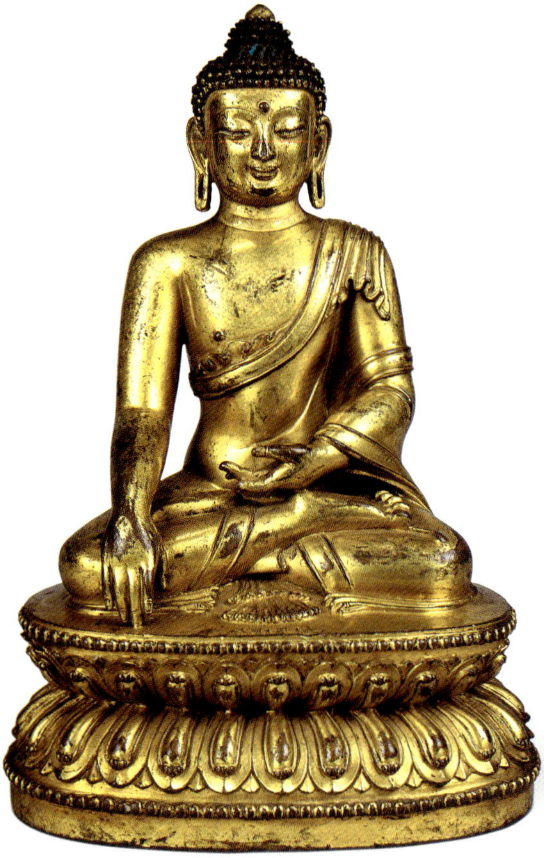

12

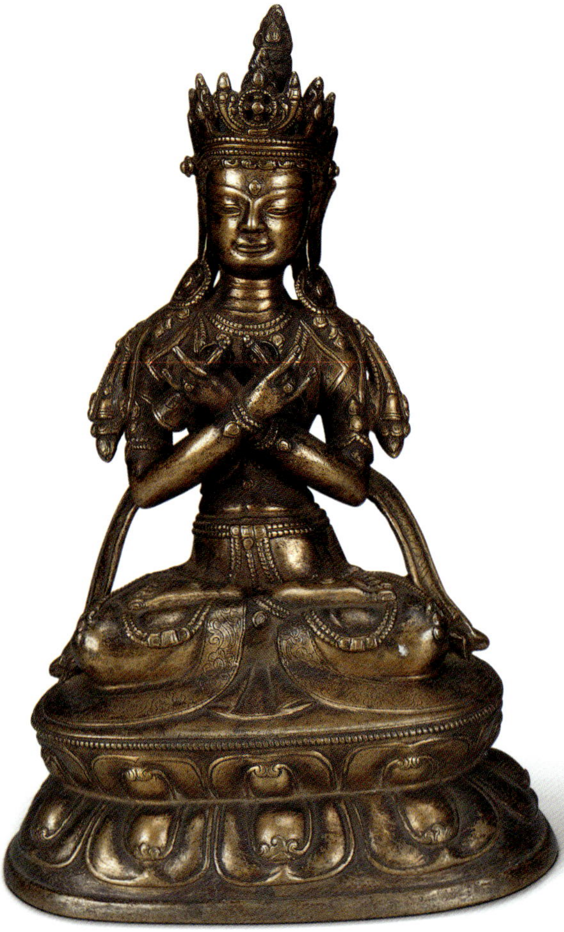

13

In order to satisfy the demand for Buddhist objects for largess and worship, the early Ming court assembled the best statuary from Central China, Tibet and even Nepal. They used Tibetan sculpture as their model, adding Chinese aesthetic concepts and expression and created the famous sculptures of the Yongle and Xuande courts that were artistic masterpieces. Bronze gold-plated sculptures from these two courts were Ming classics and later Chinese and Tibetan sculpture copied them. Furthermore, the beautiful style of this type of sculpture greatly influenced Tibetan sculpture up to the Qing dynasty. ZHANG LI

14 Bronze Tibetan statue

14th–15th century
Height 13.5 cm
West Tibet

15 Bronze gold-plated Green Tara

15th century
Height 19.5 cm
Nepal

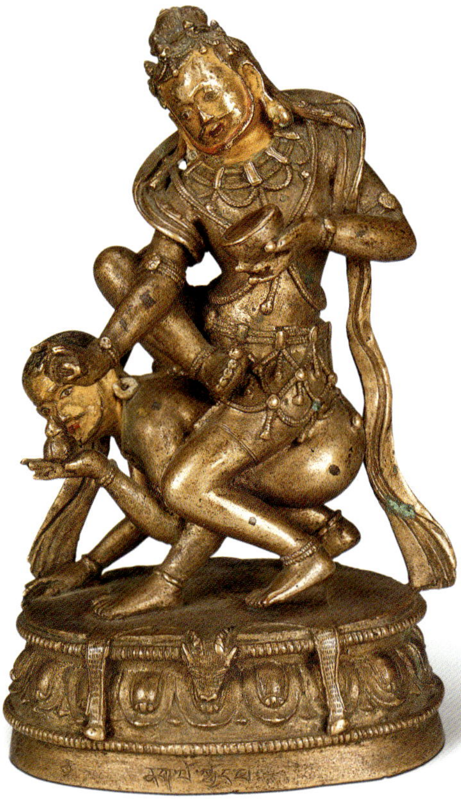

14

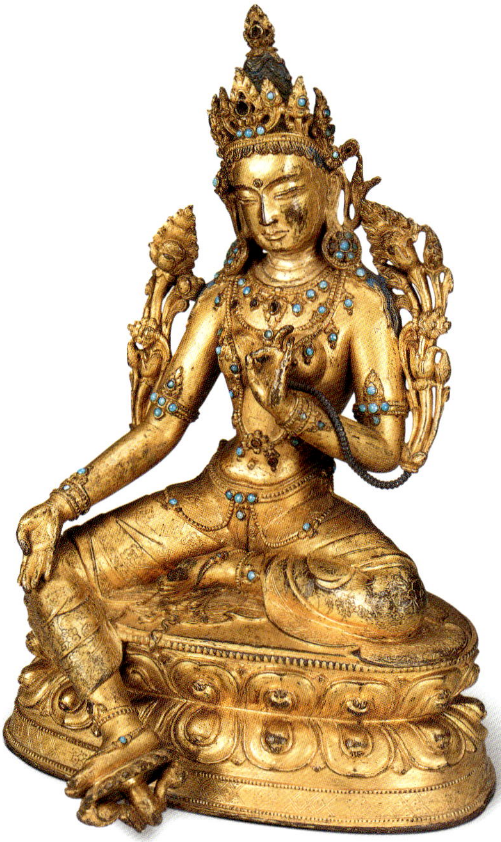

15

16 Wooden carved statue of an *arhat*

Ming dynasty (1368–1644)
Height 139 cm

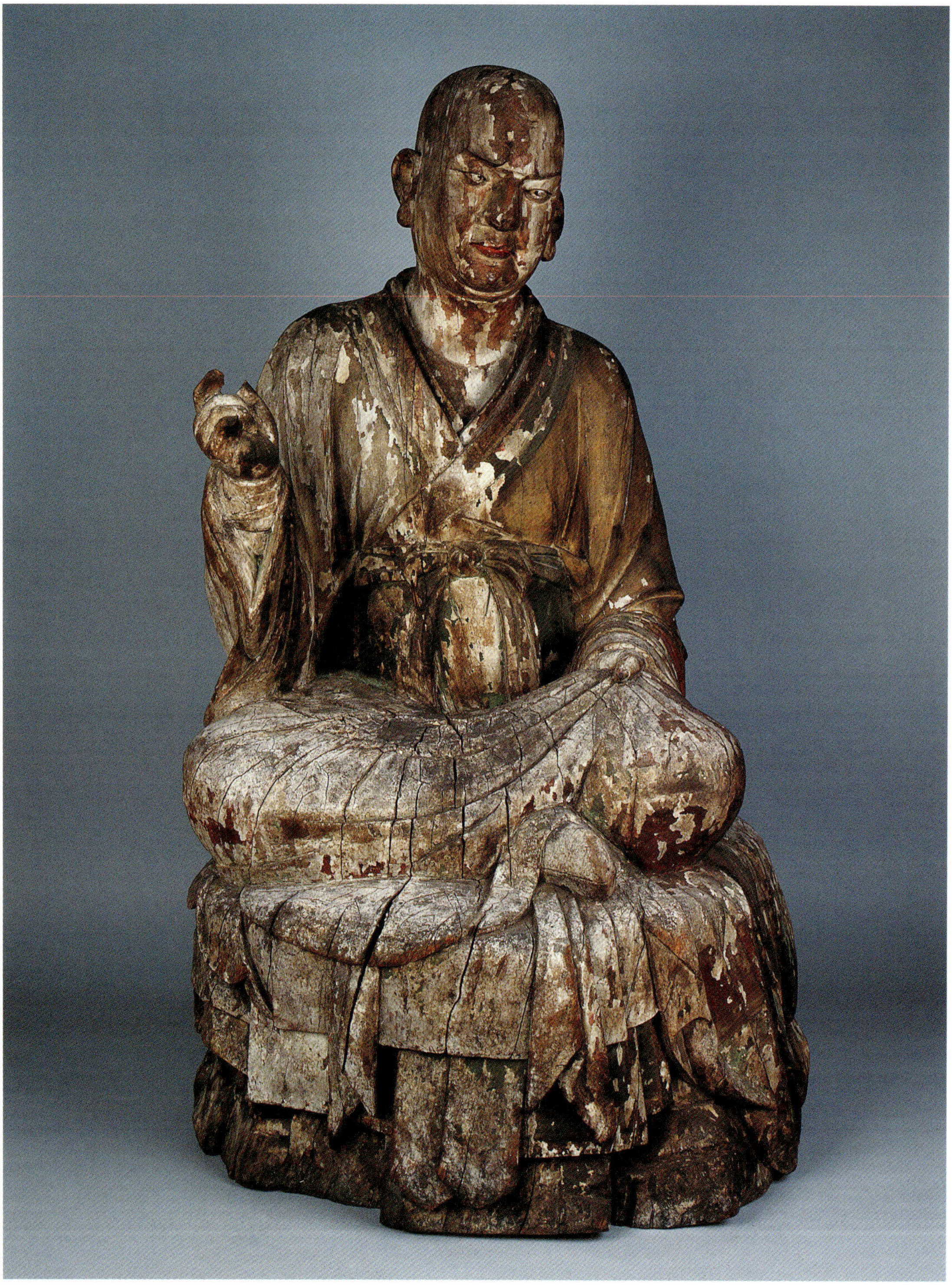

17 Silver gold-plate statue of Buton Rimpoche

15th century
Height 11.5 cm
Nepal

18 Bronze Boundless-immortality Buddha

17th century
Height 16 cm
Beijing area

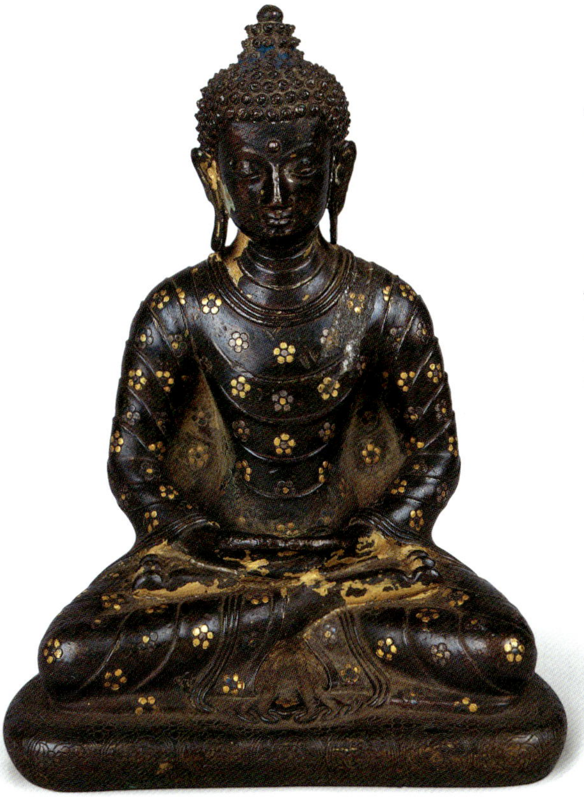

18

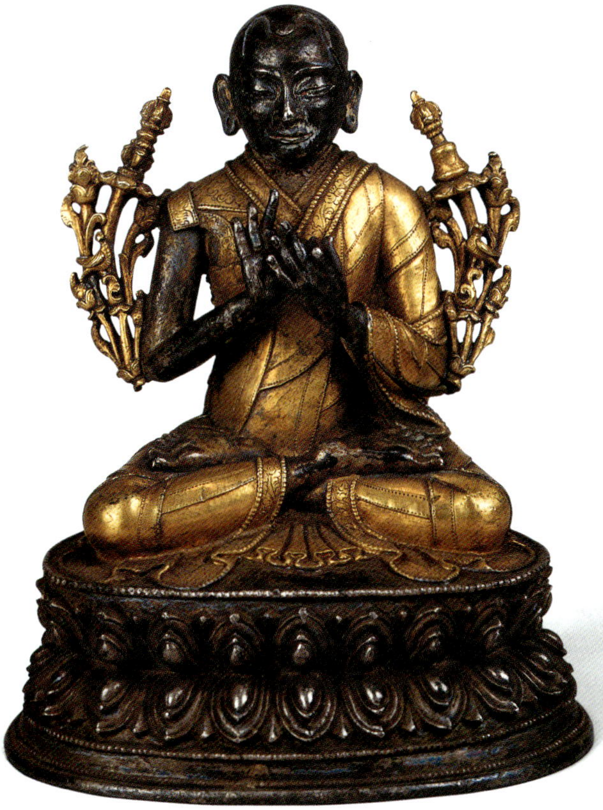

17

19 Assembly tree

18th century
Height 48 cm
Beijing area

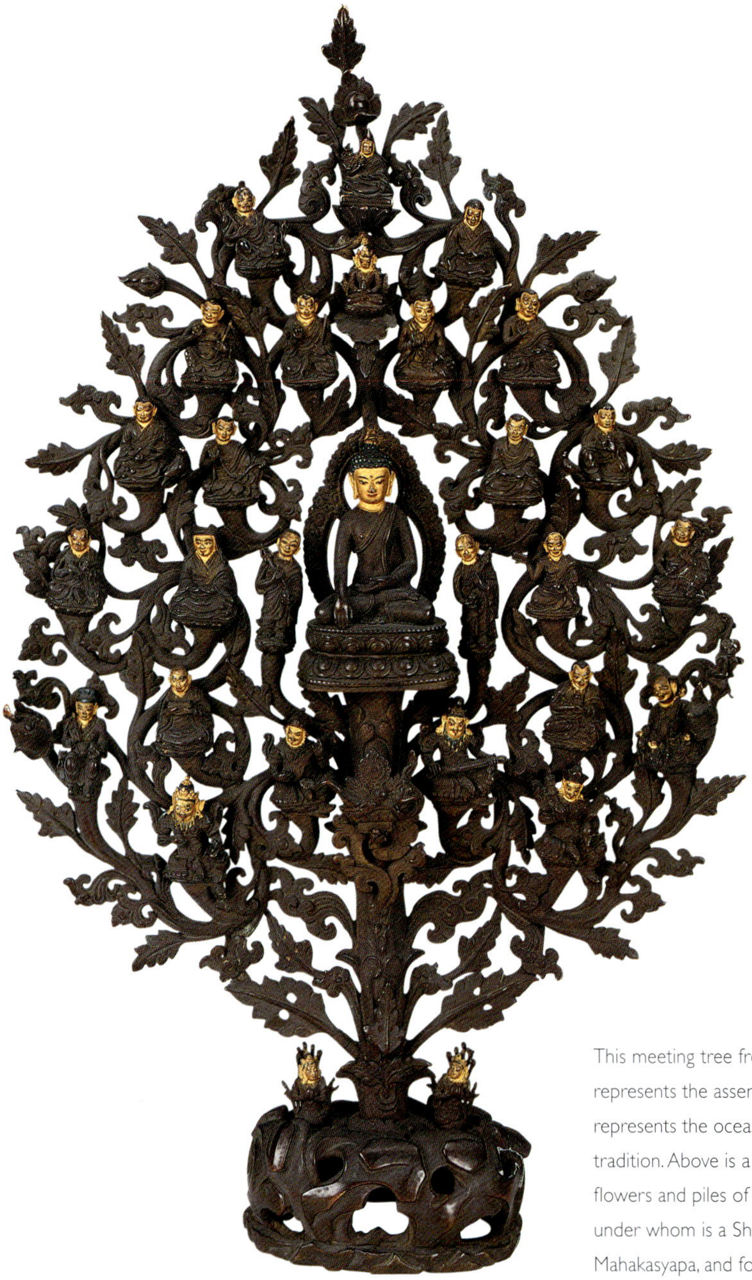

19

This meeting tree from Central China, also called the auspicious field, represents the assembly of the guru and those holding the law. The raised seat represents the ocean between the four continents according to the Buddhist tradition. Above is a lucky fruit tree with luxurious foliage and fresh open flowers and piles of fruit. Underneath this is a boundless immortal Buddha, under whom is a Shakyamuni Buddha, surrounded by eighteen *arhats*, Ananda, Mahakasyapa, and four large heavenly kings. Right at the bottom are two dragon kings, Nantuo and Panantuo. Tibetan tantric Buddhist practice ascribes most importance to transmission through guru; the guru must initiate a practitioner before they can achieve anything, hence the phrase 'A guru is like the Buddha'. Therefore, in any depictions of the levels of existence, the guru must occupy the highest, clearest position in the centre of the image. ZHANG LI

20 Bronze gold-plated Daweide diamond

Qing Qianlong period (1736–1795)
Height 23 cm
Beijing area

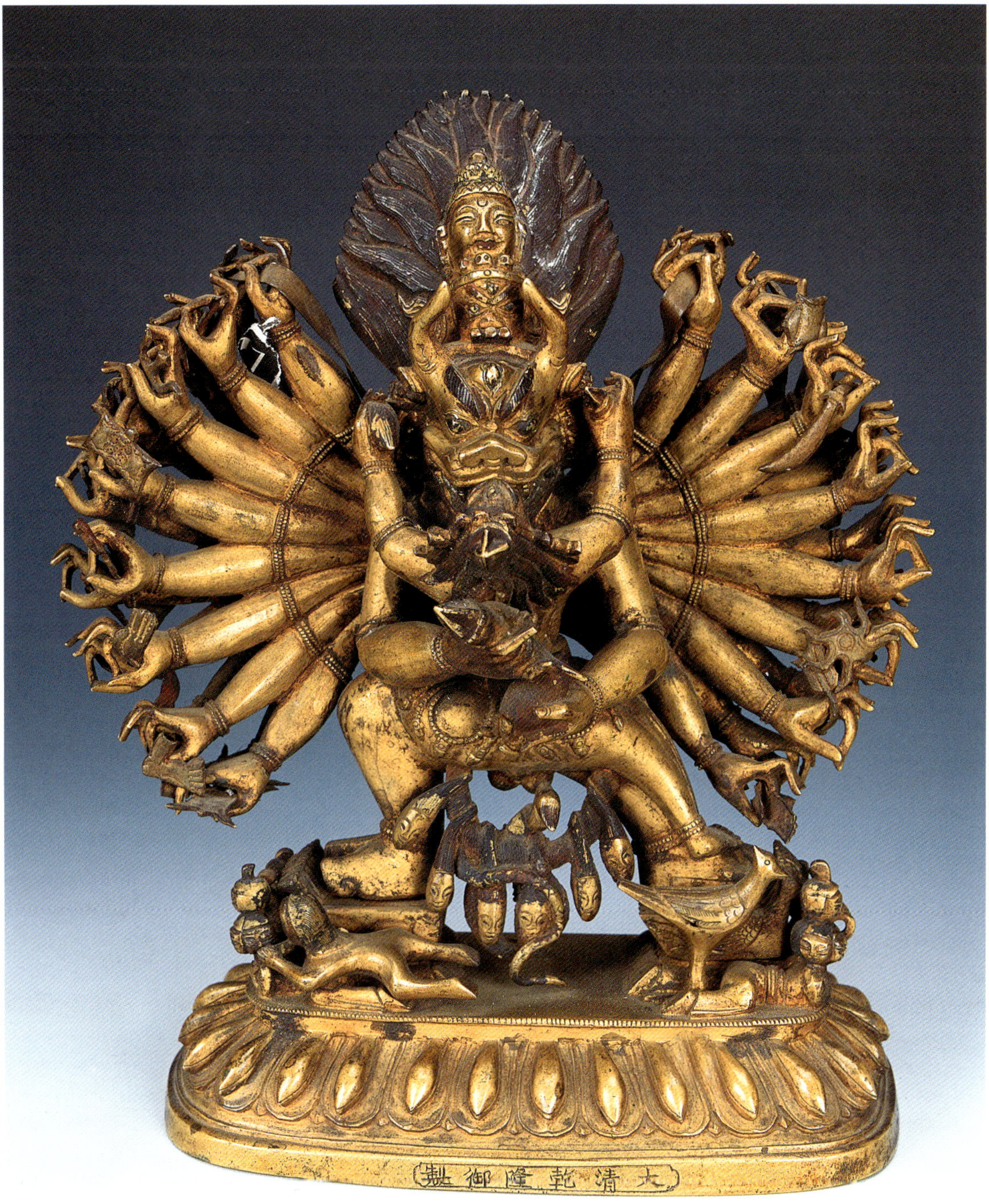

20

10

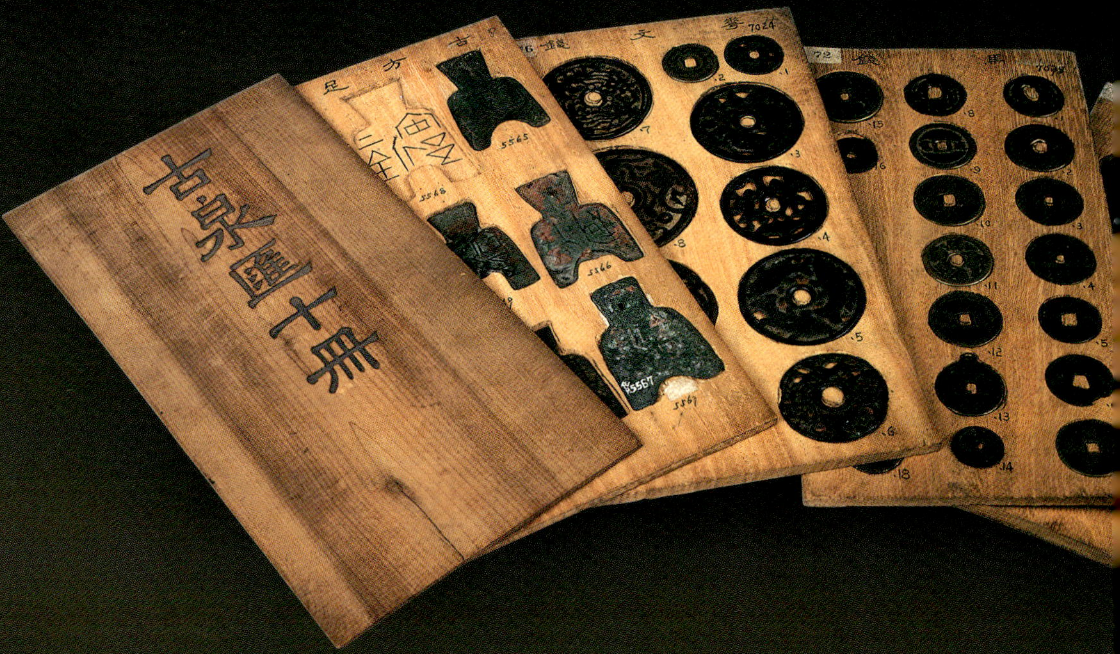

Coins and Currency

China was one of the earliest countries to use money. The emergence of a primitive coinage followed the establishment and development of an economy based on barter in the late Neolithic Age. Money went through different stages of development including metal tokens, carved coins and currency on trust, leaving a rich historical legacy. Over the course of several thousand years, Chinese money developed in isolation, receiving only little influence from other countries, and maintaining over a long period a particularly Eastern money culture.

The collection of coins and currency at the Liaoning Provincial Museum dates from the Shang to Qing periods and is a large and varied collection of high quality. It includes ancient Chinese bronze coins, modern machine-made coins, paper money from all periods, and gold and silver ingots in common use in all ages. This varied collection has provided a rich resource for researching the development of Chinese money. The most important among these include the 3,128 coins and nine moulds recorded in the famous late Qing collector Li Zuoxian's book *Collection of Ancient Coins (Gu quan hui)*. These coins range from Western Zhou primitive *bu* coins to coins carved by Wu Sangui's grandson Wu Shifan with 'Common currency of Honghua' from the late-Ming and early-Qing. It also contains coins from all ages, and the largest number are knife and *bu* coins from the Spring and Autumn and Warring States periods, altogether 1,188 pieces, accounting for nearly forty per cent of the *Collection of Ancient Coins*. Ming knife coins account for 354 pieces.

Apart from the coins from the *Collection of Ancient Coins*, Han dynasty gold horse hoofs were excavated in September 1986 in Dengta County in Liaoning Province, along with a twenty-tael golden ingot with Southern Song double-gourd stamps, some extremely rare Kaidan coins from the early Liao period, and some rare pieces of famous Tongxing coin. LIU YUN

1 *Wu* character hollow handle spade coin with sloping shoulders and arched feet

Warring States period (476–221 BC)
Total Length 6.9 cm, Width of feet 4.1 cm, Weight 13.6 g
Li Zuoxian former collection

2 Qi Jian Bang large knife coin

Warring States period (476–221 BC)
Total Length 18.4 cm, Width 2.8 cm, Weight 44.1 g
Li Zuoxian former collection

3 Wenxin round coin

Warring States period (476–221 BC)
Diameter 2.4 cm, Weight 3.2 g
Li Zuoxian former collection

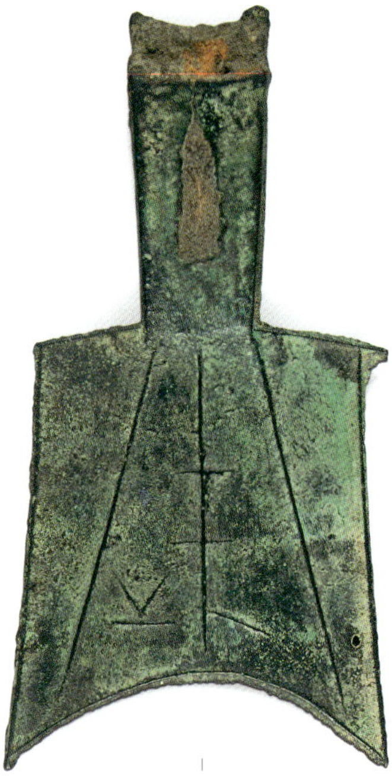

1

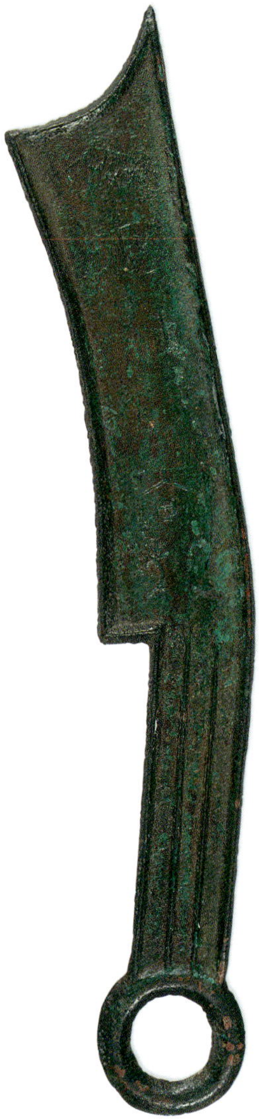

2

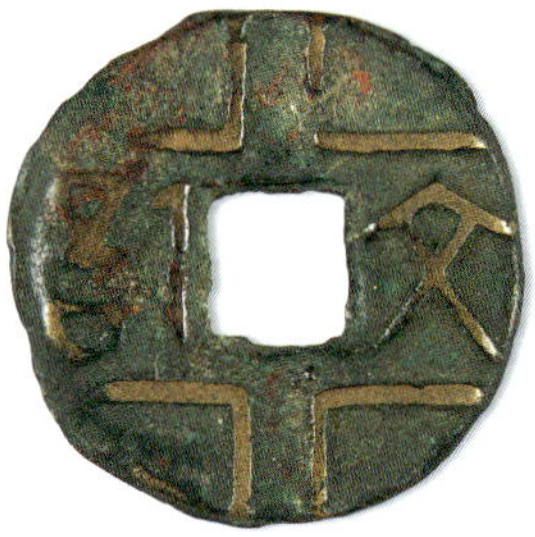

3

4 *Chi ze five zhu*

Western Han Yuan Ding 2nd year (115–8 BC)
Diameter 2.8 cm
Excavated in 1955 at Dalian, Liaoning Province

5 *Wuzhu* mould

Western Han dynasty (206–8 BC)
Length 12.2 cm, Width 4.61 cm
Li Zuoxian former collection

6 *Yi dao ping wu qian* coin

Western Han Wang Mang regent 2nd year (AD 7)
Total Length 7.3 cm, Thickness 0.37 cm, Weight 32 g
Li Zuoxian former collection

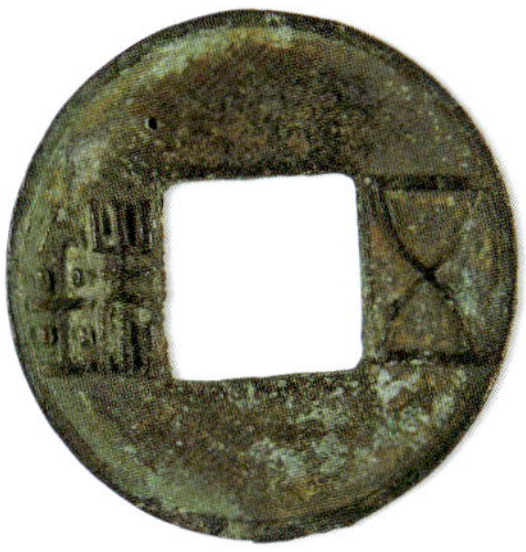

4

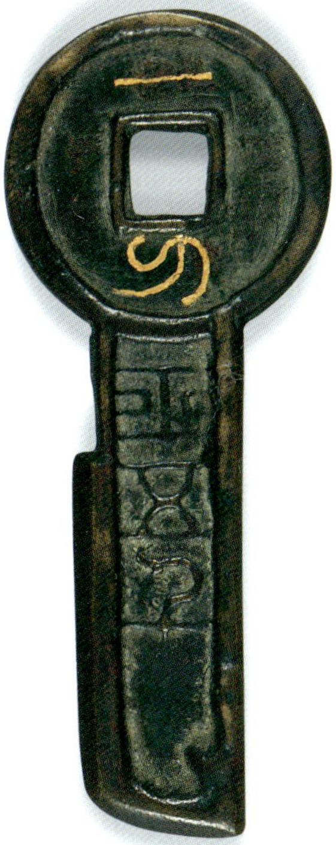

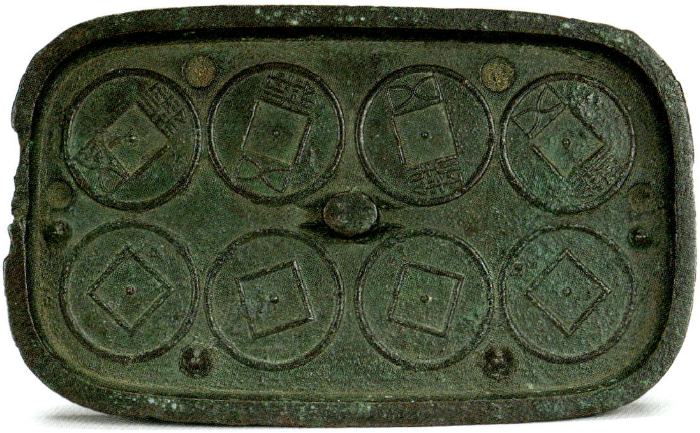

5

6

7 'Forty *zhuangquan*' money mould

Western Han Wang Mang Jianguo Second year (AD 10)
Length 12.92 cm, Width 7.93 cm
Li Zuoxian former collection

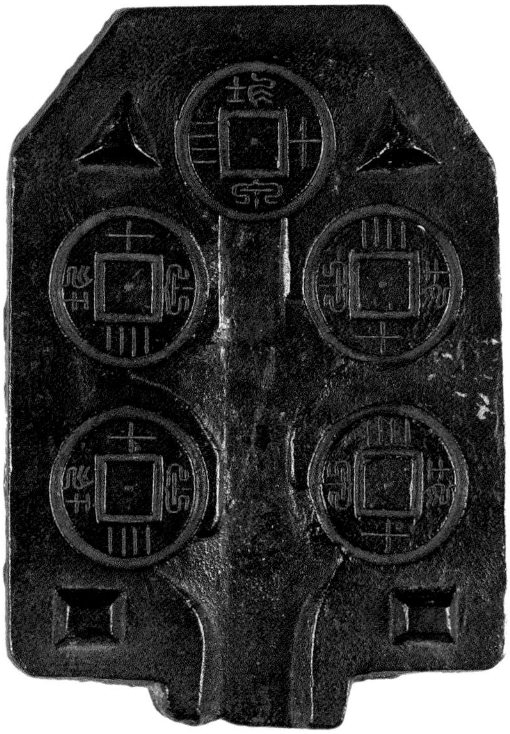

7

This coin mould is made of bronze, rectangular shaped, the top part has two corners cut off, and the bottom part has a hole for carving. Underneath this hole there is a square-shaped small protruding part, used for fixing the coin during carving. The mould is for five types of coins; in the middle one *liuzao dingduan*, on the left and right are two coins each side. All have the characters *zhuang quan si shi* carved on them. *Zhuang quan si shi* coin was one of the treasure coins used by Wang Mang two years after establishing a country in AD 10, extremely rare, and the mould is even rarer. This coin mould was a crowning piece of Li Zuoxian's collection, and was recorded in his *Collection of Ancient Coins*. Liu Yun

8 Tongxing Coin

Early Liao (901–945)
Diameter 2.8 cm
Li Zuoxian former collection

9 *Qian Qiu Wan Sui*

Early Liao (before 947)
Diameter 2.1 cm
Li Zuoxian former collection

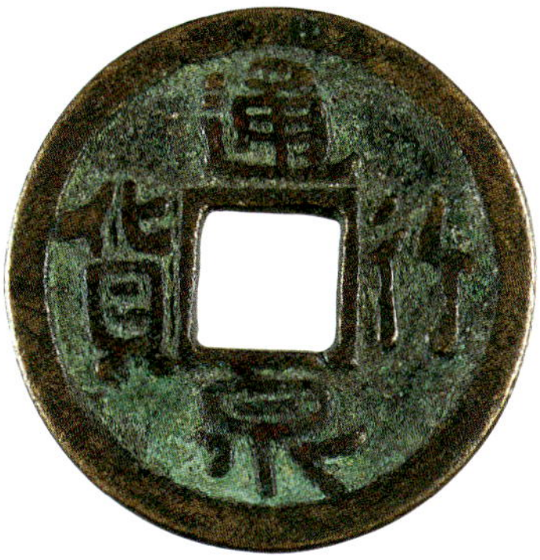

8

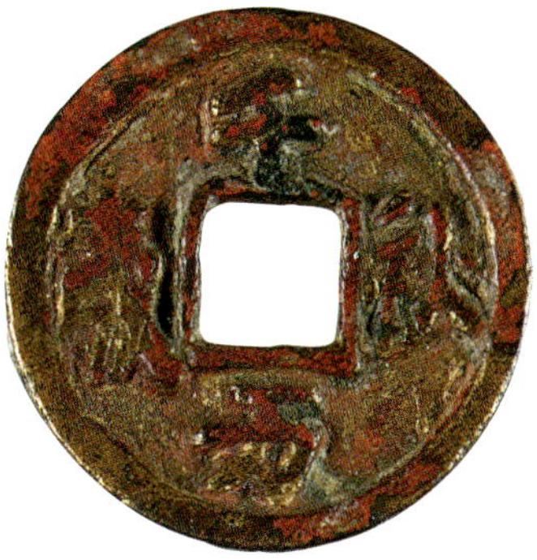

9

This bronze charm has been coated in gold on reddish bronze. The inscription reads from the right in official script and almost square characters. The characters are archaic in appearance, plain and coarse, and display stylistic elements of the late Tang and Five Dynasties period. The charm is from the early Liao without a reign period. *Qian qiu wan sui* charms can have various designs including dragons, phoenixes, dragons and phoenixes, twin phoenixes, and double swords. The charms with dragon design are commemorative currency of the Liao Tonghe emperor's birthday.

10 Gold horse hoof

Western Han (206–8 BC)
Height 3 cm, Diameter 5.1 cm, Base Thickness 0.6 cm, Weight 246 g
Excavated in 1986 from Dengta City, Liaoning Province

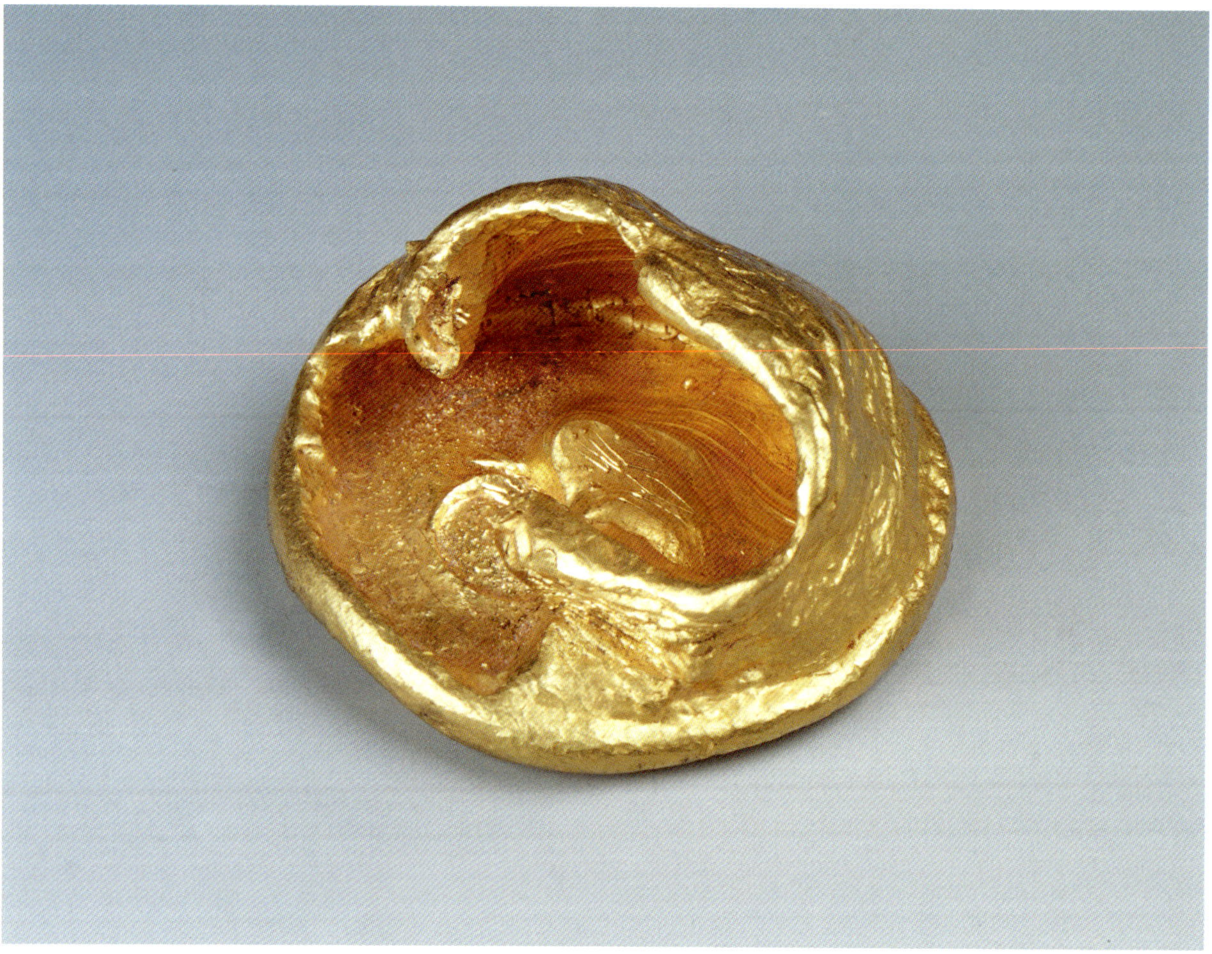

10

The base of this gold horse hoof has rings carved into it, with a *shang* character inside. Gold horse hoof first emerged in the Han dynasty, used as royal gifts or as treasures to collect. They are very rarely seen; this is the third example found in the Liaoning area. LIU YUN

11 Ten and a half tael Lu Silang gold bar

Southern Song (1127–1279)
Length 6.7 cm, Width of top 3.9 cm, Width of middle 2.4 cm, Thickness 1.2 cm, Weight 395.5 g

12 Double-gourd printed twenty tael gold bar

Southern Song (1127–1279)
Length 8.3 cm, Width of top 5.3 cm, Width of middle 3.1 cm, Thickness 1.5 cm, Weight 727 g

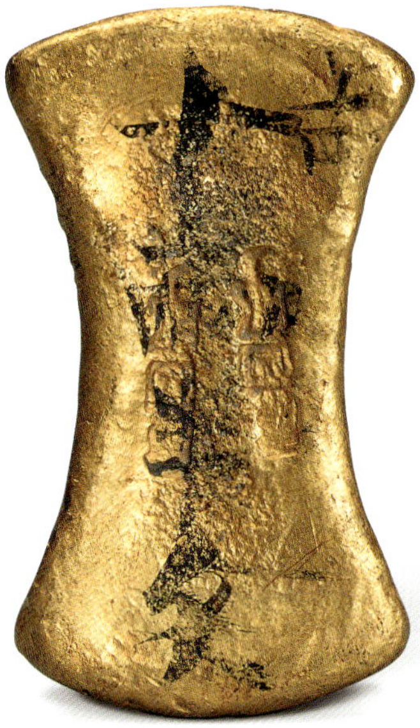

11

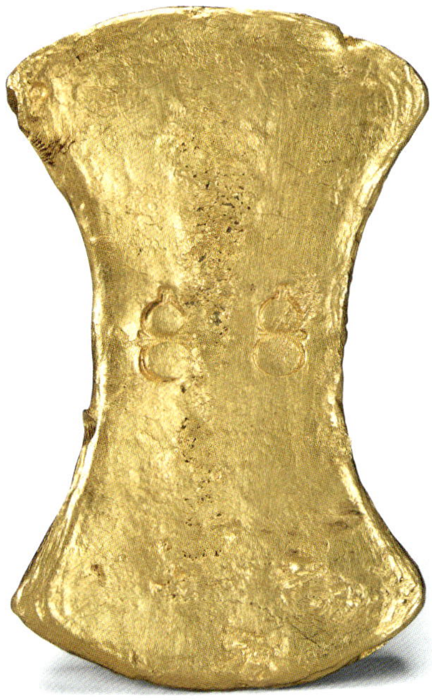

12

Both gold bars are curved with arc-shaped ends and a slender middle. On the front of the first bar, there are characters *lu silang* and *shi liang ban*, with a weight of 395.5 g. The front of the second bar has two gourds imprinted on it, with a weight of 727 g. They are both of high quality and excellently preserved. As they represented the wealth of the period, the bars are valuable for researching financial and fiscal policies, and economics of the Southern Song. Lu Silang is the name of the goldsmith, the 'gourd imprint' is a special mark of the Song dynasty: it was a security mark given by gold and silver dealers. LIU YUN

13 'Zhen hua ting yin li niansan' gourd ingot

Southern Song dynasty (1127–1279)
Length 11.6 cm, Width of Head 7.45 cm, Width of Waist 5 cm, Thickness 1.8 cm, Weight 970 g

14 Zhiyuan 14th year silver ingots

Yuan Zhiyuan 14th year, 1277
Length 14.4 cm, Width 9 cm, Weight 2,000 g

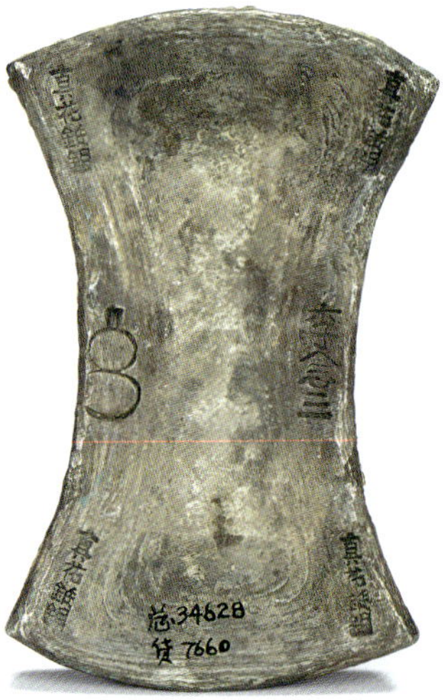

13

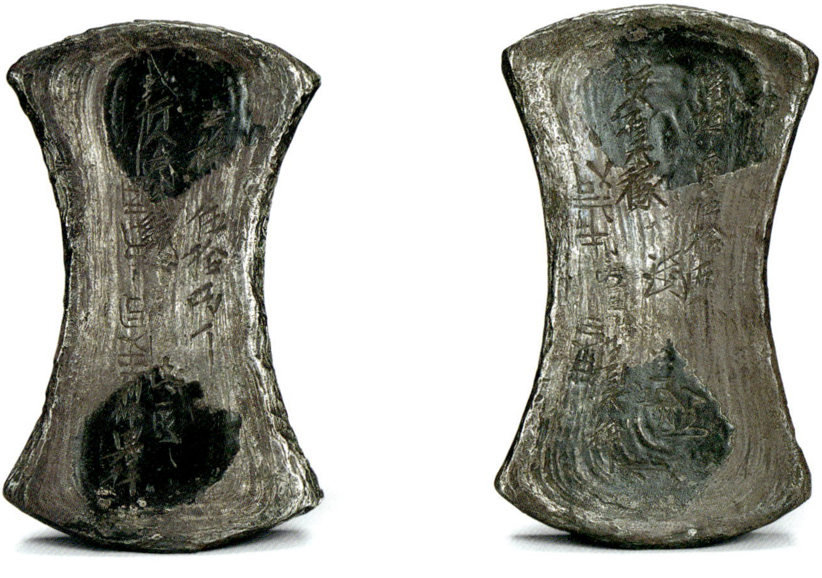

14

15 Ming currency paper note

Ming Hongwu 8th year (1375)
Length 33.9 cm, Width 22 cm

16 a: Qing paper money;
b: Ministry of Finance Bank Cheque

Qing Xianfeng 3rd year (1853)
a: Length 22.2 cm, Width 12.5 cm
b: Length 23 cm, Width 12.8 cm

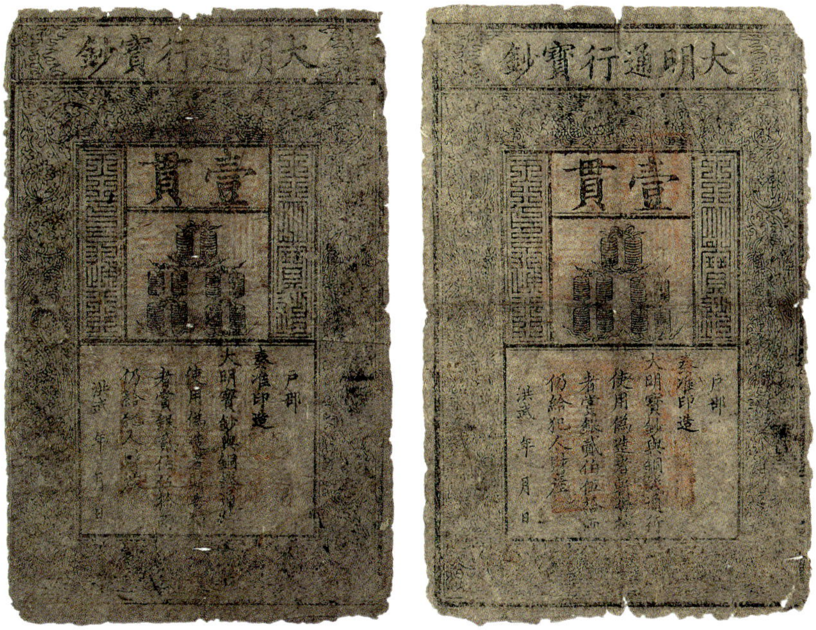

15

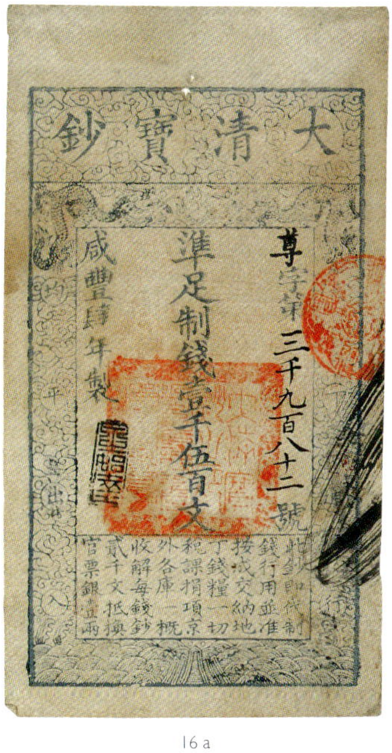

16 a

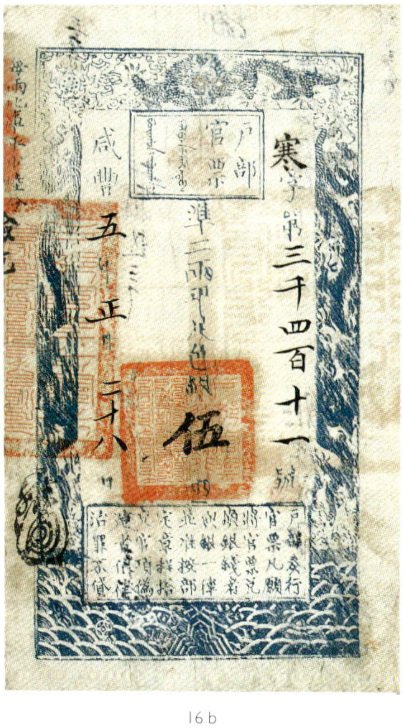

16 b

11

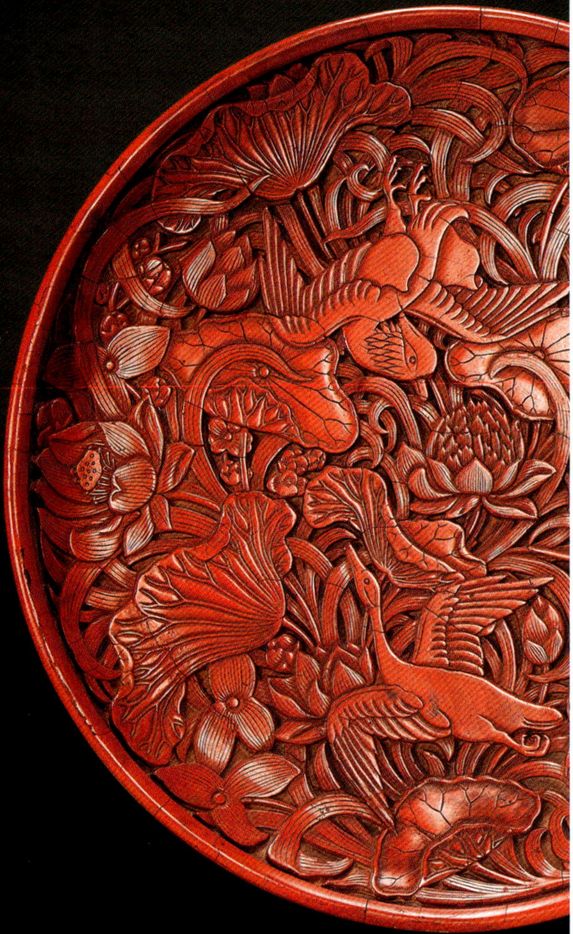

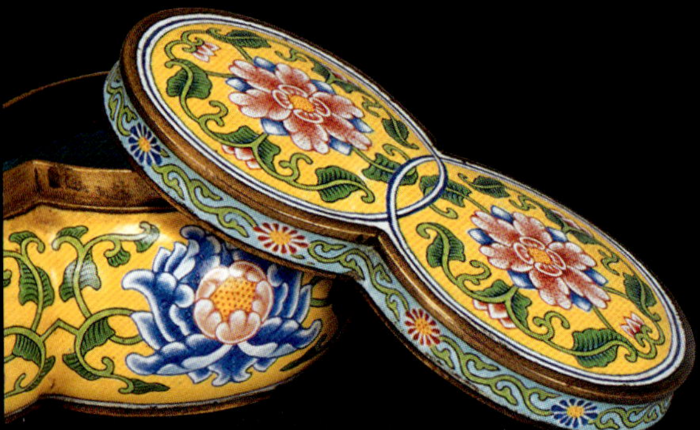

Lacquer ware

Lacquer ware is a traditional Chinese craft. It was used not only by the imperial court but also by people from all levels of society.

Liaoning Provincial Museum has more than 200 lacquer objects. The most numerous and best quality are carved red lacquer objects, many of which came from the imperial palace lacquer collection. Carved red lacquer is the main type. It is made by first coating the casting with red lacquer. Once the layer of lacquer has reached the desired level, the design is then carved on to the lacquer surface.

The centre of the carved red lacquer dish with two mandarin ducks on a lotus pond has coated lacquer on a yellow base. In the design of the two mandarin ducks on a lotus pond, the layer of lacquer is thick and solid, the carving is curved and mature, the cuts are clear, with the bottom of black lacquer, there is a vertical inscription of one single line on the left side reading 'Made in the Great Ming Yongle year'. It continues the Yuan style, and is a typical example of early Ming dynasty lacquer ware.

Carved lacquer objects of the Qianlong reign of the Qing dynasty absorbed elements from different Ming periods, creating carved lacquer ware with the simple smoothness of the early Ming and the sinuous fibres of the late Ming. There is a carved red lacquer bowl with green underneath with a Qianlong poem *San Qing Cha* inscribed. On the outer side of the main body there is an inscription of a five-syllable poem from the 11th year of Qianlong (1746) consisting of twenty-two lines and 111 characters, all in beautiful calligraphy. The six bowls all show off the mature technique and skill of the craftsmen.

The technique of mother-of-pearl inlay consists of cutting and polishing the shells of molluscs into fine pieces; and then cutting out patterns, inlaying into the casting, and coating with a layer of lacquer. When smoothly polished the shell patterns are exposed. The Ming and

Qing periods saw large-scale production of mother-of-pearl inlay. The Liaoning Museum has a mother-of-pearl case decorated with the theme of spring outing, coated in black lacquer with light-coloured mother-of-pearl inlay of a spring outing with a group of people amidst the trees and flowers, and is a masterpiece of lacquer work.

Apart from these, the Liaoning Museum also has items such as carved rhinoceroses, carved coloured lacquer, infill, coloured drawing and gold painted lacquer ware with inscriptions. ZHOU XIAOJING

Enamel ware

Enamel is a material made from glass, the main components of which are silica, soda and lime. Enamel ware is made from ground bits of enamel glaze which are glued on to the surface of metal objects, and then fired to complete the object. Gilded enamel ware was brought to China from abroad.

Techniques for producing enamel ware included cloisonné, or inlaid enamelware, and painted enamel ware. Cloisonné was the more important variety, and in Qing records, cloisonné was classified as one of the four major crafts of the Ming, along with Yongle carved lacquer ware, Xuande bronze *hu* and Tonghua *doucai* ceramics.

The cloisonné collection at the Liaoning Provincial Museum is mostly from the imperial court collection in Beijing, including items from all periods from the Yuan through to the Qing. The collection is extremely valuable.

The double-eared cloisonné censer with Indian lotus design in the Liaoning Museum collection shows a mature, elegant technique. The glaze is colourful with bright colours, and strong reflective properties. The layers of glaze are thick, with very few holes on the surface. Crystal material that has not been properly melted down is visible in the glaze, and transparent green stone is particularly obvious. It is a typical Yuan dynasty piece. The cloisonné dish with a crane and pond design at the centre uses black enamel colour to depict the water of the pond. In the pond are lotus flowers, crane and little fish, and two cranes flying in the sky. The colours are bright, especially the red, white, and yellow on blue and black backgrounds, and as such are even more striking. The design has shaken off the plain repetition of Indian lotus patterns, and is similar to the freedom of painting, showing that the cloisonné of the time of the mid to late Ming period was already very mature and confident. Cloisonné was produced on a large scale in the Qianlong period during the Qing dynasty mainly at the palace court, Guangzhou and Yangzhou. The enamel ware from these centres was of exquisite craftsmanship, and the embossed cloisonné bowl with long life characters reflects this style. The cloisonné square dish with eight steeds under a willow tree at the centre has used the dyed glaze technique as part of the enamel technique, and is a good example of the successful merging of the two techniques. The cloisonné *dou* with animal mask pattern is an imitation of Shang and Zhou bronze *dou*. It has used the cloisonné technique to decorate the surface with an animal mask pattern on a deep blue background, adding yellow, white, black and bronze glaze as decoration, ancient in colour and style.

As well as these, the Liaoning Museum has enamel interlocking peony dishes and gourd bottles with inlaid enamel from the Yongzheng period during the Qing, which are also fine works of art. ZHOU XIAOJING

1 Plum flower-shaped case with lacquered rhinoceros and cloud design

Late Yuan, Early Ming (1341–1424)

Height 13.5 cm, Diameter 25.3 cm, Base Diameter 18.1 cm

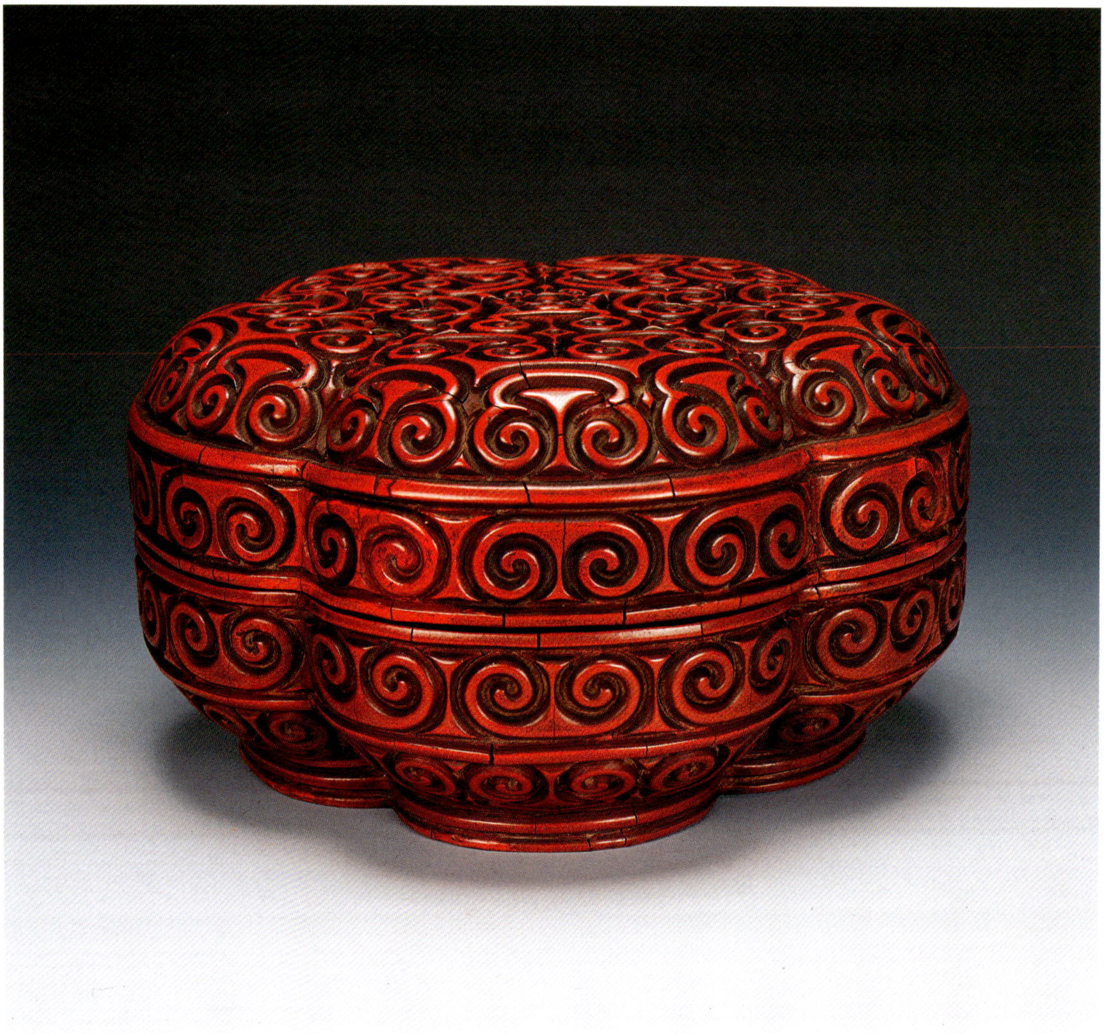

1

2 Large carved red lacquer dish with two mandarin ducks on a lotus pond

Ming Yongle reign period (1403–1424)
Height 4.2 cm, Diameter 32.4 cm, Base Diameter 25.1 cm

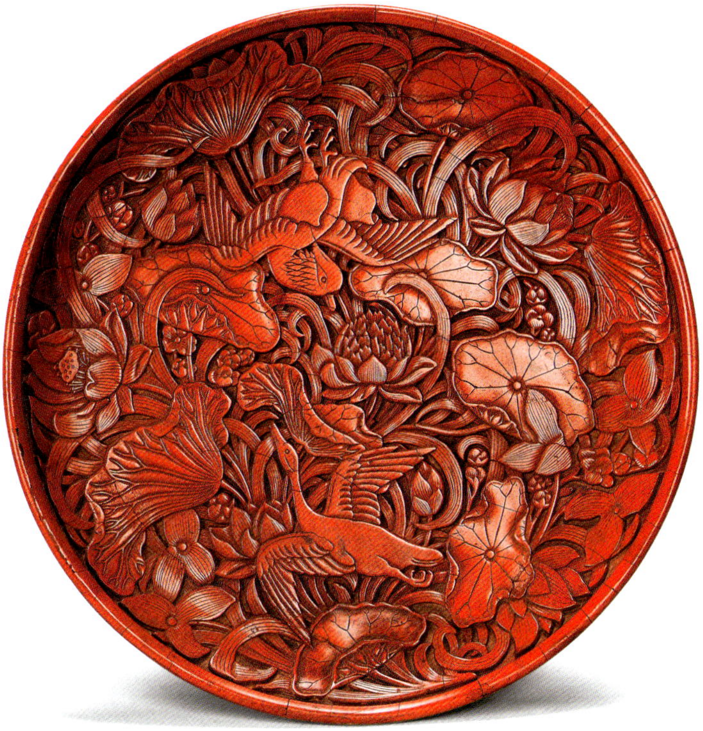

2

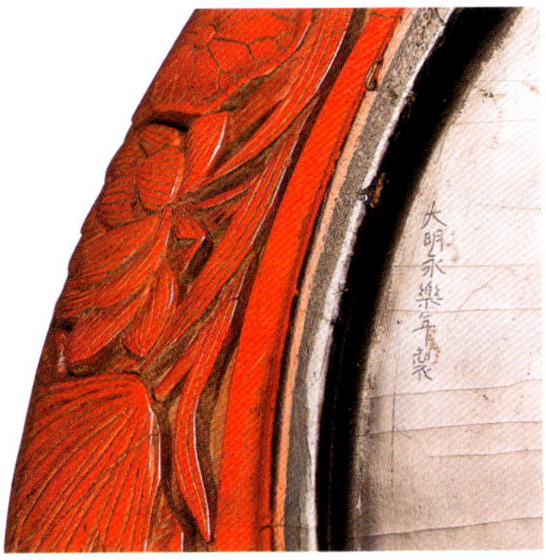

Inscription on base

The Ming Yongle Emperor (Zhu Di) was fond of carved lacquer items. When he had moved from Nanjing to Beijing, he established an imperial centre of lacquer production in the imperial palace, called the *Orchard Workshop* (*Guoyuanchang*). With patronage from the emperor, early Ming carved lacquer arts developed quickly, and created new techniques from the basis of Yuan dynasty lacquer ware. Few carved lacquer objects from the Yongle reign period are still extant, and this large lacquered dish is a fine example of lacquer work from that period. The dish is round in shape with a short round base. On the inside and outside of the dish black lacquer has been carved on to a yellow casting, with lotus flowers and leaves on water on the inside of the dish. In the middle of the flowers are a couple of mandarin ducks flying. On the base of the dish is an inscription saying 'Made in the Yongle reign period, Ming'. The rim of this dish is large and majestic. The fibres of the flowers and wings of the birds have been finely carved, in direct contrast to the large, bold lotus leaves, creating a vivid scene. The insides of the feet have been lacquered in brown and black ink showing the characters of the inscription clearly. The inscription on the base clearly records the date as the Yongle reign period, which serves as a basis for recognising other dated inscriptions on lacquer ware. Wen Kexue

3 Small lacquered round case with figure design

Jiajing reign, Ming dynasty (1522–1566)
Height 2.7 cm, Diameter 6.9 cm

4 Small case with mother-of-pearl inlay brocade pattern by Jiang Qianli

Kangxi reign, Qing dynasty (1662–1722)
Height 3.7 cm, Body Diameter 3.6 cm, Base Diameter 1.9 cm

5 Rectangular small table red-lacquered with twin phoenixes and peonies

Qianlong reign, Qing dynasty (1736–1795)
Height 27.7 cm, Length of surface 78.9 cm, Width of surface 47.5 cm

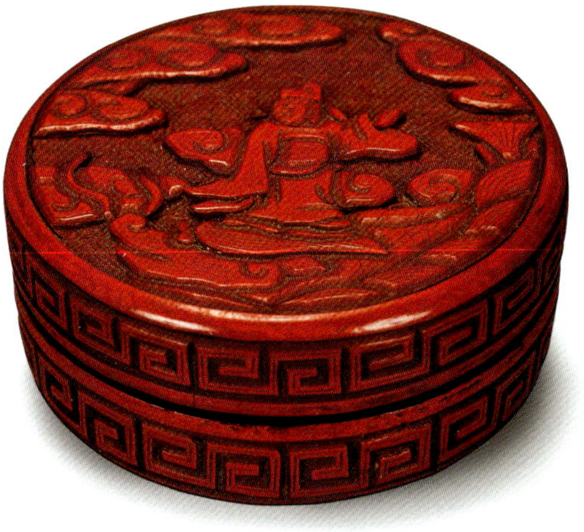

3

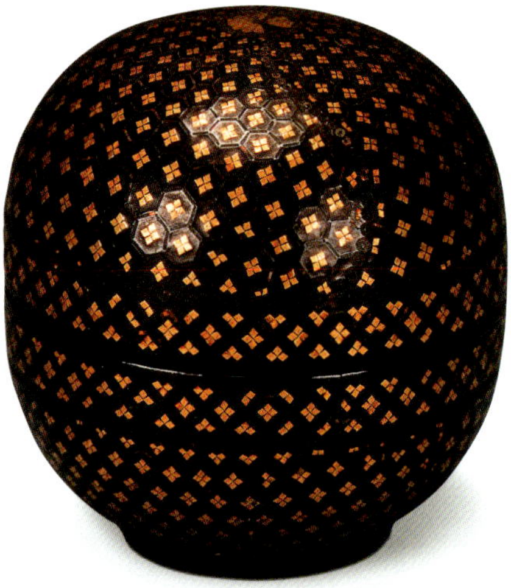

4

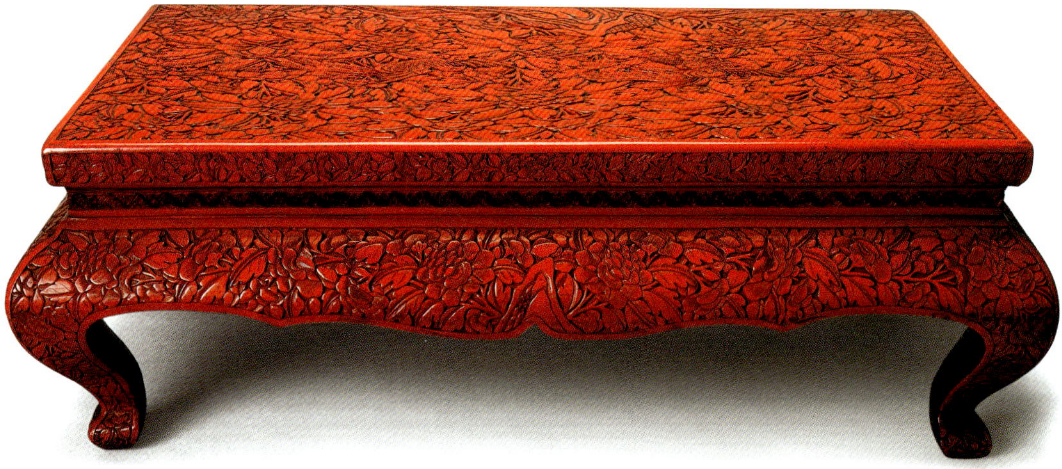

5

6 Red lacquered bowl, *san qing cha*

Qianlong reign, Qing dynasty (1736–1795)
Height 5.4 cm, Diameter 11 cm, Base Diameter 4.6 cm

7 Dish with Calendula pattern

Qianlong reign, Qing dynasty (1736–1795)
Height 5.5 cm, Diameter 34 cm, Base Diameter 26.2 cm
Height 5.3 cm, Diameter 34 cm, Base Diameter 26.4 cm

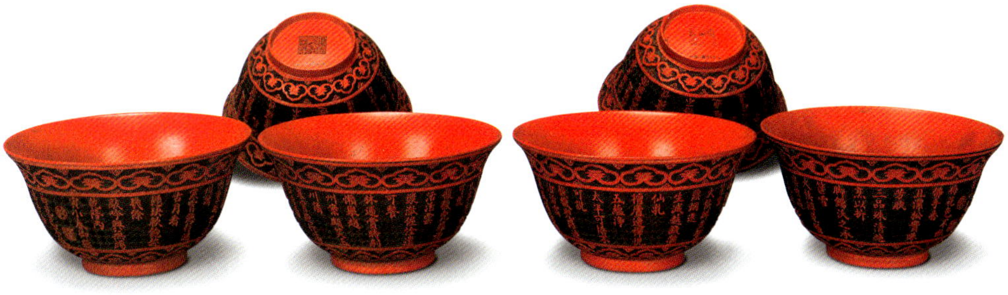

6

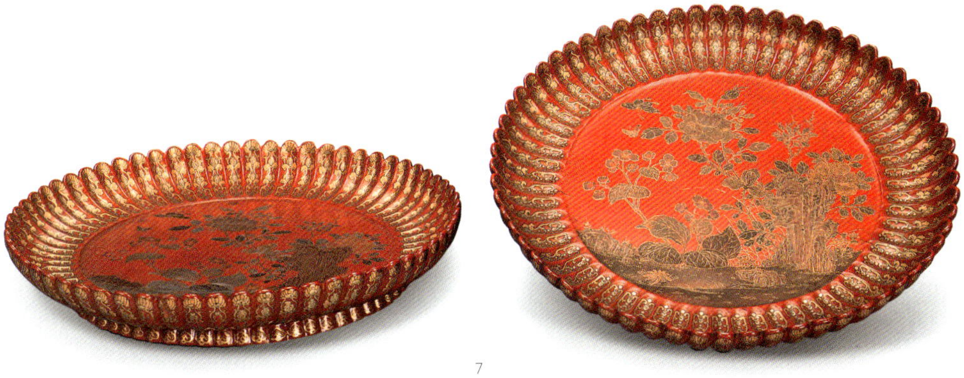

7

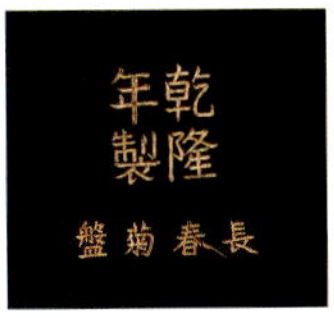

7 Inscription on base

8 Small black lacquered case with the pattern of *The Romance of the Western Chamber*

Early Qinq (1644–1661)
Height 3 cm, Diameter 8.7 cm, Base Diameter 5.5 cm

9 Dish with mother-of-pearl inlay illustrating a spring outing

Mid-Qing period (1662–1820)
Height 29.3 cm, Diameter 35.8 cm

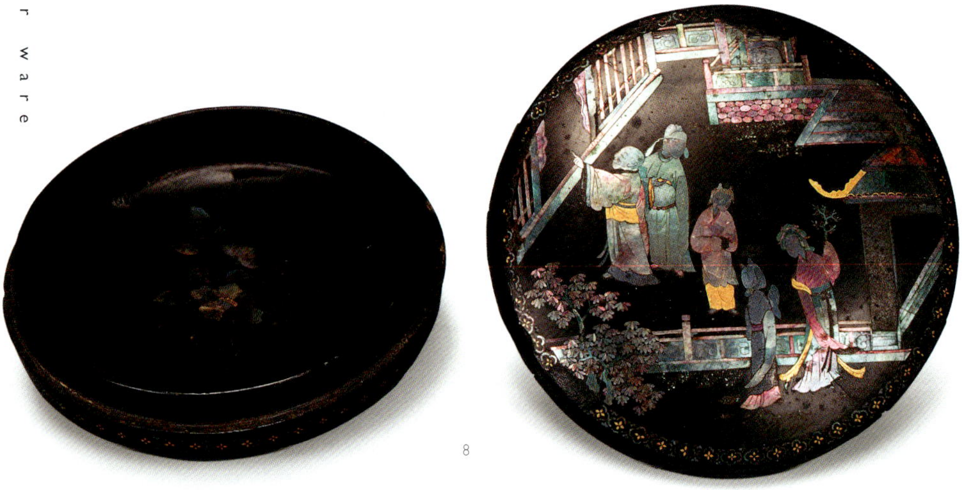

8

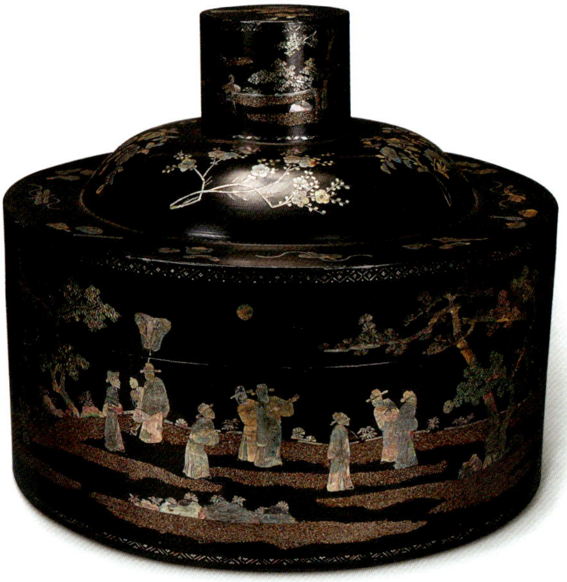

9

1 Double-eared cloisonné censer with Indian lotus design

Ming dynasty (1368–1644)
Height 7.4 cm, Diameter 12 cm,
Base Diameter 9.1 cm

2 Cloisonné dish with a crane and pond design

Late Ming dynasty (1522–1644)
Height 5 cm, Diameter 27.7 cm, Base Diameter 21.2 cm

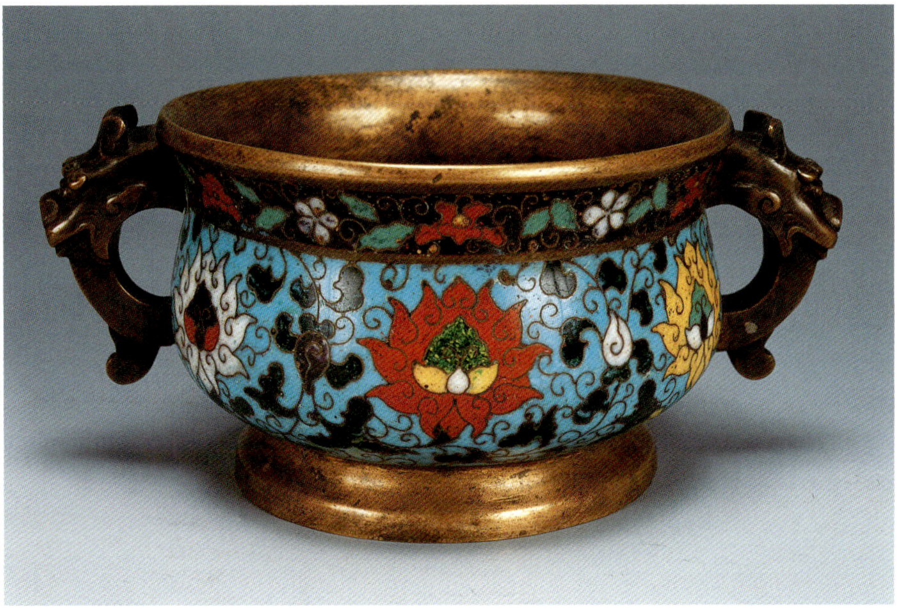

1

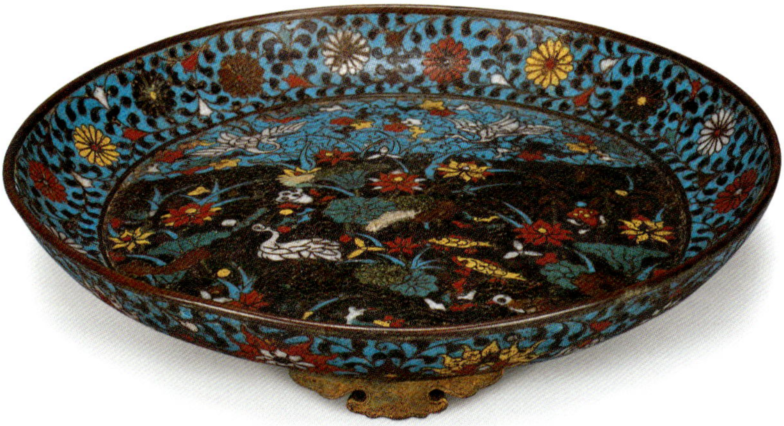

2

3 Cloisonné plum bottle with Indian lotus design

Qing dynasty (1644–1911)
Height 29.1 cm, Diameter 4.6 cm

4 Cloisonné rectangular dish with eight steeds

Qianlong reign, Qing dynasty (1736–1795)
Length 36.5 cm, Width 24.2 cm

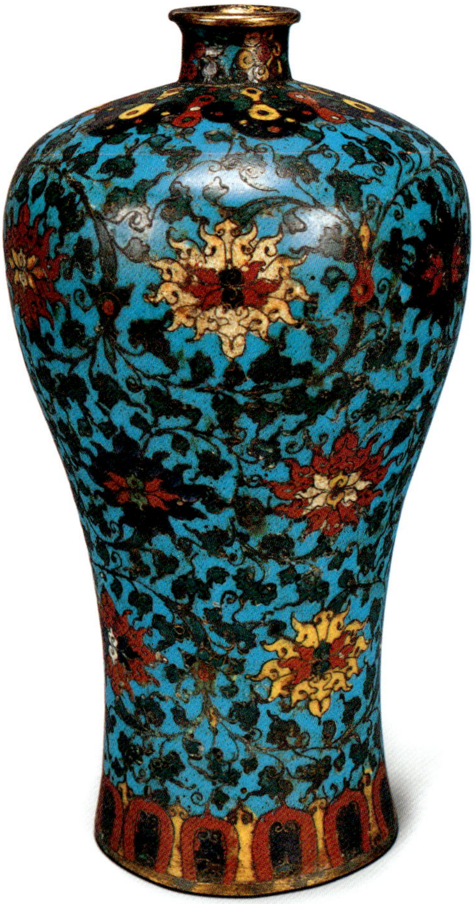

3

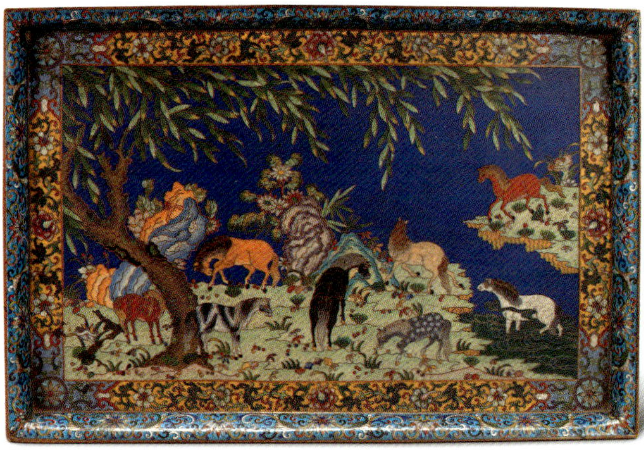

4

5 Embossed cloisonné bowl with long life characters

Qianlong reign, Qing dynasty (1736–1795)
Height 7 cm, Diameter 15.4 cm,
Base Diameter 9.7 cm

6 Cloisonné enamel *dou* with lid and design of animal face

Qianlong reign, Qing dynasty (1736–1795)
Total Height 16 cm, Diameter 6.8 cm

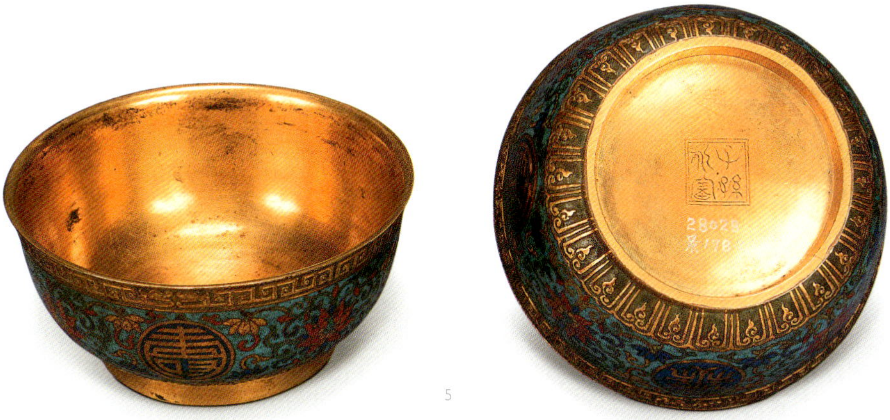

5

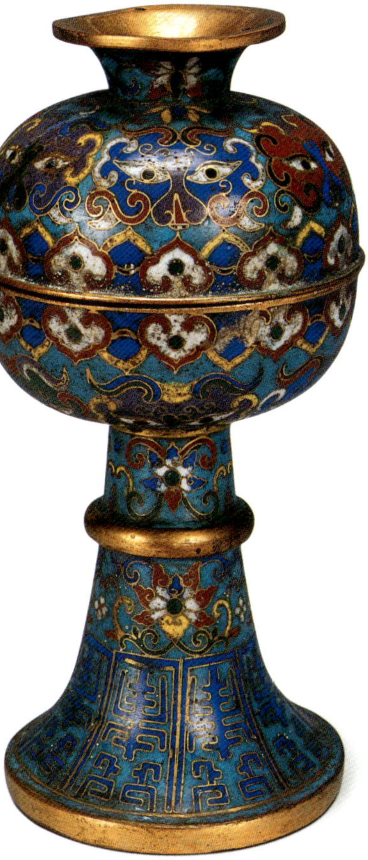

6

7 Painted enamel case and lid with interlocking peony design

Yongzheng reign Qing dynasty (1723–1735)
Height 3.9 cm, Diameter 8.3 x 4.45 cm, Base Diameter 8.8 x 4.95 cm

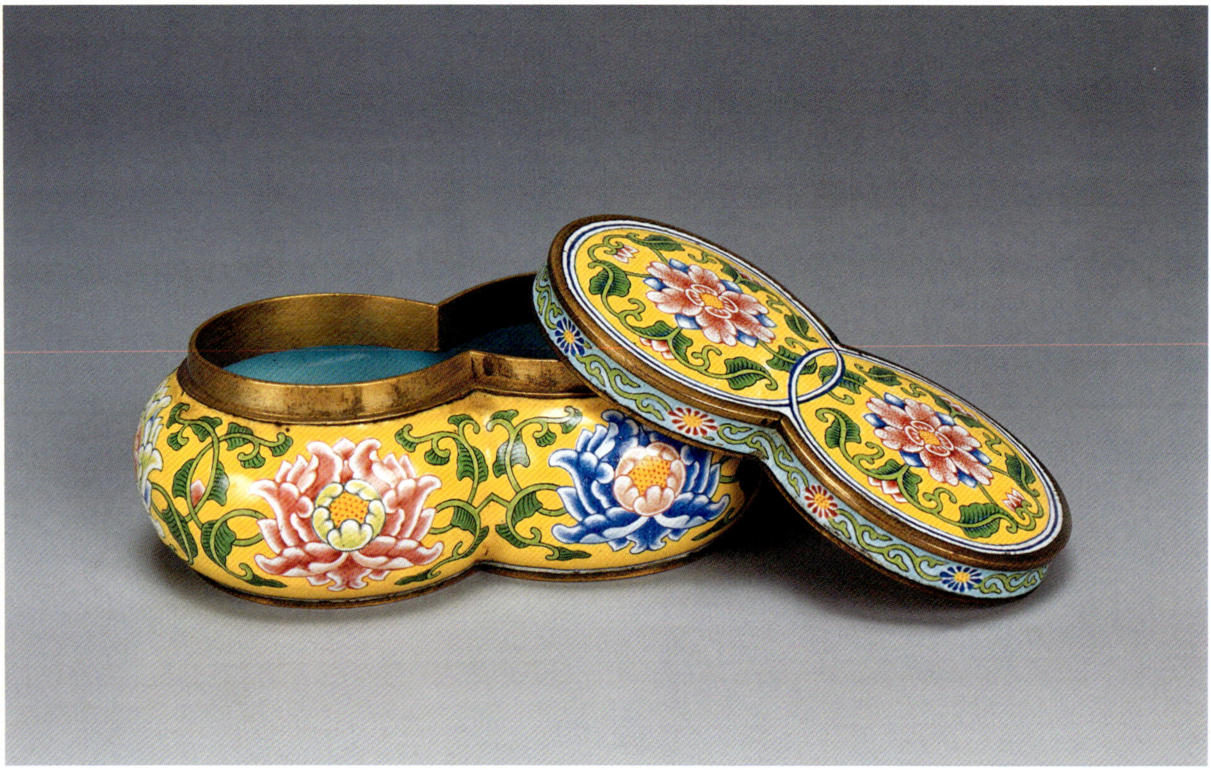

7

This case and lid with interlocking design is a typical example of copper painted with enamel, the copper glazing is thick, and the design is particular. The interior of the case is painted in turquoise. The exterior surface is painted in bright yellow with eight blooming peony flowers painted variously in pink, blue and green. The leaves of the peonies are twisting around the flowers which have their yellow pistils exposed. The brushwork is very delicate. The base of the case is in white enamel, and at the centre there is a four-character inscription reading 'Made in the Yongzheng reign period'. This case has been exquisitely designed and crafted. Coloured enamelling on copper glazing began in the Kangxi reign period, and developed quickly during the Yongzheng reign period, falling off in the Qianlong reign period, and was eventually no longer produced. This piece shows the artistic achievements in coloured enamelling on copper glazing during the prosperous Yongzheng reign period. WEN KEXUE

8 Painted enamel snuff bottle with birds, flowers, grass and insects

Qianlong reign, Qing dynasty (1736–1795)
Height 4.9 cm, Body Diameter 4.25 x 3.1 cm,
Rim Diameter 1.6 cm

9 Painted enamel dish with gilded Indian lotus design on blue background

Qianlong reign, Qing dynasty (1736–1795)
Total Height 2.7 cm, Diameter 21 cm,
Base Diameter 13.5 cm

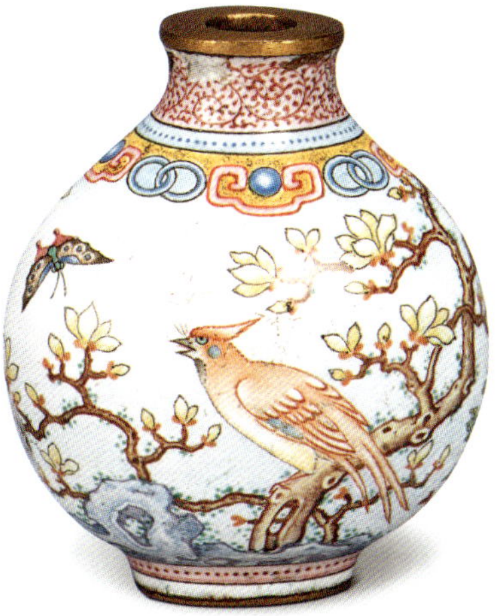

8

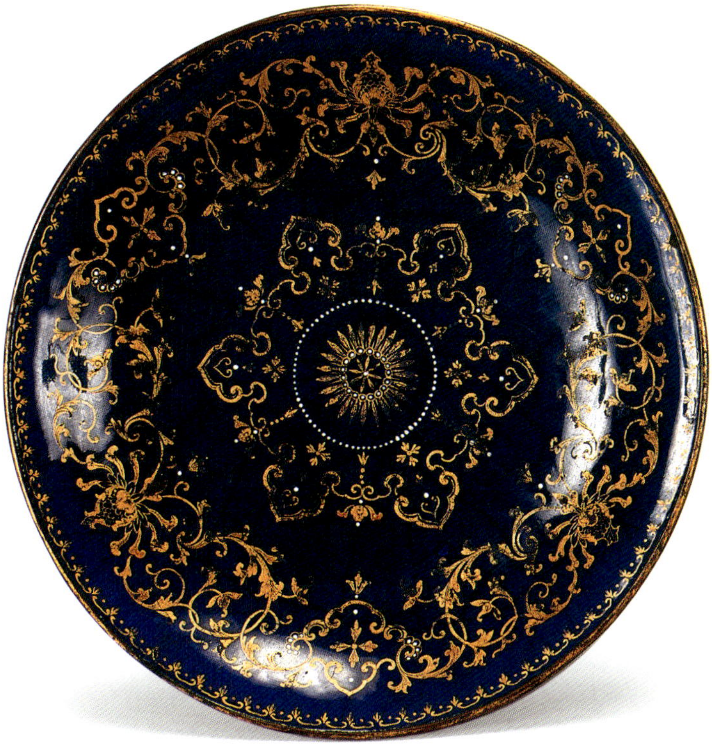

9

10 Painted enamel coloured watch with gold case

Qing dynasty (1644–1911)
Total Height 7.55 cm, Diameter 5.9 cm
Excavated from tomb at Danbaduo'erji, Nangongyingzi, Kazuo County, Liaoning Province

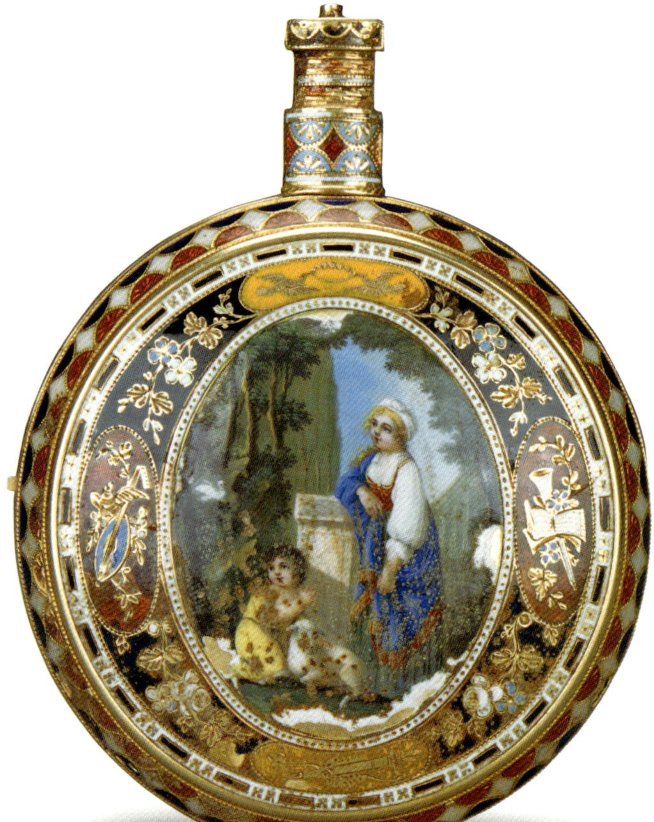

10

11 Flower pot with pomegranate flower

Qing dynasty (1644–1911)
Height 17 cm, Diameter 28.5 cm x 22 cm

12 Embossed cloisonné gourd-shaped bottle with inlaid jade

Qing dynasty (1644–1911)
Height 66.7 cm, Upper Body Diameter 27.2 cm, Lower Body Diameter 39.2 cm, Base Diameter 20.5 cm

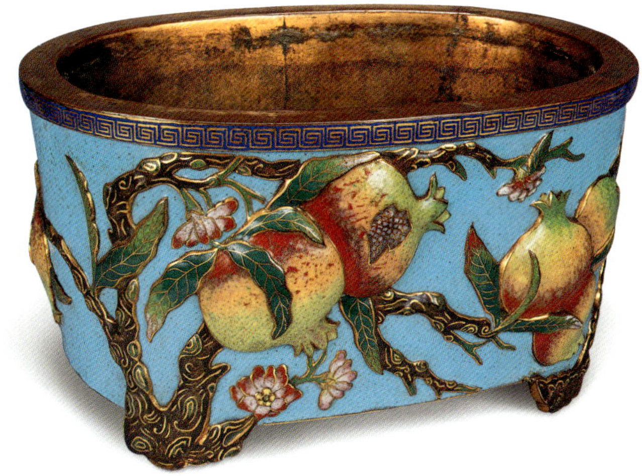

11

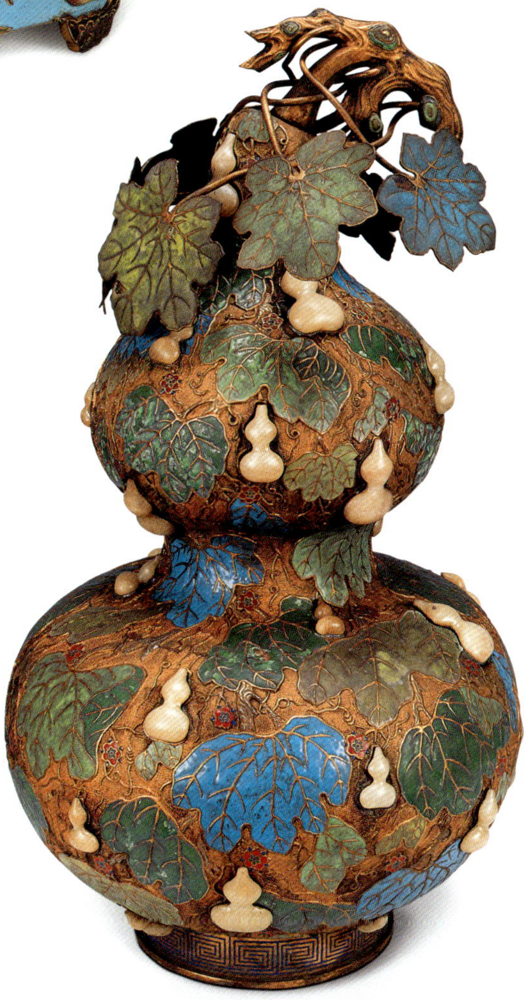

12

12

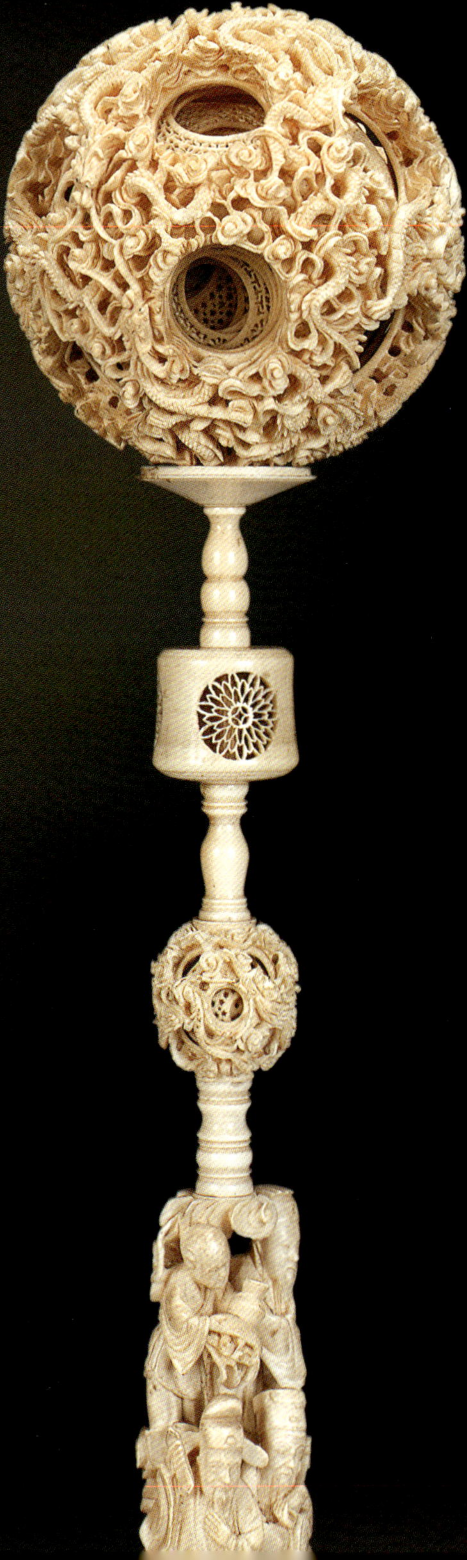

Bamboo, Wood and Ivory carving

All small decorative and everyday objects made from bamboo, wood and ivory are usually put together in one category. Bamboo, wood and ivory carving had a separate artistic development, which reached its zenith in the Ming and Qing periods. It had a strong literary appeal.

Carved bamboo is usually classified as either belonging to the Jinling school or Jiading school. With regard to carving technique, in the Ming dynasty people used deep relief carving and openwork carving, whereas in the Qing, bas-relief carving and engraving were used. They also have works that copied Ming style. In Liaoning's collection there is a Ming dynasty crab on a lotus leaf round carved from bamboo root that looks very realistic. Qing Shibi brush pots carved from bamboo also imitate Ming sculpture style.

Wood sculpture is made from materials including sandalwood, rosewood, Chinese quince, *wenge* wood, Chinese box, birch, and fruit stones. From the mid-Ming period onwards, influenced by bamboo carving, small items for the scholar's study began to be produced, called 'scholars' wood carvings', the style and carving of which were similar to bamboo carvings.

Olive stone boats are made from long olive stones, carved into boat shapes, and were popular in the Jiangsu and Guangdong areas during the Ming and Qing dynasties. The Liaoning Provincial Museum collection has a pair of olive stone boats, carved into a cabin of two stories, each boat has thirty people on it, on the hull of the boats the characters *qian chi bi fu* (The Former Red Cliff Rhapsody) are micro-carved. Mould bottle gourds were made by putting the gourd into a wooden mould with carved patterns when it had just started to grow, then growing it until it fitted the mould and the desired pattern appeared. Ordinary people began to grow real gourds into moulds in the Wanli period of the Ming dynasty. In the Qing the court also began to grow them, and they matured as an art during the Qianlong period when the characters *Qianlong shang wan* (Artefact enjoyed by Qianlong) were carved into their bases. In the late Qing cricket jars, snuff bottles or small decorative objects were mainly produced.

Ivory-carved items had already emerged in China's pre-history, and flourished in the Ming and Qing periods. Qing ivory carvings had local characteristics: Suzhou ivory carvings effectively copied bamboo carvings, achieving the style of literati painting. Guangzhou ivory carvings were very fine, emphasising the whiteness and colour decoration. Beijing ivory carvings were made into small, very delicate objects. The Qing palace merged the qualities of the Suzhou and Guangzhou techniques, creating beautiful objects according to the emperor's taste. The small screen with geese and reeds in the Liaoning Museum collection follows the Suzhou style, the ivory magic fungus follows the Beijing style, and the ivory puzzle balls are typical of the refined Guangzhou style. ZHOU XIAOJING

1 Bamboo lotus leaf

Ming dynasty (1368–1644)
Length 15.6 cm, Width 10.3 cm, Thickness 4.4 cm

2 Bamboo incense tube with pine, stone and lady

Qing dynasty (1644–1911)
Total Length 37.1 cm, Straight Diameter 6.8 cm

3 Bamboo brush pot with pine, stone and figure

Qing (1644–1911)
Height 14.35 cm, Straight Diameter 11.5 cm

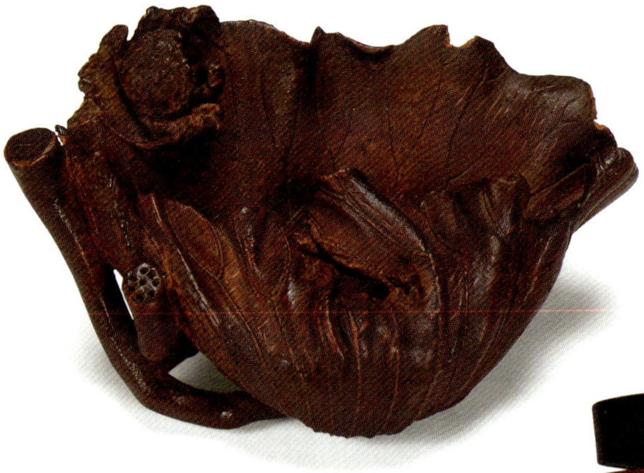

1

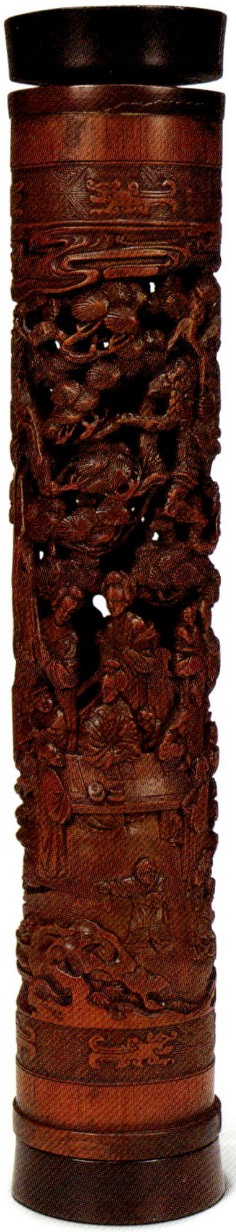

2

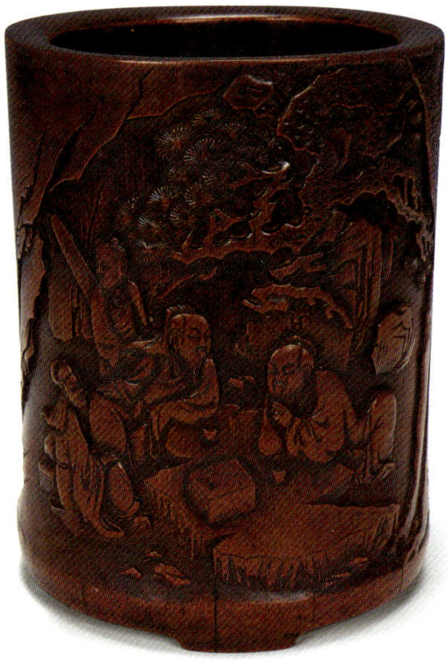

3

4 *Sanyang kaitai* case in red wood with precious objects

Qing (1644–1911)
Height 8.2 cm, Width 19.5 cm

5 Wood carving of auspicious spirit

Qing (1644–1911)
Length 57.4 cm, Width 14.4 cm,
Thickness of handle 3.1 cm

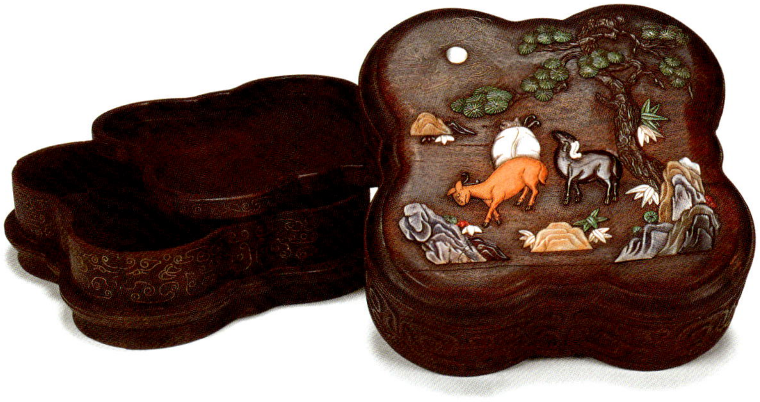

4

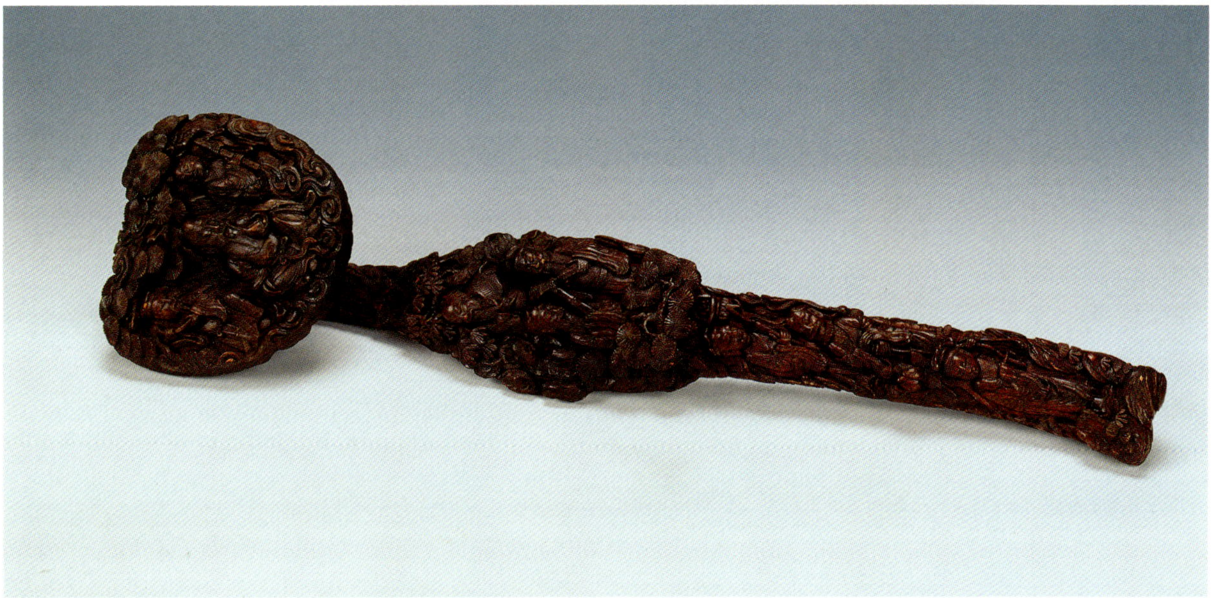

5

6 Bamboo arm rest

Qing (1644–1911)
Length 26.9 cm, Width 6.65 cm, Thickness 0.9 cm

7 Wood carving of Dharma

Qing (1644–1911)
Height 41 cm

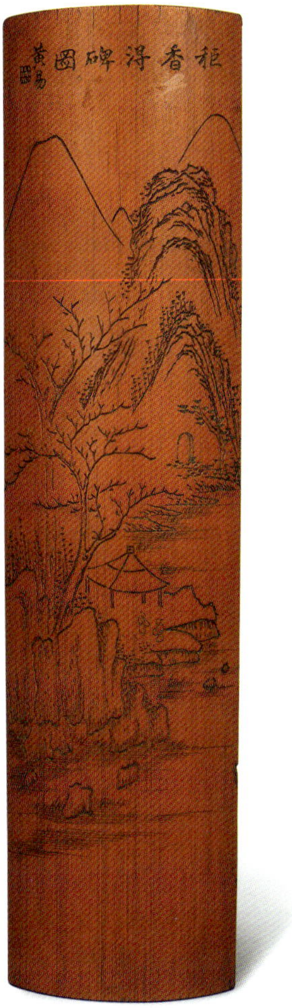

6

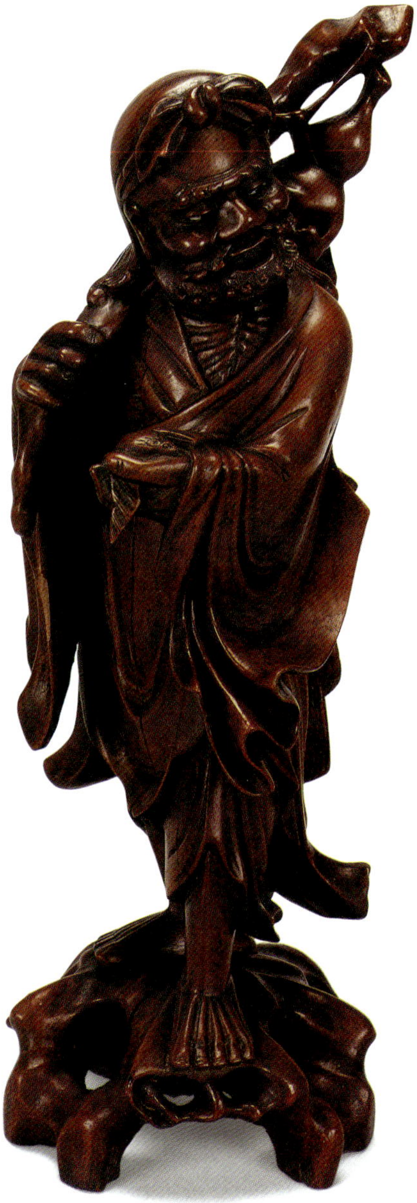

7

8 Olive stone boats

Qing (1644–1911)
Length 4.35 cm, Body Diameter 2.05 cm

9 Gold painted moulded bowl

Qing Qianlong reign (1736–1795)
Height 6 cm, Diameter 11.3 cm,
Base Diameter 4.5 cm

10 Moulded cricket pot

Qing Qianlong reign (1736–1795)
Total Height 12 cm, Diameter 6.8 cm,
Body Diameter 6.5 cm

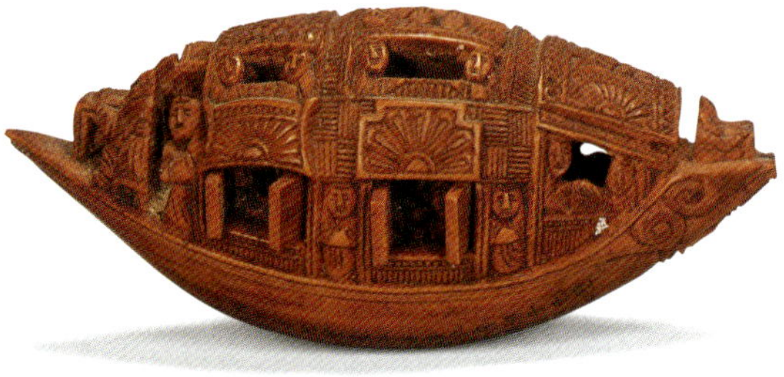

8

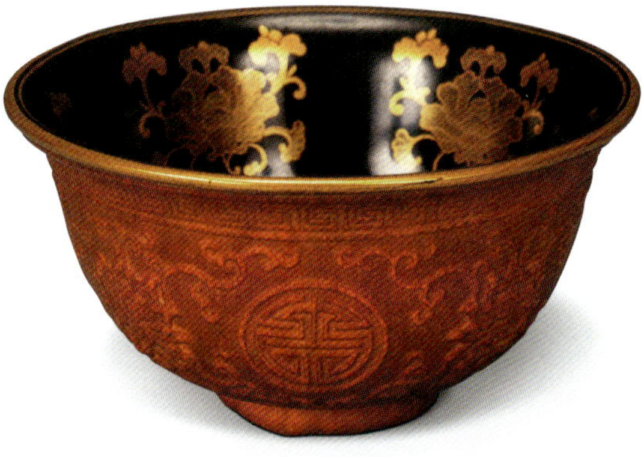

9

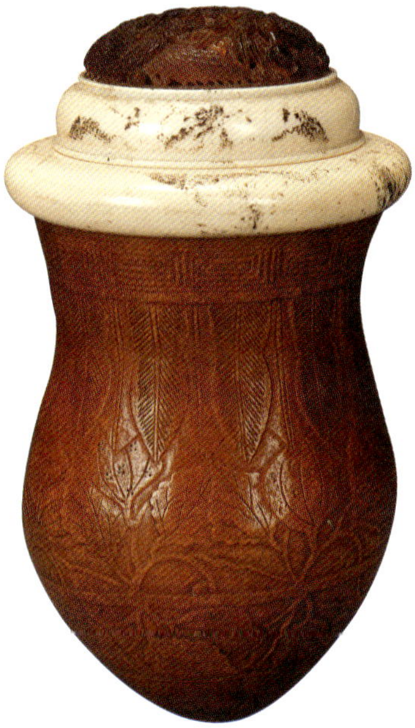

10

11 Ivory carving of brush holder with the design of figures under pine tree

Ming (1368–1644)
Height 13.7 cm, Diameter 8.9 x 9.5 cm

12 Ivory carving of old man

Ming (1368–1664)
Length 22.7 cm

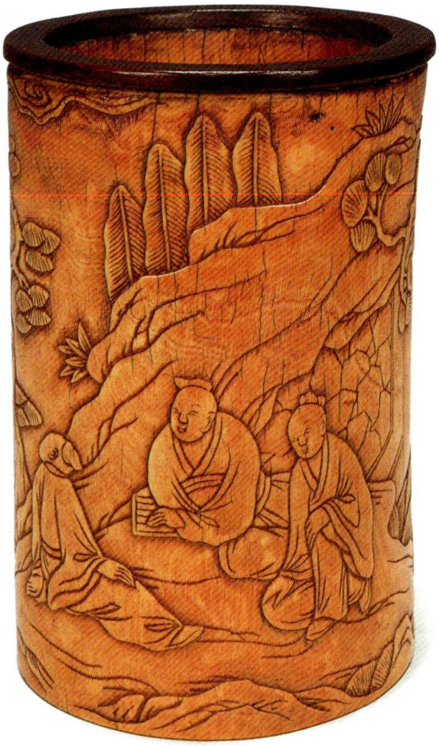

11

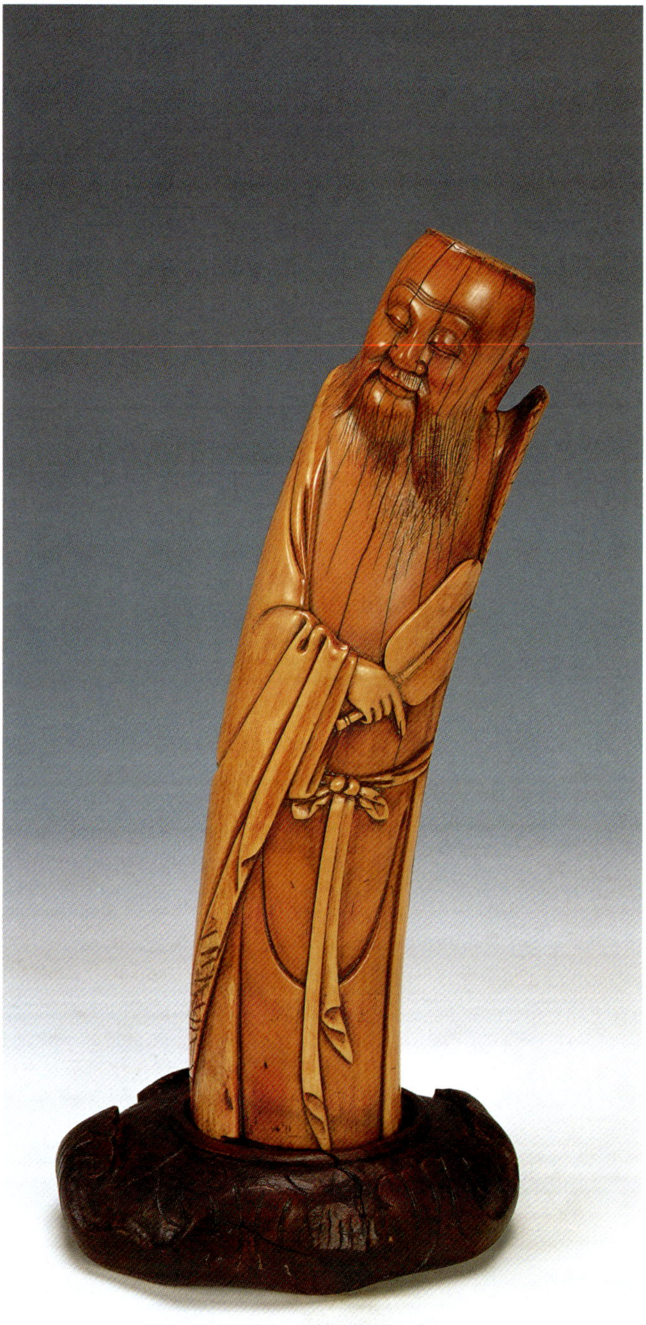

12

13 Ivory carving of court lady in traditional costume holding peaches

Qing (1644–1911)
Height 17.8 cm, Width 3.8 cm,
Thickness 2.4 cm

14 Small screen with geese and reeds made of carved ivory

Qing (1644–1911)
Height 7.05 cm, Length 10.6 cm,
Thickness 0.7 cm

15 Dish with children playing made of carved ivory

Height 1.4 cm, Length 11.8 cm,
Width 8.4 cm

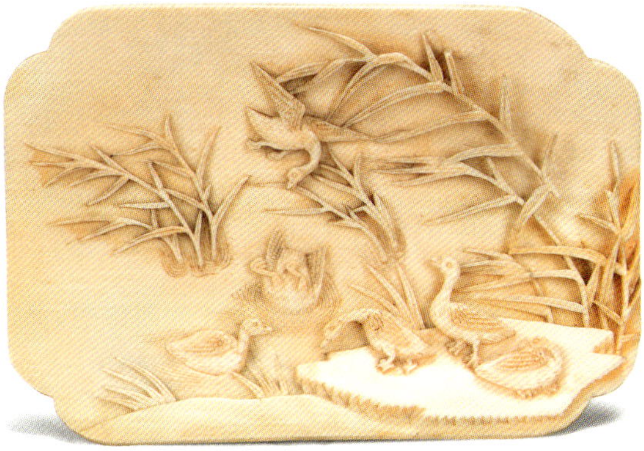

14

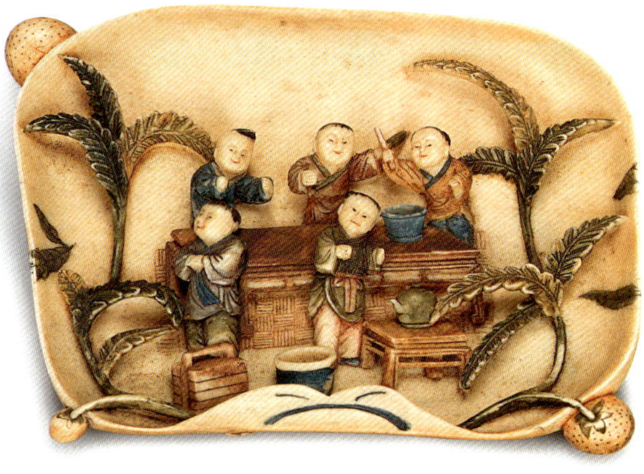

15

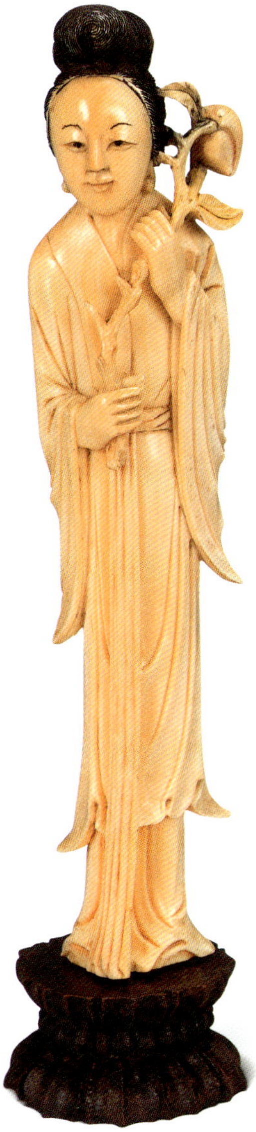

13

16 Micro-carved ivory historical story board

Qing (1644–1911)
Length 10.2 cm, Width 6.9 cm, Thickness 0.55 cm

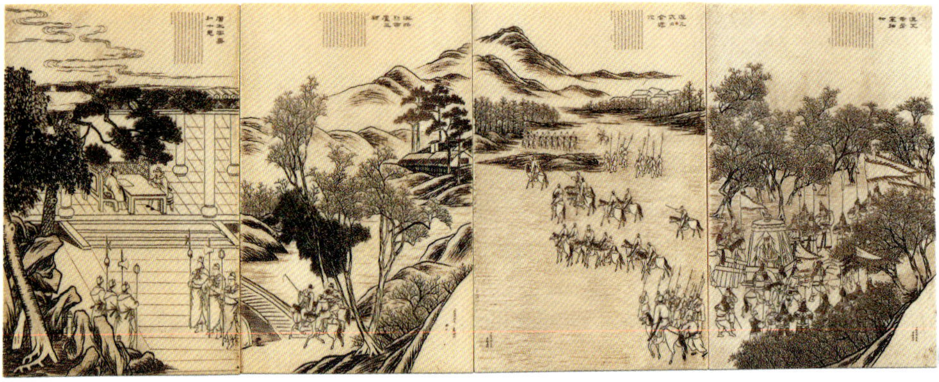

16

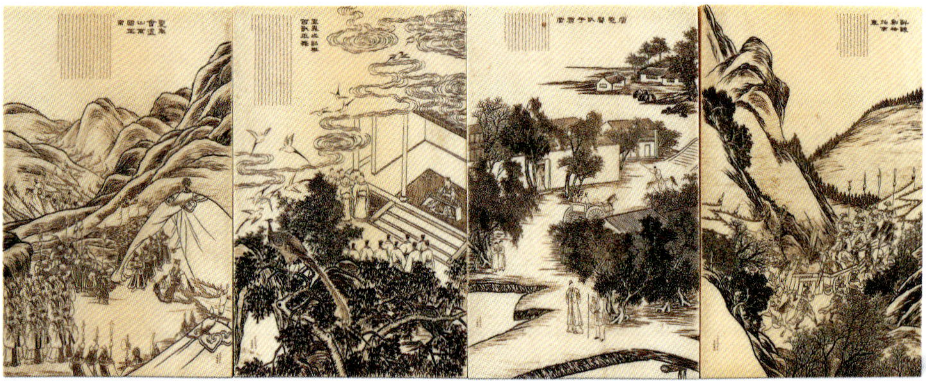

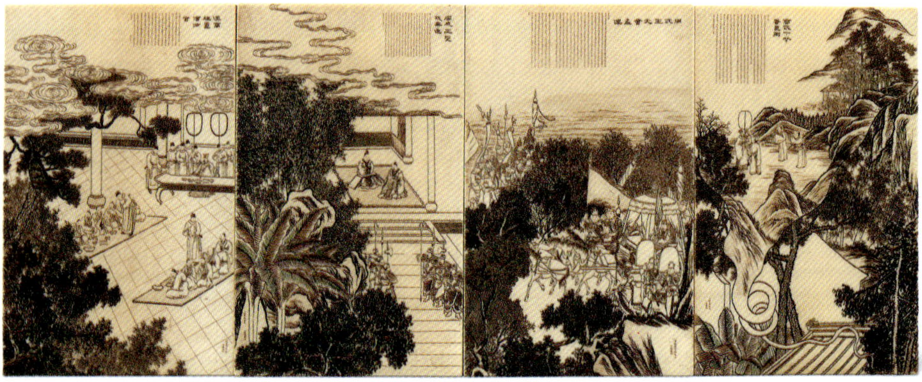

17 Ivory puzzle balls

Qing (1644–1911)
Total Height 52.2 cm, Diameter 12.9 cm, Base Diameter 12.95 cm

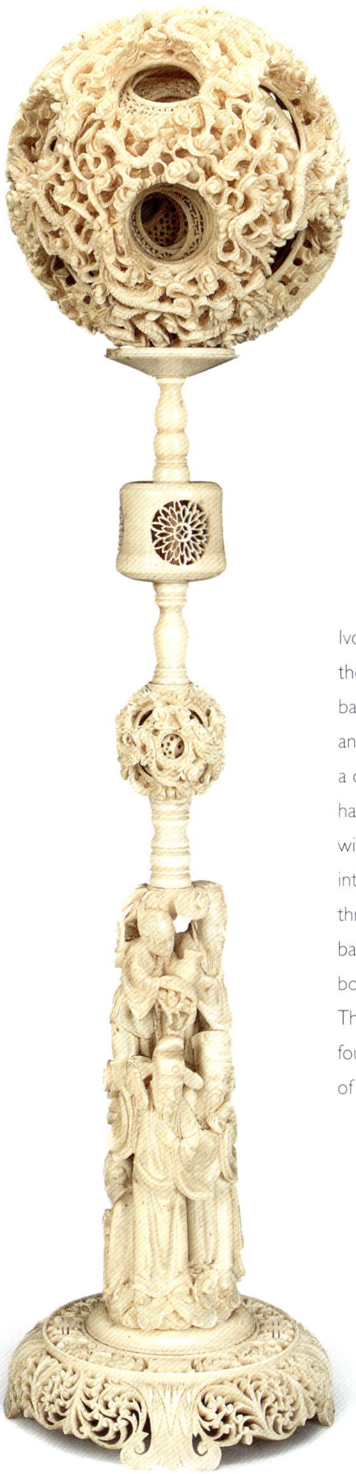

17

Ivory puzzle balls are a special Chinese craft in ivory carving. Looking from the outside, the ivory balls seem to be a body of balls, but with inner layers in the layers, with one ball inside one group. They can be freely moved, and all have the same round centre and thus are also called 'same centre balls'. Their design is highly complex. This object is a decoration, made up of a top ball, a stand, and a base. The exterior of the large ball has been delicately carved, composed of more than ten dragons among clouds either with hidden heads and exposed tails, or vice versa. The inside of the large ball is divided into layers containing twenty-one small balls all in sets, and can be turned. The stand has three parts, the top part has a carved round decoration; in the middle there is a small ball with six layers of transparent carving with a similar pattern to the large top ball; the bottom part has a group of spirit figures treading on clouds, all with serene expressions. The base has a grass, cloud and dragon design that has been transparently carved on four feet. Chinese carving technique reached its apogee in the Qing dynasty, and this set of ivory balls is an example of the fine craftsmanship achieved. Wen Kexue

13

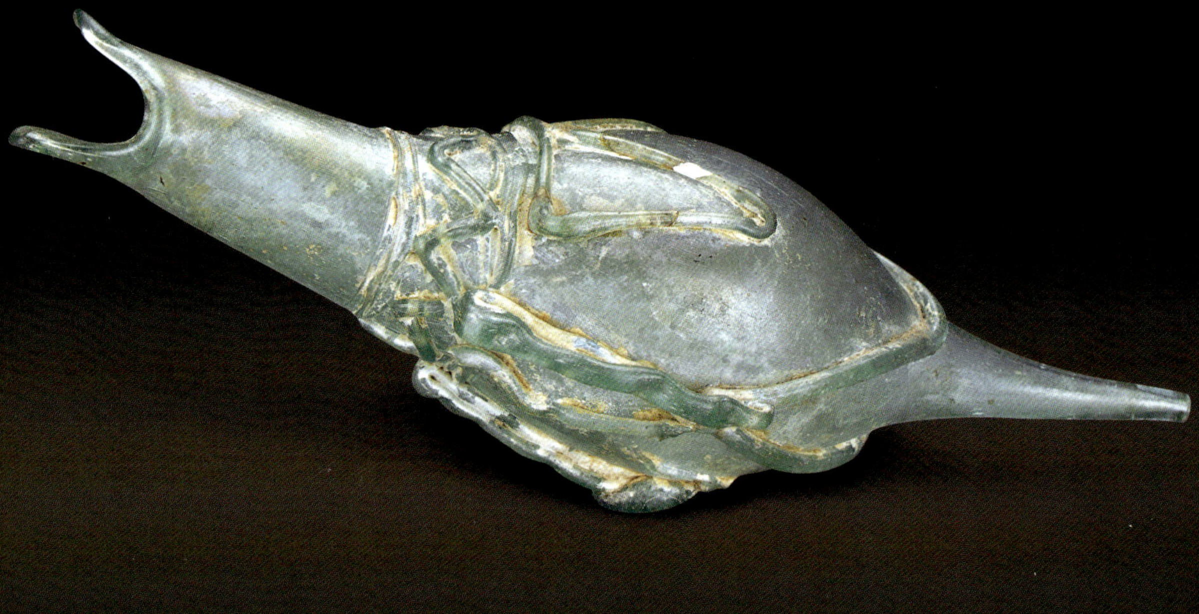

Others

The Liaoning Provincial Museum has modest collections of oracle bones, glass pieces, ancient zithers, prints and old maps that include rare items.

There are four hundred carved oracle bones, of which five have been classified as national treasures on account of their large size, number of characters and important content. These five oracle bones originally belonged to Luo Zhenyu's collection and entered the Liaoning Museum collection after 1949. The five bones record ceremonies and wars with neighbouring states, farming, weather, fertility from the Shang emperor Yi, Xin and Wuding periods. The characters are carefully formed, each passage neatly arranged, with the lines laid out in order, the characters are clear. These are rare objects and provide a precious resource for researching military affairs, astrology and calendars, and the ritual system of the Shang dynasty.

Glass ware was considered as a treasure in ancient China, a symbol of wealth and position. Glass ware from outside China was even more coveted by the higher levels of society. The duck-shaped flagon is the most precious item of glass ware in the Liaoning Museum collection. This was excavated from the northern Yan Fengsufei tomb at Beipiao in Liaoning Province, and was made in Syria on the shores of the Mediterranean. It provides useful information on Silk Road trade.

The most numerous archaeological finds were excavated at tomb number 7 at Yemaotai, Faku, Liaoning Province. A large green glass dish with an inlaid silver buckle is a precious item from the Liao dynasty. A painted wooden backgammon set is currently the best preserved ancient backgammon set to be excavated, and has important research value for popular customs and crafts. A crystal amber neck decoration is representative of Liao cultural ornaments. A bier with a small house is a rare example of a small wooden piece of architecture, and is an important indicator of the Liao assimilating culture from central China. A stone coffin carved with four deities is another rare masterpiece of Liao dynasty large-scale carving.

The collection also contains several ancient Chinese zithers (*guqin*). The *Jiuxiao huanpei* zither is the earliest and best preserved item. The shape, inscription, style of the zither and the lacquer coating indicate it was produced in the mid-Tang period, more than 1,200 years ago, thus making it extremely precious having been transmitted down to the present day.

Prints and old maps from various periods in the Liaoning Museum are mostly from the former collection of the Northeast Museum, from donations from all sections of the public, and the active collecting of the Museum. Prints mostly date from the Five Dynasties period onwards, including religious woodcuts, plain and coloured block prints, New Year paintings and Western copperplate etchings from the Ming and Qing periods. Old maps are mostly printed or painted copies and rubbings from the Ming and Qing periods. Among these of particular note are: the original colour carved *Ten Bamboo Studio Manual of Painting* from the Ming Wanli Emperor period; the wood carved colour watercolour block print of the *The Mustard Seed Garden Manual of Painting* and the *Illustrations of Tilling and Weaving*. In the old maps collection, the Ming Jiaqing period colour map on silk *Map of Nine Defence Areas* and the Wanli 31st year *Map of the Heavens and Earth as Seen from Obscurity* painted by Matteo Ricci and printed by Li Yingshi and others are all priceless works of the highest quality. Du Xiqing

1 Carved oracle ox breast bone from Wuding period

Late Shang period (13th–11th century BC)
First piece: Length 42.6 cm, Width 20.9 cm
Excavated at Yin ruins at Xiaotuncun, Anyang City, Henan Province

2 Carved oracle ox breast bone of *Diyi Dixin* period

Late Shang period (13th–11th century BC)
Length 36 cm, Width 17.5 cm
Excavated at Yin ruins at Xiaotuncun, Anyang City, Henan Province

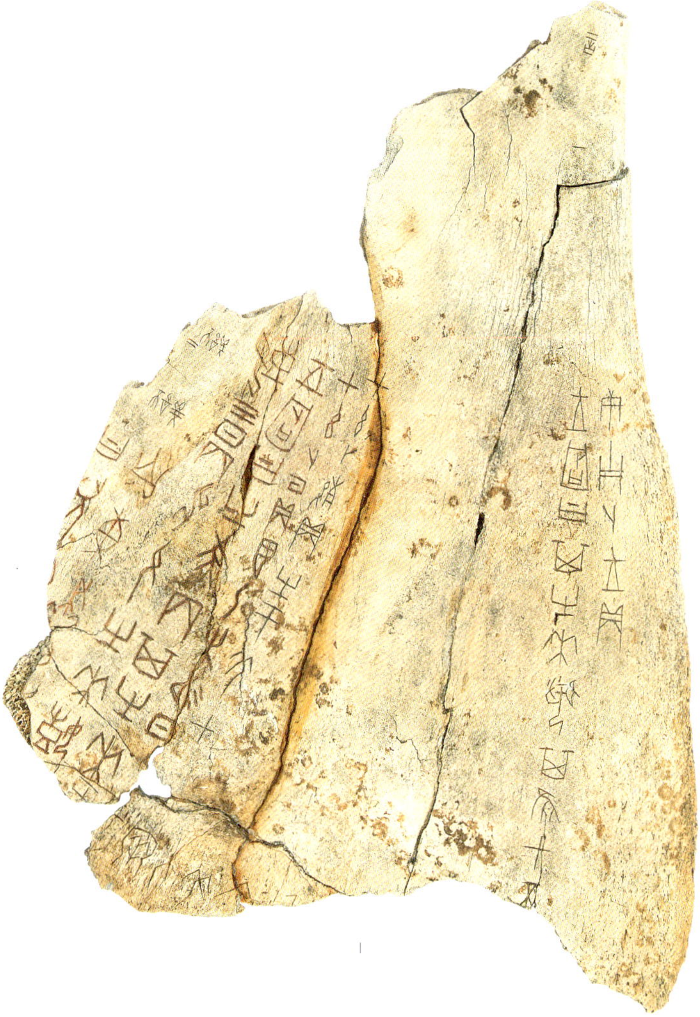

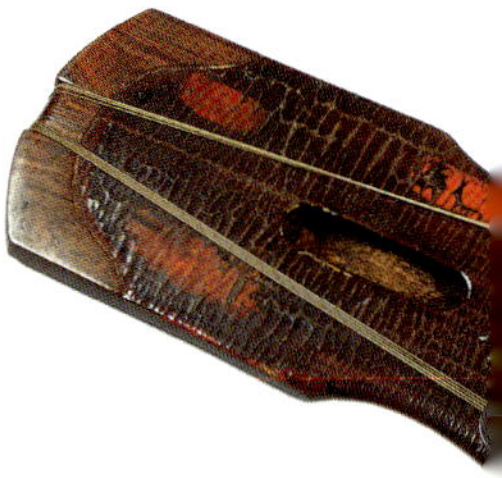

1

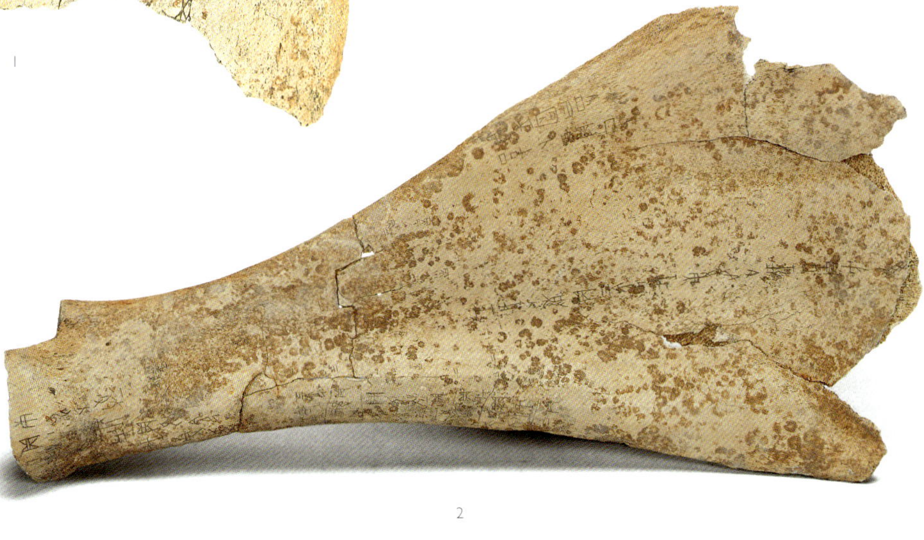

2

3 *Jiuxiao huanpei* zither

Tang dynasty (618–907)
Total Length 122.7 cm, Widest point 21.1 cm

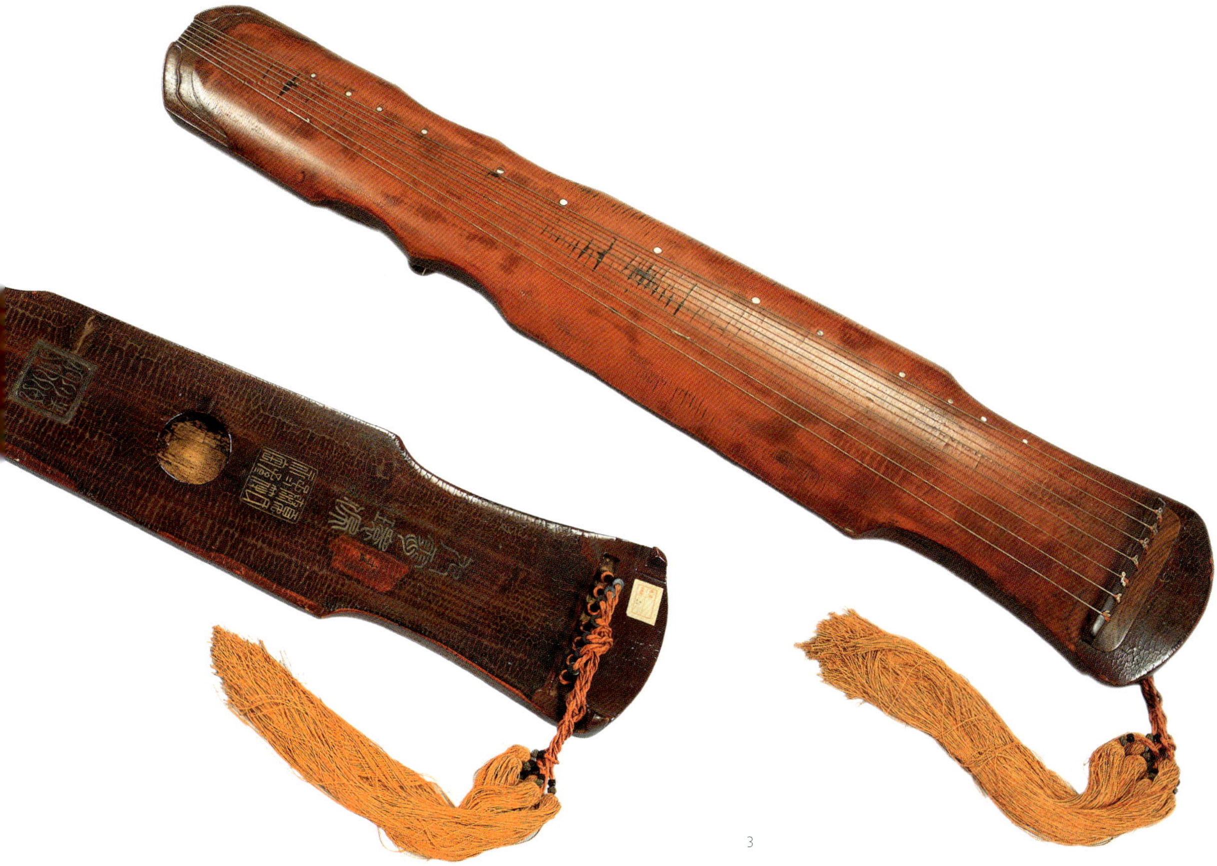

3

This patch zither's name is a *Jiuxiao Huanpei*, it is in the shape of Fuxi, made from candlenut wood, the shell has lacquer in chestnut colour, the surface of the zither has been thickly coated with deep red colour, with grey deer antler ashes padding. The surface has a craquelure-like snake skin and ox hairs, the base has one of snake skin and broken ice. On the back of the zither the four characters *jiu xiao huan pei* are carved in seal script, under which are carved three square characters from a seal. In the round *long chi* hole, there are two characters '*qing he*' in seal script. Inside the body is a long square-shaped rosewood patch pattern, with no trace of character inscription. Its feet are all decorated in red wood, both sides are smoothed flat, the top and bottom are equally round, the middle of the body is slender, with holes for threading fine floss. The round feet are trumpet-shaped and slot into the base of the instrument. On the right side of the instrument neck the characters '*xiang quan yun qing*' (ringing spring rhythm chime) are carved, as well as '*Qianlong yushang*' (Qianlong's imperial appreciation) in two lines, and a seal with the characters '*ji xia lin chi*'. From the shape of this zither, its inscriptions, stylistic characteristics, lacquer and craftsmanship it must have been produced in the mid-Tang period. YAO NAILIANG

4 Glass cup

Northern Yan (409–436)
Height 8.8 cm, Diameter 9.3 cm
Excavated in 1965 at tomb of Feng Sufu,
Xiguanyingzi, Beipiao City, Liaoning Province

5 Glass bowl

Northern Yan (409–436)
Height 4.3 cm, Diameter 13 cm
Excavated in 1965 at tomb of Feng Sufu, Xiguanyingzi,
Beipiao City, Liaoning Province

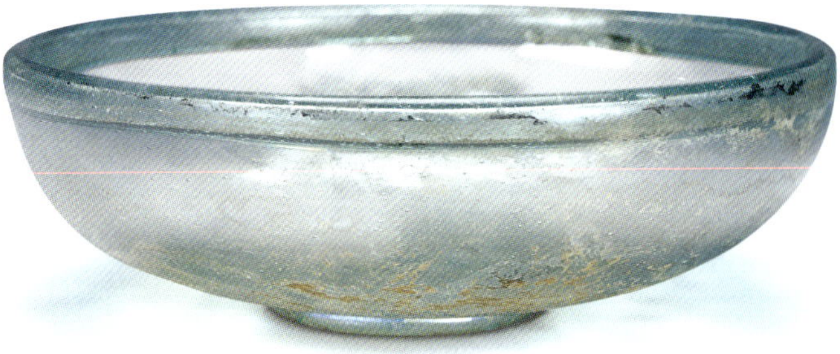

4

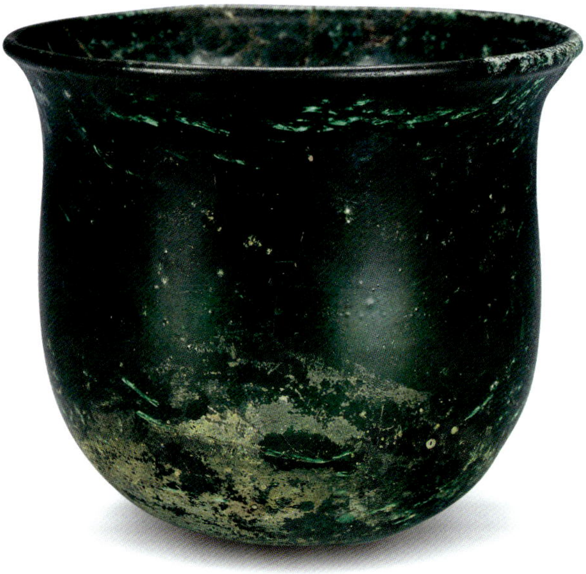

5

6 Duck-shaped *zhu* (flagon)

Northern Yan (409–436)
Length 20.5 cm, Body Diameter 5.2 cm, Weight 70 g
Excavated in 1965 at Fengsufei tomb, Xiguanyingzi, Beipiao City, Liaoning Province

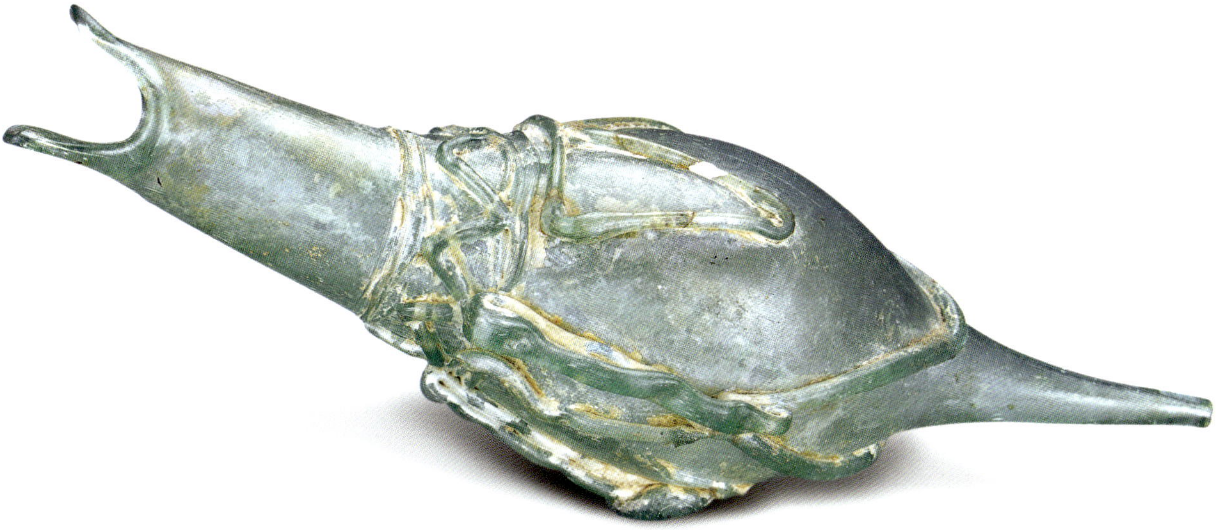

6

This duck-shaped *zhu* is made of lightly transparent blown glass, with a slight grey-green surface soaked in rust. It is long, and shaped like a duck, with a large beak, a long neck and squat body, a long thin tail; the end of the tail is slightly damaged. After it had been fired, the affixing technique was used to affix glass lines to create a pattern. The neck has a patterned ring of coloured duck feathers, the back is decorated with a pair of triangular duck wings blown out from liquid glass. On both sides of the body there are wave patterns as if made by two feet, and on the base a flat round piece of bottle-shaped glass is stuck. This piece is heavier in front. The body is half immersed in water.

This is the only extant piece of its kind of rare early glass in the world. It probably came from the Roman Empire on the Mediterranean shore of present-day Syria, and came to China through Central Asia through the countries of the steppe, finally reaching the Feng clan of the northern Yan. Yao Nailiang

7 Green glass square dish with inlaid silver buckle

Liao dynasty (916–1125)
Height 2 cm, Length 9.9 cm
Excavated in 1974 from Liao tomb number 7 at Yemaotai, Faku County, Liaoning Province

8 Crystal amber necklace

Liao (916–1125)
Length 73 cm
Excavated in 1974 at Liao tomb number 7 at Yemaotai, Faku County, Liaoning Province

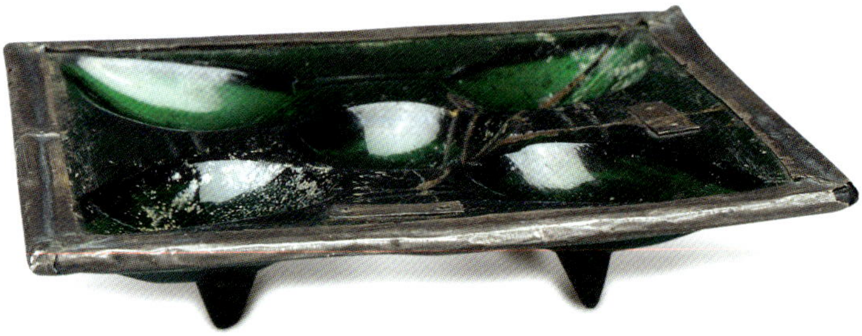

7

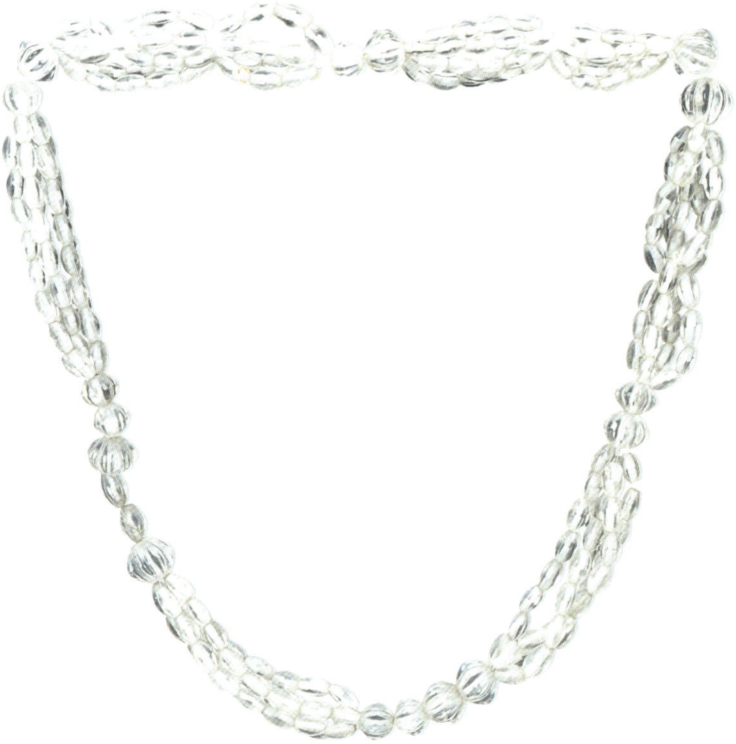

8

9 **Painted wood backgammon set**

Liao dynasty (916–1125)
Height of wooden pieces 4.6 cm, Length of board 52.8 cm, Width 25.4 cm,
Base Diameter 2.5 cm
Excavated in 1974 from Liao tomb number 7 at Yemaotai, Faku County,
Liaoning Province

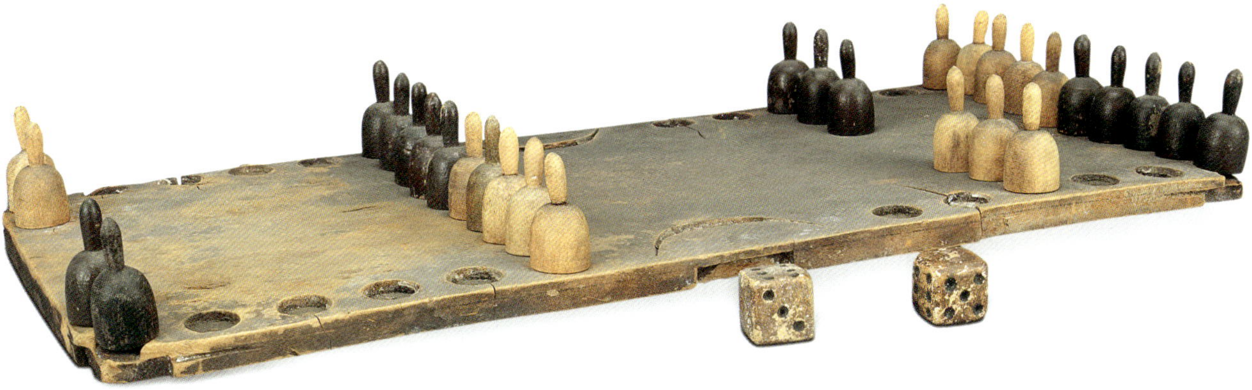

9

This is a Liao dynasty games board made up of a backgammon board and thirty pieces. There are two inlaid crescent shapes in the middle of the two facing sides of black and white pieces. On either side of these crescent 'gates' are six round 'ridge' holes. The cone-shaped pieces have pointed tops, flat bottoms and round middles. There are fifteen pieces of each colour, facing each other in different arrangements. During excavation all the pieces had yellow gauze wrappers, and there are still gauze fragments on the board. There are also two dice made from bone that were on a black lacquer dish when excavated. The dish is made from wood and pressed with ramie, is low with a flat base, coated in black lacquer, the rim has traces of sheaf inlay; we know that it originally had metal inlaid rim. It is no longer extant. It had six characters '*geng wu sui li shang lao*' in red lacquer. It was 10 cm high, had a diameter of 44.5 cm, and base diameter of 34 cm, and the dice would probably have been put on it when not in use. This is the earliest and most complete Chinese backgammon set to be excavated, complete with matching dice and dice tray, and is of great value for researching popular pastimes and craftsmanship. SUN WEI

10 A bier with a small house

Liao dynasty (916–1125)
Total Height 230 cm, Approximate Width 340 cm
Excavated in 1974 at Yemaotai, Faku County, Liaoning Province

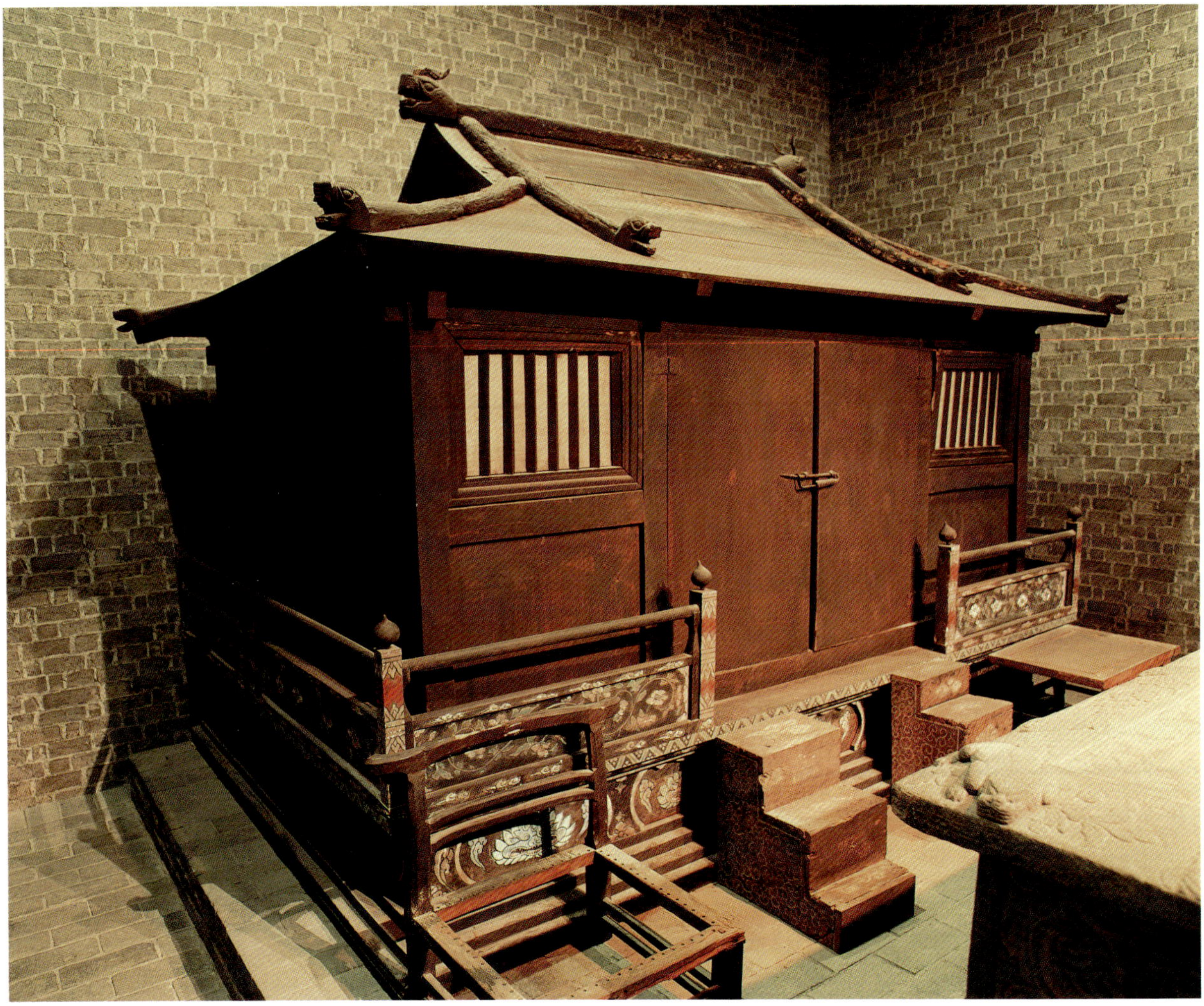

10

This is a complete small house construction in wood that holds a Liao stone sarcophagus, an example of ancient Chinese wooden architecture that is rarely seen. At excavation it was found placed at the back of the main chamber of the tomb. The bier is the base for the house, the upper part of the construction consists of a structure with a nine-ridged roof and the roof corner of the tail of a cormorant, no tiles or eave rafters. Under the eaves there are only single fittings. The front has a three-by-two bay structure with three rooms, two rooms hidden inside, surrounded by wooden walls and mullioned windows at the front. The whole small house rests on a railed rectangular Buddhist altar coffin platform. There are gourd shapes on the surrounding ballustrade, and a coloured frieze all the way around with orchid and peony designs, lion and tiger heads, a lively scene. Outside the rail are sets of three steps, also decorated in colour. This coffin platform with small house on top is an important discovery for Liao burial customs and Chinese architectural history, and is another important indication of the Khitan copying customs from Central China. Sun Wei

11 Sarcophagus carved with four gods

Liao dynasty (916–1125)
Total Height 93 cm, Length 212 cm, Width 124 cm
Excavated in 1974 at Yemaotai, Faku County, Liaoning Province

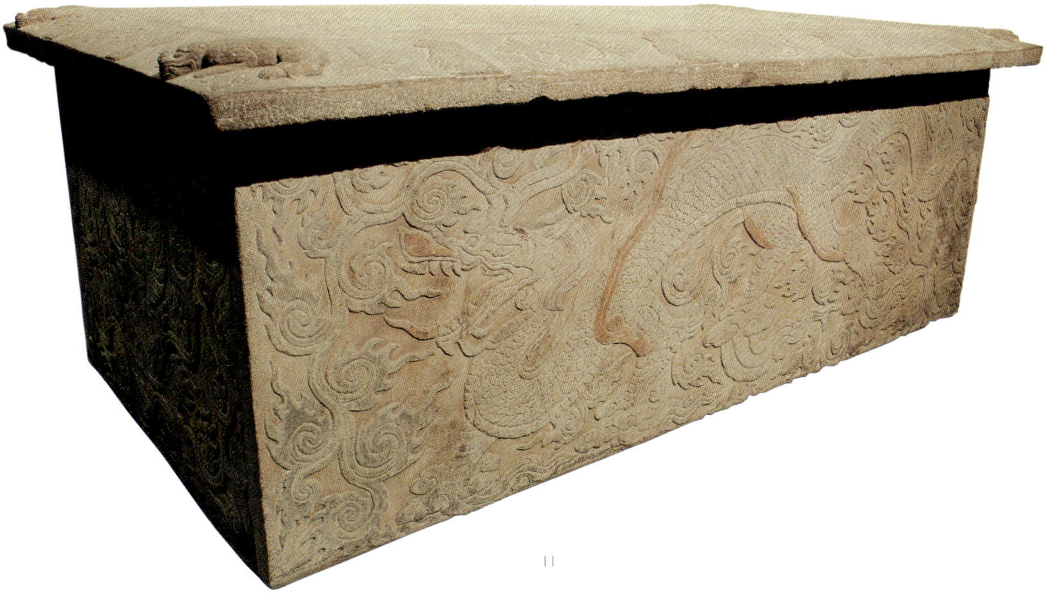

11

The sarcophagus is made by combining two equally sized chest-shape containers with six pieces of grey-white sandstone stone. Apart from the base, the rest of the sarcophagus has bas-relief patterns with added colour all over it. The lid has been incised with a large orchid plant, twelve humanised zodiacs, with lions lying on the four corners. The four surfaces of the sarcophagus have carved black dragons, white tigers, rose finch and and Xuanwu, all among flame-shaped cloud patterns. The tigers and dragons are all floating between the clouds as if riding on the wind and the rose finch is standing on a lotus flower, a vivid scene. The interior surfaces of the sarcophagus are partly incised and partly painted with decorations of male guards at either side of a two-panel, and a female opening the door, and a winged creature at the top. The whole sarcophagus has been carefully sculpted and carved, with flowing natural lines, and fully demonstrates the elegant simplicity of early Liao period art, and as such is exceedingly rare and valuable. Sun Wei

12 *Map of the Heavens and Earth as Seen from Obscurity*

Painted by Matteo Ricci

Ming dynasty Wanli period 31st year (1603)

Each panel: Height 200 cm, Width 55 cm; Eight panels joined together: Total Width 442 cm

Discovered in February 1949 in the Xiangfeng pavilion of the Shenyang Imperial Palace

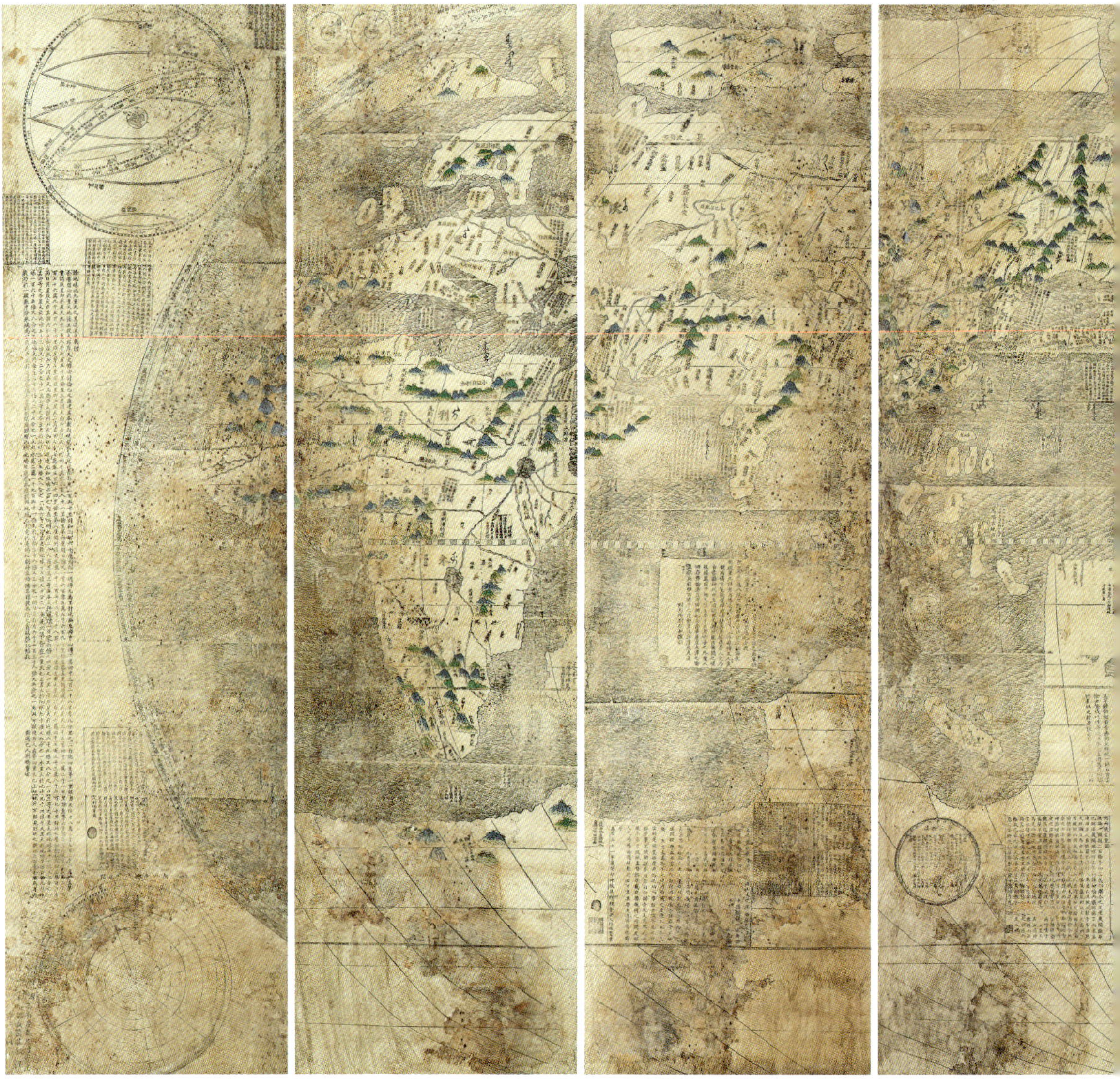

12

This is an oval-shaped world map, ink on paper, composed of eight panels joined together, and was copy printed by Li Yingshi (Baolu) in 1603 during the Ming dynasty into a cut block print of the world map from the original painting by Italian Jesuit missionary Matteo Ricci. The whole work has been produced using a western conic projection technique and longitude and latitude cartography, the equator and positions of the five large continents known at the time were painted, namely Asia, Europe, Africa and North and South America, and the South Pole, with the five areas running north to south, and the north–south Tropics, with legends and tables. There are also inscriptions by people including Matteo Ricci, Li Yingshi, Li Zhizao, Feng Yingjing, Wu Zhongming, Ruan Taiyuan and Zou chuanyan. LIU YUN

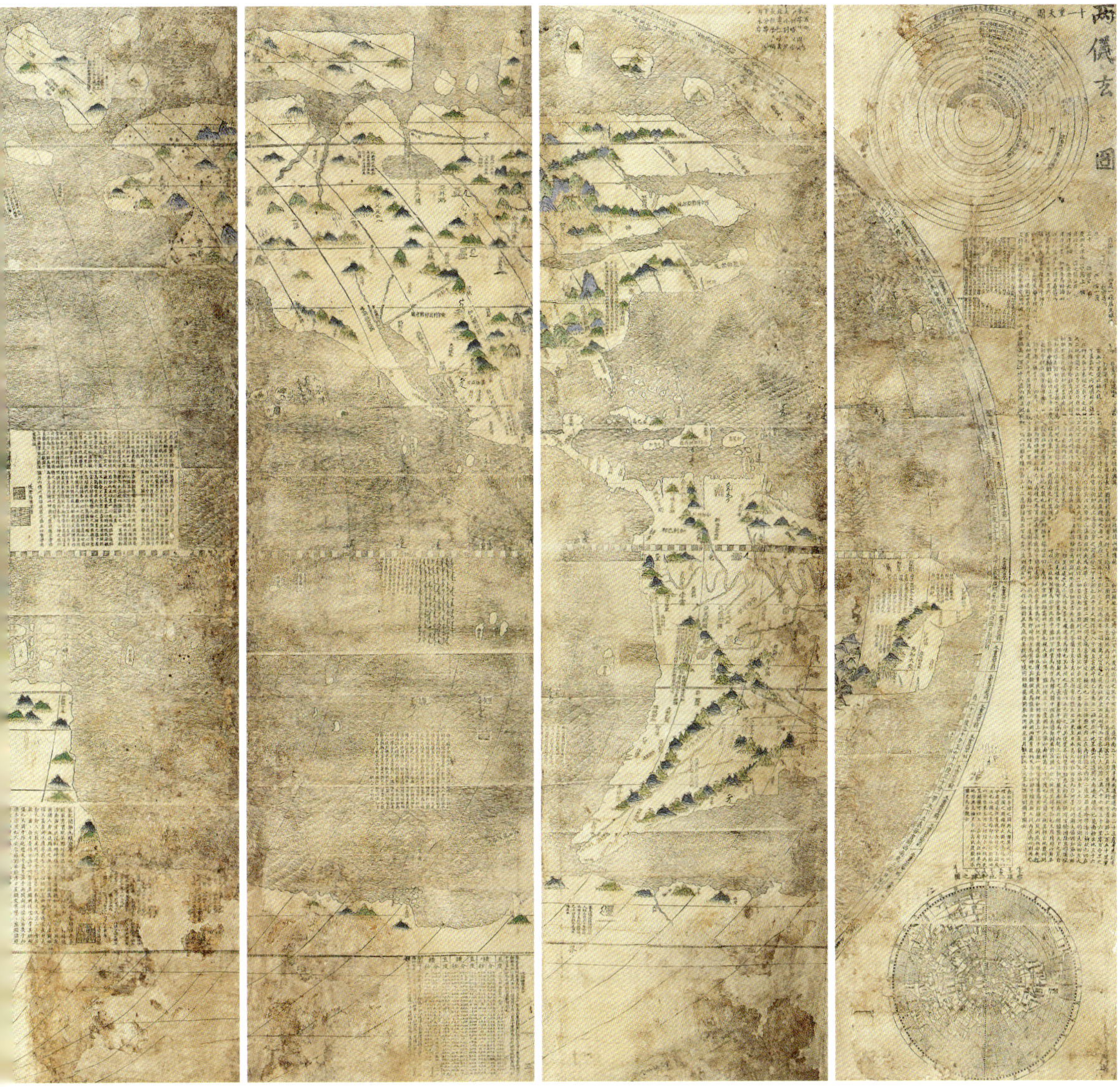
兩儀玄
圖

13 *Colour Map of the Nine Defence Areas*

Ming dynasty Jiaqing period (1522–1566)
Colour and ink on silk
Single Panel, Height: 208 cm, Width 47.3 cm; Total Width of 12 panels joined together, Width 600 cm
Discovered in April 1949 in the Xiangfeng pavilion of the Shenyang Imperial Palace

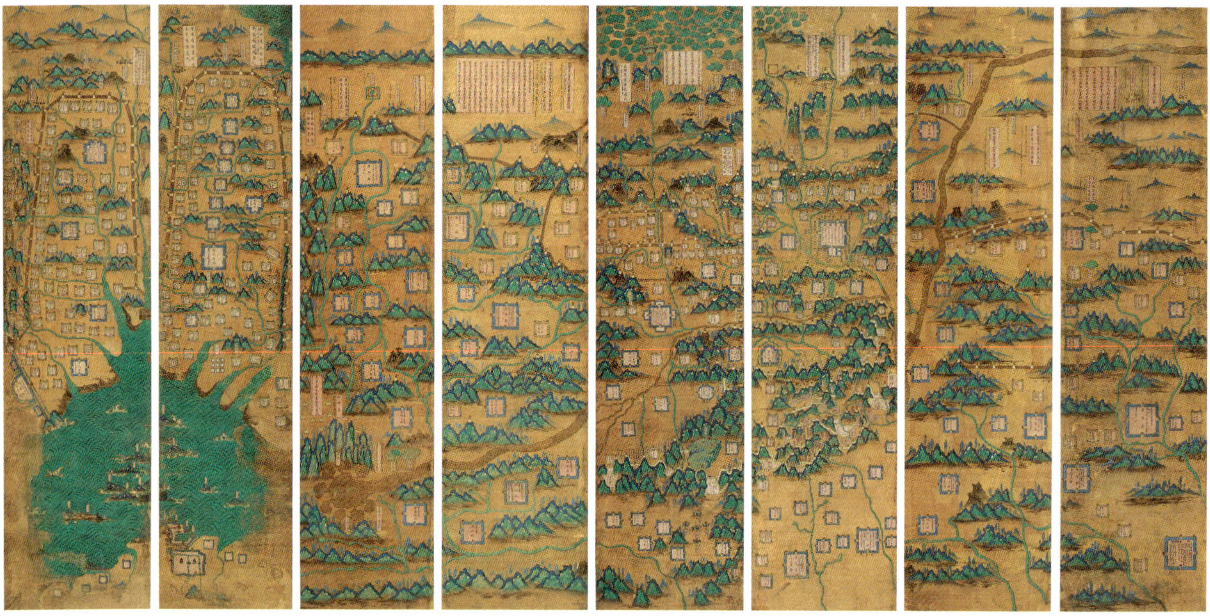

13

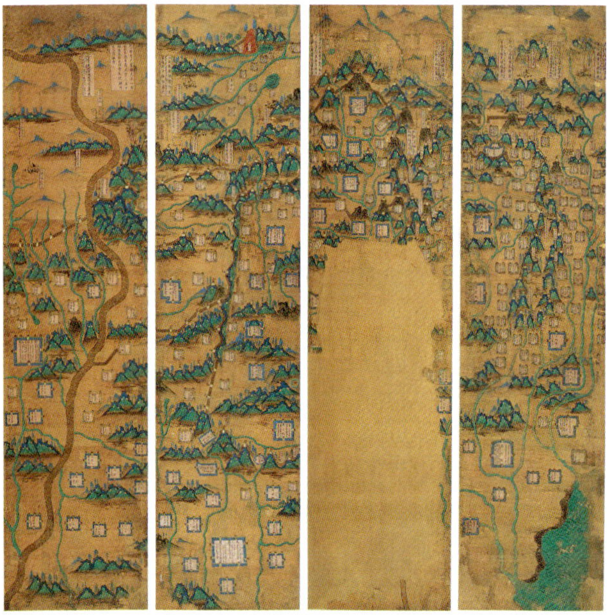

The whole map is composed of twelve panels joined together and shows the Ming dynasty 'nine border' defence areas which in order are: Liaodong, Jizhou, Xuanfu, Datong, Pianguan (Shanxi), Yulin (Yansui), Nixia, Guyuan and Gansu. The constructions, mountains and rivers, passes and fortresses of the 'nine border' area are coloured in light green, and go in a horizontal line for nearly ten thousand *li* from east to west, and vertically from north to south from the Yellow River to the Liao River Yalu tributary area for about a thousand *li*.

The 'nine border' area refers to the nine Ming border garrisons and thus this map shows the demarcation of the Ming borders. It is a useful resource for researching the military composition of the Ming border areas and military geography, as well as providing a rare insight into Ming (and earlier) painting techniques of coloured maps, and is a treasure in the history of Chinese maps. LIU YUN

14 *Ten Bamboo Studio Manual of Painting*

Ming dynasty (1368–1644)
Each section Height 27.2 cm, Width 15.1 cm

15 *The Mustard Seed Garden Manual of Painting*

Qing dynasty Kangxi period (1662–1722)
Wood block colour print
Each section, Height 26.4 cm, Width 32.6 cm

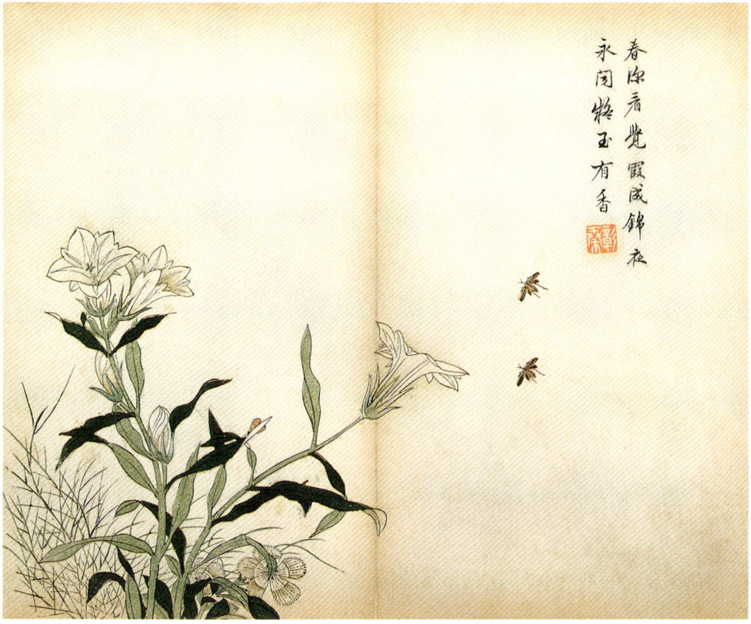

14

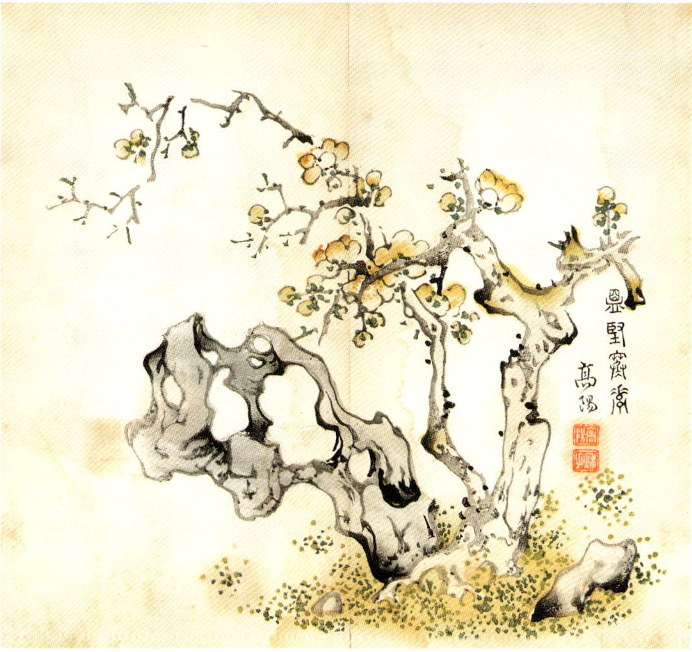

15